Second Edition

Forensic Recovery of Human Remains

Archaeological Approaches

Second Edition

Forensic Recovery of Human Remains

Archaeological Approaches

Tosha L. Dupras
John J. Schultz
Sandra M. Wheeler
Lana J. Williams

CRC Press
Taylor & Francis Group
Boca Raton   London   New York

CRC Press is an imprint of the
Taylor & Francis Group, an **informa** business

WITHDRAWN
UTSA LIBRARIES

CRC Press
Taylor & Francis Group
6000 Broken Sound Parkway NW, Suite 300
Boca Raton, FL 33487-2742

© 2012 by Taylor & Francis Group, LLC
CRC Press is an imprint of Taylor & Francis Group, an Informa business

No claim to original U.S. Government works

Printed in the United States of America on acid-free paper
Version Date: 2011928

International Standard Book Number: 978-1-4398-5030-5 (Hardback)

Library of Congress Cataloging-in-Publication Data

Forensic recovery of human remains : archaeological approaches, / authors, Tosha L.
    Dupras ... [et al.]. -- 2nd ed.
        p. cm.
    Includes bibliographical references and index.
    ISBN 978-1-4398-5030-5 (hardcover : alk. paper)
    1. Forensic anthropology. 2. Archaeology. 3. Human remains (Archaeology) 4.
Criminal investigation. I. Dupras, Tosha L.

    GN69.8.F695 2012
    599.9--dc23   2011038432

Visit the Taylor & Francis Web site at
http://www.taylorandfrancis.com

and the CRC Press Web site at
http://www.crcpress.com

Dedication

This book is dedicated to all of the law enforcement officers, fire investigators, crime scene personnel, and forensic investigators, who, through their tireless efforts, work to solve cases. The strong emotional toll that this work takes on all of those involved is great, but with each individual who is recovered, and once again remembered for who he or she was rather than for the events surrounding that person's death, the costs are overshadowed by the solace brought to families of missing loved ones.

And also to Ruger, a one-of-a-kind dog who is greatly missed but whose accomplishments live on.

Table of Contents

8   Applying Archaeological Methods in a Forensic Context   197

Foreword to the Second Edition

Welcome to the new edition of *Forensic Recovery of Human Remains*. It is designed to serve as both a field manual and a course textbook. Anybody planning a forensic field investigation would do well to read the relevant sections first, to plan their approach and to see just which of a bewildering variety of tools and technological devices might be needed. I have been doing forensic fieldwork for a quarter of a century now, and I still found ideas and information here that were new to me. These range from the extensive suite of specialized tools available for fieldwork, some of which I had never heard of, to the suggestion that the microstratigraphy at the base of a graveshaft's sides can provide some idea of the amount of time that the grave had been open. As another example, my approach to the core of a complex scene has been to work from the periphery to the center on each side consecutively, but the authors recommend a spiral approach. This has the advantage of providing a better general understanding of the scene before reaching the crucial area, and making the center more accessible with less risk of damage or loss of information. I am highlighting those sections in my copy.

In their recent review of forensic anthropology, Dirkmaat and his colleagues (2008)[*] noted that practitioners in the mid-1980s started to expand their focus, adding field recovery to the more traditional laboratory-based emphasis on identification. I started to do forensic cases at that time, and from the beginning it was fieldwork. My first case involved the documentation and recovery of the skeleton of a homicide victim that had been scattered over a wide area. The police had requested my assistance because of my archaeological field experience, not because of my osteological skills, although those were also in play. Identification is often part of my role, but usually its main purpose is just to narrow the range among an already limited set of possible identities. The police, I find, generally have a pretty good idea of whose remains we are investigating. The identification is then secured by a forensic odontologist, a radiologist or, increasingly often, a DNA specialist.

Police and coroners soon came to see the importance of good field documentation and recovery practices. Flawed fieldwork creates too many problems, like uncertainty in a suicide versus homicide determination, embarrassing gaps in the details of the physical evidence, and a plethora of

---

[*] Dirkmaat, D. C., Cabo, L. L., Ousley, S.D., Symes, S.A. 2008. New perspectives in forensic anthropology. *Yearbook of Physical Anthropology* 137:33–52.

opportunities for defense attorneys. So the police started bringing me to the scene, instead of bringing the scene to me.

There are a good number of field manuals available for archaeology and a somewhat smaller set for osteology. As useful as these are in their disciplines and as relevant as some aspects of their coverage are to forensic fieldwork, they are not adequate field guides for forensic anthropology. The legal considerations that overshadow a forensic investigation, the likely presence of soft tissue, and a host of other factors demand a very different sort of manual. One has only to look at some of the topics covered in this book to realize as much: the methods used to locate clandestine graves, the need to document continuity, the collection of entomological evidence, the spiral approach to a scene's core, etc. There are also warnings about what can go wrong in a scene investigation, and some very practical pieces of advice. Chapter 7, for example, begins with the caution that "there is an enormous amount of technology used today in recording forensic scenes, from laptops and digital cameras, to global positioning systems (GPS) and high-resolution laser surveys—all of which have an amazing capacity to fail at the most critical moment in the most remote location." So, they recommend, keep your hand-held compass, your tape measure, and your pencil and eraser close at hand.

I have come to realize that part of my job as a forensic anthropologist is to educate law enforcement personnel in proper fieldwork practices—not in a formal context like a field school (although some forensic anthropologists are doing just that), but rather by working on a scene with them as the occasion arises and carefully explaining what I am doing and why I am doing it. The goal is not to turn them into forensic anthropologists, but rather to make them aware of the sorts of things we must think about and look for, and the sorts of things we must *not* do. On one case, which turned out to be a nineteenth century burial (as many cases do), the police team that I was working with called in their colleagues from other detachments so they could all see how I handled the situation. The scene became an outdoor classroom, with me walking the police through it as they arrived.

This sort of informal education of people in the legal sphere does not stop with the field. When I was preparing for court testimony in a recent case, the judge and the lawyers (on both sides) admitted that they had no idea what a forensic anthropologist does. They did not want just a brief verbal explanation, but asked for a list of readings. The first edition of *Forensic Recovery of Human Remains* was at the top of my list. I have also given copies to the regional coroner and the pathologist with whom I frequently work. My own copy has become an indispensable piece of field equipment, well thumbed and rather dirty. Fortunately, it seems to be odor resistant.

Michael W. Spence
Professor Emeritus, Department of Anthropology, University of Western Ontario

Preface

Crime scenes involving human remains can be very complex to process. Unfortunately, standard training for many crime scene and law enforcement personnel typically does not include methods for search and recovery of human remains and associated evidence. Many investigators receive their initial training at the time when human remains are located. Insufficient knowledge of archaeological techniques and skeletal biology can lead to crime scenes that are improperly processed, and vital evidence can be destroyed or overlooked. Certain skeletal elements may be missed because the individual performing the recovery does not have a framework for identifying or locating human remains and associated evidence. Alternatively, individuals may be using search or excavation techniques that are unsuitable for the recovery of this type of evidence. The second edition of this book is intended to fill the need for an updated, comprehensive reference pertaining to the search, recovery, documentation, and excavation of human remains and associated evidence from forensic contexts.

This book is intended for advanced undergraduates and graduate students, law enforcement and death scene personnel, forensic anthropology practitioners, and forensic archaeologists. In an ideal world, individuals with expertise in forensic anthropology and forensic archaeology would be present at every crime scene that involved the search for and recovery of human remains. However, we recognize that it is not possible in every situation for law enforcement agencies to call upon these experts. Because of this, our aim is to provide readers with information that will allow them to understand and use proper search, excavation, and recovery techniques as they apply to human remains.

This book describes techniques for use at less complicated scenes such as single burials. More complicated scenes, such as multiple or mass burials, water recoveries, or cremations, should be processed with the assistance of experienced personnel. Because the primary audience of the first edition of the book was undergraduate and graduate students and death investigation personnel, we revised this book to include more of an emphasis for classroom and instruction use. Many of these changes were driven by comments from our students, field practitioners, published reviews of the first edition, as well as colleagues who used the first edition in their courses and casework. In this edition we include case studies, key terms, discussion questions, and suggested readings at the end of each chapter. We also expanded this edition to include two new chapters (Chapters 4 and 11), and we revised, reorganized, and updated existing chapters. Chapter 1 differentiates between forensic archaeology and forensic anthropology and provides the reader with information on locating experts in these areas. Chapter 2 provides descriptions of the equipment necessary to conduct searches, recoveries, and excavations of human skeletal remains. Chapter 3 highlights human skeletal terminology that assists investigators in adequately describing the scene and remains in their reports, and in understanding biological terminology used in other death investigation reports. Chapter 4 focuses on the identification of forensic and nonforensic scenes and provides an overview of the different criteria used to distinguish these types of scenes. Chapter 5 includes detailed information on search methods, including criteria for locating surface deposits and burials. Chapter 6 highlights different types of geophysical technologies that can be used for searches involving metallic evidence, graves, and submerged bodies. Chapter 7 presents step-by-step instructions for surveying and mapping techniques used to document the scene. Chapter 8 provides step-by-step instructions on how to excavate buried evidence and remains from a variety of contexts. Chapter 9 focuses on the procedures for recognizing and collecting associated botanical and entomological evidence at the scene. Chapter 10 provides information on skeletal and evidence collection, and also discusses the potential difficulty of distinguishing between human and nonhuman skeletal remains. Chapter 11 highlights the final forensic archaeological report and provides an overview of the pertinent information that should be included.

Acknowledgments

The authors would like to extend our thanks to the students, colleagues, and field practitioners who provided valuable comments that greatly improved this edition. We would also like to thank the following agencies for inviting us to work with them: Orange County Sheriff's Office, Orlando Police Department, Seminole County Sheriff's Office, Lake Mary Police Department, Ontario Provincial Police, Royal Canadian Mounted Police, and Ontario Coroner's Office. Thanks also to the following individuals and agencies for graciously allowing us to use their images and likenesses: Dave Clarke, Kelly Wood, William Hawkins, Gene Ralston, Mary Peter, Mike Warren, S. "Stacy" Barber, Jeff Brzezinski, Orange County Sheriff's Office, and Seminole County Sheriff's Office. Special thanks go to Dr. Michael Spence (University of Western Ontario) for his thoughtful suggestions and editorial comments, and willingness to write the foreword for this edition.

The Authors

Tosha L. Dupras, Ph.D., is an associate professor of anthropology at the University of Central Florida where she teaches human osteology and forensic archaeology. Dupras received a M.Sc. (1995) in human biology from the University of Guelph (Ontario, Canada) and a Ph.D. (1999) in anthropology from McMaster University (Ontario, Canada). She specializes in bioarchaeology, particularly diet reconstruction through chemical analysis, and has been associated with the Dakhleh Oasis and Dayr al-Barshā projects in Egypt where she has excavated in several cemeteries and analyzed many skeletal remains. Dupras also assists local law enforcement agencies with the search for and excavation of human remains.

John J. Schultz, Ph.D., is an associate professor of anthropology at the University of Central Florida where he teaches courses in human osteology, forensic anthropology, and archaeological sciences. Schultz received a M.Sc. (1998) in human biology from the University of Indianapolis (Indiana) and a Ph.D. (2003) in anthropology while specializing in forensic anthropology at the University of Florida. His primary research focuses on forensic and archaeological applications of ground-penetrating radar (GPR) for grave detection, and detection of buried metallic weapons using various geophysical technologies. Schultz is also a consulting forensic anthropologist in the central Florida area for various law enforcement agencies and the local Medical Examiner's Office.

Sandra M. Wheeler, Ph.D., is an instructor of anthropology at the University of Central Florida where she teaches courses in biological anthropology, cultural anthropology, and archaeology. Wheeler received an M.A. (2001) from the University of Central Florida and a Ph.D. (2009) in anthropology from The University of Western Ontario. She specializes in bioarchaeology, paleopathology, juvenile osteology, and mortuary archaeology. Wheeler has conducted fieldwork in Belize and Mexico and continues to actively work with the Dakhleh Oasis Project in Egypt. She has assisted law enforcement in Florida and Canada with the search for and recovery of human remains.

Lana J. Williams, Ph.D., is a scholar in residence at the University of Central Florida. Williams received an M.A. (2001) from the University of Central Florida and a Ph.D. (2008) in anthropology from The University of Western Ontario, where she received the prestigious Governor General's Award for her dissertation research in bioarchaeology. She specializes in biochemical analysis of human remains, mortuary archaeology, and human osteology. Williams has conducted fieldwork in Greece and Belize and is currently working with the Dakhleh Oasis and Dayr-al Barshā projects in Egypt. In addition, she has assisted law enforcement in Florida and Canada in the search, recovery, and analysis of human remains.

Introduction to Forensic Archaeology

1

Since the 1970s the discipline of forensic archaeology has received recognition for its contribution to crime scene and death investigations (Morse et al., 1976). During the 1980s there was a growing emphasis on the use of proper archaeological field methods when recovering and excavating human remains from forensic contexts (e.g., Berryman and Lahren, 1984; Morse et al., 1983; Sigler-Eisenberg, 1985; Skinner and Lazenby, 1983; Wolf, 1986). These early proponents of forensic archaeology recognized the legal importance of both the utilization of proper collection techniques for human remains and precise documentation of associated contextual information from crime scenes. Throughout the 1990s, there was an emphasis on the use of a multidisciplinary approach to detection of graves and collection of evidence, as well as continued improvement in field methods for the recovery of remains within a forensic context (e.g., Dirkmaat and Adovasio, 1997; France et al., 1992; France et al., 1997; Hunter et al., 1994; Hunter et al., 1996; Scott and Connor, 1997). Forensic archaeology is now recognized as its own discipline within academic programs, by professional and international organizations, and by the law enforcement community (Hanson, 2008; Schultz and Dupras, 2008). However, many personnel involved with the practical aspects of recovering human remains still have not been trained in or do not universally practice proper archaeological methods to successfully conduct searches, document recovery scenes, excavate burials, and collect and transport evidence.

Although the focus of this book is forensic archaeology, a brief introduction to forensic anthropology is warranted. Even though both disciplines are highly specialized, and sometimes thought of as synonymous, there are distinct differences between forensic anthropology and forensic archaeology. In North America, it is common for forensic archaeology to be encompassed within the discipline of forensic anthropology, and in such cases it may be referred to as forensic bioarchaeology (Skinner et al., 2003). However in other locations, such as in the United Kingdom and Australia, forensic anthropology and forensic archaeology are considered to be two distinct disciplines. To understand the differences between forensic anthropology and forensic archaeology and the contributions that each can make to crime scene investigation, it is important to start with a discussion of anthropology in general.

Broadly defined, anthropology is the study of humans. The word *anthropology* derives from the Greek *anthros* (man) and *logos* (the study of). Anthropologists use a holistic or biocultural approach (i.e., a combination of cultural studies and biology) to understand the many facets of human behavior, both past and present. In North America, anthropology is commonly divided into four areas of study, including cultural anthropology, archaeology, linguistics, and physical (biological) anthropology. Cultural anthropology deals with many aspects of human society including but not limited to social structure, behavior, beliefs, and ways of life. Cultural anthropologists mostly work with living societies. Archaeology is the study of past societies, through material remains such as pottery, stone tools, art, and architecture. Linguistics deals with the evolution of languages and the relationships between languages and societies. In most cases, linguistics is an important aspect of the other areas of anthropology. Physical or biological anthropology deals with the physical and biological aspects of the primate order and includes studies of humans, past and present, and nonhuman primates such as chimpanzees, gorillas, and monkeys. Some of the more specialized areas covered by physical anthropology include:

- Primatology—the scientific study of nonhuman primates (e.g., apes, monkeys, and prosimians), including their anatomy, behavior, and ecology
- Paleoanthropology—the study of ancient hominids through the fossil record in an attempt to reconstruct the evolution and behavior of humans
- Human biology—the study of modern human variation and adaptation
- Human growth and development—the study of how humans develop from conception through senescence
- Nutrition—the study of human nutrition and its effects on human development, both from a modern and evolutionary perspective
- Genetics—the study of human DNA from an evolutionary perspective
- Osteology—the study of the human skeleton including anatomy, demographics, and pathology

So where do forensic anthropology and forensic archaeology fit into all of this?

1.1 Anthropology in the Medicolegal Process

In the United States, death investigations and certifications are part of a formalized medicolegal process undertaken by either a coroner or medical examiner. There is a major difference between the two positions: A coroner is an elected official, and a medical examiner (ME) is an appointed position. Because coroner is an elected position, the chief coroner is usually not a forensic pathologist and his or her background and experience vary. The corner decides if it is necessary to perform an autopsy, which must be conducted by a forensic pathologist. Conversely, a chief medical examiner is a board certified forensic pathologist who is appointed to a government office. The role of the coroner or ME is to determine cause and manner of death, as well as identify the deceased.

When human remains are found, the law enforcement agency controls the scene, and the coroner or ME controls the body or skeletal remains. The law enforcement agency or medicolegal system involved in a death investigation has jurisdictional authority to involve, or invite, other experts in a death investigation as consultants or through formal appointments. For example, because the complexity of outdoor scenes involving skeletal remains can vary, the coroner, ME, or law enforcement agency involved can invite a number of experts to assist with the recovery of the skeletal remains, such as a forensic anthropologist or forensic archaeologist, and with the recovery of evidence such as a forensic entomologist or forensic botanist. In some instances, personnel with specialized skills not normally required during most body searches may be invited to participate in searches when machinery or technology is required, such as a backhoe operator or a ground-penetrating radar (GPR) specialist.

Although a number of experts are frequently involved as medicolegal team members, forensic anthropologists have become integral team members for death investigations involving decomposing bodies, fragmentary remains, and skeletal remains, because they provide a unique skill set in both the laboratory and the field. It is fairly common for forensic anthropologists employed at universities, colleges, or museums to consult on an as-needed basis for coroner and ME offices, because a full-time anthropologist is generally not needed on a daily basis. However, there are a number of ME offices throughout the United States that employ forensic anthropologists as full-time employees due to caseload, mass fatality preparedness, and shared expertise as investigators or autopsy technicians (Austin and Fulginiti, 2008).

1.2   What Do Forensic Anthropologists Do?

Traditionally, forensic anthropologists have been requested to assist local law enforcement agencies and coroner or ME offices with the identification of human skeletal remains. It is becoming more likely, however, that the forensic anthropologist will be asked to assist in other capacities. Table 1.1

Table 1.1   Summary of Skills and Knowledge Associated with Forensic Anthropology

- Have knowledge of and familiarity with:
  - Human soft tissue anatomy
  - Burnt and cremated remains
  - Fetal, infant, and juvenile skeletal remains (growth and development)
  - Dental development, morphology, and variation
  - Skeletal and dental pathology
- Identify human versus nonhuman skeletal remains
- Assist in determining context of human remains (e.g., forensic, anatomical, historical, archaeological)
- Understand and recognize taphonomic processes (e.g., decomposition, weathering, animal activity) and information needed for determining time since death
- Develop biological profile: skeletal indications of sex, age at death, ancestry, and stature
- Distinguish premortem, perimortem, and postmortem skeletal modification and trauma
- Identify unique skeletal traits or variations (genetic and acquired)
- Use radiologic images of dentition and skeletal remains for identification
- Understand methodology and use of mitochondrial and nuclear DNA for identification
- Understand use of facial reconstruction and superimposition identification techniques
- Provide law enforcement officials with a written report of all activities

Source: Modified from Skinner, M.F., Alempijevic, D., Djuric-Srejic, M. 2003. Guidelines for international forensic bioarchaeology monitors of mass grave exhumations. *Forensic Science International* 134:81–92; and Snow, 1982.

includes a list of skills that the forensic anthropologist should be experienced in or knowledgeable about.

In the laboratory, forensic anthropologists provide a number of important osteology skills that are pertinent to a death investigation. When the anthropologist is first presented with evidence collected from a scene, the first task is to differentiate bone from non-bone material. Once the material is identified as bone, the next task is to differentiate human bone from nonhuman bone. If the bone is identified as being human, the next task is to determine if the skeletal material is from a modern medicolegal context, more commonly referred to as a forensic context, or from a non-forensic (i.e., non-medicolegal) context, such as archaeological remains or discarded teaching materials. If the material is from a forensic context, the anthropologist's next task is to sort the remains to determine the minimum number of individuals (MNI). In some instances, the forensic context could involve a grave containing a number of individuals or a plane crash involving extreme fragmentation of multiple persons. After MNI is determined, the next task in osteological analysis is to construct a biological profile (e.g., age, sex, ancestry, stature, and individualizing traits), determine presence of antemortem and perimortem trauma, and interpret possible postmortem modifications.

The osteological analysis could also include interpreting indications of time since death and individual identification if requested.

In addition to the skills listed in Table 1.1, the forensic anthropologist, regardless of archaeological knowledge, may also be able to assist in searching crime scenes and recovering skeletal remains. Of particular importance is the fact that forensic anthropologists are also trained in recognizing patterns of taphonomy (i.e., what happens to a body after the individual dies), and they may be able to help locate remains based on these processes. Forensic anthropologists can also readily identify fetal, infant, and child skeletal remains, which often look very different from adult human skeletal remains and can be easily overlooked by the untrained eye. As previously mentioned, many forensic anthropologists are knowledgeable and trained in archaeological methods, so their expertise can also be extremely beneficial during recovery.

1.3   What Do Forensic Archaeologists Do?

As a separate discipline, or as a set of skills that the forensic anthropologist may possess, forensic archaeology involves applying archaeological techniques to the crime scene. It is important to recognize that there are fundamental differences between traditional academic archaeology and forensic archaeology (Hunter, 2002). Traditional academic archaeology is research based and question driven, where particular methodological steps are consistently followed. The forensic archaeologist, on the other hand, in addition to applying methodological steps, has to deal with law enforcement and legal procedures, major time constraints, the media, the occasional presence of soft tissues, and situations in which traditional archaeological methods will not work. Forensic archaeologists have to be much more flexible in their approach and adapt their methods to each case at hand (Hoshower, 1998).

Forensic archaeologists should be proficient in all the skills associated with traditional archaeology and know how to apply this expertise in a forensic context. A list of skills drawn from the authors' experience and modified from Skinner et al. (2003) can be found in Table 1.2. It is important to recognize that during a forensic investigation, there are five responsibilities directly associated with the forensic archaeologist: locating or eliminating areas of interest, interpreting scene context, mapping the scene, excavating remains, and collecting remains and associated evidence.

1.3.1   Locating and Eliminating Areas of Interest

Locating sites of deposition and eliminating sites as areas of interest are primary aspects of any forensic investigation. Most searches in forensic

Table 1.2   Summary of Skills and Knowledge Associated with Forensic Archaeology

- Have knowledge and recognition of:
  - Basic human soft tissue anatomy and decomposition process
  - Basic nonhuman and human (adult and juvenile) skeletal remains
  - Burnt and cremated remains
  - Associated forensic evidence (e.g., tool marks, surgical implants, bullets)
- Assist with visual and intrusive method ground searches
- Assist in determining context of human remains (e.g., forensic, anatomical, historical, archaeological)
- Direct any heavy equipment use during a ground search
- Understand and recognize taphonomic processes (e.g., decomposition, weathering, animal activity) and environmental changes associated with the burial process
- Conduct or assist with geophysical search methods (e.g., ground-penetrating radar [GPR], electromagnetic survey)
- Analyze site formation and provide detailed descriptions of soils and geotaphonomy
- Perform survey and mapping at various levels of the search and recovery process
- Establish spatial controls (e.g., Global Positioning System [GPS] data, gridding, datum points)
- Excavate and record site using archaeological methods specifically adapted to each case
- Collect, document, and preserve soil, botanical, and entomological evidence
- Collect, document, and preserve human remains and associated evidence
- Provide law enforcement officials with a written report of all activities

Source: Modified from Skinner, M.F., Alempijevic, D., Djuric-Srejic, M. 2003. Guidelines for international forensic bioarchaeology monitors of mass grave exhumations. *Forensic Science International* 134:81–92; and Snow, 1982.

investigations are initiated with a tip from an informant, followed by a visual search of the area to locate evidence associated with the missing individual or his or her remains. At times, the initial search may indicate the possible presence of remains and require further investigation. For example, authors John Schultz and Lana Williams assisted with a search in a Central Florida commercial development lot, an area of interest indicated by an informant and previously searched using cadaver dogs. Time constraints and the size of the area to be exposed necessitated the use of heavy equipment to assist with the search. After consulting with the heavy equipment operator, the area was exposed by scraping away thin layers of soil so any changes in soil layers or patterns of soil disturbance would be recognizable. Throughout the process, notes were kept on soil characteristics, depth of layers, and any inclusions and disturbances. Digging continued until the entire area was exposed and all possible means of detection had been exhausted. Although no evidence of remains was found, the expertise of the forensic archaeologists in this investigation assisted with the equally important elimination of a site as an area of further interest.

1.3.2 Interpreting Scene Context

The second role of the forensic archaeologist includes the skills and techniques needed to understand and interpret the initial context and prolonged history of crime scene transformation. The results of postdepositional events will be the first thing encountered by the team of investigators, and the interpretation of these transformations can be vital during the search and recovery process. In one instance, author Tosha Dupras realized firsthand the intensity of taphonomic processes during her involvement in a skeletal recovery near Niagara Falls, Canada. It was soon recognized that this site was exposed annually to excessive water runoff from melting snow and continual falling rock from the cliff face, which caused a great amount of landscape alteration. As a result, different parts of the body moved down the slope as the terrain changed. The skeleton was dispersed from the top of the slope as the terrain changed each year due to taphonomic processes. As the body decomposed, different parts moved down the slope as the terrain changed each year due to taphonomic processes. An understanding of the taphonomic processes at this scene aided in developing the search and excavation techniques employed in recovering this individual.

1.3.3 Mapping the Scene

Mapping techniques commonly used in forensic archaeology allow investigators to maintain an exact record of where every item of evidence was located at the scene. These techniques can also assist investigators in reconstructing the order of events that took place prior to recovery. An example of this occurred when author Sandra Wheeler assisted with the mapping and recovery of an individual found among tall reeds along a canal embankment. The slope of the embankment caused the skull to slide away from the body during the decomposition process and become lodged in the reeds farther downhill. To aid the mapping and recovery of evidence from the slope, the crime scene unit carefully trimmed the reeds surrounding the skull and the additional remains. During the autopsy, the forensic anthropologist working with investigators identified a possible perimortem fracture in two of the facial bones of the skull. However, the forensic anthropologist and investigating detective needed to eliminate the possibility of the fracture being caused by the postmortem movement of the skull. The investigators examined the original scene map to evaluate the slope of the hill and distance that the skull traveled (Figure 1.1). The map shows that the skull did not travel far from the body and that the reeds most likely blocked it from rolling farther down the slope. It was determined that the postmortem movement of the skull could not have caused the force needed to result in the type of fracture identified by the forensic anthropologist. Although photographs were taken at the scene,

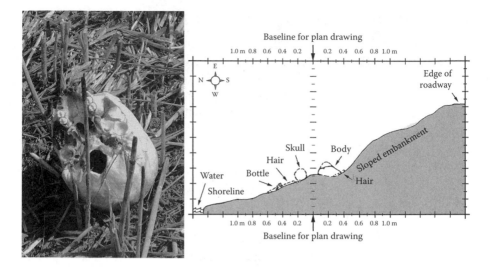

Figure 1.1 Field photo (left) taken from downhill of the skull to show its position among reeds, which were cut to aid in the recovery of the remains. The section drawing of the embankment (right) shows the position of the skull on the slope in relation to the body at the time of recovery.

they did not supply the level of detail needed to evaluate the exact location of the skull on the embankment in relation to the body at the time of recovery. In this instance, proper mapping techniques used in forensic archaeology, which included plan and section drawings, assisted with the reconstruction of events and provided support for the identification of perimortem trauma to the individual.

1.3.4 Excavation of Remains

Forensic archaeologists also play a key role in the reconstruction and interpretation of events that occur as the scene was being created and the evidence or body deposited. Meticulous archaeological techniques can also be used to corroborate or disprove assailant stories about what happened at a particular scene. For example, authors Sandra Wheeler and Lana Williams assisted in the recovery of an individual who was placed in a hole in a cement floor that was initially dug for the installation of a water pump. During burial, the assailants undercut the cement floor to remove enough soil to accommodate the body. The assailants then used the soil and large fragments of cement, which were removed earlier for the water pump installation, to backfill over the victim's body. During excavation, everything was meticulously mapped and recorded with top and bottom depths noted for each object and layer encountered. The head of the victim was positioned in the undercut with no other debris or cement fragments in the immediate vicinity. During review by the coroner, it was discovered that the victim had multiple fractures to the skull, which were most likely sustained during beating at the time of death. The assailants, however, claimed that the fractures were caused during burial, when the fragments of cement were tossed in over the body. When the records from the excavation were consulted, it was evident that the victim's head was covered with a soil layer and located approximately 15 centimeters below the depth of the nearest cement fragment. Moreover, it was also evident that any material used to backfill the hole could not have dropped directly on the victim's head. By using proper excavation and recording techniques throughout recovery, the coroner and the investigating detectives were able to eliminate any possible damage to the victim's skull during burial and attribute the fractures to injuries sustained during the last moments of the individual's life.

1.3.5 Collecting Remains and Evidence

Because forensic anthropologists are trained in recognizing human skeletal remains, they may be able to provide valuable assistance in locating missing skeletal elements. This was true in a Central Florida case where authors Tosha Dupras and Lana Williams assisted in analyzing human skeletal remains that were recovered during a forensic investigation without the assistance of a forensic anthropologist. After taking inventory of the recovered remains, which were intermingled with a matting of plant roots and the individual's clothing, initial skeletal analysis and examination of the scene photos revealed that several bones that should have been present were missing. Upon revisiting the site, several more bones were recovered (Figure 1.2). To the layperson it may seem that missing a few bones would be inconsequential, but these bones could be the ones that hold the key to the individual's identification and also aid in reconstructing what happened to the individual at the time of death. In

Figure 1.2 Sorting through plant materials and remains removed from a crime scene (left). The remains were recovered from the scene without the help of a forensic anthropologist or forensic archaeologist. Author Tosha Dupras later recovered missing bones and evidence (right) when she assisted the homicide detective at the site.

addition, it may also save time, money, and resources in the future by avoiding a situation in which someone might discover the missing bones well after the case is closed, therefore creating what appears to be a new case.

1.4   Education and Training

In North America it is expected that a forensic archaeologist will be trained not only in archaeological techniques but also in human osteology. Typically forensic archaeologists and forensic anthropologists will begin their education in physical anthropology and specialize in human osteology or human skeletal biology. Once the skills of human osteology are mastered, it becomes possible to apply the methods and techniques of analyzing skeletal remains to cases of legal importance.

In recent years, the number of forensic anthropologists receiving training in archaeological field methods has increased. This increase, in part, is due to many graduate students in forensic anthropology understanding the importance of receiving training in archaeological methods and taking advantage of training in both areas in the same academic department. However, it is possible that the skills of the forensic anthropologist will not include knowledge of archaeological techniques, and the forensic archaeologist will not necessarily have knowledge of human osteology. Therefore, when searching for the appropriate individual to assist in crime scene excavations, local law enforcement agencies should be aware of an individual's skill set before asking for that individual's assistance.

There are also numerous short courses offered in North America that include training in archaeological methods. Although this text is written to assist law enforcement personnel, death investigation personnel, students, and professional forensic anthropologists and archaeologists, it is not meant to replace training in these methods. If an individual with skills in forensic archaeology is not available to assist with a case, at minimum one, if not all, personnel involved with field collection, search, or recovery should attend a forensic archaeology short course. Information on these courses can be found by doing an Internet search, or through the website for the American Academy of Forensic Sciences (http://www.aafs.org). Once at this site, select the "Meetings" button at the top of the screen, and then "Other" from the pull-down menu to see a list of upcoming short courses and other meetings.

1.5   Employment in Academic and Nonacademic Settings

In most instances, forensic archaeologists do not have full-time positions in which they actively work on forensic cases. The majority of forensic anthropologists and forensic archaeologists in North America are employed as professors at universities or other academic institutes. When their field or lab skills are needed, law enforcement agencies, medical examiners, and coroners consult with practicing forensic anthropologists. In rare instances, forensic anthropologists and forensic archaeologists may be employed by museums. For example, when the Federal Bureau of Investigation (FBI) needs the expertise of a forensic anthropologist, it turns to the Smithsonian Institution (http://www.si.edu), which has a number of physical and biological anthropologists who specialize in forensic anthropology (Ubelaker and Scamell, 2000). In addition, forensic anthropologists are employed in jobs outside of academics. As mentioned earlier, coroner or ME offices occasionally hire forensic anthropologists for additional roles in the office and to work on forensic anthropology casework when the need arises. They may also be hired full time by coroner or ME offices if they are located in regions that support a heavy caseload.

The single largest employer of forensic anthropologists and forensic archaeologists in the United States is the Joint POW/MIA Accounting Command, or JPAC (http://www.jpac.pacom.mil), located on the island of Oahu in Hawaii. JPAC was formed in October 2003 with the joining of the U.S. Army Central Identification Laboratory Hawaii (CILHI), and the Joint Task Force–Full Accounting. One of the missions of JPAC is to account for all Americans missing as a consequence of any conflicts involving the United States. As a result, forensic anthropologists and forensic archaeologists perform searches and recoveries in countries where there are reports of remains belonging to American citizens.

Forensic anthropologists and forensic archaeologists are also recognized for their expertise in the identification of individuals involved in mass disasters such as plane crashes (e.g., TWA Flight 800), earthquakes, floods, or bombings (e.g., Oklahoma City Federal Building and World Trade Center in New York City). In the United States, most state and federal mass disaster teams, known as the Disaster Mortuary Operational Response Teams (DMORT) (http://www.dmort.org), have several forensic anthropologists and forensic archaeologists on their rosters. In addition, other government agencies that employ forensic anthropologists in a full-time capacity include the National Transportation and Safety Board (NTSB) (http://www.ntsb.gov) and the Armed Forces Institute of Pathology (AFIP) (http://www.afip.org).

Since the 1980s, forensic anthropologists and forensic archaeologists have become vital team members in the search, recovery, and identification of victims of human rights violations around the world. Agencies such as Physicians for Human Rights (PHR) and the United Nations International Criminal Tribunals routinely employ forensic anthropologists and forensic archaeologists in locations such as Guatemala, Argentina, Bosnia, Rwanda, and East Timor to assist in the identification of individuals who have died as a result of their ethnicity, political affiliation, or religious beliefs.

1.6   Locating a Forensic Anthropologist or Forensic Archaeologist

The American Academy of Forensic Sciences (AAFS) is a nonprofit organization composed of forensic specialists in the following 11 sections: criminalistics, digital and multimedia, engineering sciences, general, jurisprudence, odontology, pathology and biology, physical anthropology, psychiatry and behavioral sciences, questioned documents, and toxicology. The AAFS has members representing all of the United States, Canada, and 50 other countries worldwide. To achieve recognition within the broader discipline of forensic sciences in North America, most forensic anthropologists belong to the Physical Anthropology section of the AAFS. There are certain qualifications that must be met to become a member of the AAFS. For the Physical Anthropology section, members must demonstrate through casework, teaching, or research that they are active in the discipline. Please note however, that this does not mean that the individual has been certified as an expert in forensic anthropology.

One option for locating members of the discipline is to visit the website for the AAFS. Unfortunately, access to the membership directory is now restricted to Academy members. If you or your agency has a membership, you can find a list of Academy members in your area by following these instructions:

1. Log on to the official website for the Academy of Forensic Sciences, which can be found at http://www.aafs.org.
2. Select "Membership" at the top of the page, and then select "Find a Member" from the pull-down menu.
3. Enter desired "State" and leave "Last Name" and "City" blank.
4. Under "Section" choose "Anth."

This should result in a list of forensic anthropologists with contact information.

A growing number of members of the Physical Anthropology section of the AAFS have received certification or Diplomat status from the American Board of Forensic Anthropology (ABFA). Diplomat status is the highest recognized form of certification in the discipline of forensic anthropology in North America. To obtain this certification, individuals must have a doctoral degree in anthropology with an emphasis in physical anthropology, have three years of professional experience, and must pass a comprehensive written and practical examination. Currently, there are approximately 85 members listed as board certified, while perhaps only about 70 of these are practicing forensic anthropologists. For a list and contact information for forensic anthropologists with Diplomat status, visit the American Board of Forensic Anthropology website (http://www.theabfa.org).

Unfortunately, at this time, there are no recognized associations or boards specifically for forensic archaeology, and because of this, there are no easy ways to find individuals who have skills in forensic archaeology. The Society for American Archaeology keeps a forensic archaeology recovery roster, but this information can only be accessed on their website (http://www.saa.org) if you are a member of the organization. The best way to find these specialists, particularly in North America, is to contact individuals who identify themselves as forensic anthropologists and inquire as to their skills in the realm of forensic archaeology. Another option, if forensic specialists are not available in your area, is to contact local universities that have field archaeologists on staff. Even though these individuals may not be trained in the forensic context, they will still possess all the necessary archaeological skills to conduct excavations.

Case Study 1: The Flexible Approach

Two of the authors, Dupras and Schultz, were asked to assist in a case that involved the search for a missing adult female. She had been missing for approximately 12 years, and the police received a tip that she may have been deposited in a currently unused subterranean city sewage-holding tank that was not easily accessible. One of the suspects in this case had previously been employed by the city and had worked at the treatment facility when the holding tank was in use. Shortly after the woman's disappearance, this holding tank was sealed off and no longer used.

This case truly was a challenge, and there was no possible way to apply traditional archaeological techniques throughout the recovery process. An adaptable and flexible approach was required. The first obstacle was gaining access to the small opening at the entrance to the large subterranean holding tank, which required city workers to remove part of the wall of a small structure located directly above the tank (Figure 1.3). A sturdy tripod was set up over the opening so that individuals could be lowered into the tank, and exhaust tubes were also inserted into the tank to provide some ventilation.

Representatives from environmental health and safety deemed this to be a hazardous site due to the nature of the material in the holding tank, particularly due to the presence of lethal gases. This meant that a traditional-style excavation of the holding tank could not be performed. The potential lethal nature of this site required that the material had to first be removed from the holding tank before it could be thoroughly examined. This was accomplished by lowering heavily protected individuals into the tank, who were outfitted with oxygen so they would not succumb to deadly gases (Figure 1.4).

Figure 1.3 Search at the sewage-holding tank with removal of the outer wall to gain access to the holding tank opening (left), and a tripod with safety lines set up over the opening (right) with exhaust vents.

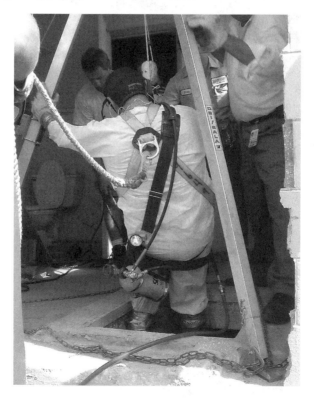

Figure 1.4 Lowering a well-protected city worker (note biohazard suit, mask, and oxygen tank) through the opening into the sewage-holding tank.

Figure 1.5 Large vacuum truck dumping materials from the holding tank into a prepared area lined with heavy plastic.

Once in the tank, workers used a large vacuum to suction the material into the tank of an industrial vacuum truck. When filled, the vacuum trucks separated the sediment from the liquid and then moved the material to a large dumping area lined with heavy plastic, which was created for the drained material (Figure 1.5). Large screens were set up in the bucket of a backhoe to sieve the material and recover any remains (Figure 1.6). The thick and wet nature of the soil required the use of a wet screening method (Figure 1.7). It took three days to remove and process all the material from the holding tank, and no evidence of human remains was recovered. If this missing individual was placed in the holding tank, the passage of 12 years in this particular environment most likely completely destroyed all traces of her remains. She currently remains a missing person.

Figure 1.6 Author Tosha Dupras (center), Orange County, Florida, crime scene investigator Kelly Wood (back), and Orange County homicide detective Dave Clarke (right) sieving through materials removed from the sewage-holding tank.

Figure 1.7 Crime scene investigator (right) using water to flush material through the screen while author Tosha Dupras (left) carefully examines all fragments held on the screen.

Key Words and Questions

AAFS
ABFA Diplomat
antemortem
biological profile
DMORT
forensic anthropology
forensic archaeology
forensic botany
forensic entomology
forensic odontology
JPAC
medical examiner
osteology
perimortem
PHR
physical anthropology
postmortem

1. Under the following circumstances, would it be appropriate to request assistance from a forensic archaeologist? What special skills or knowledge would a forensic archaeologist provide in the recovery of the remains?
   - Five large bones were uncovered while digging a trench for a new utility line.
   - During autopsy, partially skeletonized human remains recovered from an abandoned warehouse are found to be incomplete.
   - The neighbor's dog, Marley, left a pile of dirt-covered, chewed bones on your front porch, one of which resembles a human femur.
   - Workers turn up skeletonized remains of an individual in a cemetery plot that should have been empty.
   - A local man, digging the foundation for a backyard shed, uncovers a group of cut and chipped burnt bones.
   - During a police investigation, an individual in a fairly advanced state of soft tissue decomposition is said to be under a concrete slab in a backyard.
   - In the woods, a hunter finds what may be portions of a child's skull and some additional small bones sticking out of the ground.
2. Relate the skills and areas of knowledge listed in Table 1.2 to each of the five responsibilities directly associated with the forensic archaeologist during an investigation.

3. Forensic archaeologists have been involved in many mass disaster and human rights investigations around the world. What organizations would they most likely be working with in these instances? How do the skills of a forensic archaeologist assist with the identification of individuals recovered during these types of investigations?

Suggested Readings

Austin, D., Fulginiti, L. 2008. The forensic anthropology laboratory in a medical examiner setting. In: Warren, M.W., Walsh-Haney, H.A., Freas, L.E., eds. *Forensic Anthropology Laboratory*, pp. 23–46. Boca Raton, FL: CRC Press.

Dirkmaat, D.C., Adovasio J.M. 1997. The role of archaeology in the recovery and interpretation of human remains from an outdoor forensic setting. In: Haglund, W.D., Sorg, M.H., eds. *Forensic Taphonomy: The Postmortem Fate of Human Remains*, pp. 39–64. Boca Raton, FL: CRC Press.

Dirkmaat, D.C., Cabo, L.L., Ousley, S.D., Symes, S.A. 2008. New perspectives in forensic anthropology. *Yearbook of Physical Anthropology* 51:33–52.

Mann, R.W., Anderson, B.E., Holland, T.H., Webb Jr., J.E. 2009. Unusual "crime" scenes: the role of forensic anthropology in recovering and identifying American MIAs. In: Steadmann, D.W., ed. *Hard Evidence: Case Studies in Forensic Anthropology,* 2nd ed., pp. 133–140. Upper Saddle River, NJ: Prentice Hall.

Schultz, J.J., Dupras, T.L. 2008. The contribution of forensic archaeology to homicide investigations. *Homicide Studies* 12:399–413.

Skinner, M.F., Alempijevic, D., Djuruc-Srejic, M. 2003. Guidelines for international forensic bioarchaeology monitors of mass grave exhumations. *Forensic Science International* 134:81–92.

Sledzik, P.S. 2009. Forensic anthropology in disaster response. In: Blau, S., Ubelaker, D.H., eds. *Handbook of Forensic Anthropology and Archaeology*, pp. 374–387. Walnut Creek, CA: Left Coast Press.

Steadman, D.W., Haglund, W.D. 2005. The scope of anthropological contributions to human rights investigations. *Journal of Forensic Sciences* 50:23–30.

References

Austin, D., Fulginiti, L. 2008. The forensic anthropology laboratory in a medical examiner setting. In: Warren, M.W., Walsh-Haney, H.A., Freas, L.E., eds. *Forensic Anthropology Laboratory*, pp. 23–46. Boca Raton, FL: CRC Press.

Berryman, H.E., Lahren, C.H. 1984. The advantages of simulated crime scenes in teaching forensic anthropology. *Journal of Forensic Sciences* 20:699–700.

Dirkmaat, D.C., Adovasio, J.M. 1997. The role of archaeology in the recovery and interpretation of human remains from an outdoor forensic setting. In: Haglung, W.D., Sorg, M.H., eds. *Forensic Taphonomy: The Postmortem Fate of Human Remains*, pp. 39–64. Boca Raton, FL: CRC Press.

France, D.L., Griffin, T.J., Swanburg, J.G., Lindemann, J.W., Davenport, G.C., Tramell, V., Travis, C.T., Kondratieff, R., Nelson, A., Castellano, K., Hopkins D. 1992. A multidisciplinary approach to the detection of clandestine graves. *Journal of Forensic Sciences* 37:1145–1458.

France, D.L., Griffin, T.J., Swanburg, J.G., Lindemann, J.W., Davenport, G.C., Tramell, V., Travis, C.T., Kondratieff, R., Nelson, A., Castellano, K., Hopkins, D., Adair, T. 1997. NecroSearch revisited: further multidisciplinary approaches to the detection of clandestine graves. In: Haglund, W.D., Sorg, M.H., eds. *Forensic Taphonomy: The Postmortem Fate of Human Remains*, pp. 497–509. Boca Raton, FL: CRC Press.

Hanson, I. 2008. Forensic archaeology: approaches to international investigations. In: Oxenham, M., ed. *Forensic Approaches to Death, Disaster and Abuse*, pp. 17–28. Brisbane: Australia Academic Press.

Hoshower, L.M. 1998. Forensic archaeology and the need for flexible excavation strategies: a case study. *Journal of Forensic Sciences* 43:53–56.

Hunter, J.R. 2002. Foreword: a pilgrim in forensic archaeology—a personal view. In: Haglund, W.D., Sorg, M.H., eds. *Advances in Forensic Taphonomy: Method, Theory, and Archaeological Perspectives*, pp. xxv–xxxii. Boca Raton, FL: CRC Press.

Hunter, J.R., Heron, C., Janaway, R.C., Martin, A.L., Pollard, A.M., Roberts, C.A. 1994. Forensic archaeology in Britain. *Antiquity* 68:758–769.

Hunter, J., Roberts, C., Martin, A. 1996. *Studies in Crime: An Introduction to Forensic Archaeology*. London: B.T. Batsford.

Morse, D., Crusoe, D., Smith, H.G. 1976. Forensic archaeology. *Journal of Forensic Sciences* 21:323–332.

Morse, D., Duncan, J., Stoutamire, J. 1983. *Handbook of Forensic Archaeology and Anthropology*. Tallahassee, FL: Rose Printing.

Schultz, J.J., Dupras, T.L. 2008. The contribution of forensic archaeology to homicide investigations. *Homicide Studies* 12:399–413.

Scott, D.D., Connor, M. 1997. Context delecti: archaeological context in forensic work. In: Haglund, W.D., Sorg, M.H., eds. *Forensic Taphonomy: The Postmortem Fate of Human Remains*, pp. 27–38. Boca Raton, FL: CRC Press.

Sigler-Eisenberg, B. 1985. Forensic research: expanding the concept of applied archaeology. *American Antiquity* 50:650–655.

Skinner, M.F., Alempijevic, D., Djuric-Srejic, M. 2003. Guidelines for international forensic bioarchaeology monitors of mass grave exhumations. *Forensic Science International* 134:81–92.

Skinner, M., Lazenby, R.A. 1983. *Found! Human Remains: A Field Manual for the Recovery of the Recent Human Skeleton*. Burnaby, BC: Archaeology Press Simon Fraser University.

Snow, C.C. 1982. Forensic anthropology. *Annual Review of Anthropology* 11:97–131.

Ubelaker, D., Scammell, H. 2000. *Bones: A Forensic Detective's Casebook*. New York, NY: M. Evans and Company.

Wolf, D.J. 1986. Forensic anthropology scene investigations. In: Reichs, K., ed. *Forensic Osteology: Advances in the Identification of Human Remains*, pp. 3–23. Springfield, IL: Charles C. Thomas.

Tools and Equipment

2

The forensic archaeologist should be well prepared and have all the tools and equipment required to perform recoveries and excavations, and should not rely on local law enforcement to provide the necessary tools. Because the search and recovery of human remains is not a common type of crime scene for most law enforcement agencies, it is not surprising that most agencies will not have this specialized equipment. The variety of tools and equipment used by forensic archaeologists during excavation is practically limitless, but this chapter provides descriptions of the basic, most helpful tools commonly used in the forensic recovery of human remains. A checklist of basic field equipment is located at the end of the chapter. More specialized search equipment is discussed in Chapters 5 and 6, and associated equipment needed for the procurement of entomological and botanical evidence is discussed in Chapter 9. Although some of the tools and equipment are purchased through specialty stores (see Table 2.1), a majority of them are available at local hardware and home improvement stores. However, metric measurement tools may not be readily available locally. If this is the case, they can easily be obtained through online specialty stores.

2.1 Search and Site Preparation Equipment

Certain tools are necessary during a search and for site preparation (Figure 2.1). When beginning a search, each individual should be equipped with a bundle of brightly colored survey flags that can be used to mark the locations of scattered evidence. These flags usually have metal posts; however, if a geophysical survey is being conducted, or will be conducted after a foot search, it is best to use flags with a fiberglass post to avoid interfering with geophysical signals. Survey flags and survey tape may also be used to mark the entrance and exit locations to the site. A handheld Global Positioning System (GPS) device may also be useful to record site location and data points for evidence. Be sure you keep spare batteries on hand, and it is always recommended to test any electronic equipment before going to the field. A handheld compass is also useful for determining directionality when conducting a search over a large area and can also be useful for recording the orientation of evidence, including graves and body position. Small hand machetes and handsaws are helpful

Table 2.1   Companies Selling Equipment Used in Forensic Archaeology

Company and Contact Information	Equipment Available
Forestry Suppliers, Inc. 205 West Franklin Street, Jackson, MS 39201 Phone: 1-800-647-5368 Fax: 1-800-543-4203 Email: contact form on website http://www.forestry-suppliers.com/	Chaining pins Metric measuring tapes Compasses and global positioning system devices Probes and trowels
Ben Meadows Company P.O. Box 5277, Janesville, WI 53547-5277 Phone: 1-800-241-6401 Fax: 1-800-628-2068 Email: contact form on website http://www.benmeadows.com/	Field survey equipment Survey flags and tape Chaining pins Plumb bobs Compasses
Evident Crime Scene Products 739 Brooks Mill Road, Union Hall, VA 24176 Phone: 1-800-576-7606 Fax: 1-888-384-3368 Email: contact@evident.cc http://www.evidentcrimescene.com/	Photographic scales North arrows Evidence markers Protective clothing Entomology kits
Lynn Peavey Company 10749 West 84th Terrace P.O. Box 14100, Lenexa, KS 66214-3612 Phone: 1-800-255-6499 Fax: 1-913-495-6787 Email: lpv@pvcorp.com http://www.lynnpeavey.com/	Barrier tape Evidence packages Casting materials Filter masks Latex and nitrile gloves Camera equipment
Arrowhead Forensic Products 14400 College Boulevard, Suite 100, Lenexa, KS 66215 Phone: 1-913-894-8388 Fax: 1-913-894-8399 Email: info@arrowheadforensics.com http://www.crime-scene.com/	Evidence packages Casting materials Photographic scales Evidence markers Disinfectant kits
Forensic Source 13386 International Parkway, Jacksonville, FL 32218 Phone: 1-800-852-0300 Fax: 1-800-588-0399 Email: contact form on website http://www.forensicsource.com	Casting materials Photographic supplies Magnifiers Odor inhibitors Cleaners and disinfectant
Stoney Knoll Archaeological Supplies, Inc. P.O. Box 493, Stockton Springs, ME 04981 Phone: 207-548-0080 Fax: 207-548-0116 Email: info@stoneyknoll.com http://www.stoneyknoll.com	Screening equipment Field survey equipment Excavation equipment Recording supplies Photographic supplies

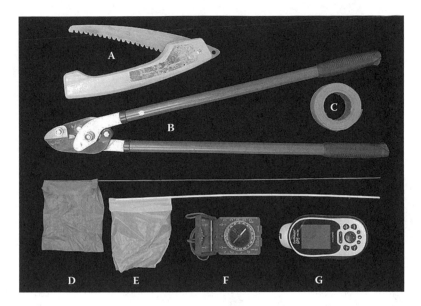

Figure 2.1 Equipment used during survey and clearing: (a) handsaw, (b) hand loppers, (c) survey tape, (d) metal post survey flags, (e) fiberglass post survey flags, (f) handheld compass, and (g) handheld global positioning system (GPS) device.

in clearing plant growth from the surrounding work areas and around any associated evidence. Investigators should be especially vigilant when clearing underbrush or leaf cover, because evidence can be lodged at the base of trees or in other plant materials. Hand loppers are useful for cutting thick underbrush or branches, fencing wire or landscaping cables, and any other heavy materials that impede investigation or obstruct the work area.

When specifically searching for buried bodies or evidence, a variety of probes can be used and should be included as standard field equipment. The most common probes used are the basic T-bar probe (Figure 2.2) and a soil-coring probe, used to detect soil disturbances. A detailed description of different types of probes and their proper uses can be found in Chapter 5.

2.2   Field Excavation Equipment

Excavations normally begin with surface clearing and require general tools such as rakes, shovels, and screens (Figure 2.2). When removing surface debris such as leaf litter and vegetation, a fan-shaped rake (plastic preferred) should be used. Shovels are useful when removing large quantities of soil, but they should never be used as excavation tools once the burial site has been located. Spade, or round-point, shovels should only be used to backfill holes or move soil that has already been screened from one location to another. Flat-blade, or square-point, shovels are typically used for removing very thin

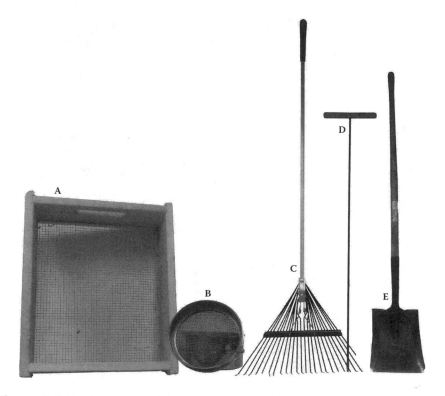

Figure 2.2 Equipment used for site clearing and excavation: (a) handheld box screen, (b) stacked sieves, (c) fan-shaped rake, (d) T-bar probe, and (e) flat-blade shovel.

layers of soil from surface areas or to cut and remove sod from yards or fields. All materials removed from a site should be sifted with a screen, and smaller items can be sorted by using stacked sieves.

Before excavation begins, a grid is usually constructed over the area to be excavated (see Chapter 7). The size of the grid depends on the area to be excavated, and a calculator can be useful to determine the dimensions of the grid. The equipment necessary to construct a grid (Figure 2.3) consists of chaining pins or wood stakes to establish the perimeter, and a mallet is used to secure the stakes into the ground. A brightly colored nylon cord or mason's line is used to establish the internal and external grid lines, and a line level is used to assure that the grid lines are level. Evidence markers can be used to establish references for each grid square.

Smaller and finer tools are used once excavation begins (Figure 2.4). Hand trowels are used for precise excavation, especially when removing soil surrounding bones or objects where larger tools would damage or displace evidence. With a bit of practice, a pointed hand trowel with a straight blade can be used for extremely delicate work and may prove to be the most effective tool in the field kit. Four- or five-inch (10 or 12 centimeters) cement

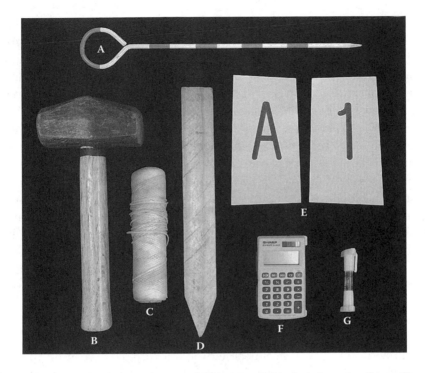

Figure 2.3 Equipment used to establish a grid: (a) chaining pin, (b) mallet, (c) mason's line, (d) wooden stake, (e) evidence markers, (f) calculator, and (g) line level.

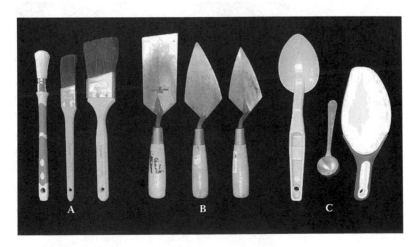

Figure 2.4 Equipment used during excavation: (a) a variety of different-sized brushes, (b) pointed and square-edged margin trowels, and (c) a variety of different-sized scoops and spoons.

trowels made of drop-forged steel are recommended, as the handles, blade welds, and points are more resistant to breakage. Square-edged margin trowels are perfect for excavating in sandy or wet soils. Some of the more popular brands of trowels used by archaeologists include Marshalltown or Goldblatt. Cheaply constructed trowels will bend or break and can quickly put an end to any excavation if the site is miles from the nearest hardware store. Garden-variety trowels with curved blades are not suited for excavation and should not be used in any recovery of human remains. In addition, garden claw tools should never be used for excavating.

Soft horsehair, China bristle, or other natural bristle brushes, such as paint or makeup brushes, are recommended in excavation to clear loose soil from the remains before photographing or drawing (Figure 2.4). Natural bristle brushes tend to last longer than synthetic bristle brushes and have less of a tendency to clump in sandy or wet clay soils. These brushes are also less likely to lose bristles. A variety of different sized brushes should be included in each kit. Makeup brushes are a smaller, softer alternative for very delicate excavation.

Wood sculpting tools, splints, bamboo skewers, makeup brushes and toothbrushes, and various sizes of plastic spoons are ideal for detailing around bone surfaces to avoid scratching, nicking, or damaging the bone (Figure 2.5). Bulb syringes may also be useful for blowing away dirt particles, particularly when preparing the skeleton for a photograph. Dental picks may also be used, but only with extreme care to avoid producing any misleading or erroneous marks on the bone surfaces. Small tweezers are useful for removing small items or for evidence collection. In some cases, it may be

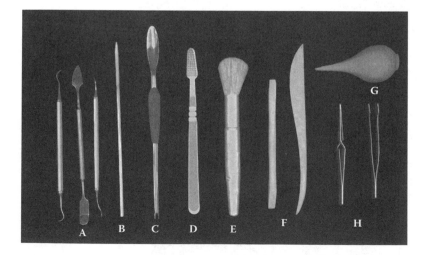

Figure 2.5 Equipment used during excavation: (a) dental picks, (b) bamboo skewers, (c) powder spatula, (d) toothbrush, (e) makeup brush, (f) wooden tools, (g) bulb syringe, and (h) tweezers.

Figure 2.6 Equipment used for clearing and excavation: (a) spackle bucket, (b) whisk broom, (c) dust pan, (d) paint brush, and (e) root clippers.

preferable to use disposable skewers or plastic items when detailing around remains in extremely wet conditions or if any soft tissue is still present.

Root clippers are needed for trimming roots and small ground cover (Figure 2.6). Large brushes and whisk brooms are useful in removing loose dirt from surrounding areas but should never be used directly on the remains as they may become displaced or damaged. Heavy plastic or metal dustpans can be used along with whisk brooms when collecting loose soil from larger cleared spaces within the excavation or in the surrounding area. Avoid the use of flimsy metal or plastic dustpans that will bend or break when they are used with heavy soil. Sturdy metal or plastic buckets (spackle and paint buckets work best) are used to transport soil for screening.

Screens with 1/4-inch (#3) mesh are typically used for sifting through soil removed from the excavation to recover materials that may otherwise be overlooked (Figure 2.2). A smaller gauge screen (#7 mesh) may be attached to an 8 × 10 inch wooden picture frame for screening very small elements, such as fetal bones or insect casings, that would normally be missed using the larger gauge screens. Mesh can be either metal or plastic; however, metal is recommended, as it is more durable, especially when working with heavier or damp soils. All screens should be thoroughly cleaned after use. Collapsible sawhorses are an excellent platform for screening materials. By laying the screen across the sawhorses, there is a clear view of the materials and a relatively flat, level working surface. Plastic sheeting or tarps should be placed beneath the screens to catch the screened soil. This method also allows for the screened material to be kept separate in cases where finer screening is necessary. After each bucket of soil is completely screened, simply change out the plastic sheeting or tarp from under the work area. The tarp or sheeting can be used to keep the soil separate for further screening or to move the soil to a collection pile. Tarps and plastic sheeting can also be used to cover an excavation in case of rain or to protect the excavation overnight.

2.3 Mapping and Measuring Equipment

A transit is used with a stadia rod for measuring precise angles and distances from fixed points. These points are used to plot the survey map, plan, and section drawings of the site. A total station can also be used for this purpose; however, it is an expensive piece of equipment and requires a trained operator. A hand compass is useful in the site survey and also in determining the orientation of graves relative to other features, such as posts, trees, or buildings.

Metric measuring tapes are indispensable tools during the mapping and excavation processes, and the more and different kinds that are available, the better (Figure 2.7). A 5-meter steel tape that can be clipped to the belt is a must. At least two 20- to 50-meter field tapes should be included in the toolkit, as these are needed for mapping any areas of recovery. Metric folding stick tapes are also handy for drawing and taking depth measurements. Plumb bobs with a 2- to 5-ounce weight and string line levels are crucial for plotting the exact location of evidence and for measuring depths.

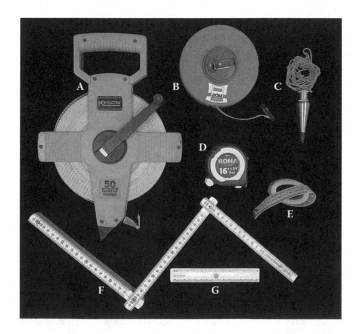

Figure 2.7 Equipment used for measurement: (a) 50-meter field tape, (b) 20-meter field tape, (c) plumb bob, (d) 5-meter steel tape, (e) flexible fiberglass tape, (f) folding stick tape, and (g) ruler.

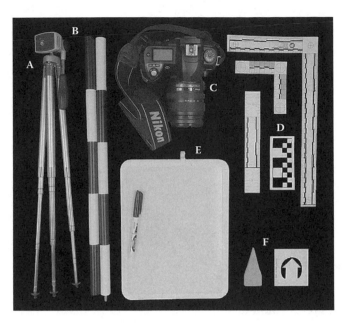

Figure 2.8 Equipment used for photography: (a) tripod, (b) collapsible meter stick, (c) digital camera, (d) various scales, (e) writing board, and (f) north arrows.

2.4 Drawing and Recording Equipment

Recording equipment (Figures 2.8 and 2.9) is an essential part of every excavation kit. Photographic accessories such as scales and a north arrow (a pointed trowel can substitute for a north arrow) should be used in all photography to note scale and orientation of any evidence. A camera tripod and writing board (used to include site information in photographs) should also be included in the kit. All necessary blank forms, paper evidence bags, labels, tags, notebooks, pens, permanent markers, and pencils should be on hand to properly record and collect materials. Tools needed for a detailed drawing of the excavation would include several mechanical pencils with extra lead and erasers, nails or chaining pins, mason's line, compass, handheld measuring tapes, folding stick tapes, line level, plumb bob, a pad of 5- or 10-squares-per-centimeter graph paper, and a drawing board, clipboard, or field desk. A waterproof field notebook can also be very useful in bad weather conditions.

2.5 Optional Equipment

With field conditions varying from scene to scene, it is always best to keep a few optional items available in case any adverse conditions or special circumstances arise (Figure 2.10). A first aid kit is a necessity in the field. Any cuts or scrapes acquired during excavation should be attended to as soon as

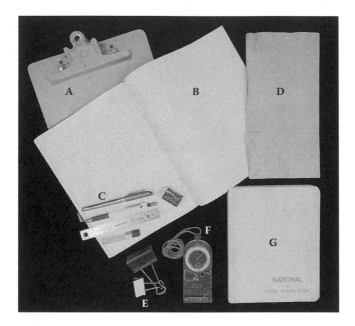

Figure 2.9 Equipment used for recording data: (a) clipboard, (b) notebook with graph paper, (c) writing utensils and rulers, (d) paper evidence bags, (e) binder clips, (f) handheld compass, and (g) waterproof survey record book.

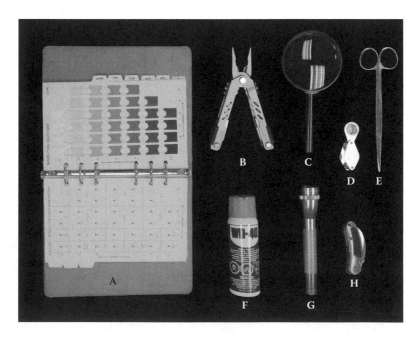

Figure 2.10 Optional equipment: (a) soil color chart, (b) multipurpose tool, (c) magnifying lens, (d) handheld lens, (e) scissors, (f) rust inhibitor, (g) flashlight, and (h) folding utility knife.

possible to prevent severe infections. Filter breathing masks are helpful in extremely dusty or odorous conditions as well as cases with heavy infestations of insects.

Additional items that may be useful include:

- Multipurpose tool, utility knife, and scissors for any minor tool needs that may occur
- Hand lens or magnifying glass for close inspection of remains or associated evidence
- Flashlight for illuminating shadowed areas
- Water spray bottles to keep the sides of an excavation from collapsing in sandy or dry soils
- Soil color charts for accurate color identification of the soils associated with the remains
- Antimicrobial or disinfectant for cleaning all equipment
- Rust or corrosion inhibitor for treating metal tools after use

Other useful items that can make your work environment much more tolerable when spending time doing detailed tasks include (Figure 2.11):

- Fresh drinking water
- Snacks
- Bug spray
- Sunscreen
- Odor inhibitor

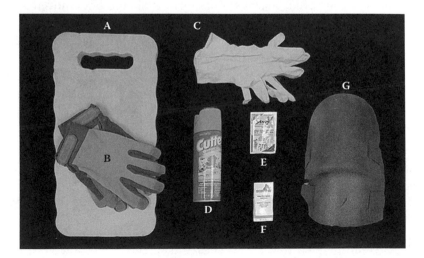

Figure 2.11 Optional comfort items: (a) kneeling pad, (b) gloves, (c) latex or nitrile disposable gloves, (d) bug spray, (e) sunscreen, (f) odor inhibitor, and (g) knee pads.

- Hats
- Extra batteries for all equipment
- Latex gloves and canvas or leather work gloves
- Foam knee pads or mat
- Hand sanitizer
- Disposable coveralls
- Extra clothing
- Extra pair of shoes and socks

2.6 Caring for Your Equipment

Field equipment can be exposed to various environments, and taking proper care of your equipment is vital to extend its life span. Time should be budgeted after each excavation to completely clean all tools. Forensic contexts such as moist, wet soils can have deleterious effects on tools, particularly those that have metal components such as trowels, shovels, and screens. If left wet, these tools will start to rust and corrode. To prevent this from happening, tools should be thoroughly cleaned after use to remove all dirt and stains. Before storing tools, a standard lubricating oil or rust inhibitor should be applied to the surface. Tools should be stored in a dry place. If your toolkit has to be stored in a humid area, commercial desiccant packages can be added, or, if these are not available, uncooked rice placed into a porous bag can serve as an improvised desiccant package. Desiccants or rice bags should be replaced regularly to keep the humidity down and prevent rust and corrosion buildup. In the event that rust does form, it should be removed as soon as possible. This can be achieved by washing the tool with hot water and dish detergent to remove any dirt or grit. After this, use a wire brush to scrub the outer surface until all rust is removed. Rinse again with hot water. A water displacing spray can help remove light rust and corrosion by applying it to the metal surface and rubbing it with steel wool or medium-grain sandpaper. Once again, the surface should be treated with a rust inhibitor or lubricant before storage.

Tools with a sharp edge, such as shovels, trowels, pruning shears, and root clippers, can become dull with use and should be sharpened on a regular basis. Smaller tools can easily be sharpened with a flat hand file or a honing stone that can be kept in the toolkit. A sharp trowel can aid in removing heavier soils and cutting small roots when excavating. You may also consider bringing your tools into a tool shop to have them sharpened.

It is recommended that all brushes and screens be cleaned with a 2% bleach-to-water solution after each excavation to avoid any possibility of contamination and transfer of materials to the next recovery scene. Keep in mind that decomposition molecules can permanently attach themselves to any organic component in tools such as certain brushes, paper, or any fabric items. For example, one author spent an entire week tracking down an item in a toolkit that was carrying a decomposition odor. After repeatedly cleaning all the tools, it was finally discovered that a simple pad of notepaper was the culprit. In cases where the smell of decomposition is especially pungent even after cleaning, you may want to replace these kinds of tools with ones that are easier to clean and maintain. Special odor inhibitor sprays and cleaning disinfectants are available to treat tools for extreme decomposition smell.

2.7 Basic Field Equipment Checklist

- Survey transit, tripod, and stadia rod
- Photo gear, north arrow, and scales
- Field notebook and drawing supplies
- Flat-blade shovel and leaf rake
- Soil probe and corer
- Large screen (30 × 30 in, #3 mesh)
- Small screen (8 × 10 in, #7 mesh)
- Wood stakes and chaining pins
- Survey flags and survey tape
- Whisk broom and dustpans
- Plumb bob and line levels
- Natural bristle brushes
- Tweezers and magnifying glass
- Plastic tarp and rope
- Paper bags and tags
- Hand compass
- 20- or 50-m field tapes
- 5-m steel tape
- Folding stick tape
- Handsaw
- Mason's line
- Mallet and hand tools
- Utility knife
- Spoons and wooden skewers
- Large nails
- Loppers
- Root clippers
- Trowels
- Plastic buckets
- Blank forms

Key Words and Questions

50-meter field tape
box screen
chaining pin
flat-blade shovel
folding stick tape
grid marker
hand trowel
natural bristle brush
photographic scale
plumb bob
soil color chart
T-bar probe

1. The practice of using the correct tools for the job prevents injury and also prevents unnecessary loss or destruction of critical information in a forensic context. Under the following circumstances, which tool(s) would be appropriate for the task described? Are there any evidence recovery or safety concerns associated with using tools in these tasks?
    - A bucket of loose soil from the surface of a grid needs to be examined.
    - Heavy underbrush and a layer of leaf cover needs to be removed from a search area.
    - The locations of cut and chipped bones, found in an open field, need to be marked for mapping.
    - The location of burnt remains, found scattered across the cement floor of a warehouse, needs to be marked for mapping.
    - The position and orientation of an old shed, relative to a tree line within a search area, needs to be determined.
    - A thin layer of surface soil needs to be removed from a suspected burial site, and a hole from a previous test excavation needs to be backfilled.
    - During excavation of a burial, the edges of some small bones need to be detailed and photographed.
    - A small area with city utility lines and landscaped bushes needs to be examined for possible soil disturbances.
2. Forensic archaeologists depend on their tools for every aspect of their work. What kinds of maintenance should be performed on digging and cutting equipment after every use? Why is it important to carefully clean each of your tools after every use?

Human Skeletal Terminology

3

Even though we advocate that it is preferable to include an osteology expert such as a forensic anthropologist for processing scenes involving human skeletal remains, this is not always possible. Investigators are generally expected to write detailed reports and create scene maps for all types of crime scenes; therefore, investigators should also be expected to keep detailed notes and create well-documented scene maps for scenes that involve human skeletal remains. As the purpose of this book is to provide investigators with a guide to properly process scenes involving human skeletal remains, we recognize that most field investigators, whether homicide detectives or crime scene personnel, will not have a basic osteology background. The reason for including information on human skeletal terminology is not so the reader will become an expert in human osteology. This chapter is designed to help the reader create scene maps in which bones are illustrated and to help in describing specifics in scene notes about the body position, any dispersal of remains, and the condition of bones. In addition, processing of a scene involving skeletal remains does not end after the remains are collected or excavated, particularly with a homicide investigation. This chapter is also designed to provide a better understanding of terminology used in reports on skeletal material that may be provided by a medical examiner, coroner, or forensic anthropologist.

The authors strongly caution that this chapter is not to be used as a definitive guide for bone identification, as only very basic information on the human skeleton is provided. Information such as sex, age at death, population ancestry (also termed *race*), stature, pathology, and trauma should only be determined by a qualified expert; therefore, the methods required for determining this information are not included here. A qualified forensic anthropologist or medical examiner should handle final identification of all skeletal material. If further references are needed for documentation, several human anatomy books contain excellent skeletal descriptions, and there are also books written by physical anthropologists and anatomists that deal specifically with the human skeleton. These include *Human Osteology* by Tim White, Michael Black, and Pieter Folkens (2011), *Human Osteology and Skeletal Radiology: An Atlas and Guide* by Evan Matshes and colleagues (2004), *Human Osteology: A Laboratory and Field Manual* by William Bass (1995), *Skeleton Keys* by Jeffrey Schwartz (2006), and *Anatomy and Biology of the Human Skeleton* by Gentry Steele and Claude Bramblett (1988). Because these texts are mainly concerned with adult skeletal morphology, the following can be used as references for juvenile skeletal remains: *The Osteology of Infants and Children* by Brenda Baker, Tosha Dupras, and Matthew Tocheri (2005), *Developmental Juvenile Osteology* by Louise Scheuer and Sue Black (2000), and the condensed version of the previous book, *The Juvenile Skeleton* also by Louise Scheuer and Sue Black (2004).

3.1   Terms Associated with Bone Morphology

When human skeletal remains are processed at a crime scene, specific bone identification, including siding, can be provided onsite when an osteology expert is part of the recovery team. However, when this is not possible, scene investigators still need to provide a description of the types of bones that are located, and a well-documented map can still be created even without using the proper bone names. If a specific bone is not readily identifiable, investigators should document the bone based on its shape and size (e.g., maximum length of the bone). Bones have a number of different shapes, such as long, flat, irregular, tubular, and rounded, that can be used as general identifiers in notes and map legends (Figure 3.1). Table 3.1 provides a description of these common bone identifiers based on shape. If needed, the scene investigator can later work with an osteology expert to provide the specific names of each bone if the scene was documented properly. For example, the osteology expert would need scene photographs of each bone or grouping of bones, and

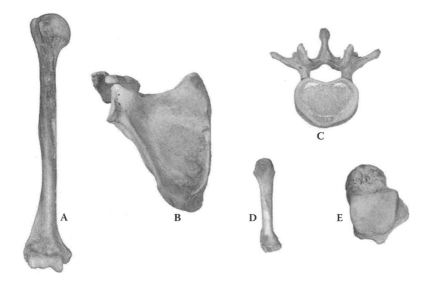

Figure 3.1 Examples of basic bone shapes: (a) long bone, (b) flat bone, (c) irregular bone, (d) short tubular bone, and (e) small, rounded bone.

Table 3.1 Common Descriptive Bone Identifiers Based on Shape

Long	Bones that are longer than they are wide such as a humerus and femur
Flat	Bones with broad, flat plates or muscle attachment surfaces such as the parietals or scapulae
Irregular	Bones with a peculiar form to support nervous tissue or anchor multiple muscle attachments such as the vertebrae and sacrum
Tubular	Bones that are shaped like long bones but are much smaller in size such as the metacarpals
Rounded	Bones that are approximately as wide as they are tall, such as the tarsals

this information can then be added to the scene notes, map legend, and corresponding evidence descriptions.

Osteologists use broad terms to describe the gross morphological portions of the long bones. During the growth and development phase of mammalian bone, bones do not grow as one unit. For example, long bones, such as those of the arms and legs, will ultimately form from multiple bony elements. Each of the growth components has a specific name. The portion that makes up the shaft of the bone is referred to as the diaphysis, while the expanded ends of the shaft are called metaphyses, and the ends of the long bones, which exist as separate bones until fusion occurs, are called epiphyses (Figure 3.2). During development, there are cartilaginous soft tissue layers between the metaphyses and the epiphyses, known as epiphyseal growth plates, which allow for growth at the ends of long bones.

In life, when long bones are articulated, the articular surface is covered with cartilage, and the bone surface under this cartilage is referred to as

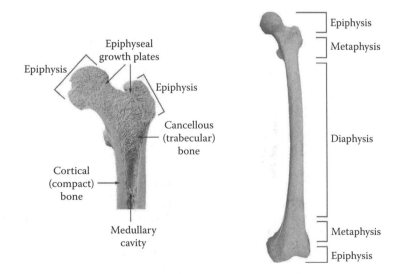

Figure 3.2 Gross morphology of a long bone: (left) cutaway and (right) anterior views of a left femur.

Table 3.2 Terms Used to Describe the Gross Morphology of Long Bones

Nutrient foramen	External opening of nutrient canal in bone; facilitates blood and nerve supply
Periosteum	Fibrous membrane covering the outer surface of bone
Diaphysis	Shaft of a long bone
Metaphysis	Expanded, growth portion of a long bone found between the diaphysis and epiphysis
Epiphysis	End of long bone; separates from metaphysis during development and becomes fused when growth has ceased
Epiphyseal growth plate	Layer of cartilage between metaphysis and epiphysis
Medullary cavity	Central cavity of bone that holds bone marrow
Subchondral bone	Area of bone at the joint covered by cartilage
Cortical (compact) bone	Dense, thickened outer layer of bone
Cancellous (trabecular) bone	Light, porous interior structure of bone

subchondral bone. The diaphysis of the long bone is made up of thick, dense cortical bone, while the ends are composed of cancellous or trabecular bone. Cortical bone is covered by a fibrous soft tissue called the periosteum. The diaphysis of the long bone also has a feature called the nutrient foramen, which allows for the passage of blood vessels and nerves into the bone. Each long bone also has a hollow center referred to as the medullary cavity. During life, this cavity is filled with yellow marrow, which consists mainly of fat cells, and red marrow, which consists of tissues involved in the formation of red and white blood cells. See Table 3.2 for a summary of the terminology associated with the gross morphology of the long bones.

3.2 Terms Associated with Bone Features

Each bone of the skeleton has numerous visible external features that are named according to their appearance. Many of the terms used to describe these features commonly appear in forensic reports. Please refer to Table 3.3 for a summary and description of these terms.

3.3 Anatomical or Relative Position

When presenting the human skeleton in reports, the forensic anthropologist will describe the skeleton and its components in relation to the standard anatomical position (Figure 3.3). In standard anatomical position, the human body is standing erect, facing forward with feet together, arms raised slightly out from the body, and with the hands supinated so the palms are facing forward. In this position almost all the bones are visible, and none

Table 3.3   Terms Used to Describe Bone Features

Ala	Wing-like structure
Alveolus	Angular cavity or pit
Articular surface	Where one bone comes in contact with another
Condyle	Large, rounded articular projection
Crest	Sharp border or ridge
Dens	Tooth-shaped projection
Epicondyle	Small projection superior to a condyle
Facet	Smooth, flattened articular surface
Foramen	Opening or hole passing through bone
Fossa	Shallow depression
Groove (sulcus)	Furrow on bone surface
Line (ridge)	Long, thin elevation with roughened surface
Notch	Indentation at an edge
Pit	Tiny pocket or depression
Process	A bony projection
Ramus	Arm-like bar of bone
Sinus	Hollow area within a cranial bone
Spine	Relatively long, slender projection
Suture	Joint between cranial bones
Trochanter	Large, blunt elevation for muscle attachment
Tubercle	Small, round elevation with roughened surface
Tuberosity	Large, round elevation with roughened surface

are crossed over one another. If the hands are pronated, with the palms facing backward, the radius is crossed over the ulna causing much of the ulna to be hidden. Most skeletal data recording sheets will include a drawing of a skeleton in the standard anatomical position, and this may be a common inclusion in reports by medical examiners, coroners, or forensic anthropologists (see Appendix A). These drawings may be used to indicate the absence or presence of skeletal elements or may also be used to illustrate pathology or trauma.

The skeleton and independent skeletal elements may be referred to in reference to anatomical planes (Figure 3.4). The median (or sagittal) plane runs through the center of the body from the head to the feet and divides the body into right and left halves, while the frontal (or coronal) plane divides the body into front and back halves. The horizontal (or transverse) plane passes through the body perpendicular to the median and frontal planes and is used to divide the body at any level into upper and lower sections. An oblique plane is any plane passing through the body that is not parallel to the other three planes and is used to divide the body diagonally.

The skeleton may also be divided into particular regions. The skull (i.e., cranium plus the mandible) and the hyoid are usually treated as one complex

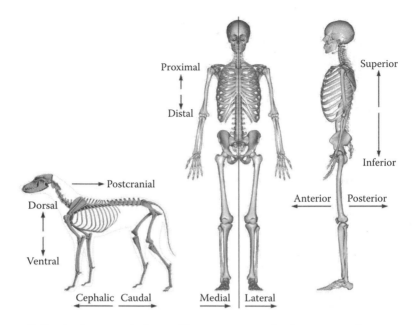

Figure 3.3 The human skeleton illustrating standard anatomical position and terms commonly used to describe relative position in anterior view (center) and lateral view (right). The canine skeleton (left) illustrates positional terms that are more suited for describing the quadrupedal skeleton.

structure referred to as the cranial skeleton. The term used to describe the entire region below the skull in the human skeleton would be infracranial. Although the investigator may come across the term *postcranial* to describe the skeleton located below the skull, this term is more accurately used to describe the skeleton of a quadrupedal animal as it literally translates to "behind the cranium" (see Figure 3.3). The human infracranial skeleton can also be divided into two further areas, the axial and the appendicular skeleton. The axial skeleton is found at the midline of the body and consists of 80 bones, including the skull, the auditory ossicles, the hyoid, the vertebral column, and the ribs. The appendicular skeleton is composed of 126 bones, including all the bones of the shoulder girdle, pelvic girdle, the limbs, and the hands and feet.

There are several other terms that may appear in relation to the anatomical and positional description of the skeleton, or even in descriptions of a skeleton in relation to additional evidence at the scene (e.g., carnivore chewing), pathology (e.g., healed fractures), or trauma (e.g., a gunshot wound or sharp-force trauma). These terms may also be used in field reports to describe the relative position of particular skeletal elements, or to describe the spatial relationship between objects and the skeleton. For example, a bullet found beside the upper portion of the humerus may be described as being located by the proximal or superior end of the humerus. The upper portion

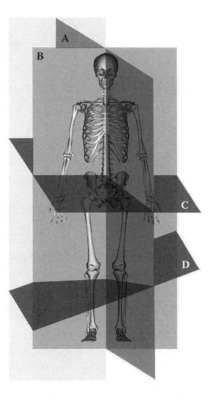

Figure 3.4 The anatomical planes of reference for the human skeleton are the (A) median or sagittal plane, dividing the body into right and left halves; (B) the frontal or coronal plane dividing the body into front and back halves; (C) horizontal or transverse plane, dividing the body into upper and lower sections at any level; and (D) the oblique plane, which divides the body diagonally.

or most superior end (i.e., toward the head) of a long bone is referred to as the proximal end of the bone, and its most inferior portion (i.e., toward the feet) is referred to as the distal end. Superior and inferior may also be used to describe portions of bones in relation to where they are positioned within the skeleton. For example, the surface of the vertebra that is toward the cranium is the superior surface, and the surface that is toward the feet is the inferior surface. The directional terms *cephalic* (i.e., toward the head) or *caudal* (i.e., toward the tail) are better used to describe quadrupedal skeletons; however, some medical examiners may use these terms when describing the human skeleton. Any part of the skeleton or bone that is found toward the middle of the body, or midline, is referred to as *medial*, while any part of the body that is away from the midline is called *lateral*. Any portion of the skeleton or bone located toward the front of the body is described as *anterior* (or ventral), and anything toward the back is described as *posterior* (or dorsal). See Table 3.4 for a summary of the terms commonly used in forensic reports to describe anatomical and relative position.

Table 3.4 Terms Used to Describe Anatomical and Relative Position

Standard anatomical position	Body standing erect, face forward, feet together, arms slightly raised, palms of hands facing anteriorly
Pronation	Rotation of hand so palm faces posteriorly
Supination	Rotation of hand so palm faces anteriorly
Median (sagittal) plane	Plane runs through body from head to feet, dividing body into left and right halves
Frontal (coronal) plane	Plane runs through body from head to feet, dividing body into front and back halves
Horizontal (transverse) plane	Plane perpendicular to median and frontal planes; divides body into upper and lower sections at any level
Oblique plane	Any plane through the body not parallel to the median, frontal, or horizontal planes; divides body diagonally at any level
Cranial skeleton	The skull (cranium and mandible) and hyoid
Infracranial skeleton	All skeletal elements except the skull and hyoid
Axial skeleton	Infracranial bones of the midline (include skull, auditory ossicles, hyoid, ribs, and vertebral column)
Appendicular skeleton	Bones of the shoulder girdle, pelvic girdle, and limbs
Superior	Upper or above; toward the head
Inferior	Lower or below; toward the feet
Anterior	Toward the front
Posterior	Toward the back
Proximal	End of bone closest to axial skeleton
Distal	End of bone farthest from the axial skeleton
Medial	Toward the midline
Lateral	Away from the midline
Dorsal	On the back of the hand or top of the foot
Palmar	On the palm of the hand
Plantar	On the sole of the foot
Bilateral	On both sides
Unilateral	On one side
Cephalic	Toward the head of a quadruped
Caudal	Toward the tail of a quadruped
Dorsal	Toward the back of a quadruped
Ventral	Toward the chest of a quadruped
Postcranial	All bones of quadrupedal skeleton except the skull

3.4 Basic Adult Human Skeleton

The average adult human skeleton contains 206 bones (see Figure 3.5). Take note, however, that human variation may exist in the number of skeletal elements that each individual has, so there may be more or less than 206 bones, depending on genetics, development, and life history. For example, one common area of the human skeleton where variation may be found is in the number of specific types of vertebrae within the spinal column. Table 3.5 contains an inventory of the average adult human skeleton, and Appendix A includes

A) Cranium
B) Mandible
C) Hyoid
D) Cervical vertebrae
E) Clavicle
F) Scapula
G) Sternum
H) Ribs
I) Humerus
J) Thoracic vertebrae
K) Lumbar vertebrae
L) Sacrum & coccyx
M) Innominate
N) Radius
O) Ulna
P) Carpals
Q) Metacarpals
R) Phalanges
S) Femur
T) Patella
U) Tibia
V) Fibula
W) Tarsals
X) Metatarsals
Y) Phalanges

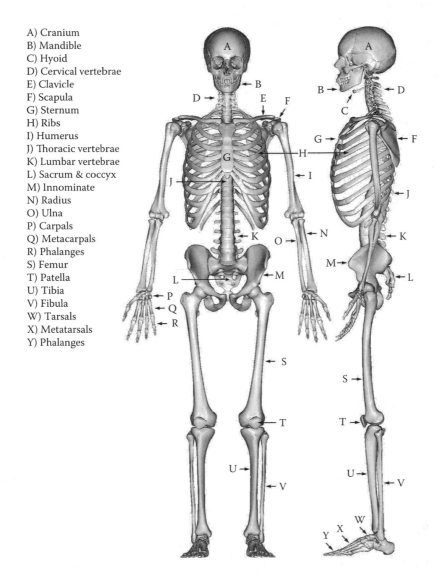

Figure 3.5 Elements of the human skeleton shown in their anatomical position.

Table 3.5   Inventory of Bones in the Average Adult Human Skeleton

Axial Skeleton

Facial Bones (Splanchnocranium)

Mandible	1	Nasal	2
Vomer	1	Lacrimal	2
Maxilla	2	Palatine	2
Zygomatic	2	Nasal concha	2

Cranial Vault Bones (Calvarium)

Frontal	1	Sphenoid	1
Occipital	1	Temporal	2
Ethmoid	1	Parietal	2
Auditory ossicles	6		

Total Bones in Skull: 28

Infracranial Bones

Hyoid	1	Sacrum	1
Cervical vertebra	7	Coccyx	1
Thoracic vertebra	12	Sternum	1
Lumbar vertebra	5	Ribs	24

Total Bones in Infracranial Axial Skeleton: 52

Appendicular Skeleton

Clavicle	2	Scapula	2
Humerus	2	Carpals	16
Ulna	2	Metacarpals	10
Radius	2	Hand phalanges	28
Femur	2	Patella	2
Tibia	2	Tarsals	14
Fibula	2	Metatarsals	10
Innominate (os coxae)	2	Foot phalanges	28

Total Bones in Appendicular Skeleton: 126

Total Bones in Adult Human Skeleton: 206

an inventory sheet that can be used for documentation of skeletal elements at the scene.

The adult skull contains an average of 29 bones when the hyoid (Figure 3.6) is included. Please note that some anatomy textbooks may include the hyoid as part of the skull, while many texts include it as part of the infracranial axial skeleton. Although there are many situations in which the cranial bones may become separated (e.g., in unfused juvenile remains, during exposure to high-temperature fires, in cases of high-impact blunt force trauma or a gunshot wound), typically the majority of the cranial elements will be found articulated. The exception to this would be the mandible, the hyoid, and the

Figure 3.6 Superior view of the hyoid bone: (a) fused and (b) unfused.

auditory ossicles, all of which may easily become disarticulated after soft tissue decomposes. Figure 3.7 shows the skull in four views with all the different bones identified. It is useful to be familiar with the different bones of the skull as both medical examiners and forensic anthropologists will refer to the separate bones of the skull when documenting the location of pathology or trauma.

For the purposes of mapping and greater understanding of field and forensic reports, we provided illustrations of articulated portions of the

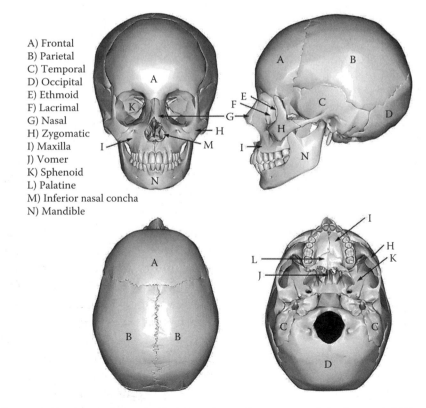

A) Frontal
B) Parietal
C) Temporal
D) Occipital
E) Ethmoid
F) Lacrimal
G) Nasal
H) Zygomatic
I) Maxilla
J) Vomer
K) Sphenoid
L) Palatine
M) Inferior nasal concha
N) Mandible

Figure 3.7 Bones of the skull shown from the anterior view (upper left), lateral view (upper right), superior view (lower left), and inferior view (lower right).

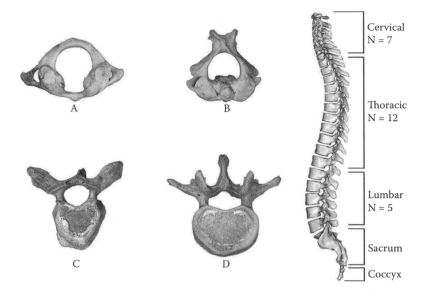

Figure 3.8 Articulated bones of the vertebral column are shown on the right with the number of elements assigned to each category. Superior views of individual vertebra illustrate some of the differences between categories: (a) first cervical vertebra (C1 or atlas); (b) second cervical vertebra (C2 or axis); (c) thoracic vertebra #6 (T6); and (d) lumbar vertebra #2 (L2).

human skeleton as well as singular bones, because it is just as likely to find dispersed bones as it is to find a fully articulated skeleton in a forensic case. The vertebral column (Figure 3.8) and the thoracic area (Figure 3.9) make up the infracranial axial skeleton, which is an area of the body that is most likely to bear evidence of sharp force trauma (i.e., stab wounds) and therefore it is important that all bones be collected from the scene if possible. The shoulder girdle (Figure 3.9) and the pelvic girdle (Figure 3.10) form the attachments between the axial and appendicular skeleton. The bones of the arm (Figure 3.11) consist of the humerus, the ulna, and the radius. The hand is made up of eight carpals, five metacarpals, five proximal phalanges, four intermediate phalanges (the first digit, or thumb, does not have an intermediate phalanx), and five distal phalanges (Figure 3.12). The bones of the leg (Figure 3.13) consist of the femur, the patella, the tibia, and the fibula. Each foot consists of seven tarsals, five metatarsals, five proximal phalanges, four intermediate phalanges (the first digit, or big toe, does not have an intermediate phalanx), and five distal phalanges (Figure 3.14). Although the hand and foot bones are small, it is very important that they are recognized and collected from a scene. Forensically relevant information such as defense wounds to the hands may be present on these small bones and may be vital for reconstructing the events surrounding an individual's death. See Table 3.6 for a list of the separate hand and foot bones.

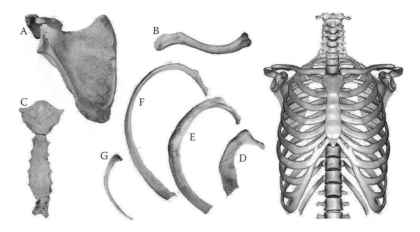

Figure 3.9 Bones of the shoulder girdle and thoracic area are shown articulated on the right. The shoulder girdle is composed of the scapulae and clavicles, with the right scapula shown in anterior view (a) and the right clavicle shown in superior view (b). The thoracic area is composed of the sternum (c), ribs (d–g), and thoracic vertebrae (shown in Figure 3.8). From the superior view, most ribs can be distinguished by their morphology: rib #1 (d); rib #2 (e); rib #8 (f); and rib #11 (g).

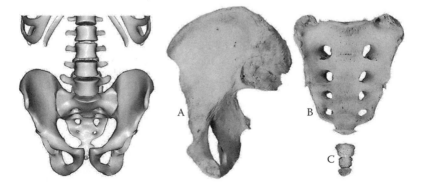

Figure 3.10 Bones of the lower portion of the vertebral column and the pelvic girdle are shown articulated on the left. The pelvic girdle is composed of the left and right innominates (os coxae). The right innominate (a) is shown in medial view, and the sacrum (b) and coccyx (c) are shown in anterior view.

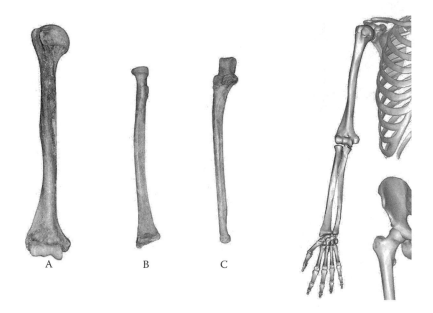

Figure 3.11 Bones of the arm and hand are shown articulated on the right. The right humerus (a), right radius (b), and right ulna (c) are all shown in anterior view.

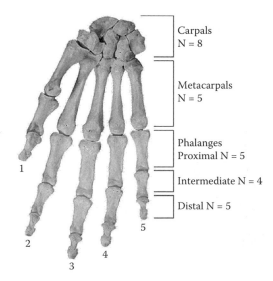

Figure 3.12 Articulated bones of the right wrist and hand shown in standard anatomical position (palm facing forward). Digits are numbered starting with the thumb (1) through the little finger (5).

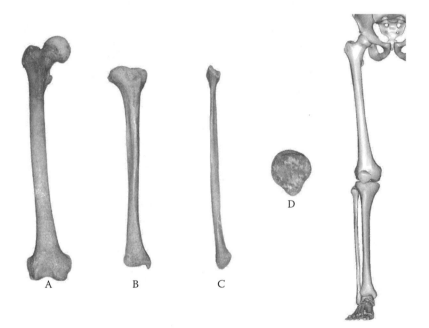

Figure 3.13 Bones of the leg and foot are shown articulated on the right. The right femur (a), tibia (b), fibula (c), and patella (d) are all shown in anterior view.

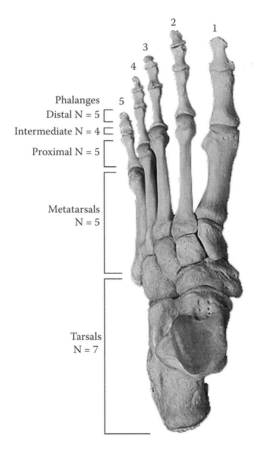

Figure 3.14 Articulated bones of the left foot shown in superior view. Digits are numbered starting with the big toe (1) through the little toe (5).

Table 3.6   Inventory of Bones in the Adult Hands and Feet

Hands and Wrists		Feet and Ankles	
Carpals (Wrists)		Tarsals (Ankles)	
Lunate	2	Calcaneus	2
Scaphoid	2	Talus	2
Triquetral	2	Navicular	2
Pisiform	2	Cuboid	2
Trapezium	2	First cuneiform	2
Trapezoid	2	Second cuneiform	2
Capitate	2	Third cuneiform	2
Hamate	2		
Metacarpals (Palms of Hands)		Metatarsals (Arches of Feet)	
Metacarpal #1	2	Metatarsal #1	2
Metacarpal #2	2	Metatarsal #2	2
Metacarpal #3	2	Metatarsal #3	2
Metacarpal #4	2	Metatarsal #4	2
Metacarpal #5	2	Metatarsal #5	2
Phalanges (Fingers)		Phalanges (Toes)	
Proximal	10	Proximal	10
Intermediate	8	Intermediate	8
Distal	10	Distal	10
Total in Hands and Wrists	64	Total in Feet and Ankles	62

3.5   Basic Juvenile Human Skeleton

It should be noted that the fetal, infant, child, and teenage or adolescent skeleton has a significantly different morphological appearance and can contain far more bones than the adult skeleton (Figures 3.15 and 3.16; see Appendices B and C for inventory illustrations of the juvenile skeleton). At 11 weeks before birth there are usually about 800 bony elements of the skeleton, while at birth there are about 450 (Baker et al., 2005). There are several small, bony elements called epiphyses that will eventually fuse to the shafts of the long bones and other skeletal elements (refer to Figure 3.2). As an individual grows, more skeletal elements will develop and eventually all these elements will fuse together to form the adult skeleton. By adulthood, normally between the ages of 21 to 25, all of the epiphyses have fused and an average of 206 bones remain in the body (White and Folkens, 2005). Refer to Figure 3.17 for an example of how a long bone changes during growth of the skeleton.

Bones of an infant or fetal skeleton are commonly light brown in color and may appear to the untrained eye as small twigs and debris, or be mistaken

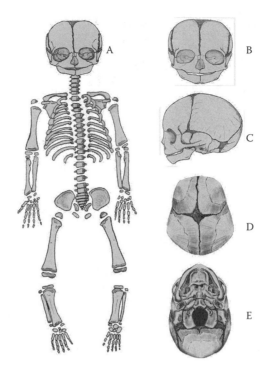

Figure 3.15 Bones of the infant skeleton: (a) shows the articulated skeleton, demonstrating that there are many more skeletal elements at this stage of development. The skull, (b) in anterior view, (c) lateral view, (d) superior view, and (e) inferior view, is also not fused and consists of more elements than found in an adult skull.

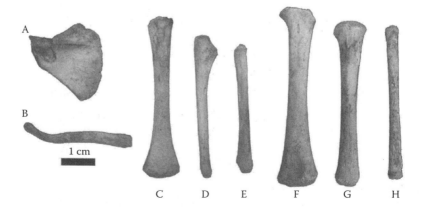

Figure 3.16 The scapula (a), clavicle (b), and long bones of the fetal skeleton are shown in anterior view: (c) humerus, (d) ulna, (e) radius, (f) femur, (g) tibia, and (h) fibula.

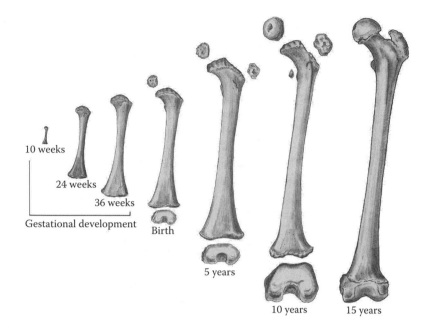

Figure 3.17 Comparison of various stages of growth of human femur. The anterior view of the left femur illustrates the appearance of epiphyses and the diaphysis during development.

as the skeleton of a nonhuman animal. As a result, they are easily missed at the scene. Occasionally, it may be necessary to identify fetal bones in a field situation if a female victim was pregnant, or in a case where a fetus or infant is part of a scene. Although it may seem like this would be a rarity, the authors have participated in forensic cases in which the identification and estimation of fetal age greatly assisted in the identification of the victim. Care should be taken when removing dirt and debris from the pelvic area of any human skeleton, as this would be the most likely location of fetal remains, if they were present. (See Chapter 10 for more information on the recovery of juvenile human skeletal remains.)

3.6 Basic Human Dentition

Humans typically have two sets of teeth, the deciduous, also called the primary, baby, or milk teeth, and the permanent, also called the secondary or adult teeth. Teeth can be a very important part of a forensic investigation, as positive identification of the individual can be made with comparisons to dental records. The dentition is the only part of the human skeleton that comes into regular contact with the environment during a person's life. For that reason teeth can retain modifications that occur during the life of the individual, be it intentional or unintentional. For example, trips to the dentist may alter the teeth (e.g., fillings, tooth extraction, root canals) in a distinct manner that can be used to identify the person after death.

3.6.1 Terms Associated with Dental Morphology and Position

Each tooth is made up of a crown, root, pulp cavity, and a root canal (Figure 3.18). The structural components of a tooth include the enamel, dentin, and cementum. The point at which the enamel ends and cementum begins is referred to as the cemento-enamel junction (CEJ). During life, the tooth is held in the tooth socket by the periodontal ligament.

Four morphological tooth types are found in human dentition: incisors, canines, premolars, and molars (Figure 3.19). Incisors are so named because of their chisel-like appearance and sharp cutting edges. Canines are typically longer than incisors and have a cone-shaped appearance; however, over time their tips can become flattened due to wear or chipping. Premolars are smaller and shorter than canines and have two pointed cusps on their chewing surface, which is why they are sometimes referred to as *bicuspids*. Molars are the largest teeth and have broad chewing surfaces adapted for grinding food.

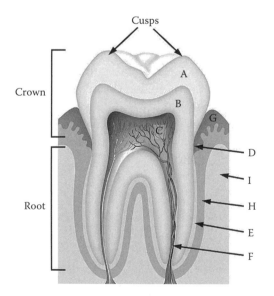

Figure 3.18 Gross morphology of a tooth: (a) enamel, (b) dentin, (c) pulp chamber, (d) cemento-enamel junction, (e) cementum, (f) root canal, (g) gingival tissue, (h) periodontal ligament, and (i) bone.

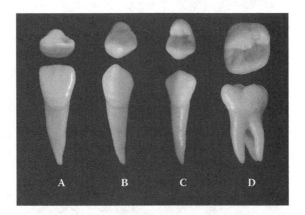

Figure 3.19 Comparison of the four basic tooth types in human dentition. The occlusal surface of each tooth type is shown in the upper row; the lower row shows the incisor (a) and canine (b) in labial view and the premolar (c) and molar (d) in buccal view.

When describing the dentition, the teeth are separated into four quadrants by dividing the mouth into an upper and lower half (i.e., the maxilla and the mandible) and left and right halves at the median plane. This creates upper right, upper left, lower right, and lower left quadrants (Figure 3.20). The deciduous dentition is made up of five teeth in each of the four dental quadrants for a total of 20 teeth. In each deciduous quadrant there are two incisors, one canine, no premolars, and two primary molars. The permanent dentition is made up of eight teeth in each of the four dental quadrants for a total of 32 teeth. In each permanent quadrant there are two incisors, one canine, two premolars, and three molars. During middle childhood an individual will have mixed dentition (i.e., both deciduous and permanent teeth).

As with the skeleton, there are directional and descriptor terms that are used by the dentist, medical examiner, and forensic anthropologist to describe teeth and any notable modifications. Each tooth has six directional planes (Figure 3.20) that are commonly used to describe the location of modifications such as cavities or fillings. The chewing surface of the tooth is called the occlusal surface (this may be called the incisal surface on incisors). The surface or direction toward the tip of the tooth root is referred to as the apical surface. The surface of premolars and molars facing the anterior of the mouth and the surface of the canines and incisors facing the midline of the mouth is called the mesial surface, while the opposite surface is called the distal surface. The surface of the tooth facing the tongue is called the lingual surface, while the opposite side on molars and premolars is referred to as the buccal surface, and on the canines and incisors is called the labial surface. Refer to Table 3.7 for a summary of terms associated with human dentition that may be used in forensic reports.

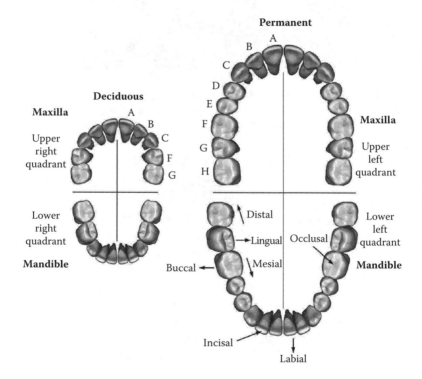

Figure 3.20 Comparison of deciduous (left) and permanent (right) dentition. Permanent dentition has eight teeth in each quadrant (32 teeth): (a) first incisor, (b) second incisor, (c) canine, (d) first premolar, (e) second premolar, (f) first molar, (g) second molar, and (h) third molar. Deciduous dentition has five teeth in each quadrant (20 teeth) and follows the same general tooth type pattern as permanent dentition but lacks premolars and third molars. Directional terms associated with dentition are illustrated on the permanent dentition.

Table 3.7 Terms Associated with Gross Morphology and Relative Position of Human Dentition

Crown	Visible portion of the tooth; covered by enamel
Cusp	Elevation on occlusal surface of tooth; primarily found on premolars and molars
Root	Portion of tooth embedded in jaw; covered by cementum
Enamel	Hard, white mineral portion of the tooth; makes up majority of tooth crown
Dentin	Softer core tissue of crown and root of tooth; surrounds pulp chamber
Cementum	Hard tissue covering tooth root; provides attachment surface for periodontal ligament
Cemento-enamel junction (CEJ)	Point at which enamel ends and cementum begins; found at junction of crown and root
Pulp chamber	Inner portion of tooth crown containing blood and nerve supply
Root canal	Narrow end of pulp chamber at root end of tooth
Periodontal ligament	Soft tissue ligament holding tooth in tooth socket
Occlusal	Chewing surface of all teeth
Incisal	Chewing surface of the incisors
Labial	Surface of incisors and canines facing the lips
Buccal	Surface of premolars and molars facing the cheek
Lingual	Surface of the tooth facing the tongue
Apical	Toward the tip of the tooth root
Mesial	Toward the anterior or median plane of the mouth
Distal	Toward the posterior of the mouth

3.6.2 Dental Numbering Systems

Worldwide there are many different systems that dentists use to assign identity to each tooth. Here we present the two most widely used systems so that investigators can interpret which teeth are being discussed in a report. For example, if a forensic odontologist uses the dentition to make a positive identification, they will commonly discuss singular teeth used to make the match, and these teeth will be referred to according to a dental numbering system. In North America, the standard system used by dentists to number teeth is called the Universal or National dental numbering system. The alternate standard system accepted worldwide is called the International system or the FDI (*Fédération Dentaire Internationale)* system.

In the Universal system (Figure 3.21), dentists use a simple number or letter to identify each tooth. The deciduous dentition is identified using letter identifiers, A through T, starting with the upper right, second deciduous molar labeled as "A" and the lower right, second molar labeled as "T." The permanent dentition is identified using numerical identifiers, 1 through 32,

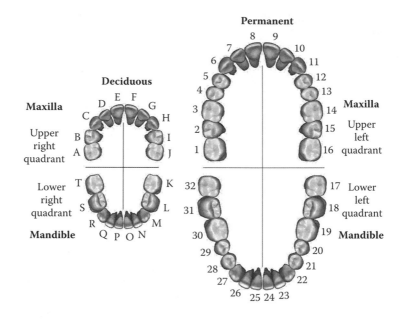

Figure 3.21 Comparison of deciduous (left) and permanent (right) dentition using the Universal (or National) numbering system.

starting with the upper right, third permanent molar labeled as "1," and the lower right, third molar labeled as "32."

The International system (Figure 3.22) is a little more complicated, using a double-digit numbering system that considers both the quadrant and the specific tooth type. In some respects, it is easier to start the description of this system with the permanent teeth. When identifying a tooth using this system, the first number represents the quadrant where the tooth is located. Quadrants for the permanent teeth are numbered as follows:

- Upper right quadrant—1
- Upper left quadrant—2
- Lower left quadrant—3
- Lower right quadrant—4

The second number in this system identifies specific tooth types that are numbered as follows:

- First incisor—1
- Second incisor—2
- Canine—3
- First premolar—4
- Second premolar—5

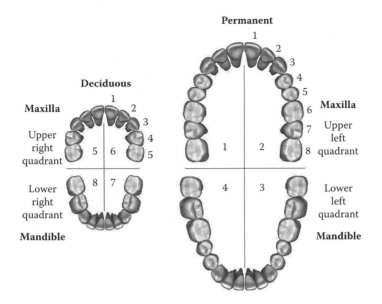

Figure 3.22 Comparison of deciduous (left) and permanent (right) dentition using the International (*Fédération Dentaire Internationale,* FDI) numbering system.

- First molar—6
- Second molar—7
- Third molar—8

Thus, a tooth labeled as "36" would be a permanent lower left first molar, while a tooth labeled as "14" would represent a permanent upper right first premolar. The deciduous dentition follows a similar pattern, with the first number identifying the quadrant and the second number identifying the specific tooth type. The quadrant designations for the deciduous teeth are a continuation of the permanent dentition, and are numbered as follows:

- Upper right quadrant—5
- Upper left quadrant—6
- Lower left quadrant—7
- Lower right quadrant—8

Because there are only five teeth in each of the deciduous quadrants they are numbered as follows:

- First incisor—1
- Second incisor—2
- Canine—3

- First molar—4
- Second molar—5

Therefore, a tooth labeled "73" would represent a deciduous lower left canine, and one designated as "55" would be a deciduous upper right second molar.

Key Words and Questions

anterior/posterior
appendicular skeleton
axial skeleton
buccal/lingual
cranial skeleton
crown
deciduous teeth
diaphysis
epiphysis
frontal plane
horizontal plane
infracranial skeleton
medial/distal
medial/lateral
median plane
occlusal/apical
permanent teeth
proximal/distal
root
standard anatomical position
superior/inferior

1. You have been asked to take notes on a group of bones located during a search, but you have no osteological training. How would you describe the bones (a–f) in Figure 3.23?
2. How many bones are there in the average adult human skeleton? How many bones are there in the average human skeleton at birth?
3. The upper limbs of the human skeleton are made up of what three paired long bones? The lower limbs are made up of what three paired long bones?
4. How many bones are there in the human hand and wrist? How many bones are there in the human foot and ankle?
5. What are the four types of teeth found in the human mouth? How many teeth are there in a complete set of permanent dentition?

Figure 3.23 Describe the shapes of bones (a) through (f) using terminology presented in Chapter 3.

6. Why is it important to learn and use the proper terms for anatomical and relative position in the human skeleton and dentition? Using the proper terms presented in the chapter, how would you describe the positions of the following skeletal elements?
   - The lumbar vertebrae in relation to the sacrum
   - The thoracic vertebrae in relation to the sternum
   - The metatarsals in relation to the foot phalanges
   - The radius in relation to the ulna
   - A lower left permanent second molar in relation to a lower left canine

7. When reading a report concerning remains recovered from a crime scene in Europe, you find that the dental anthropologist has used the International system for recording dental information. Unfortunately, you need to use this information in a report you are writing. Change the following International tooth identifications to Universal identifications and list the tooth each one represents:
   - 48
   - 63
   - 14
   - 21

References

Baker, B.J., Dupras, T.L., Tocheri, M.W. 2005. *The Osteology of Infants and Children.* College Station, TX: Texas A&M University Press.

Bass, W.M. 1995. *Human Osteology: A Laboratory and Field Manual.* Columbia, MO: Missouri Archaeological Society.

Matshes, E., Burbridge, B., Sher, B., Mohamed, A., Juurlink, B. 2005. *Human Osteology and Skeletal Radiology: An Atlas and Guide.* Boca Raton, FL: CRC Press.

Scheuer, L., Black, S. 2000. *Developmental Juvenile Osteology.* San Diego, CA: Elsevier Academic Press.

Scheuer, L., Black, S. 2004. *The Juvenile Skeleton.* San Diego, CA: Elsevier Academic Press.

Schwartz, J. 2006. *Skeleton Keys: An Introduction to Human Skeletal Morphology, Development, and Analysis,* 2nd ed. New York: Oxford University Press.

Steele, D.G., Bramblett, C.A. 1988. *Anatomy and Biology of the Human Skeleton.* College Station, TX: Texas A&M University Press.

White, T.D., Black, M.T., Folkens, P.A. 2011. *Human Osteology*, 3rd ed. San Diego, CA: Elsevier Academic Press.

White, T.D., Folkens, P.A. 2005. *The Human Bone Manual.* San Diego, CA: Elsevier Academic Press.

Understanding the Forensic Context

4

Upon arrival at a scene, one of the important tasks of the investigators, in conjunction with the forensic archaeologist, is to establish whether or not the scene is of forensic significance. The context of the scene will dictate who becomes involved in the recovery and examination of the remains. There are many potential contexts in which human remains may be found, and the preservation and documentation of these contexts can significantly aid in determining in which category the remains belong. Contextual information such as location, body position, associated artifacts, and taphonomic modifications to the remains will assist in determining whether the scene and remains are of recent and forensic significance. It should be noted, however, that forensic archaeologists might be involved in recovering burials that have been disturbed due to a variety of processes (e.g., gravesite erosion or backhoe use during construction) that can destroy contextual evidence and make it difficult to determine forensic significance. No matter what the initial setting may present, the scene should be treated as being medicolegally significant until determined otherwise. In some instances forensic significance may not be determined until a forensic anthropologist or medical examiner fully examines the remains. General categories used by forensic archaeologists and forensic anthropologists for non-forensic skeletal remains include archaeological prehistoric, archaeological historic, war trophies, and teaching material, which includes commercially prepared specimens and autopsied material. Before considering the scene context, the various types of deposition and body position must be discussed.

4.1 Defining a Forensic Context

Context can be referred to as an object's exact place in time and space and its association and relationship with other items. A forensic context differs from what we consider to be an archaeological context, with depth of time and intent of placement being the primary variables. When defining a forensic context, investigators must consider the interrelated circumstances in which something of medicolegal significance occurs or is found, such as the association and relationship between skeletal remains, personal possessions, location of burial, and environment. Depending on the circumstances, a forensic context or setting can be officially determined by the local law enforcement or medical examiner/coroner's office. For example, Section 872.05 of the Florida Statutes (2010) dictates that any remains over 75 years of age are deemed to be non-forensic and therefore jurisdiction may shift from the medical examiner to the state archaeologist.

4.2   Indications of a Forensic Context

4.2.1   Location of Remains

Because of the nature of bodies disposed as the result of criminal activity, the location of forensic contexts can be extremely varied. Outside of surface deposits, primary burials are one of the most common types of burial encountered in a forensic setting (Killam, 2004). Although multiple burials are occasionally found in a forensic context, the most common occurrence is in cases of human rights violations where many individuals will be deposited into one large grave (Haglund, 2002; Schmitt, 2002; Simmons, 2002; Skinner et al., 2002; Stover and Ryan, 2001).

4.2.1.1   What Are Surface Deposits?

Surface deposits are remains situated either completely on the ground surface or partly exposed, typically with little to no effort of concealment. In most cases surface deposits retain some soft tissues (e.g., skin, hair, nails) indicating a more recent disposal, as taphonomic processes will usually destroy these kinds of tissues in a given period of time. Due to the likelihood that remains in surface deposits will be disturbed (Dirkmaat and Adovasio, 1997), they are usually recorded in relation to a primary or secondary deposit site. A primary deposit site is the location where the body was originally placed, which may include an abundance of skeletal remains still in relative anatomical position and the presence of soil stained by decomposition fluids. Secondary deposit sites can be created by many different types of taphonomic processes, such as movement of the remains by natural environmental forces, the perpetrator, or by animals. In most cases secondary deposit sites are marked by the presence of minimal or partial skeletal remains and very little to no evidence of decomposition.

4.2.1.2   What Is a Burial?

As a general definition, *burial* is the practice of concealing a body in the ground (Sprague, 2005). Determining forensic significance of a burial becomes more difficult when postdepositional disturbances occur, as these disturbances may result in the loss of valuable contextual evidence. A disturbed burial is one that has been altered at some point after the initial burial, but not necessarily moved to a new location (Hester et al., 2008). Burrowing animals, gravesite erosion, heavy equipment, or human activity are common causes of burial disturbance. In most cases, a few skeletal elements may be disarticulated or missing while the remaining elements are preserved in their original anatomical position. Missing skeletal elements, either due to erosion or animal activity, may be recovered by tracing the routes of removal. Identification of human activity, such as someone returning to the burial to remove or add specific items, may play a crucial role in later legal aspects of the investigation. The following descriptions of the main types of burials encountered can provide useful information when trying to determine context.

4.2.1.2.1 Primary In a primary burial, the body remains in the location where it was originally deposited and the context of the burial has not been disturbed (Hester et al., 2008; Sprague, 2005). When excavated, the bones will appear to be articulated; that is, all the bones will remain in correct anatomical position in relation to one another as if soft tissues were still present (Figure 4.1). The presumption is that the relationships of the skeletal articulations have not been altered since the decomposition of the soft tissue.

4.2.1.2.2 Secondary A secondary burial consists of skeletal elements that have been removed from their original burial location by human activity and deposited in another location, thus disturbing their original context (Hester et al., 2008; Sprague, 2005). If sufficient time has elapsed to allow for complete decomposition of the soft tissue, the bones removed from the primary burial will not remain in an articulated or anatomical position unless purposefully placed in this fashion. Consequently, a secondary burial commonly consists of a jumbled arrangement of skeletal remains (Figure 4.2). In addition, it is not unusual for skeletal elements to be missing, as most secondary burials contain skulls and larger long and flat bones such as those found in the pelvis and limbs.

4.2.1.2.3 Multiple A multiple burial consists of a single grave containing the remains of two or more articulated individuals (Hester et al., 2008; Sprague, 2005), either neatly aligned or in a haphazard fashion. The individuals may either have been buried all at once as a primary deposit, or as a

Figure 4.1 Primary burial found in an archaeological context in Egypt.

Figure 4.2 Secondary burial found in an archaeological context in Egypt.

combination of primary and disturbed burials due to reentering an existing grave to deposit additional remains. Although commonly confused in the literature, a multiple burial can be differentiated from a mass burial based on the level of articulation. A multiple burial consists of articulated individuals, and a mass burial (including ossuaries) consists of disarticulated individuals with the possibility of articulated fragments (Sprague, 2005). A multiple burial or mass burial can be created through different actions, including cultural practices (e.g., Native American ossuaries), human rights violations, and homicide.

4.2.1.3 What Are Cremains?

In a forensic investigation, cremated remains, or cremains, may originate as the result of criminal activity or as a result of normal cultural practices of disposal. In the case where remains are cremated as the result of the perpetrator deliberately trying to dispose of the remains, the remains will most likely range from charred to incompletely burnt, as it takes extremely high temperatures (above 1600°C/2912°F) to destroy bone (Iserson, 2001). It is almost impossible to completely destroy all evidence of a body through burning. Because of this fact, cremations produced by modern crematoriums are normally reduced to very small particles, depending on the type of processor used to reduce the volume of the remains.

4.2.2 Position and Orientation of the Body

In a forensic context, the body may be found in any position, and in many cases the position is directly related to the size of the grave. Position is best described through the relationship of legs, arms, and head to each other and to the trunk of the body (Hester et al., 2008; Sprague, 2005). The description should relate to only the body with no reference to the grave, compass directions, or any other natural features. In other words, "it should be as if the body is floating in space" (Ubelaker, 1999: 16). Orientation is the cardinal direction in which the head lies in relation to the body's central axis and should be recorded in directional terms using a compass, natural features, or human-made structures, but preferably in some combination of these reference points (Hester et al., 2008; Sprague, 2005). For example, an individual placed north of a nearby barn with his or her head to the east and feet to the west, would be oriented east–west outside the northern wall of the structure.

In a primary burial, the body may be described as being in an extended, flexed, or semi-flexed position as shown in Figure 4.3. An extended position indicates that the legs are straight, forming a 180° angle with the trunk. The body can either be supine (i.e., lying on back) or prone (i.e., lying face down). An extended position is a common formal burial position, particularly with cemetery remains, where the hands are crossed over the chest or pelvis (see Figure 4.1). A flexed position signifies that the body is at an angle of 90° or less between the legs and the trunk, and semi-flexed refers to burials in which the angle of the legs is between 90° and 180° from the trunk. In forensic contexts, bodies are usually placed within a hole that is dug quickly and may not be large enough to place the body neatly within the grave. As a result, bodies are found in many different positions with limbs situated in directions consistent with tossing or rolling a body rather than formally positioning a body prior to filling in the grave.

It is extremely important to note how the arms and legs are positioned in relation to the rest of the body. For instance, arm and hand bones positioned behind the body might indicate that the individual's hands had been bound behind the back when placed in the grave, even though traces of a ligature may have long since disintegrated. Noting these details in positioning might assist in determining the context of the burial. The position of the body may also give some indication as to what postmortem state the body was in when placed in the grave. If the body was in full rigor (i.e., temporary stiffness of muscles after death) it is unlikely that the individual would be placed in a grave in a tightly flexed position. A tightly flexed position would indicate that the individual was placed in the grave prior to the onset of full

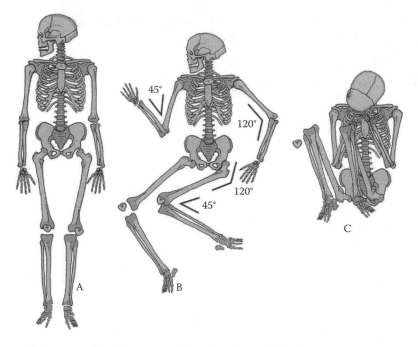

Figure 4.3 Examples of a primary burial in (a) extended position, (b) semi-flexed position, and (c) flexed position. The semi-flexed burial (b) shows an example of differing angles for the left and right arms and superior and inferior joints in the left leg.

rigor or after rigor had dissipated. The onset and length of time that rigor lasts is dependent on multiple variables (such as age, sex, physical condition, musculature) but is particularly influenced by the ambient temperature (Adams, 2009).

4.2.3   Preservation of the Remains

When determining the context of human remains, it is important to consider preservation and taphonomic conditions. The state of decomposition or preservation can contribute significant information regarding the postmortem interval (PMI). In many cases the presence of soft tissue such as remnants of desiccated skin, ligaments, and tendons, as well as costal cartilage, hyaline cartilage, tracheal rings, and thyroid cartilage are consistent with a short PMI and therefore indicate a forensic context. In the absence of soft tissue structures, other evidence such as the smell of decomposition or a yellowish-hue and greasy texture due to the retention of fats, fluid, and collagen may also indicate a short PMI. However, retention of soft tissue through mummification or buildup and retention of fats during decomposition can preserve soft tissue for significant periods of time in the right environment

(Hester et al., 2008). In these cases the presence of soft tissue cannot be used as an indicator of forensic context. For these reasons it is useful to have some background on the process of decomposition.

4.2.3.1 What Is the State of Preservation?

Active decay or decomposition of the body involves two processes after death: autolysis and putrefaction (DiMaio and DiMaio, 2001). Autolysis is a chemical process that results in the destruction of tissues or cells by intracellular enzymes within an organism. Environmental conditions such as heat can accelerate autolysis, while cold can slow this process. Putrefaction is the result of bacterial flora spreading in the gastrointestinal tract and decomposing or breaking down organic matter. Bloating is a recognizable by-product of putrefaction that can accelerate in hotter climates and occur more slowly or be delayed in colder climates.

Further changes to the body may occur, such as skin slippage of the fingers and toes as well as the scalp and hair, as decomposition progresses. At this stage, depending on environmental conditions, the skin can desiccate and mummify while internal organs and muscle tissue will still decompose. Furthermore, adipocere development may occur when bodies are deposited in moist conditions or submersed in water. Adipocere, an insoluble fatty acid resulting from slow hydrolysis of the body's fat, is also referred to as grave wax because it has a firm and wax-like texture with a grayish white coloration. This material accumulates wherever fats are present in the body and forms during putrefaction (DiMaio and DiMaio, 2001).

The final stage in soft tissue decomposition is skeletonization. This is a highly variable process that is dependent on many factors such as temperature, humidity, access by insects, and animal scavenging. The state of bone after skeletonization can also be an indication of forensic context. Relatively recent skeletal remains may have a greasy texture and be yellowish in color, also due to the retention of fats, indicating that the remains are potentially recent with a short PMI. Bones with a thick cortical layer such as the femur will also be quite heavy, and the bone surface will be smooth. Bone that has been skeletonized for significant periods of time, depending on the environment, may be very lightweight, brownish in color, and have a roughened surface.

It is also important to note that in addition to various forms of soft tissue preservation and skeletonization, human remains can be subject to cremation or thermal damage. Cremation is a process that uses intense heat to rapidly reduce a body to ashes and small bone fragments (Iserson, 2001). Bodies are typically burned prior to burial or within the grave and may be charred, or partially, incompletely, or completely burned depending on the intensity of the fire to which the body was exposed (Correia and Beattie, 2002), and the purpose behind carrying out the cremation. Also, the remains may be mixed in with other elements of the burial (e.g., clothing, wood), left as a surface deposit, or held in some type of container.

4.2.3.2 *What Is Taphonomy?*

When the term *taphonomy* is used in forensic archaeology, it is in reference to the postmortem time period and the changes or modifications that occur to bodies, skeletal remains, and any associated evidence, such as clothing or personal possessions. Taphonomic agents can include animals, bacteria, chemicals, temperature, geological processes, humans, plants, and water (Haglund and Sorg, 1997). A solid understanding and detailed documentation of these processes may help to determine the context of the remains. Please see Chapter 5 for a more comprehensive discussion concerning common taphonomic processes encountered in forensic archaeology.

4.2.4 Associated Artifacts and Evidence

Associated artifacts are those that have some direct association with the body, and they may vary significantly in type and number. Clothing and other personal possessions can assist in determining the forensic context of the remains. Items related to the crime or the creation of a burial may also be present as associated artifacts or as indirect evidence, providing indications of a forensic context. These can include weapons, disposal artifacts (e.g., digging tools, tarps), and natural (e.g., tree limbs) or cultural (e.g., concrete blocks) materials used to cover the deposit. Evidence of modern surgical procedures and dental work can also provide clues concerning the forensic context of skeletal material.

4.2.4.1 *Are Personal Belongings or Cultural Materials Associated with the Remains?*

Personal belongings or cultural materials can help to give some context to the skeletal remains. Personal belongings would be those items associated with an individual on a regular basis. These can include items such as clothing, eyeglasses, and jewelry, and may belong to either the suspect or the victim. Styles and brands of clothing (e.g., Adidas), dates found on tags or on other associated artifacts (e.g., tool patents), or certain kinds of materials (e.g., PVC plastic) could be used to indicate a forensic context simply by the period of time that these items have been in production. Other cultural items, such as a coffin, might indicate a modern or historic context, but may also signify that the remains are not of a forensic nature. However, it is always wise to remember that over time, anything and everything has been used to conceal a body. Even though a style of clothing or a coffin may indicate that the remains of an individual are not of forensic significance, one can never be sure and should treat each case as if it was a forensic context.

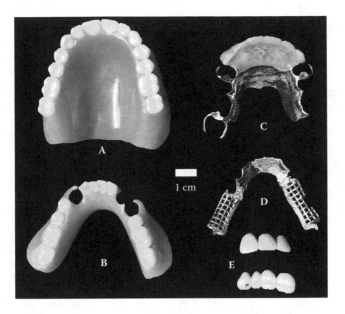

Figure 4.4 Examples of dental prosthetics: (a) full denture plate, (b) partial dental plate, (c) partial bridge, (d) bridge plate, and (e) porcelain teeth.

4.2.4.2 Are There Medical or Cultural Modifications to the Body?

Modifications to the body or skeleton that were made during life can also help to indicate context. Skin or dental tattoos, prosthetic devices (e.g., artificial joints or limbs, glass eyes), surgical implants (e.g., pacemakers), birth control devices (e.g., intrauterine devices), dental work (e.g., fillings, crowns, false teeth, and bridges), dental modification (e.g., inlays, tooth filing, and tooth evulsion), skeletal alterations (e.g., cultural cranial or foot modification), and other medical procedures are all modifications that can be used to indicate cultural affiliation and time period of that individual (Figures 4.4 and 4.5). Cultural modifications made to the body during funerary preparations (e.g., trocar plugs, eye caps, and wires to close the jaws) would indicate either a historic or modern context, but not necessarily a forensic context.

4.3 Common Non-Forensic Contexts

4.3.1 Prehistoric Finds

Common criteria that can indicate a prehistoric context include proximity of burials to known prehistoric archaeological features (e.g., middens), the position of the skeleton, and associated artifacts. The placement of remains across the landscape in prehistoric contexts usually follows some kind of pattern, such as those seen in cemeteries or burial grounds, or social arrangement, for

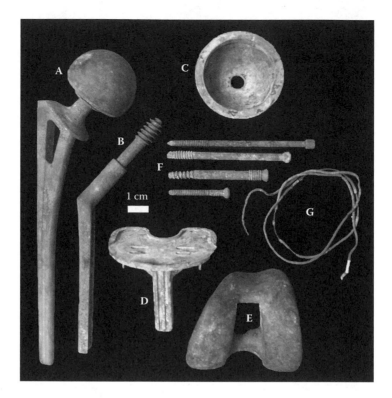

Figure 4.5 Examples of surgical prosthetics: (a) prosthetic hip joint, (b) femoral neck fracture post, (c) acetabular prosthetic, (d) tibial plateau prosthetic, (e) distal femoral prosthetic, (f) internal fixation (i.e., fracture) screws, and (g) pacemaker lead wire.

instance using natural caves or crevasses for disposal (Ucko, 1969). Although primary burials are common, prehistoric skeletons may also be found in secondary, multiple, and mass burials. Skeletons from primary burials in prehistoric contexts are commonly found in a flexed or semi-flexed position (Roberts, 2009; Ubelaker, 1999), although this is highly dependent on the culture and time period being investigated. In most instances, grouped prehistoric burials also follow patterns of orientation, possibly toward a specific feature or event such as a body of water or the rising of the sun (Ucko, 1969).

Associated burial artifacts can include lithics (e.g., chipped stone tools and debitage) as well as ceramic vessels and sherds. Skeletal and dental alterations may also be present such as artificial cranial modifications, dental inlays, or filing of teeth. These practices are usually culture specific and in most cases indicate an archaeological context. Taphonomic modifications of prehistoric skeletons include bones that are lighter in weight, and the overall quality of the bone surface may be eroded and cracked rather than smooth and greasy in texture. Prehistoric bones generally display a uniform staining ranging from light tan to darker colors, dependent on the type of soil and moisture leaching from the surrounding area. In some cases, however, it must also be noted that cultural treatment of the body during funerary preparation may create purposeful preservation of soft tissues. In this case all contextual information must be weighed together to form an opinion of context.

4.3.2   Historic and Modern Cemetery Settings

Identification of skeletal remains belonging to the historic period is easily performed if skeletal remains can be analyzed *in situ*. Historic remains are found in a variety of marked and unmarked locations including pioneer graves, small family cemeteries, small community cemeteries, graves within the documented boundaries of an existing cemetery, and graves in close proximity to an existing cemetery. In cemetery burials individuals are usually placed in an extended position with hands at the side or placed over the chest or abdomen. It should be noted, however, that certain cultural customs might influence body position and orientation. For example, many slave burials from the mid 1700s to late 1800s are positioned facing a body of water in a west–east orientation to ensure that the soul of the deceased will follow the water to the seas and eventually return to Africa (Handler, 1994). Items associated with historical remains are also very telling. These can include remnants of coffin wood, coffin hardware and adornment, evidence of embalming, adhered fabric from the coffin lining or pillow, and period jewelry or clothing artifacts (e.g., buttons, textiles, clasps, and pins) that are either adhered to the remains or are in direct association. As mentioned above, clothing and personal items are very useful in estimating PMI, as most textiles and fashions can be dated to particular time periods. Evidence of purposeful preservation or embalming of remains such as trocar plugs, eye caps, mouth formers, and embalming fluid bottles can aid in establishing a modern or historic cemetery context.

4.3.3   Ritualistic or Anatomical Use of Remains

It is also important to consider that there may be situations that are not easily classified into the contexts discussed previously. Examples of such contexts would include a scene where skeletal remains, which are not forensic in nature, have been used in ritual ceremonies or situations that include discarded skeletal material used for teaching in anatomy labs or associated with historic hospitals (see Case Study 3, this chapter). In these cases the location, position and orientation, preservation, and associated evidence will be very important. Remains associated with rituals are usually found in suggestive locations (e.g., on an altar or in a charm fetish), and will also be associated with specific items used in the rituals such as cauldrons, feathers, or candle wax. In these cases the remains are usually incomplete, and there may be multiples of the same skeletal element. In some instances the remains may still have tags or associated receipts showing where the remains were purchased. Discarded materials that may have been used as teaching specimens in anatomy labs will also have specific recognizable modifications. Wires for holding elements together, drill holes or cuts, markings to demonstrate muscle attachments, and a shiny patina due to handling are all indications that the remains were used in teaching anatomy. Remains discarded from historic medical schools and hospitals will also be specific in their nature. These remains will usually possess cut marks, and the discarded skeletal elements will most likely represent amputated limbs. One of the best contextual identifiers for these remains will be historic documentation of building location such as a hospital or university.

Every potential forensic scene is unique. When bones are discovered, regardless of context, it is not unusual for law enforcement or the medical examiners/coroner's office to become involved in the scene. What will become very important during the initial assessment of the site, and subsequent excavation and procurement of evidence, is to note all the characteristics of the site. What is the site's location? Where are the remains? How are they positioned? What is the associated contextual evidence? All of this information can help investigators determine the context of the scene, whether it is forensic, archaeological, historical, or modern. Establishing of the context will dictate what happens to the remains during subsequent investigation.

Case Study 2: Dog Days

In July 2006 investigators received information that there may have been a possible unattended death and burial of a child. The supposed burial site was located on a wooded residential property, and the informants indicated that the grave had been marked with a wooden cross. Investigators arrived to find a small grave marked with a wooden cross (Figure 4.6), which had a piece of purple, black, and white material draped around it. There were also two sets of artificial flowers on the ground in front of the cross. The ground around the cross did not appear to be disturbed, and vegetation around the cross and surrounding area was consistent. The current residents of the property had only lived there for four months and indicated that the cross was there when they moved in. Permission was given by the residents to excavate the burial.

Crime scene analysts began to process the scene by probing the area to locate the limits of the burial. A grid was created around the area, and all vegetation was cleared from the grid (Figure 4.7). Dirt was removed layer by layer, and at a depth of approximately 15 inches (38 centimeters) a degraded black plastic bag was discovered (Figure 4.8). Once masses of fur were discovered, it became evident that the burial was that of someone's pet. Dupras and Schultz later confirmed that the skeletal remains were those of an elderly dog.

Figure 4.6 Makeshift wooden cross wrapped with fabric and used to mark the location of a dog burial. (Photo courtesy of Seminole County Sheriff's Office.)

Figure 4.7 Grave and surrounding area gridded and cleared for excavation. (Photo courtesy of Seminole County Sheriff's Office.)

Figure 4.8 Degraded plastic bag (a) and remains of an elderly pet dog (b).

Case Study 3: Fence Line Forensics

In July 2008 authors Williams and Wheeler assisted in the excavation and recovery of skeletal elements found while digging postholes for a new fence on the property of a day-care center. The displaced bones, some of which displayed cut marks, were identified as possibly being human. Law enforcement and the coroner's office requested assistance for the recovery of the remaining skeletal elements. Upon arrival at the scene, we recorded the area that had been cleared for the new fence and the holes dug for the fence posts. Although some skeletal elements had been displaced, we could see that there were more bones still in the ground.

After photographing the site, we began by defining the limits of the burial feature surrounding the partially exposed skeletal elements (Figure 4.9). We recovered several old glass medicine bottles from the soil layers (Figure 4.10). After clearing the soil around the remaining skeletal elements, we noted there were two nearly complete and fully articulated limbs: a left foot, leg, and hip (including the left innominate, the left half of the sacrum, and the left halves of three lower lumbar vertebrae), and a right hand, arm, and shoulder (including the right scapula and lateral half of the right clavicle) (Figure 4.11). The foot and lower leg were doubled back tightly beneath the femur, and the lower arm and hand were doubled back beneath the humerus. The skeletal remains of a small mammal, likely a cat, were also found in the same pit as the human skeletal remains. The only other items found in the backfill with the human remains were two nails.

Figure 4.9 Author Lana Williams defining the limits of a burial pit along a fence line by removing thin layers of soil and groundcover with a flat-blade shovel.

Figure 4.10 Antique glass medicine bottles recovered from the soil layers above the human remains.

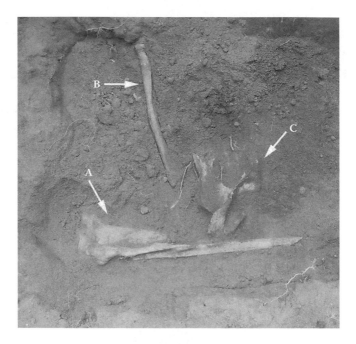

Figure 4.11 Human remains found in the burial pit along the fence line: (a) tibia and fibula, (b) radius, and (c) scapula.

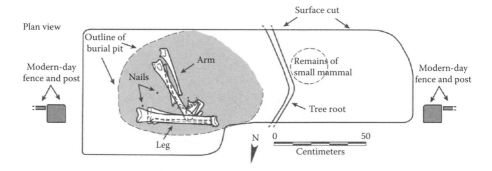

Figure 4.12 Plan view map of the recovery area and burial pit along the fence line.

All of the soil was screened, including what was removed from the new postholes, to ensure full recovery of all skeletal elements and associated evidence. After photographing and mapping all remains (Figure 4.12), we noted the dark staining of the human remains, discoloration of cut surfaces and saw marks, and some cortical surface deterioration, all of which suggested that the deposit was not recent. When removing the leg, we also saw that this individual had suffered a severe fracture of the tibia that also showed evidence of an active infection at the time of death. The presence of a well-healed nonaligned fracture and evidence of untreated infection led us to believe that this was not a case of forensic significance.

Further skeletal analyses indicated that the pelvis and articulated leg were from an adult male; however, it was not possible to say whether the arm was from the same person. The right arm and shoulder had been detached by sawing through the midpoint of the clavicle, and the left leg and hip had been detached by sawing through the lumbar vertebrae and the sacrum. Analyses of the cut surfaces indicate that a hand-powered saw with a straight blade and alternate-set teeth was used. Placement of the saw cuts was found to be consistent with 18th and 19th century medical school dissections. The recovered nails were identified as being 19th century machine-cut nails. It was also discovered that the remains were found near the location of a 19th century medical school. All of this evidence indicated that the recovered remains were likely buried in an attempt to dispose of medical school specimens illegally acquired through grave robbing, a common method of obtaining cadavers for medical schools during this time. Therefore, all evidence pointed to the remains as being historic anatomical specimens rather than forensic in nature.

Key Words and Questions

adipocere
autolysis
bloating
cremation
extended position
flexed position
forensic context
mass burial
multiple burial
orientation
PMI
primary burial
primary deposit
putrefaction
secondary burial
secondary deposit
semi-flexed position
skeletonization
surface deposit
taphonomy

1. You have been asked to take notes on a group of bones located during a search, all of which appear to be piled on the ground surface. You recognize that many of the skeletal elements are missing, especially the smaller bones of the skeleton. What additional indications would you look for in determining the context of these remains?
2. Does the presence of soft tissue always indicate that you are working with remains in a forensic context? Why or why not?
3. What does body position have to do with determining the context of the remains? Why is it important to note the details of hand and foot position for an individual prior to removing the remains for further analyses?
4. What is adipocere, and what is its forensic and taphonomic relevance?
5. Remains of an individual were recovered from a shallow grave located near a river. The individual was in an extended position and oriented west–east. Explain how the following artifacts found in direct association with human remains could indicate that the remains are potentially of forensic significance:
   • Leather shoes
   • Wire-rimmed eyeglasses
   • U.S. quarter with Washington's profile
   • Glass eye
   • Brass handle from a coffin lid
6. Using the information from Question 5, explain how the position, orientation, and associated artifacts could potentially indicate that the remains are from a historical context.

Suggested Readings

Bell, E.L. 1990. The historical archaeology of mortuary behavior: coffin hardware from Uxbridge, Massachusetts. *Historical Archaeology* 24(3):54–78.

Berrymann, H.E., Bass, W.M., Symes, S.A., Smith, O.C. 1997. Recognition of cemetery remains in the forensic setting. In: Haglund, W.D., Sorg, M.H., eds. *Forensic Taphonomy: The Postmortem Fate of Human Remains*, pp. 165–170. Boca Raton, FL: CRC Press.

Harrington, J.M., Blakely, R.L. 1995. Rich man, poor man, beggar man, thief: the selectivity exercised by graverobbers at the Medical College of Georgia. In: Saunders, S.R., Herring, A. eds. *Grave Reflections: Portraying the Past through Cemetery Studies*, pp. 153–178. Toronto, Ontario, Canada: Canadian Scholar's Press.

Nawrocki, S.P. 1995. Taphonomic processes in historic cemeteries. In: Grauer, A.L., ed. *Bodies of Evidence: Reconstructing History through Skeletal Analysis*, pp. 49–66. New York: Wiley-Liss.

Sledzik, P.S., Wilcox, A.W. 2009. Corpi aquaticus: the Hardin Cemetery flood of 1993. In: Steadmann, D.W., ed. *Hard Evidence: Case Studies in Forensic Anthropology*, 2nd ed., pp. 256–264. Upper Saddle River, NJ: Prentice Hall.

Wetli, C.V., Martinez, R. 1981. Forensic sciences aspects of Santeria, a religious cult of African origin. *Journal of Forensic Sciences* 26:506–514.
Willey, P., Leach, P. 2009. The skull on the lawn: trophies, taphonomy, and forensic anthropology. In: Steadmann, D.W., ed. *Hard Evidence: Case Studies in Forensic Anthropology*, 2nd ed., pp. 176–188. Upper Saddle River, NJ: Prentice Hall.

References

Adams, V.I. 2009. Medicolegal autopsy and postmortem toxicology. In: Waters, B.L., ed. *Handbook of Autopsy Practice*, pp. 7–20. Towata, NJ: Humana Press.
Correia, P.M., Beattie, O. 2002. A critical look at methods for recovering, evaluating, and interpreting cremated human remains. In: Haglund, W.D., Sorg, M.H., eds. *Advances in Forensic Taphonomy: Method, Theory, and Archaeological Perspectives*, pp. 435–450. Boca Raton, FL: CRC Press.
DiMaio, V.J., DiMaio, D. 2001. *Forensic Pathology*, 2nd ed. Boca Raton, FL: CRC Press.
Dirkmaat, D.C., Adovasio, J.M. 1997. The role of archaeology in the recovery and interpretation of human remains from an outdoor forensic setting. In: Haglund, W.D., Sorg, M.H., eds. *Forensic Taphonomy: The Postmortem Fate of Human Remains*, pp. 39–64. Boca Raton, FL: CRC Press.
Florida Statutes § 872.01-06. 2010. Offenses Concerning Dead Bodies and Graves.
Haglund, W.D. 2002. Recent mass graves, an introduction. In: Haglund, W.D., Sorg, M.H., eds. *Advances in Forensic Taphonomy: Method, Theory, and Archaeological Perspectives*, pp. 243–262. Boca Raton, FL: CRC Press.
Haglund, W.D., Sorg, M.H. 1997. Method and theory of forensic taphonomic research. In: Haglund, W.D., Sorg, M.H., eds. *Forensic Taphonomy: The Postmortem Fate of Human Remains*, pp. 13–26. Boca Raton, FL: CRC Press.
Handler, J.S. 1994. Update # 4: New York's African Burial Ground. *African American Archaeology* 12:1–2.
Hester, T.J., Shafer, H., Feder, K. 2008. *Field Methods in Archaeology*, 7th ed. Walnut Creek, CA: Left Coast Press.
Iserson, K.V. 2001. *Death to Dust: What Happens to Dead Bodies?* 2nd ed. Tucson, AZ: Galen Press.
Killam, E.W. 2004. *The Detection of Human Remains*, 2nd ed. Springfield, IL: Charles C. Thomas.
Roberts, C.A. 2009. *Human Remains in Archaeology: A Handbook*. York: Council for British Archaeology.
Schmitt, S. 2002. Mass graves and the collection of forensic evidence: genocide, war crimes, and crimes against humanity. In: Haglund, W.D., Sorg, M.H., eds. *Advances in Forensic Taphonomy: Method, Theory, and Archaeological Perspectives*, pp. 277–292. Boca Raton, FL: CRC Press.
Simmons, T. 2002. Taphonomy of a karstic cave execution site at Hrgar, Bosnia-Herzegovina. In: Haglund, W.D., Sorg, M.H., eds. *Advances in Forensic Taphonomy: Method, Theory, and Archaeological Perspectives*, pp. 263–276. Boca Raton, FL: CRC Press.

Skinner, M., York, H.P., Connor, M.A. 2002. Postburial disturbance of graves in Bosnia-Herzegovina. In: Haglund, W.D., Sorg, M.H., eds. *Advances in Forensic Taphonomy: Method, Theory, and Archaeological Perspectives*, pp. 293–308. Boca Raton, FL: CRC Press.

Sprague, R. 2005. *Burial Terminology*. Oxford: Altimira Press.

Stover, E., Ryan, M. 2001. Breaking bread with the dead. *Historical Archaeology* 35(1):7–25.

Ubelaker, D.H. 1999. *Human Skeletal Remains: Excavation, Analysis, Interpretation,* 3rd ed. Washington, DC: Taraxcum.

Ucko, P. 1969. Ethnography and archaeological interpretation of funerary remains. *World Archaeology* 1:262–280.

Search Techniques for Locating Human Remains

5

In forensic investigation, searches are performed to locate clandestine graves, bodies deposited on the surface, and any missing body parts, skeletal elements, and associated evidence. At the same time, searches can also be utilized in clearing areas so investigations can continue in other suspected areas. Before conducting a search, a search plan should be formulated that identifies the personnel and equipment that will be needed and the specific search techniques that will be used.

Most searches will have a greater rate of success employing multiple methods (France et al., 1992, 1997). Search techniques can be either nonintrusive or intrusive. Nonintrusive searches are primarily used when searching for remains deposited on the ground surface and surface changes consistent with a clandestine grave. Nonintrusive searches use nondestructive methods, which include visual searches, the use of cadaver dogs, and almost all geophysical prospecting methods. Conversely, intrusive searches use destructive methods that can damage bodies and evidence; therefore they should only be used as a follow-up to visual search methods or when nonintrusive methods are not successful. Intrusive searches include probing and coring the soil, shovel shining and digging test excavations, and using heavy equipment.

In addition to having a forensic archaeologist involved in the search, it can be beneficial to have a forensic anthropologist on-site during the search phase for the *in situ* identification of potentially significant physical evidence. Forensic anthropologists can provide a quick evaluation of remains to determine the following:

- Bone versus nonbone material
- Human versus nonhuman bones
- Forensic versus nonforensic skeletal remains (e.g., historic and prehistoric)
- Missing skeletal elements that may still be within the search area

5.1 Types of Search Areas

There are three basic types of areas that can be defined when searching for human remains: open, obstructed, and submerged areas (Killam, 2004).

Open areas can be searched using aerial reconnaissance, walking grids, or remote sensing techniques. These areas include fields, flatlands, backyards, or any area that is primarily open to a 360° field of vision. Searchers tend to have the most success in locating remains in open areas. Urban developments, wooded areas, caves, and any other landscape features that impede search techniques are defined as obstructed areas where it becomes more difficult to locate remains. Underwater searches require specialized equipment and personnel. The search and mapping techniques used in submerged areas are specific to each individual case and are less commonly utilized.

5.2 Planning the Search

Preparation for a search is just as important as the search. The planning phase should include a preliminary physical reconnaissance of the search area to learn more about the terrain, the different search methods that can be used, and any specialized equipment that may be necessary. Prior to beginning every search, carefully determine the boundaries of the area to be searched and the different methods that will be used. If a large area is to be searched, geographic or topographic maps and aerial photographs can be helpful in providing specific information about the terrain and area to be searched (see Chapter 7 for various photograph and map sources). Maps and aerial photographs are typically used to determine how the area can be divided for the search and which search methods may produce the best results. Maps and photographs are also used to show any changes in the terrain that may have occurred since the body was buried. For example, an aerial photograph of the proposed search area from the estimated or reported date of burial and a photograph from present day should be compared to determine any changes in the landscape and whether the suspected area is still accessible. If a structure, pavement, or roadway was placed over the body after it was buried, traditional visual search methods will not work.

The planning phase should also entail learning as much as possible about the disposal of the body or burial process. Many offenders will go to great lengths to dispose of their victims in a manner intended to avoid detection. However, according to Killam (2004), most individuals will dispose of bodies in one of two ways: those that are dumped quickly within an area little known or unknown to the perpetrator; and those that are deposited in an area where the landscape is well known through ownership, holidays, or frequent visits. Killam (2004) also states that some 90% of victims are recovered downhill to facilitate carrying or deposition from vehicular access points along roadways. Specific information obtained about the disposal process may dictate which search methods will be appropriate. For example, if a search

Table 5.1 Questions for Investigators to Ask Suspects or Informants about a Burial Prior to a Search

- When did the event occur?
- How large (height and weight) was the missing individual?
- How deep was the body buried?
- Was the body wrapped in anything and was the body clothed when it was buried?
- Was anything placed over the body (e.g., boards, concrete, metal debris, or even a pet or a second individual) before the grave was filled?
- What were the local conditions of the area (e.g., dry or moist ground, open or wooded area)?
- Was anything placed over the grave after it was filled (e.g., brush, trash, tree limbs) to conceal its location?
- Were there any unique landmarks near the grave that may be helpful in locating the burial during the search?
- Has the landscape changed since the body was buried?

is planned to locate a buried homicide victim, detectives and investigators need to learn as much about the burial process as possible when talking to informants and suspects. See Table 5.1 for specific questions to ask about bodies that have been buried to conceal their location. Finally, on the day of the search, make sure there are enough personnel to carry out the search in the designated area and that all the equipment and experts are arriving when expected. Also, make sure that refreshments are provided for the personnel involved in the search. Providing water, snacks, and hot or cold drinks can help the search team to easily avoid instances of heat stroke or overexposure to cold depending on the weather.

5.3 Visual Foot Searches

Visual foot searches in archaeology and forensic investigations involve visually searching an area using nonintrusive techniques to locate archaeological sites or various types of forensic evidence. When searching large areas or areas with obstructions, the total search area should be divided into smaller zones that are easily managed in a day or less. These smaller, manageable areas commonly follow existing boundaries formed by natural and cultural (i.e., human-constructed) obstructions or features. For example, natural obstructions can include streams, other bodies of water, hills, and cliffs. Cultural obstructions can include buildings, fences, roads, and parking lots. After boundaries of the search area have been determined, a pattern must be chosen for an effective and thorough search of the defined area. The pattern should maximize available personnel for the most efficient results. Three of the most effective patterns for visually searching the surface of an area on foot are a strip (or line) pattern, a grid pattern, and a spiral pattern.

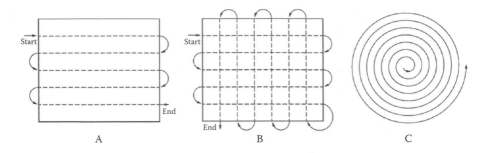

Figure 5.1 Search patterns: (a) line or strip search, (b) grid search, and (c) spiral search.

5.3.1   Strip or Line Pattern

The most frequently used search method is a strip or line pattern (Figure 5.1a) and provides 100% coverage if performed properly. Search team members line up in a straight line and are positioned close enough to one another so that their field of view overlaps (Figure 5.2). Depending on the size of the search team and the area to be searched, the individuals will search an area by walking first in one direction, completing one strip, or transect, of the search area, and then walk in the opposite direction, completing the transect adjacent to the first. This is repeated until the entire search area has been covered. Using flagging tape or survey flags, the end persons in the search line should mark the boundaries of the transect being searched. Each search line should be directed by a team leader who is positioned in the middle of the search line, or behind the line, to maintain the pace of the search. Also, if the search team is looking for human remains or evidence of a burial, a forensic anthropologist or forensic archaeologist can follow behind the line and inspect any item that a searcher thinks might be bone or help identify suspicious surface changes that could be related to a grave.

Figure 5.2 Searchers performing a line or strip search.

The line should move at a pace that is slow enough to allow all of the searchers ample time to view the ground in their line of sight. It is the job of the team leader to ensure that individual personnel do not search too far ahead of the line. Whenever individuals in the line move too far ahead, the leader should direct the pace of the line to get team members back in a straight line, or stop the line to allow those working at a slower pace to catch up. If the line is stopped, only the leader can direct the line to resume the search. Team members should carry survey flags and mark any evidence or anything potentially significant in their respective lanes. When one team member locates potential evidence he or she should call out to the team leader and everyone in the line should stop to perform a detailed search of the immediate area. After everyone has finished the detailed search, the team leader can then direct the line to resume the search.

5.3.2   Grid Pattern

A more time-consuming variation of the strip or line search is the grid pattern (Figure 5.1b). Once the line search pattern is completed, the team will search the same area again in a direction perpendicular to the first search. This pattern provides 200% coverage because the ground is visually searched twice. The main advantage of this method is that the ground is searched from two directions and multiple angles. Using this pattern increases the potential for discovering skeletal material or evidence that may have been concealed from another angle. In areas with uneven terrain, heavy brush, or ground cover, it may be difficult to visually inspect every angle of the ground when moving in only one direction across the landscape. Also, depending on the amount of sunlight, certain surface changes related to a grave may be more evident from a different angle of approach in the search line.

5.3.3   Spiral Pattern

A spiral pattern (Figure 5.1c) works best when the search team and search area are small, or if the search starts on the top of a hill. Killam (2004) suggests using the spiral pattern as a one-person search method in which the searcher moves in decreasing concentric circles within a small search area (i.e., moving from the outer edges toward the center). This method is commonly used to ensure that evidence is not inadvertently trampled during the initial search. However, there are instances when it is more appropriate to reverse this pattern, starting the search initially inside and moving in a spiral pattern toward the outside. This reversed search pattern is often used when searching for bones that might have been dispersed from a known primary deposition site by carnivores or other taphonomic processes. The circular pattern would begin at the location of the primary deposition site and continue outward in increasing concentric circles, as more bones are located.

5.3.4   Other Recommendations for Visual Searches

The degree of difficulty in conducting a visual search is directly related to the landscape features. An open field provides ideal landscape conditions for searching. However, as the number of obstructions increase in the search area, it becomes more difficult to locate bones and associated evidence. In search areas with scrub brush or other forms of ground cover, team members should be placed closer together to allow for more detailed searching in and around undergrowth. In addition, when detailed searching is required, the leader should instruct team members to search on hands and knees. The leader should slow the pace of the search in areas of dense undergrowth to increase the amount of time the team is searching each area. It is also important to remember that crime scenes can be three dimensional. Bones and associated evidence can be found in other locations in addition to being deposited on the ground. In forested areas, it is sometimes helpful to look up because remains can be deposited in trees by various means. For example, when searching a scene involving a plane crash in a wooded area, it is recommended that a visual search of the forest canopy be included to locate evidence that may be lodged in the tree limbs.

5.4   Briefing Team Members Prior to Search

After the search plan is devised, all team members must be briefed on the rules and procedures for the search. It should not be assumed that all team members have prior experience in conducting visual foot searches. When large searches are conducted, there could be numerous volunteers with no experience in searching for bones or burials. As a result, they would not be familiar with indicators that would signify a possible grave or recognize evidence of scattered remains. If a search line consists of experienced and inexperienced personnel, they should be intermixed along the line so the personnel with experience can help the inexperienced. Prior to starting the search, all search team members should be fully briefed on the following:

- Areas and types of terrain to be covered
- Patterns to use for the search
- Specific directions for the visual search
- Possible visual indicators
- Time constraints and local weather

5.5   Indications of Surface Deposit of Remains

A body deposited on the ground surface will obviously be easier to locate than a body that was buried to hide its location. However, there are numerous helpful indicators to look for when searching for remains deposited on the ground surface. Surface deposits will be identified by visually locating bones and soft tissue, clothing and personal possessions, and other forms of evidence that are associated with the remains, such as material used to wrap a body (e.g., rugs, tarps, plastic sheeting, plastic bags). It is also important to search through piles of trash and natural brush, as these are quite often placed over a body to conceal its whereabouts. Search teams should also look for any evidence of animal activity and scavenging, which may indicate scattering of a surface deposit over a larger area. Recent surface deposits can also be located via decomposition scent using cadaver dogs (see Section 5.7). However, deposits that have been on the surface for multiple years can be difficult to recognize. Over time, the bones, clothing, and other evidence can deteriorate from weathering and plant growth and become difficult to recognize on the ground surface. For example, weathered bones can turn white in color from sun bleaching, or dark in color from soil staining. In addition, bones can become more difficult to locate over time as they become covered by fallen leaf litter or partially buried due to soil erosion, decay of organic material, and other environmental variables. When bones become partially buried, searchers may need to remove all organic material from the ground surface to locate bones and associated evidence. Table 5.2 provides a summary of indicators used to locate surface deposits.

5.5.1   Common Taphonomic Processes of Dispersal

As discussed in Chapter 4, the term *taphonomy* as it is used in forensic archaeology refers to the postmortem time period and the changes or modifications that occur to bodies, skeletal remains, and any associated evidence, such as clothing or personal possessions. Taphonomic analysis begins at the scene with the reconstruction of the postdepositional history of the body or

Table 5.2   Summary of Indicators Used to Locate Surface Deposits

- Skeletal remains and soft tissue
- Clothing, personal objects, and weapons
- Decomposition odor and staining
- Insect activity
- Loose trash or brush heaps
- Animal activity and scavenging
- Materials used for wrapping body

skeleton in question. One of the more common postdepositional processes that must be reconstructed is disarticulation and dispersal of decomposing bodies. There is usually some degree of dispersal of skeletal remains deposited in outdoor environments due to numerous active processes, such as animal activity and environmental changes. To correctly interpret disarticulation and dispersal patterns of bodies deposited in outdoor environments, the application of archaeological methods is vital so that valuable contextual information can be documented. In addition, when dispersal patterns are correctly interpreted, there will be a higher probability of delineating scene boundaries, locating additional skeletal elements, locating the primary depositional site of scattered remains, locating secondary depositional sites of scattered remains, and determining the original position of the body. The more common natural postmortem modifications that can disarticulate, modify or damage, and disperse skeletal remains include weathering, carnivore activity, rodent gnawing, and botanical activity. These taphonomic processes are described in more detail to assist the forensic archaeologist in interpreting and reconstructing the scene.

5.5.1.1 Weathering

After a body is skeletonized, the remaining hard tissues will break down at a much slower rate. The destruction of bone is the result of numerous mechanical and chemical forces that include weathering. The processes of weathering can result in modifications to bone such as soil staining, sun bleaching, cracking and flaking, and eroding of skeletal elements. According to Behrensmeyer (1978: 153), bone weathering is defined as "the process by which the original microscopic organic and inorganic components of bone are separated from each other and destroyed by physical and chemical agents operating on the bone *in situ*, either on the surface or within the soil zone." The critical factor with weathering appears to be time, but the relationship between time and weathering is not straightforward (Lyman, 1994). Although buried bones weather, they weather at a much slower rate than exposed bones on the surface.

Skeletal remains that have been exposed to an outdoor environment for a minimal time period may display early signs of weathering such as sun bleaching and soil staining (Figure 5.3). Continued exposure of bone leads to cracking, exfoliation, and erosion of the surfaces of skeletal elements (Figure 5.4). Although burying a body does not stop weathering, it significantly reduces its effect (Behrensmeyer, 1978). As the acidity, clay and moisture content, and organic content increase in the soil, bone degradation will increase, leading to generalized erosion of skeletal elements (Grupe et al., 1993). Preservation of skeletal remains is most favorable in dry, alkaline, sandy soils (Hedges, 2002).

Bone survivability and the effects of weather can be related to differences in density due to the size of the bone, the type of bone, the age of

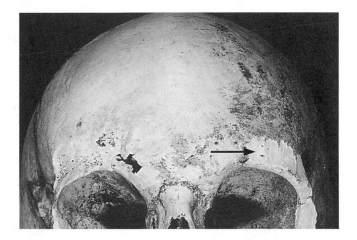

Figure 5.3 Superior portion of a human crania that was partially exposed to the environment, resulting in sun bleaching (left) and soil staining (right). Note the soil staining has been removed by rodent gnawing around the left eye orbit (arrow).

Figure 5.4 Long bone surfaces showing no taphonomical modifications (left), the beginning stages of weathering with cortical exfoliation (center), and extreme weathering with cracking and surface exfoliation (right).

the individual, and the nutritional and pathological status of the individual. Smaller bones will weather more quickly than larger ones due to a higher surface-to-volume ratio. The bones of a juvenile or an older individual with osteoporosis will degrade much more quickly than a healthy adult with normal bone density. Cortical bone has a higher degree of survivability than cancellous bone. For example, the epiphyses of long bones are composed of porous cancellous bone and will weather and erode more quickly than the diaphysis, which is composed of dense cortical bone.

5.5.1.2 *Carnivore Activity*

It is fairly common to find animal damage on human skeletal remains deposited in an outdoor setting, including those on the surface and in shallow burials. Animal involvement results in modification and consumption of soft tissue and bone, as well as significant disarticulation and dispersal of body parts. The most frequently reported canids responsible for scavenging and dispersal of human remains are dogs and coyotes (Haglund et al., 1988; Rossi et al., 1994). Although not as frequent, the forensic literature discusses modifications to bone from other animals, including bears (Carson et al., 2000), mountain lions and domestic cats (Murad, 1997), alligators (Harding and Wolf, 2006), sharks (Iscan and McCabe, 1995; Rathbun and Rathbun, 1984), birds (Komar and Beattie, 1998), rodents (Haglund, 1997a), and pigs (Berryman, 2002). Each type of animal will produce its own unique modifications and patterns of damage.

Carnivore gnawing is recognized as a crenulated or ragged edge on the ends of long bone shafts (Binford, 1981; Maguire et al., 1980) and other bones that have been chewed. When carnivores gnaw on long bones, they begin first on the ends of the bones where the softer cancellous bone is located and then progressively reduce the size of the shaft (Figure 5.5a). The four types of carnivore tooth marks described in the taphonomy literature (Binford, 1981; Haglund et al., 1988; Haynes, 1980; Maguire et al., 1980) include scoring, punctures, pitting, and furrows. Scoring or striations (Figure 5.5b) are scratches on the surface of the diaphysis of a long bone, usually perpendicular to the long axis of the bone, resulting from the teeth being scraped over the

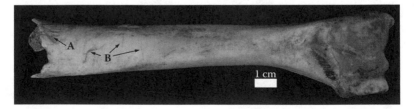

Figure 5.5 Nonhuman long bone showing an example of the reduction of cancellous bone at the end (a) due to carnivore gnawing, and canine scoring (b) as a result of removal of soft tissue along the diaphysis.

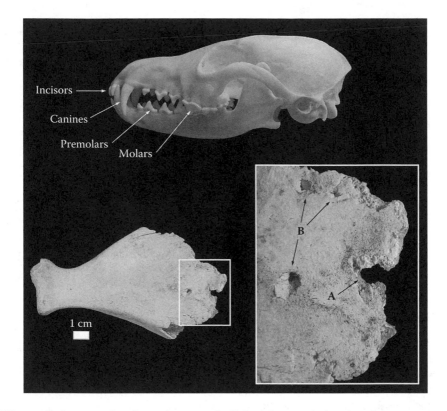

Figure 5.6 Example of a carnivore skull (red fox, top) showing large canines, premolars, and molars. Canine taphonomic modifications of a nonhuman scapula include crenulated edges (bottom, left) created by the premolars and molars, and punctures (a) and pits (b) created by the canines.

bone to remove soft tissue. Punctures (Figure 5.6a) are oval defects resulting from cortical and cancellous bone collapsing under the force of a single tooth cusp or canine tooth. Conversely, pits (Figure 5.6b) are conical indentations on the cortical surface caused by a failure of the tooth cusp or canine tooth to puncture the bone. Furrows are deep channels created by the cusps of carnivore premolars and molars crushing the cortical bone and underlying cancellous bone (Figure 5.7). Extreme furrowing results in a scooped or hollowed-out appearance in significant portions of the metaphyses and epiphyseal ends in long bones.

To the inexperienced eye, carnivore modifications to bone can be confused with nicks or incisions caused by sharp force trauma. A common way to differentiate between a tooth mark versus an incision is to look at the cross-sectional shape of the defect using a dissecting microscope. Sharp force trauma will exhibit more of a V-shaped cross section, whereas carnivore modifications on bone (e.g., pits and scoring) will more commonly have a more rounded U-shaped cross section.

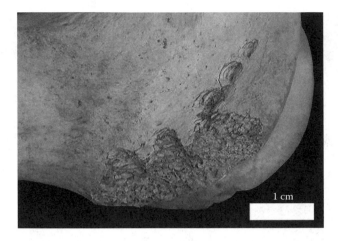

Figure 5.7 Furrowing on nonhuman bone epiphysis produced by the premolars and molars of a carnivore.

5.5.1.3 Rodent Activity

All rodents share a dentition that is highly specialized for the process of gnawing, "a type of incisive movement capable of reducing hard fibrous substances in which the separated material is not always ingested" (Moore, 2009: 177). Rodents are distinguished by the presence of a large pair of ever-growing upper and lower central incisors (Figure 5.8). Enamel is only present on the anterior and lateral surfaces of the incisors. As a result of this unique dental characteristic, differential wear of the harder enamel and softer dentin produces a sharp, chisel-like beveled edge (Carleton, 1984). Rodents do not have lateral incisors or canines, which leaves a gap (called a diastema) between the incisors and molars. In addition, rodents have a unique jaw joint that is loose in nature, allowing the lower jaw to move forward and backward to facilitate gnawing and chewing (Carleton, 1984; Moore, 2009).

Rodents must continually gnaw on hard fibrous objects, such as bone, to prevent their incisors from growing too long. Rodents will modify remains in varying postmortem periods, including fresh bodies, mummified bodies, and dry and fresh bone, and they are also noted to be vectors of transport (Haglund, 1997a). It is common to find gnaw marks on bone deposited in an outdoor context. Rodent gnaw marks are recognized as patterns of shallow, parallel channels, or furrows, as shown in Figure 5.8. The adjacent linear and shallow pattern of the channels can be easily differentiated from the more irregular furrows from carnivore damage. Also, the width of the channel may provide general clues as to the size of the rodent (Hillson, 2005).

5.5.1.4 Botanical Activity

Plant activity can have profound effects on the survivability and dispersal of skeletal remains. Two of the more common botanical effects on the outer

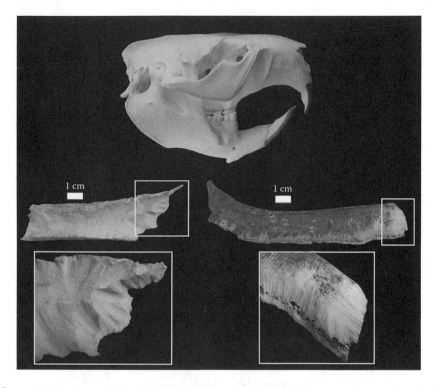

Figure 5.8 Example of rodent skull (beaver) exhibiting large, ever-growing incisors (top). The size of the parallel rows of rodent gnaw marks can indicate the general size of rodent (larger rodent gnaw marks shown lower left, and those of a smaller rodent shown on the lower right).

surface of bones are a green staining caused by algae growth and a brown staining caused by organic decomposition. Contact between bone and roots can result in root staining on the bone surface. Root staining is recognized as a dendritic pattern of stains, and possibly adhered root material, on the surface of bones. Prolonged contact between roots and bone may cause root etching that is recognized by shallow grooving and is common with archaeological remains but infrequent with forensic remains. The roots of many plants secrete humic acid, and the grooves found in root etching are interpreted as the "result of dissolution by acids associated with the growth and decay of roots or fungus in direct contact with bone surfaces" (Behrensmeyer, 1978: 154). It is also possible to observe staining and etching on bone resulting from contact with pine needles (Figure 5.9). Pine needles are highly acidic and tend to mark the bone surface as they decompose, leaving an unorganized pattern of linear staining or shallow etching. Roots can also destroy bone by perforating the outer surface and growing into and within bone, resulting in additional mechanical damage. It is common to find roots growing through holes in the skull, such as the eye orbits and the nasal aperture (Figure 5.10).

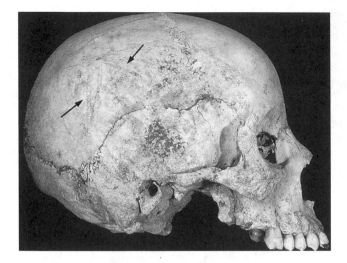

Figure 5.9 Pine needle staining (arrows) shown on lateral surface of cranial vault (brain case). (Photo courtesy of the Department of Anthropology, University of Florida.)

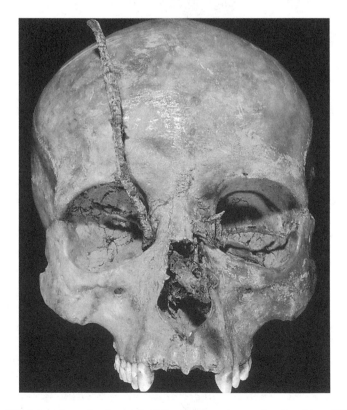

Figure 5.10 Root growth through the nasal cavity and eye orbits. (Photo courtesy of the Department of Anthropology, University of Florida.)

Smaller roots can cause extreme damage to bone by invasive growth within cancellous bone, which can result in the porous regions of long bones, vertebrae, carpals, and tarsals to break apart or disintegrate over time.

5.5.2 Dispersed Remains

Remains deposited in outdoor environments usually exhibit some degree of dispersal of skeletal elements. Some common causes of skeletal dispersal include taphonomic processes such as animal or human activity, gravity, and fluvial transport (e.g., rivers and streams), as well as mechanical alterations to sediments due to burrowing animals, plant root growth, tree falls, frost heaves and ice thaws, and slumping of the soil layers. Proper search strategies are therefore important in delineating site boundaries, locating primary and secondary depositional sites of remains, determining the original position of the remains, and locating scattered skeletal elements.

In many instances, dispersal of skeletal remains results from carnivores scattering skeletal elements over a large area. It is therefore important to focus visual foot searches on areas with the highest concentration of skeletal elements as well as outlying zones where fewer scattered elements may exist. When searching for missing bones, the search team should be thorough and adapt their search methods to the particulars of the site. For example, because scavenged skeletal remains may be dispersed and deposited under thick brush by animals, team members need to search on their hands and knees when thick brush or heavy ground cover is encountered in the search area. Rodent burrows found within the search area should be thoroughly and carefully examined. If birds have scavenged the remains, nests in the proximity of the scatter should also be searched (if possible, by an avian expert).

When skeletal remains are located, the ground surface should be carefully searched to ensure that small bones, bone fragments, teeth, and associated evidence are not missed. Using proper tools and methods, all organic material and debris in the primary site must be removed from the ground surface and screened. After the primary site has been properly cleaned of debris to expose the ground surface and all exposed skeletal elements and evidence have been mapped, the organic layer of the ground surface should be scraped with a trowel. The loose soil should then be screened to locate any remaining small bones, fragments, teeth, or evidence that might have slumped into the soil layers over time.

After cleaning the site of debris and mapping the location of known skeletal elements, it may be possible to infer the directional pathway that missing bones might have been dragged from the primary deposit. For instance, if there are missing elements and it is noted that the dispersal of bones occurs in a single direction from the primary deposit, you would then know in what direction to begin searching for missing elements or a possible secondary deposit of bones. This is very helpful to search teams in wooded environments with thick underbrush or heavy ground cover. As additional bones are located along the directional path of dispersal, team members can spread out into a directed search pattern if needed. Natural landscape features may also direct dispersal patterns and should be considered when searching for missing elements. For example, if a body was deposited on or near an incline, gravity, wind, and water flow could move skeletal elements farther down the hill to a lower level. In this example, locating missing elements would require searching downhill from the primary deposition site. It is important to note that proper search patterns and recovery methods are still required when searching the directional pathways and secondary deposits. All of the organic material and debris must also be removed and screened from these areas, followed by mapping and proper collection procedures, and scraping the ground surface and screening the loose soil to ensure that all evidence has been collected.

The most difficult skeletal elements to locate in the field are the teeth because of their small size and ease of separation. Incisors and canines separate from their sockets early in the decomposition process. Incisors and canines separate much easier because they have single roots, as opposed to premolars and molars that typically have two or more roots (refer to Figure 3.19, for example). It is important to locate as many teeth as possible for identification purposes and this can be accomplished using appropriate search strategies. Haglund (1997b) outlines search strategies used in locating missing teeth associated with remains scattered by medium-sized canids. Teams should search the primary deposition site for teeth, but also along any directional pathways that skeletal elements may have traveled, secondary deposition sites, and possibly areas containing animal scat. Haglund (1997c) also brings attention to special circumstances that might bias predictable patterns of canid bone scattering, such as preexisting facial trauma, terrain, or purposeful dismemberment by humans. In these circumstances, it may not be possible to predict the correct location of missing teeth, and an extended, thorough search must be conducted.

5.6   Indications of Burial of Remains

A grave is much more difficult to locate than a surface deposit because in most cases a body is buried to conceal its location. In many instances, it may be impossible to find a clandestine grave without information providing the exact area where a body was buried. When searching for buried remains, surface indicators may be the best clues for locating a grave. A variety of surface changes occur during the disposal process, some of which may still be present long after burial (Figure 5.11). During the initial digging of a grave, the soil

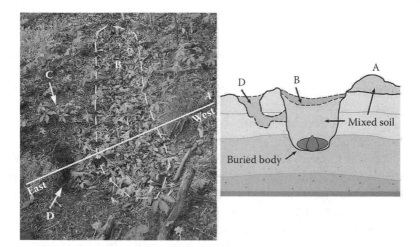

Figure 5.11 Image (left) showing (a) mounding of excess dirt remaining after backfilling process, (b) the primary burial depression filled with leaf litter, (c) ground cover that varies from surrounding plant growth due to disturbance of topsoil, and (d) a burrow possibly from a scavenging animal. The east–west transect line in the image corresponds with the section drawing for the burial (right).

that is removed will normally be placed adjacent to the grave and on top of any associated vegetation. Soils are typically layered and vary in color and texture in relation to depth. The layers of soil removed from the grave become intermixed with each other and with existing topsoil, plants, and other surface materials (e.g., crushed rock, landscaping mulch, trash items). On average, assuming that the original intent is to bury the body in an extended position, the dimensions of the disturbed area may be approximately the same length as the body and at least twice as wide as the body, due to the displaced soil next to the grave. This entire area is referred to as the burial site. The terrain, type of soil, and effort expended in digging a grave will influence how deep the burial will be and how much soil is displaced. In general, hand-dug graves are only as deep as is necessary to conceal the body due to the fact that digging a hole of this size is physically demanding and time consuming.

When filling a grave, there will generally be some original soil that cannot be returned to the burial pit due to the soil becoming less compact and the volume of the body displacing a portion of the original fill. Excess soil is usually scattered around the edges of the grave or left with no attempt to level the surface with the surrounding area, resulting in a small ridge or rise next to the grave (Figure 5.11a). The surface of the soil covering the body will typically have a different color and texture than the surrounding surface soil due to the intermixing of the soil layers during digging and backfilling. In cases where a body is buried at a shallow depth or placed in a natural depression, extra holes may be dug around the burial site in an attempt to gather enough soil to completely conceal the body.

Naturally, there is a high probability that surface changes will occur at the site, making the appearance of the grave differ significantly over time. These changes include depressions that form over the body, variations in localized areas of plant growth, and variations in plant composition. A primary burial depression will normally occur as a result of compaction of the loose soil that was placed over the body and the collapsing of the thorax and abdominal areas of the body during decomposition. Depending on the length of time that the body has been buried and the regional landscape being searched, seasonal leaf litter may naturally build up in the primary depression and indicate the surface outline of the burial (Figure 5.11b). Furthermore, smaller secondary depressions may form within the primary depression due to additional soil compaction and soft tissue decomposition.

In many instances, there are noticeable changes in vegetation over and around the grave because of damage to existing ground cover and disturbance of soil layers. The intermixing of soil layers may limit or destroy the high level of organic nutrients commonly found on or near the ground surface. In addition, the mixing of these layers will affect the number and types of plants that germinate in the disturbed soil. If the soil surface was left bare, plant composition over the grave is initially dominated by species that tend to colonize in disturbed or bare soil, such as grasses. A typical sequence of plant composition would then follow, such as herbaceous plants, shrubs, and trees. However, if tree seeds are present in the disturbed soil, they will germinate as conditions become suitable, and a concentration of young seedlings will be evident. Germination and growth of tree seedlings can also assist in determining when the burial occurred. For example, if a body was buried in autumn, when most tree seeds are prevalent, the surface of the grave might be populated with tree seedlings the following spring. In addition, localized areas of sparse, new ground cover surrounded by dense, mature ground cover may indicate some kind of recent disturbance to the soil layers, most likely within at least one or two seasons of growth (Figure 5.11c). Localized variations in plant growth may be due to a number of factors. If a body is buried in soil that lacks nutrients, plants over or around the burial may be more lush and vibrant green in color than surrounding vegetation. This can be attributed to the aerated soil promoting seed germination and by-product nutrients being released into the soil during body decomposition. If a whole plant or a portion of one (e.g., stems or a few leaves) is covered with soil and unable to photosynthesize for a period of time, it can become yellowed, lose vigor, and appear stunted. In addition, if remains are wrapped or covered (e.g., cement blocks, sheet metal, plastic tarps) when placed in a shallow grave, root growth may be limited and result in weak stems and sparse leaf cover.

It may also be possible to locate burials by searching for surface indicators of animal scavenging (Figure 5.11d). There is a higher probability that animals

Table 5.3   Summary of Indicators Used to Locate Buried Bodies

- Skeletal remains and soft tissue brought to the surface
- Clothing or personal effects
- Insect activity
- Evidence of animal digging and scavenging
- Abandoned tools or weapons
- Soil or vegetation disturbances (e.g., growth, color changes, and lack of growth)
- Depressions, soil disturbances, or unnatural mounding of soil
- Soil coloration changes from mixing soil layers
- Decomposition odor
- Decreased soil compaction
- Areas where bushes or tree limbs have been moved to conceal something buried

will detect and scavenge shallow graves rather than deep ones as decomposition odors are more evident in surface deposits and shallow graves. Areas of localized animal digging encountered during the search should be examined for skeletal elements or personal possessions (e.g., clothing, jewelry, wallets, backpacks) that were brought to the ground surface by scavenging. In special circumstances, digging tools and weapons that may have been discarded or accidentally left behind most likely indicate that a grave is in the vicinity. Table 5.3 provides a list of indicators used to locate buried bodies.

5.7   Cadaver Dogs

Cadaver dogs, or human remains detection (HRD) dogs, can also be invaluable during searches for clandestine graves as they locate bodies through the detection of decomposition odor. However, a cadaver dog may only indicate a localized area where a body is buried and not necessarily the exact spot. This may be due to environmental factors that carry the decomposition odor to another location (see discussion below). Because of this possibility, it is always important to search the area surrounding where the dog indicated, using traditional search methods to determine where the decomposition odor may have originated.

It is important to understand the capabilities and limitations of cadaver dogs and their handlers when choosing and working with an HRD team during a body search. The purpose of this section is to educate anyone requiring the assistance of an HRD team for a body search. This section is not about handling cadaver dogs. For information on choosing, training, and handling cadaver dogs, please see *Cadaver Dog Handbook: Forensic Training and Tactics for the Recovery of Human Remains* by Andrew Rebmann, Edward David, and M.H. Sorg (2000), and *Buzzards and Butterflies: Human Remains Detection Dogs* by J.C. Judah (2008).

5.7.1   What Is a Cadaver Dog?

Cadaver dogs are specially trained in detecting the scent of human decomposition and assisting in locating human cadavers, body parts, and body fluids. They are conditioned to give their handlers an alert when they detect odors associated with human decomposition and to ignore other odors including scents associated with nonhuman animal decomposition (Figure 5.12). Cadaver dogs can be trained to recognize and alert to a variety of decomposition by-products such as gases, liquids, acids, adipocere, and the musty odor

Figure 5.12 Cadaver dog, Ruger, with master canine trainer, Mary Peter. Ruger is searching while on a leash (a), allowing for a more detailed search in particular areas of interest, and (b) searching a defined area without a leash.

from mummified tissue (Rebmann et al., 2000), and also to provide assistance in locating buried bodies, disarticulated remains, bodies submerged in water, or those hidden in vehicles or structures (Lowy and McAlhany, 2000). They will alert to bodies that lack any signs of decomposition detectable by humans (i.e., those with a very short postmortem interval), remains in advanced stages of decomposition, skeletal remains, and even soil and other materials (e.g., carpets and fabrics, truck beds, wood surfaces) containing fluids from human decomposition (Rebmann et al., 2000).

When scent molecules from decomposing human remains are dispersed into the air, the dogs register a sensory reaction in the brain that categorizes these molecules and recognizes them as a unique "total odor" effect, allowing for scent-specific work. This sensory reaction also allows the dog to detect the relative concentration of scent and follow it, as it disperses through the environment in a scent cone, to its place of origin or a secondary scent pool. Rebmann et al. (2000) discuss the basic principles of scent cone presence and distortion (Table 5.4) that are key in understanding the actions and alerts provided by cadaver dogs when conducting searches. The scent molecules shed from decomposing remains form a primary scent cone around and above the body when the air is stagnant (Figure 5.13a). This effect can be intensified with the addition of thermal uplift caused by heat from the sun, at times dispersing the scent well above the ground surface (Figure 5.13b). With wind, a horizontal scent cone forms with the scent becoming more and more dispersed as it is carried away from the body (Figure 5.13c). Conditions with light and variable winds may produce multiple horizontal scent cones, which disperse the scent away from the body in different directions. Many additional factors can alter or distort the position of the scent cone in relation

Table 5.4 Understanding the Presence and Distortion of Decomposition Scent Cones

- Primary scent pools form above and around decomposing remains
- Scent cones form as scent molecules are dispersed away from the source by airflow or thermal uplifting
- Variable winds can cause uneven dispersal of scent molecules or multiple scent cones around the remains
- Water may move the scent away from the source in response to currents, gravity, surface or underground waterways, erosion, or drainage patterns
- Scent barriers, such as vegetation or terrain, may form remote secondary scent pools and scent cones
- Scent voids near the remains can form in areas where water flow interrupts the absorption of decomposition fluids into the soil or in cases where the body is elevated in relation to the ground surface (e.g., a body hanging from a tree)

Source: Adapted from Rebmann, A., David, E., Sorg, M.H. 2000. *Cadaver Dog Handbook: Forensic Training and Tactics for the Recovery of Human Remains.* Boca Raton, FL: CRC Press.

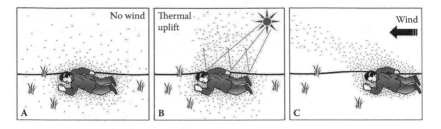

Figure 5.13 Presence of a primary scent pool and distortion of scent cone around decomposing remains in a surface deposit with (a) no wind, (b) no wind and thermal uplift due to radiating heat, and (c) wind from a single direction.

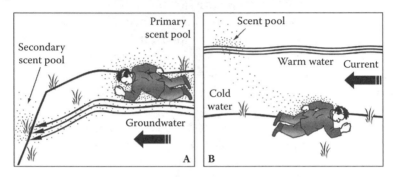

Figure 5.14 Presence of a primary and remote secondary scent pool around decomposing remains: (a) a surface deposit with groundwater transporting scent molecules to a secondary pool downhill from the body, and (b) currents and thermal uplift in water transporting scent molecules from the body to a remote surface location.

to the position of the body, such as terrain, vegetation, water flow, climate, and seasonal weather. For example, scent molecules of a decomposing body located on the ground surface or buried in a shallow grave can be carried away from the body by flowing groundwater and reappear in areas remote from the disposal site (Figure 5.14a). In this example, the cadaver dog would most likely indicate the presence of a buried body or surface deposition at a remote location. In addition, cadaver dogs can detect bodies submerged in water because the decomposition odor of the body can be carried to the surface of the water by currents or natural turbulence. However, like wind, water currents can carry the scent of a submerged decomposing body away from the remains, leaving a scent void in the water directly above the body (Figure 5.14b).

5.7.2   Limitations of Cadaver Dogs

A successful search using cadaver dogs depends on numerous factors including the investigation prior to the search, type of search method, the

Table 5.5 Understanding Limitations of Cadaver Dog Scent Detection

- Are the remains actually present within the search area?
- Are the remains creating a scent pool and a scent cone above ground?
- Is there significant air movement between the scent pool and the dog?
- Is the temperature in range for detection (between 32°F/0°C and 90°F/32°C)?
- Does the handler guide the dog to the correct area?
- Does the handler correctly interpret the dog's behavior?

Source: Adapted from Rebmann, A., David, E., Sorg, M.H. 2000. *Cadaver Dog Handbook: Forensic Training and Tactics for the Recovery of Human Remains.* Boca Raton, FL: CRC Press.

dog handler's skills, weather during the search, terrain of the search area, circumstances leading to death and deposition of the body, and time since death (Rebmann et al., 2000). Table 5.5 provides a few questions that may help in understanding the limitations of cadaver dogs and scent detection during body searches. The primary thing to remember is that the dog's ability to pinpoint the exact location of a buried body depends on decomposition odor reaching the surface. Decomposition odor may not reach the ground surface if the depth of the body is too deep, if the soil type is too compacted, and if the body is wrapped in material that will not release the odor. The soil may need to be vented when a cadaver dog is not able to locate a suspected burial in a given area or when a dog does not indicate the exact location of a buried body. The search area can be vented with a T-bar probe (see following sections in this chapter) to bring decomposition odor to the ground surface. Rebmann et al. (2000) suggest venting every 18 inches (46 centimeters) utilizing grid lines and offsetting the holes between adjacent lines.

5.7.3 Locating a Cadaver Dog

Although there is an obvious need for cadaver dogs, they have been minimally represented in the law enforcement canine population across the United States, and smaller law enforcement agencies may not have their own dog (Lowy and McAlhany, 2000). The canine HRD specialty has not been given the same attention as dogs that are trained in the explosive and narcotic specialties, because it may not be feasible to include another canine specialty in smaller law enforcement agencies for the occasional search. Smaller agencies can usually request the services of a larger nearby department, thereby justifying not having a cadaver dog program. When agencies seek the assistance of an HRD team, it is essential to determine their level of expertise because the experience and abilities of teams vary. It is important to ask questions about team qualifications including training, certifications, and the number of cases handled (Lowy and McAlhany, 2000). A number of national organizations provide cadaver search certification, such as the National Narcotics Dog Detector Association (NNDDA), the National Association of Search and Rescue (NASAR), and the North American Police Working Dog Association (NAPWDA). To receive a cadaver search certification, testing of the dog's abilities requires alerting to human bone, fluid, and tissue, while ignoring nonhuman remains. Various county, state, and federal law enforcement agencies may be able to provide you with recommendations of HRD teams throughout your area.

5.8   Intrusive Search Methods

After the nonintrusive search techniques have been exhausted, there are a number of intrusive techniques that can be used to further explore areas of interest. One caution is that intrusive methods can ultimately destroy the site, so the decision to use these methods must be made carefully.

5.8.1   Probe Searches

The most common intrusive search method is using a probe to locate a clandestine grave and the outline of the grave. Numerous authors have discussed the effectiveness of using probes to locate forensic and archaeological graves (e.g., Boyd, 1979; Imaizumi, 1974; Killam, 2004; Morse et al., 1983; Owsley, 1995; Ruffell, 2005). This method should be used systematically across a search grid and can also be used as a follow-up method after a visual search to further inspect areas of interest.

The most common probe used is called a T-bar probe (refer to Figure 2.2d). Probing is conducted by pushing a pointed metal or fiberglass rod, typically 4 feet (1.2 meters) in length and around ½ inch (approximately 1 centimeter) in diameter with a crossbar handle at the top, into the ground at regular intervals (Figure 5.15). This method is used to determine the qualitative differences in density of subsurface materials, because the disturbed soil of the grave will be less dense than the surrounding undisturbed soil. When using equal amounts of pressure, the probe will penetrate deeper and easier into disturbed soil than it will into undisturbed soil. Because probing is based on relative and subjective resistance, a single person should use the probe within the survey grid if time permits. With practice in the given search area, an individual can determine the amount of pressure needed to probe to a specific depth, or through a specific type of soil layer. As individuals systematically work their way systematically through the grid, areas where the probe easily penetrates the soil are noted and marked for further investigation.

Another type of probe that can be used in forensic investigation is a penetrometer, which is more commonly used for agricultural applications. A

Figure 5.15 Author John Schultz demonstrates the use of a T-bar probe to detect differences in soil compaction in a depression.

Figure 5.16 Using a penetrometer probe with a gauge to measure differences in soil compaction.

penetrometer has a pressure gauge at the junction of the rod and the crossbar (Figure 5.16) that measures soil compactness, or density, by providing a quantitative measurement. A normal T-bar probe can also be modified and used as a penetrometer by attaching a pressure or weight gauge to record pressure measurements (Ruffell, 2005).

The third type of probe is a soil-coring probe (Figure 5.17). This probe is not used to determine whether the soil compactness has changed, instead it is used to determine whether soil horizons are mixed. This is done by removing and examining a vertical core of soil. Soil-coring probes are generally 3½ feet (1 meter) in length, and the end that is inserted into the ground has a hollow soil coring tube that is ½ to ¾ inches (1 to 2 centimeters) in diameter and around 8 inches (20 centimeters) in length. One side of the coring tube is open so the stratigraphy, or layers, of the soil can be viewed. Once a core of the undisturbed natural stratigraphy is extracted (Figure 5.17b), cores of disturbed soil

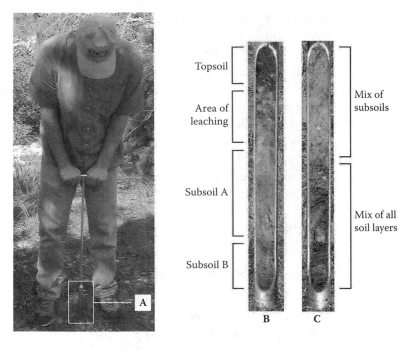

Figure 5.17 Author John Schultz demonstrates the use of a soil-coring probe (a) to detect the presence of disturbed soil layers. Shown on the right is a comparison of soil cores from (b) undisturbed natural soil layers and (c) mottled and mixed soil layers.

will be easily recognized as having a mottled appearance (Figure 5.17c) that is produced from the mixing of the soil layers. An advantage of this method over standard probes is that it is not pushed into the ground as far and there is less of a chance of damaging the body and any associated evidence.

If a T-bar probe is going to be used as a primary search instrument, a grid pattern should be used across the search area. Grid lines should be placed close enough together so that the buried item in question will not be missed between two adjacent lines. A recommended grid interval is approximately 1 foot (30 centimeters) or less. There should be one person using the probe and one person taking notes and marking a scaled map of the search area (see Chapter 7 for information on scaled maps). The individual using the probe should indicate to the note taker whether the soil is more or less compacted. Pin flags should be carefully placed in the areas that require further evaluation. Isolated or suspicious areas exhibiting lower pressure measurements can then be probed with smaller transects to narrow down the size of the area of interest. If the size of the area is consistent with the size of a grave, then further invasive testing will be required to discern if the burial site has been located.

Some inherent difficulties exist in using the soil probe method. It is not normally a search method used systematically over large areas because it can be very time consuming. Also, this method is invasive and can damage a body or evidence. Soil probes should only be used to locate the disturbed soil of a grave and not the exact location of the body within the grave. For example, when performing a search with a soil probe, special care must be taken not to push the probe through the body or skeleton. If a probe was used to locate a grave and possibly caused damage to the body or skeleton in the process, the medical examiner or coroner should be informed so he or she does not mistake postmortem damage as perimortem trauma. It is important to note that the use of probes may not work in soil composed of homogenous sands. Because a probe can be easily pushed through undisturbed homogenous sands, it is generally not possible to discern disturbed areas in this type of soil. Probes will work best in compacted soils, or soils that contain dense layers, where pressure differences from disturbances may persist for many years.

5.8.2   Shovel Testing and Shovel Shining

Although invasive testing with a shovel is not a recommended search method, there are cases when this may be the only alternative after other search methods are exhausted or as a follow-up to a visual or probe search. There are two ways to use a shovel when trying to locate or delineate the boundaries of a grave. The first method is digging a test pit in an attempt to locate evidence of a burial or a body. In this instance, a small test hole is dug with a spade shovel, and all removed soil should be screened so that no potential evidence is missed. However, we caution that this should be used as the absolute last alternative because it is very destructive.

If there are possible indicators of a burial from either visual or invasive search methods, a sharpened flat-blade shovel (refer to Figure 2.2e) may be used to delineate the boundaries of the burial feature. When removing soil, the proper method is to keep the back of the shovel almost parallel with the ground surface. By applying pressure in a forward skimming motion, also known as shovel shining (Figure 5.18), the sharpened edge of the flat shovel blade shaves soil in ½ to ¾ inch (1 to 2 centimeters) layers from the surface. This method does not involve digging, only the removal of thin layers of soil at very slight depths, and keeps the surface over the area as level as possible. This is to ensure that if the outline of a grave appears, it will not be missed (Figure 5.19).

5.8.3   Heavy Equipment Searches

Most forensic anthropologists have heard the obligatory story of law enforcement using a "forensic backhoe" to excavate a burial. For obvious reasons, such as extreme damage to skeletal remains or evidence, a backhoe is not an ideal piece of equipment to use for a forensic search. However, in certain

Figure 5.18 Orange County Sheriff's Office homicide detective Dave Clarke (left) and authors Lana Williams (center) and Sandra Wheeler (right) shovel shining an area of interest while searching for a buried body at a forensic scene.

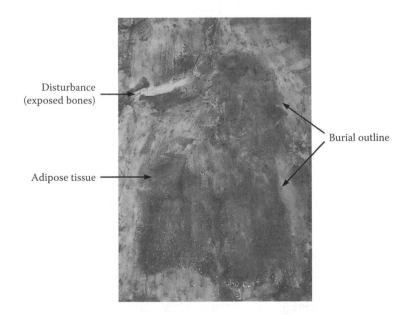

Figure 5.19 Grave outline and associated remains revealed after shovel shining.

Figure 5.20 Heavy equipment (Caterpiller 320B trackhoe excavator with extended boom) being used to search a suspected location of a buried car containing two bodies.

instances, a backhoe with a flat-blade bucket (i.e., without teeth, also called a "clean-up bucket") or an elevated scraper may be a final alternative when all other methods have been exhausted, or when it may not be possible to use traditional methods in searching for a clandestine grave (Figure 5.20). In some cases, a backhoe may be the only realistic option, such as in landfills, heavily flooded areas, and large areas where the soils or groundcover are not suitable for geophysical methods. Backhoes and other heavy equipment can also be valuable tools in lifting or removing cement slabs used to conceal the location of a grave (Hawley et al., 1994). The greatest advantage in using a backhoe is that it can remove a considerable amount of soil in a short period of time. However, backhoes have also been used in archaeology to locate burials by carefully scraping sterile topsoil and exposing the burial outline of cemetery or historic period graves (Bass, 1963; Ubelaker, 1989). Because the use of a backhoe involves extending the bucket over a smaller area of interest, the heavy equipment will not damage material by driving over the search area. An experienced operator can meticulously control the bucket so that the soil is removed a few inches at a time, leaving a relatively smooth surface with a single soil layer exposed at each depth (Figure 5.21).

Bulldozers should not be used in forensic searches as they can quickly and significantly damage evidence as well as the search area. Bulldozers are designed to push soil around, creating a greater chance of mixing soil layers and damaging evidence when their metal tracks drive over and compress the soil. Nevertheless, use of a "forensic bulldozer" can be warranted through the trench-and-shift technique (Christensen et al., 2009). This method involves first digging a trench adjacent to the search area and carefully scraping soil

Figure 5.21 A backhoe (Case 680 loader with Extendahoe) being used to clear an area of interest. Note the smooth, level surface of the cleared area and exposure of a dark, highly organic soil layer (a), located below a lighter-colored sand layer (b). Information provided by the land owner indicated that the organic layer was the original ground surface, while the sand layer was added later to level the property after an old grove of trees had been removed.

from the side of the trench, rather than the heavy equipment moving over the top of the search area and possibly damaging a potential grave.

There should always be a forensic archaeologist guiding the backhoe operator and checking the ground as the soil is being scraped to determine whether a grave or soil change, has appeared. Depending on the angle and amount of sunlight, soil changes, and early indications of grave outlines may appear differently from various perspectives. Therefore, as the ground is scraped, additional team members should be watching for differences in color changes in relation to the surrounding undisturbed soil and taking notes on depths for each soil layer. Designated team members should periodically check suspicious areas with trowels as well as soil probes to discern differences in soil compaction. Soil in a grave is generally a different color from the surrounding layer or may appear mottled due to mixing of the soil layers and decomposition products. If the soil profile consists of multiple discernable soil layers such as a hardpan or clay horizon, the entire layer can be exposed using the backhoe (Figure 5.21b). It may then be possible to locate a clandestine grave by noting the isolated soil changes within the layer, much like the changes seen in the smaller-scale process of shovel shining. During a backhoe search it is also important to have someone visually checking each bucket of removed soil for any evidence. If possible, it is recommended to have someone experienced with human skeletal remains at the scene assisting with the search. Once anything suspicious is located in the area being scraped, all work with the backhoe must cease, and less destructive methods should then be used to determine whether a burial is present. After all evidence has been cleared, or in cases where no evidence was found, the forensic archaeologist should coordinate with law enforcement investigators and the backhoe operator about backfilling all areas that were investigated.

Case Study 4: Try and Try Again

In May 2005 authors Schultz and Dupras were asked to participate in the search for the grave of a 12-year-old female. Law enforcement officials had received a tip from an informant that the girl had been killed a year and a half before and buried approximately 6 feet (1.6 meters) deep in a residential backyard. Investigators felt the information was credible because a cadaver dog had alerted in the suspected area. This case utilized several types of search methods prior to using a backhoe to assist in locating the grave. Upon arriving at the scene, we first conducted a search survey using ground-penetrating radar (GPR). (See Chapter 6 for discussion of GPR equipment and use.) However, this technique was inconclusive due to interference from tree roots in the area. Probes were then used in the area, though soil compaction differences were not detected. We next used flat-edged shovels to shovel shine the search area, and we used trowels for detailed work in clearing the area. Although large networks of undisturbed tree roots were present, we noted that a number of surface roots were previously cut (Figure 5.22), but this had not been a recent

Figure 5.22 Network of large tree roots present in the suspected area. This image shows two large uncut roots (a) and a cut root with smaller roots growing from the cut end (b).

Figure 5.23 Author John Schultz shovel shining the bottom of the trench dug by a backhoe with a rock bucket (circled).

occurrence as several of these roots had developed root balls with smaller roots growing out of them. This was consistent with information concerning one of the children at the residence periodically digging in the backyard for worms used as fishing bait. None of these search methods yielded evidence of a clandestine grave.

In order to completely clear the area, the detective in charge requested that we follow up with a backhoe search. We were provided a city-owned backhoe, but the city was not able to provide one with a flat-blade bucket, and instead, we received one with a "rock" bucket (i.e., a toothed bucket) (Figure 5.23). Because it was not possible to scrape the ground surface with this bucket, we decided to improvise by first digging a trench outside the search area. This allowed us to view the natural stratigraphy of the soil profile, which consisted of distinct and contrasting soil horizons. Shovel shining was used to check the bottom of the trench before the work continued. Using the trench-and-shift technique, the backhoe proceeded to slowly remove soil from the exposed wall of the trench, working toward the main area of interest. Each time the backhoe removed a strip of soil,

Figure 5.24 Author John Schultz scraping the wall of the trench with a trowel to discern any disruption of the natural stratigraphy.

we would scrape the newly exposed surface with trowels to discern any soil changes that might indicate a grave outline (Figure 5.24). The entire area was cleared using this method, which confirmed our previous search results that a grave was not within the search area.

Case Study 5: The Good, the Bad and the Muddy

In September 2001 authors Dupras, Williams, and Wheeler were asked to assist in the search for the remains of a 22-year-old male who had been missing for approximately 15 months. Information from one of the suspects, already incarcerated for another offense, led the police to search an abandoned pig farm. The suspect indicated that the victim had been lured to the area with false hopes of a romantic rendezvous, and upon his arrival four individuals proceeded to beat him to death and then bury him on the property.

The police had set a perimeter before we arrived on the scene. The suspect had been brought out to the scene the previous day and had indicated areas of interest. The area marked as searchable by the police was approximately 50 by 75 feet (15 by 23 meters) in size and was bordered on the north by a tree line and fire trench, on the south by a dirt road, and on the east and west by low brush cover. The area to be searched included tall grass, brush, and brambles. Police cadaver dogs had been brought in to assist with the search, and they had alerted at two particular spots (Figure 5.25). A walking survey was very difficult as the surface features

Figure 5.25 Cadaver dog search in the suspected burial area. Note the growth of grasses, low brush, and trees that needed to be cleared before a detailed search could be conducted.

were not discernable through the vegetation, so a decision was made to clear the area. A large field mower was brought in to clear low brush and small trees, and a prison detail of 10 inmates cleared the remainder of the ground cover (Figure 5.26). After the ground was cleared, there were two disturbed areas that were investigated in addition to the areas that the dogs alerted on earlier. All of the disturbed areas were first shovel shined to discern any grave outlines and then excavated with trowels to examine any suspected features. These areas revealed only butchered pig bones and turtle shells. Toward the late afternoon, heavy rainfall caused the search to be suspended for the day.

On the second day of the search, the suspect was brought back out to give us further indication of where to search and provide a description of the burial site. The suspect had a difficult time indicating where to search because the environment had been changed dramatically after removal of the foliage. It was decided at this point to use a backhoe so the entire area could be searched in a timely manner (Figure 5.27). Initially, there were a few minutes of anxious anticipation when the backhoe overturned a turtle shell. With only part of the shell exposed, it looked remarkably like a human skull! But alas, no human bones were uncovered, and, like the day before, a torrential downpour began around 3:00 P.M., creating a very muddy area. The search was once again suspended for the day.

Figure 5.26 Area of interest after all vegetation was removed with a large field mower and prison detail.

Figure 5.27 View of scene showing backhoe (front center), command vehicles, and the two areas (arrows) cleared by the backhoe on the second day of the search. (Photo courtesy of the Orange County Sheriff's Office.)

On the morning of the third day, the cadaver dogs were brought back out to search the area. On occasion, a secondary canine search is performed once vegetation is removed or soil is disturbed by a backhoe, as this can potentially cause the release of decomposition molecules triggering a canine alert. The cadaver dogs hit on one area that was further explored.

By this time, our search area had turned into a giant mud bowl. The summer of 2001 had been a particularly bad year for rainfall, and the ground was already saturated with water before we started searching the new area indicated by the canine unit. With the addition of multiple days of heavy rain, the water was unable to drain from the ground surface and pooled in every depression created by the backhoe. It is also imperative at this point to emphasize the importance of having a backhoe operator who is experienced and skilled at his or her job (i.e., can take direction and knows how to remove soil in small, level increments). In this case, the operator actually contributed to the difficulties in excavation. The operator did not listen to our needs and instead created large holes and piles of dirt in areas that, when combined with the rain, created unsteady and hazardous working conditions. Because of the condition of the terrain, a special type of backhoe, called a spider backhoe, was brought in to continue excavations. The spider backhoe has extension legs that allow for the stabilization of the machine on uneven terrain. At 2:45 P.M. on the third day of the search, the bucket of the spider backhoe snagged and exposed what appeared to be a human leg bone. All excavations were suspended until the local medical examiner arrived at the scene to verify that the bone was human and then instructed us to continue with the recovery.

The rain continued, and a temporary shelter was erected over the site where the bone was discovered (Figure 5.28). The large quantities of standing water, however, made excavation very difficult. The sides of the excavation area were unstable and continued to collapse. Water continually ran down the sides of the excavation area and also seeped in from the surrounding walls. Efforts were made to construct drainage trenches around the area so the water could be diverted. The spider backhoe was used to dig a reservoir pit, so the water would accumulate there instead of the grave. Because of these difficult conditions, we knew we had to work faster than normal to recover the remains.

Flat-blade shovels were used to shovel shine the area, revealing the outline of the grave (Figure 5.29). Because this area was an abandoned pig farm, there was a thick, decomposed organic layer of soil over the sand. When the grave was dug and filled, these two soils were intermixed, making the grave outline very evident. The burial pit, 2.5 feet in width by 4 feet in length (0.76 by 1.2 meters), was clearly defined as a dark area in comparison to the surrounding white sterile sand layer. Traditional excavation techniques, such as setting up a grid, were impossible in this

Figure 5.28 Temporary shelter erected over burial site. This image also shows the mess that was made by the backhoe operator and the pooled rainwater.

case due to the muddy, unstable conditions and the continual water flow. The site and excavation were primarily documented using photography. Layers of soil in the feature were removed slowly and carefully with a flat-blade shovel until the skull was located. At this point trowels and small excavation tools were used to excavate and reveal the entire individual. Although the individual had been interred for 15 months, the burial environment and the copious amount of rain created a condition that was conducive to the development of adipocere; therefore, much of the soft tissue was still present on the postcranial portion of the body. Once the body was completely uncovered it was removed as a single unit and placed in a body bag. The area under the body was excavated to make sure that none of the smaller bones or any associated evidentiary items were missed.

As a follow-up to this case, the four individuals responsible for this crime were charged and convicted of first degree murder and are all currently serving their sentences.

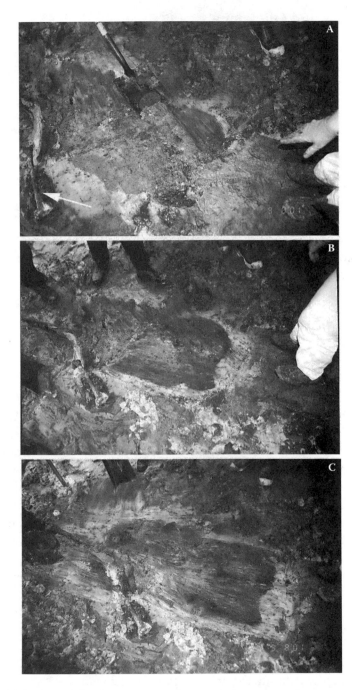

Figure 5.29 Shovel shining process showing the progressive exposure of the burial feature: (a) first portion of the burial exposed. The tibia dislodged by the backhoe is present in the lower left part of the image (arrow); (b) burial pit half exposed; and (c) entire burial pit exposed.

Key Words and Questions

backhoe
burial depression
burial site
cadaver dog
clandestine burial
dispersal patterns
dispersed remains
etching
gnawing
grid pattern
HRD team
penetrometer
scent cone
scent pool
shovel shining
soil-coring probe
strip (line) pattern
T-bar probe
transect
weathering

1. During a search, the remains of an individual who has been missing for five years are found scattered across an open area surrounded by low-lying scrub brush and trees. The majority of the remains are bright white in color on their posterior portions. The right femur is found approximately 35 feet (10.5 meters) to the east of the individual's pelvis, and the lower right leg and foot have not been found. The surface of the femur is rough in texture and bright white in color on the posterior side but stained a darker brown color on the anterior side. In addition, the distal end of the right femur is missing, and the remaining edges have a very ragged and hollowed-out appearance. On the basis of this information, answer the following:
    - What is the taphonomic significance of the condition of the femur? What kinds of information does it provide in relation to the search?
    - Describe how you would follow the methods presented in this chapter to locate the missing skeletal elements.
2. The local police receive a tip concerning an individual who had gone missing three years ago. The informant stated that the individual was buried in an old apple orchard that is no longer harvested. The general landscape of the orchard is flat with tall grass and trees and

covers about one square mile (1.6 square kilometers). Considering these factors, answer the following:

- How would you go about searching for the remains? What search pattern would you use?
- How many people would be needed on the search team? What would the spacing be between individuals?
- When would you consider using an invasive method in your search? What method(s) would you use and why?

3. A hiker disappeared two years ago in some rocky terrain in a river valley. Cadaver dogs were used in a recent search for the missing hiker and alerted to an area at the bottom of a 20 foot (6 meter) cliff that ran along a closed mountain bike trail. The local police searched the area and along the edge of the river, which was approximately 15 feet (4.5 meters) away from the bottom of the cliff. No bones or associated evidence were found in the area indicated by the dogs. Considering these factors, answer the following:

- What processes would cause the dogs to alert to this area even though no remains were found? Describe the possible scenario of scent pool and scent cone formation.
- What would you do at this point in the search? Explain your reasoning using the information provided.
- Is there any additional information that the HRD team could provide that may help explain why the cadaver dogs alerted to this area?

4. You are assisting in a search that is using a backhoe and have been asked to keep a set of notes for the lead forensic archaeologist. What kinds of information should you be collecting? What other method(s) of data collection might you use to go along with your written notes?

Suggested Readings

Haglund, W.D. 2007. Scattered skeletal human remains: search strategy considerations for locating missing teeth. In: Haglund, W.D., Sorg, M.H., eds. *Forensic Taphonomy: The Postmortem Fate of Human Remains*, pp. 383–394. Boca Raton, FL: CRC Press.

Lasseter, A.E., Jacobi, K.P., Farley, R., Hensel, L. 2003. Cadaver dog and handler team capabilities in the recovery of buried human remains in the Southeastern United States. *Journal of Forensic Sciences* 48:617–621.

Nawrocki, S.P. 2009. Forensic taphonomy. In: Blau, S., Ubelaker, D.H., eds. *Handbook of Forensic Anthropology and Archaeology*, pp. 284–294. Walnut Creek, CA: Left Coast Press.

Owsley, D.W. 2005. Techniques for locating burials. *Journal of Forensic Sciences* 40:735–740.

Sledzik, P.S., Dirkmaat, D., Mann, R.W., Holland, T.D., Mundorff, A.Z., Adams, B.J., Crowder, C.M., DePaolo, F. 2009. Disaster victim recovery and identification: forensic anthropology in the aftermath of September 11. In: Steadmann, D.W., ed. *Hard Evidence: Case Studies in Forensic Anthropology*, 2nd ed., pp. 289–302. Upper Saddle River, NJ: Prentice Hall.

References

Bass, W.M. 1963. The use of heavy power equipment in the excavation of human skeletal material. *Plains Anthropologist* 8(20):122–123.

Behrensmeyer, A.K. 1978. Taphonomic and ecologic information from bone weathering. *Paleobiology* 4:150–162.

Berryman, H.E. 2002. Disarticulation pattern and tooth mark artifacts associated with pig scavenging of human remains: a case study. In: Haglund, W.D., Sorg, M.H., eds. *Advances in Forensic Taphonomy: Method, Theory, and Archaeological Perspectives*, pp. 487–496. Boca Raton, FL: CRC Press.

Binford, L. 1981. *Bones: Ancient Men and Modern Myths*. New York: Academic Press.

Boyd, R.M. 1979. Buried body cases. *FBI Law Enforcement Bulletin* 48(2):6–11.

Carleton, M.D. 1984. Introduction to rodents. In: Anderson, S., Jones, K.J., eds. *Orders and Families of Recent Mammals of the World*, pp. 255–265. New York: John Wiley and Sons.

Carson, E.A., Stefan, V.H., Powell, J.F. 2000. Skeletal manifestations of bear scavenging. *Journal of Forensic Sciences* 45:515–526.

Christensen, A.M., Lowe, W.M., Reinecke, G.W. 2009. The "forensic bulldozer" as a clandestine grave search tool. *Forensic Science Communications* 11(4): http://www.fbi.gov/hq/lab/fsc/current/technical/2009_10_Technical_Note.html.

Clark, A. 1996. *Seeing Beneath the Soil: Prospecting Methods in Archaeology*. New York: Routledge.

France, D.L., Griffin, T.J., Swanburg, J.G., Lindemann, J.W., Davenport, G.C., Tramell, V., Travis, C.T., Kondratieff, R., Nelson, A., Castellano, K., Hopkins, D. 1992. A multidisciplinary approach to the detection of clandestine graves. *Journal of Forensic Sciences* 37:1145–1458.

France, D.L., Griffin, T.J., Swanburg, J.G., Lindemann, J.W., Davenport, G.C., Tramell, V., Travis, C.T., Kondratieff, R., Nelson, A., Castellano, K., Hopkins, D., Adair, T. 1997. NecroSearch revisited: further multidisciplinary approaches to the detection of clandestine graves. In: Haglund, W.D., Sorg, M.H., eds. *Forensic Taphonomy: The Postmortem Fate of Human Remains*, pp. 497–510. Boca Raton, FL: CRC Press.

Grupe, G., Dreses-Werringloer, U., Parsche, F. 1993. Initial stages of bone decomposition: causes and consequences. In: Lambert, J.B., Grupe, G., eds. *Prehistoric Human Bone: Archaeology at the Molecular Level*, pp. 257–274. Berlin: Springer-Verlag.

Haglund, W.D. 1997a. Rodents and human remains. In: Haglund, W.D., Sorg, M.H., eds. *Forensic Taphonomy: The Postmortem Fate of Human Remains*, pp. 405–414. Boca Raton, FL: CRC Press.

Haglund, W.D. 1997b. Scattered skeletal human remains: search strategy considerations for locating missing teeth. In: Haglund, W.D., Sorg, M.H., eds. *Forensic Taphonomy: The Postmortem Fate of Human Remains*, pp. 383–394. Boca Raton, FL: CRC Press.

Haglund, W.D. 1997c. Dogs and coyotes: postmortem involvement with human remains. In: Haglund, W.D., Sorg, M.H., eds. *Forensic Taphonomy: The Postmortem Fate of Human Remains*, pp. 367–382. Boca Raton, FL: CRC Press.

Haglund, W.D., Reay, D.T., Swindler, D.R. 1988. Tooth mark artifacts and survival of bones in animal scavenged human skeletons. *Journal of Forensic Sciences* 51:674–677.

Harding, B.E., Wolf, B.C. 2006. Alligator attacks in Southwest Florida. *Journal of Forensic Sciences* 33:985–997.

Hawley, D.A., Harruff, R.C., Pless, J.E., Clark, M.A. 1994. Disinterment from paving materials: use of heavy equipment for exhumation and examination of bodies. *Journal of Forensic Sciences* 39:100–106.

Haynes, G. 1980. Prey, bones and predators: potential ecological weathering from analysis of bone sites. *Ossa* 7:75–97.

Hedges, R.E.M. 2002. Bone diagenesis: an overview of processes. *Archaeometry* 44:319–328.

Hillson, S. 2005. *Teeth*, 2nd ed. New York: Cambridge University Press.

Imaizumi, M. 1974. Locating buried bodies. *FBI Law Enforcement Bulletin* 43(8):2–5.

Iscan, M.Y., McCabe, B.Q. 1995. Analysis of human remains recovered from a shark. *Forensic Science International* 72:15–23.

Judah, J.C. 2008. *Buzzards and Butterflies: Human Remains Detection Dogs*, 2nd ed. Wilmington, NC: Coastal Books.

Killam, E.W. 2004. *The Detection of Human Remains*, 2nd ed. Springfield, IL: Charles C. Thomas.

Komar, D., Beattie, O. 1998. Identifying bird scavenging in fleshed and dry remains. *Canadian Society of Forensic Science Journal* 31:35–43.

Lowy, A., McAlhany, P. 2000. Human remains detection: the latest police canine detector specialty. *FDIAI News* April/June: 6–8.

Lyman, R.L. 1994. *Vertebrate Taphonomy*. New York: Cambridge University Press.

Maguire, J.M., Pemberton, D., Collett, M.H. 1980. The Makapansgat Limeworks Grey Breccia: hominids, hyaenas, hystricids, or hillwash? *Paleontologia Africana* 23:75–98.

Moore, W.J. 2009. *The Mammalian Skull*. New York: Cambridge University Press.

Morse, D., Duncan, J., Stoudamire, J. 1983. *Handbook of Forensic Archaeology and Anthropology*. Tallahassee, FL: Rose Printing.

Murad, T.A. 1997. The utilization of faunal evidence in the recovery of human remains. In: Haglund, W.D., Sorg, M.H., eds. *Forensic Taphonomy: The Postmortem Fate of Human Remains*, pp. 395–404. Boca Raton, FL: CRC Press.

Owsley, D.W. 1995. Techniques for locating burials, with emphasis on the probe. *Journal of Forensic Sciences* 40:735–740.

Rathbun, T.A., Rathbun, B.C. 1984. Human remains recovered from a shark's stomach in South Carolina. *Journal of Forensic Sciences* 29:269–276.

Rebmann, A., David, E., Sorg, M.H. 2000. *Cadaver Dog Handbook: Forensic Training and Tactics for the Recovery of Human Remains*. Boca Raton, FL: CRC Press.

Rossi, M.L., Shahrom, A.W., Chapman, R.C., Vanezis, P. 1994. Postmortem injury by indoor pets. *American Journal of Forensic Medicine and Pathology* 15:105–109.

Ruffell, A. 2005. Burial location using cheap and reliable quantitative probe measurements. *Forensic Science International* 151:207–211.

Ubelaker, D.H. 1999. *Human Skeletal Remains: Excavation, Analysis, Interpretation,* 3rd ed. Washington, DC: Taraxcum.

Methods of Geophysical Survey 6

Conducting a geophysical survey in a forensic context is important for not only locating buried bodies and forensic evidence but also equally as important for clearing suspected areas so law enforcement can direct investigations elsewhere. Geophysical prospecting is the study of locating and mapping hidden objects or features that are underground or underwater. In most instances, methods of geophysical prospecting are nonintrusive or nondestructive. Therefore, one advantage of using geophysical methods in forensic and archaeological searches is scene or site preservation because the ground is not disturbed. Methods of geophysical prospecting can be used as a follow-up technique to searching potential areas after a visual search has been conducted, as well as in isolating smaller areas for further investigation. In addition, geophysical prospecting methods can be effective in search areas where traditional search methods are inadequate, such as over concrete and pavement. For example, a geophysical survey can be performed over a house foundation without any initial destruction to the slab. If there are potential areas under the slab that need further investigation, there will be only minimal destruction because the exact areas to search will have been highlighted using methods of geophysical prospecting.

The purpose of conducting a geophysical survey is to systematically detect subsurface anomalies, which are recognized as localized areas of contrasting physical properties such as a metallic weapon buried in the soil. In this case, the buried metallic weapon may be detected with various geophysical prospecting tools because it would have different electrical properties (e.g., an increased ability to conduct electrical current, or higher conductivity) than the surrounding soil. (See Table 6.1 for a summary of commonly used tools and their applications.) However, the only way to determine what produces the anomaly is to then use a destructive follow-up method such as probing or excavating. Geophysical prospecting methods can be classified into two basic types: active and passive (Reynolds, 1997). Active methods send an induced signal into the ground by a transmitter and then measure the returning signal via a receiver. Conversely, passive methods only contain a receiver that measures variations within the natural forces of the earth, such as gravitational and magnetic fields, which are generally produced by buried metallic objects.

Table 6.1   Summary of Commonly Used Geophysical Prospecting Tools[a]

	Applications	Disadvantages
Electromagnetic (EM) induction meters[b]	• Metallic weapons and other large metallic objects • May detect graves	• Expensive • Require expert operator • Shallow detection
Resistivity meters[b]	• Metallic weapons and other large metallic objects • May detect graves	• Moderately priced • Require some ground disturbance
Magnetometers	• Metallic weapons and other metal evidence	• Expensive • Require expert operator
Magnetic locators	• Metallic weapons and other metal evidence	• Only detect objects at shallow depths
Metal detectors	• Metallic weapons and other metal evidence	• Only detect objects at shallow depths
Side-scan sonar	• Water search for bodies and large objects	• Expensive • Requires expert operator

[a]   Information regarding use of ground-penetrating radar (GPR) can be found in Table 6.2.

[b]   These tools may not be useful for detecting graves due to insufficient contrast between the burial and the surrounding undisturbed soil. We suggest these meters be used only in cases where conditions are unsuitable for ground-penetrating radar (GPR) systems.

The following description of geophysical prospecting tools is not an exhaustive list of those used in forensic and archaeological applications. The purpose of this chapter is to discuss the best equipment to use in various contexts when searching for buried bodies and metallic forensic evidence and to explain the operation and use of the equipment in the field. The chapter reviews the more common tools used in forensic and archaeological surveys, such as ground-penetrating radar (GPR), electromagnetic (EM) induction meters, electrical resistivity meters, magnetometers, magnetic locators, metal detectors, and side-scan sonar. These methods provide excellent resolution of many types of archaeological features and can be operated under a wide range of conditions. Of all these, GPR is generally the best option when searching for buried remains. However, if it is not possible to use a GPR system, either due to equipment availability or unsuitable site conditions, or when searching for smaller metallic evidence, then one of the alternate geophysical methods described in this chapter may be useful.

6.1   Ground-Penetrating Radar

Ground-penetrating radar has proven to be the best geophysical tool to use when searching for a grave in archaeological, forensic, and controlled contexts. For example, GPR has been used to locate or verify the location of historic or archaeological graves (Bevan, 1991; King et al., 1993; Vaughn,

Figure 6.1 Author John Schultz demonstrating how the ground-penetrating radar (GPR) is operated when using a survey cart with the 500 MHz antenna secured to the bottom of the cart.

1986) and increasingly has been used to locate clandestine graves involving bodies interred in varying environments and over various postmortem intervals (Calkin et al., 1995; Davenport, 2001a; Mellett, 1992; Nobes, 2000; Schultz, 2007). At the same time, controlled studies using buried pig cadavers have demonstrated that a GPR system is the most effective geophysical prospecting tool used to delineate graves in forensic contexts (France et al., 1992, 1997).

Standard GPR systems consist of four main components: the control unit, the transmitter, the receiver, and the display unit. Systems used in archaeology and forensics typically have monostatic antennas where the transmitter and receiver are contained within the same antenna housing. GPR systems can be configured a number of different ways for use in the field. The most common configuration is to mount all of the GPR components onto a cart that can be operated by one individual (Figure 6.1). The second option has one individual pulling the antenna and operating a control unit that is attached to the body via a harness (Figure 6.2). The last option is to have the antenna and control unit separate from one another, where one individual pulls the antenna across each transect on a grid while another individual monitors the GPR signal on the control unit and directs the antenna operator. For a geophysical survey performed outdoors, this last option would only be used

Figure 6.2 Author John Schultz demonstrating how the ground-penetrating radar (GPR) is operated when one individual is pulling the 500 MHz antenna with the monitor secured to the body via a shoulder harness.

if a cart-mounted GPR system were not available. However, if a geophysical survey was performed inside a house or structure, using an antenna and control unit separated by a longer cable may be preferable because this configuration allows for more detailed work. Operating the GPR system begins with placement of the antenna on, or near, the ground surface and then moving it over the area being surveyed. When the GPR system is active, it emits continuous EM pulses of short duration that propagate from the transmitting unit in the antenna downward into the ground. As the signal penetrates into the subsurface, it will be reflected, refracted, and scattered as it encounters materials of contrasting electrical properties (Figure 6.3). The receiving portion of the antenna records the returning signal and sends it back to the control unit. The control unit amplifies and formats the raw, reflected signal for immediate display on a video monitor. The GPR data files can also be downloaded to an external computer and stored for further viewing and processing (e.g., to increase resolution of the reflection profile) using a variety of commercially available software programs.

Antennas for GPR systems come in standard frequencies that are designated by the frequency corresponding to the peak power of the radiated spectrum, or the center frequency. The most common GPR systems available from commercial manufacturers employ pulsed radar energy of one center frequency. Antenna choice is a compromise between depth of penetration and

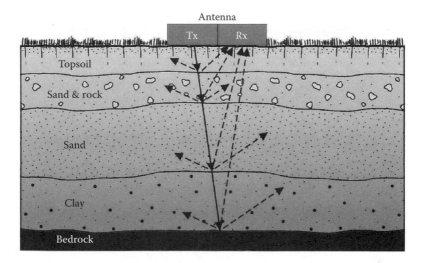

Figure 6.3 Radar waves transmitted (Tx) from the antenna are either received (Rx) or reflected and scattered as they encounter soil–horizon interfaces with differing properties of conductivity and density.

subsurface resolution. Lower-frequency antennae (e.g., 250 MHz) are used for much deeper surveys but have a lower resolution of small subsurface targets. In some instances, a higher-resolution antenna (e.g., 900 MHz) may yield so much detail or clutter (i.e., small discontinuities that reflect energy but are not the target of the survey) that the target may not be readily identified (Nobes, 2000; Schultz, 2003). Antennae with frequencies from 400 to 500 MHz are generally appropriate for most forensic and archeological applications because they provide an excellent compromise between depth of penetration and resolution of subsurface features (Schultz, 2008; Schultz et al., 2006). However, soil type must also be considered when choosing antenna size because depth of penetration of the EM wave will be reduced in certain soil types. In particular, soils composed of a high clay percentage will dissipate or attenuate the radar signal. When soil properties limit the depth of penetration, a lower-frequency antenna, such as 250 MHz, must be considered. Pre-survey testing with more than one antenna can be very beneficial in determining the optimal antenna frequency for a particular soil type.

It is important to note that an exact picture of the subsurface is not provided with a GPR system. Instead, it produces a GPR reflection profile that represents a grid transect line in the search area and is a cross section of the subsurface, providing length and depth. Features are generally detected by GPR systems due to increases in conductivity, changes in density, and voids. Increases in conductivity are primarily due to an increase in water content in certain soils or stratigraphic horizons such as clay. For example, when soil is disturbed during the digging of a grave, the space between the particles increases and results in greater moisture retention and conductivity

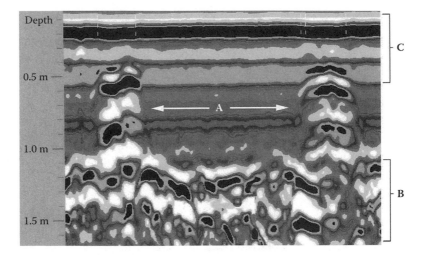

Figure 6.4 Ground-penetrating radar (GPR) reflection profile of two pig cadavers buried at approximately 60 cm. The reflection profile shows two point sources from the buried pig cadavers (a). A planar surface (b) is demarcated by a clay horizon in the bottom portion of the reflection profile, while ringing (c) is evident in the horizontal banding in the top portion of the profile.

in the backfill compared to the surrounding undisturbed soil. Conductivity increases also occur with buried metallic objects and buried electric lines. When a subsurface feature is detected and noted on the GPR reflection profile, as shown in Figure 6.4, it is called a reflection, or anomaly, which can be produced from a feature described as either a point source or planar surface (Conyers and Goodman, 1997). Reflections are nonspecific features, and in many instances limited exploratory probing or excavation may be required to determine the exact item or feature that was detected. Point sources, or small hyperbolic reflections commonly referred to as anomalies, are due to smaller features such as tunnels, voids, pipes, graves, buried remains, small archaeological features, and weapons (Figure 6.4a). Planar surfaces that are detected can be due to interfaces of stratigraphic horizons (e.g., sand, clay, loam), water tables, or large archaeological features, such as floors and foundations (Figure 6.4b). In addition, prominent horizontal bands of antenna noise, known as ringing (Figure 6.4c), may appear in the top portion of most GPR reflection profiles (Shih and Doolittle, 1984; Sternberg and McGill, 1995). If the ringing obscures the GPR reflection profile, it can be removed during processing of the data.

Hyperbolic reflections visible on the GPR profile are produced from the wide angle of the transmitted radar pulse, which is in the shape of an elliptical cone. The long axis of the ellipse is parallel to the direction that the antenna travels, and the radiation pattern on a horizontal plane is directed below the

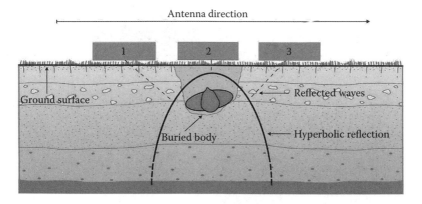

Figure 6.5 Illustration of how a ground-penetrating radar (GPR) system detects a feature or buried object. A point source or hyperbolic reflection is generated from one single subsurface feature due to the wide angle of the transmitted radar beam. The hyperbolic characteristics of the reflection are due to the increased travel time of the radar signal before and after the subsurface feature is detected.

antenna, as well as in front, behind, and to the sides as it travels across the ground surface (Conyers and Goodman, 1997; Schultz, 2007). As the antenna is dragged over a subsurface object, it will detect the object prior to arriving directly over it, as well as when it is directly over it, and will continue to detect the subsurface object after passing it (Figure 6.5). When the point source is detected prior to and after the antenna has passed, it is recorded as if the point source is directly beneath the antenna, but the travel time of the radar signal to the object is increased. The hyperbolic characteristics, or the addition of the tails, are due to the increased travel time of the radar signal before and after the subsurface feature is detected. This shape is important because it allows the GPR operator to note when a feature is located on the GPR profile.

By incorporating GPR profile data into a search grid, the operator can also provide horizontal slices, which show a plan view of the data at designated depths. The GPR software interpolates the distance between the grid lines, which are represented by the GPR profiles, to make a cube (Figure 6.6). The software can then "slice" through the cube to view the subsurface at different depths. However, if horizontal slices are incorporated, it is recommended that assessment of individual GPR profiles is also included so that the forensic search does not rely solely on data obtained from horizontal slice reflections. In addition, while GPR data can be assessed in the field when performing the geophysical survey, it is a good idea to process and clean the data back at the lab to determine if additional reflections become discernable with processing.

There are many advantages for using a GPR system in forensic contexts. The data are displayed in real time and, for forensic surveying, the

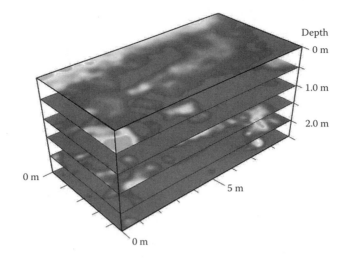

Figure 6.6 Vertical ground-penetrating radar (GPR) profiles can be processed into a cube and then horizontal slices can be produced to view the subsurface layers. These slices are akin to plan map views, which represent different depths.

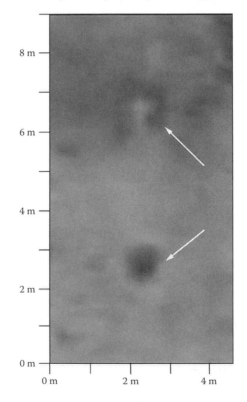

Figure 6.7 Horizontal slice detecting two controlled burials (arrows) containing animal cadavers.

excellent resolution of subsurface features is only surpassed by side-scan sonar (described below). Also, it is possible to estimate the depth of forensic targets in the field without having to dig up the target producing the reflection or post-processing the data. Geophysical surveys using GPR systems work best in dry, sandy soils with little subsurface debris, but the equipment can also be used in a variety of contexts such as over concrete, pavement, and hard-packed surfaces. In addition, GPR systems can be used to search for large metallic evidence. For example, the contrast of a grave will be increased if a large metallic object, such as a shotgun or rifle, was buried in a grave with a body. Although GPR components can be used in a boat over fresh water to search for large submersed metal drums or vehicles, this equipment should only be used in this manner if side-scan sonar is not available.

There are a number of disadvantages that will limit or prevent the use of a GPR system as a search tool. First, the equipment is expensive, and it requires an experienced operator to interpret the data. Also, the search area must be fairly level, smooth, and open with few trees, and must have relatively few buried large metal objects, as they can produce a reflection similar in size and shape to that of a buried body. However, experienced operators may be able to rule out specific reflections based on their experience and the relationship of the reflections to specific site features. For example, if reflections are detected near a large tree, it is possible that the tree roots are producing the reflections. Soil properties will also affect GPR system use because the system may not produce quality signal profiles in water-saturated soils, and it may be very difficult to locate a buried body or forensic evidence in clayey soils. In addition, it could take quite a long time to perform a geophysical survey using a GPR system depending on the size of the search area. For example, it would not be feasible to perform a GPR geophysical survey in an area that consists of many acres. Table 6.2 summarizes advantages and disadvantages of GPR use in forensic contexts.

Table 6.2 Advantages and Disadvantages of Ground-Penetrating Radar (GPR) System Use in Forensic Searches

Advantages	Disadvantages
• Real-time display	• Expense of equipment
• Immediate results in the field	• Requires experienced operator
• Excellent resolution	• Slow coverage speed
• Detection of graves and metallic objects	• Ground must be relatively level, smooth, and open
• Estimation of depth of forensic targets	• Poor penetration in clayey and saturated soils
• Penetration of concrete and pavement	

6.2   Electromagnetic Induction Meters

Electromagnetic (EM) induction meters, more commonly called EM conductivity meters, are active EM instruments that contain a transmitter and a receiver and are used to measure differences in the electrical conductivity of the ground. The transmitter projects a primary low-frequency EM field into the ground that generates a small eddy of current on the surface of conducting (ferrous and nonferrous) objects or features. The eddy of current in turn creates a secondary EM field that is measured by the receiver (Figure 6.8). Therefore, the operator must remove all metal items from their person such as car keys, belt buckles, and steel-toed boots before conducting a search using an EM induction meter. Conductivity is measured in millisiemens per meter (mS/m), and measurements should be recorded along a grid with data saved in a data logger. Data can then be downloaded to a mapping program and plotted similar to a surface contour map for interpretation and detection of conductivity anomalies.

The most popular EM induction method for forensic and archaeological contexts is the horizontal loop or slingram method. A typical EM induction meter (e.g., Geonics EM31 model) used in archaeological contexts (Figure 6.9), contains a long antenna rod measuring 4 meters (smaller models are available) with transmitting and receiving units mounted on opposite ends. Generally, the greater the distance the receiver and transmitter

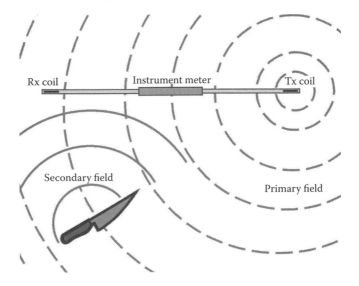

Figure 6.8 A primary electromagnetic field is transmitted into the ground from the transmitting coil (Tx) that generates a small eddy of current on the surface of conducting objects (e.g., knife). This eddy of current in turn creates a secondary electromagnetic field that is measured by the receiver coil (Rx).

Figure 6.9 The slingram EM induction method shown here consists of a long antenna pole with transmitting (Tx) and receiving (Rx) coils mounted at opposite ends of the pole. The unit is operated by one person and should be carried horizontally above the ground.

are separated, the deeper the maximum depth of detection. The unit is operated by one person and is carried horizontally above the ground. An EM induction meter of this type averages conductivity measurements to a depth of approximately 6 meters with the highest sensitivity for features located in the top meter of soil. Therefore, in a forensic context this type of EM induction meter is best suited for detecting buried metal objects at shallow depths or large metallic objects at deep depths. More commonly, a smaller EM induction meter (e.g., Geonics EM38 model) is used in forensic geophysical surveys because of its size (approximately 1 meter in length), portability, and ease in maneuvering (Figure 6.10). The maximum depth for this kind of meter is limited because the signal strength peaks at 40 centimeters for the deepest mode with signal strength decreasing as depth increases (Geonics, 2006).

A major advantage of using EM induction methods is that the units do not have to be in contact with the ground surface (Davenport, 2001b; Reynolds, 1997). All EM induction meters will detect metallic objects such as guns, knives, and other metallic evidence, and in certain instances, it might be possible to detect a grave if there is enough contrast between the backfill and undisturbed soil. A recent study has shown that the more popular small-sized EM induction meter was able to detect a variety of buried weapons. The largest weapons, including shotguns and a rifle, were detected at a depth of 75 centimeters (Dionne et al., 2010), which is a greater depth than the detection limits of less-expensive options, such as a metal detector or magnetic locator (both tools discussed below). Most EM induction meters can be used in wooded areas and over hard ground and concrete. In addition, large open areas can be surveyed in a timely manner using a combination of EM

Figure 6.10 Field assistant William Hawkins demonstrating the use of the more popular small-sized electromagnetic (EM) induction meter during a controlled study.

induction and GPR methods. For example, Nobes (2000) first used an EM induction meter over a large open area during a forensic search and then used a GPR system to perform a more detailed survey of a number of localized areas of interest when locating a grave.

Davenport (2001b) notes a number of limitations using EM induction to measure conductivity. One disadvantage is that the measurements produced by an EM induction meter are only averages of all ground conductivities within the depth range. As a result, a basic conductivity contour map does not provide an accurate depth of forensic targets. Instead, there may only be a range of depth based on the unit settings at the time of data collection. Another major disadvantage of using an EM induction method concerns the signal noise or "clutter" created by metallic objects in the vicinity, such as fences, pipes, or power lines. In addition, certain geologic features that have high conductivities, such as clayey soils, may quickly dissipate the EM fields and not permit signal penetration.

6.3 Electrical Resistivity Meters

Resistivity is a measure of how strongly a material opposes the flow of electrical current, and it is the reciprocal of conductivity. Resistivity meters are typically mounted on a square frame with four electrodes, called probes, sticking downward and placed 50 centimeters apart along the base of the frame. The electrodes are inserted into the ground at 1 meter intervals along a grid transect, and an induced weak electrical current is passed between a positive and negative current electrode. The current does not jump in a single direct line between the electrodes but fans out to form a zone of electrical potential that is measured by two low-voltage electrodes (Figure 6.11). Moisture content is essential to the level of resistance in the soil, as the electrical current is conducted through the soil by mineral salts in water. Any deviations from the predicted flow of current are due to variations in the electrical resistance of the soil or presence of added features. Features that readily allow for the flow of an electrical charge (e.g., graves) have low

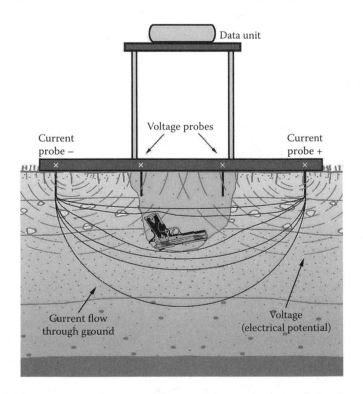

Figure 6.11 Current probes in an electrical resistivity meter introduce current into the earth, while voltage probes measure the voltage (electrical potential) of the current as it passes through the ground, indicating localized resistivity. The buried handgun shown here allows movement of an electrical charge more readily than the surrounding soils. This results in a low-resistivity anomaly.

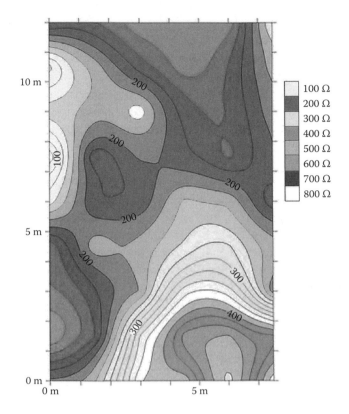

Figure 6.12 Resistivity contour distribution map showing varying levels of soil resistivity across a survey area. The areas of higher resistivity (lower right corner) contained backfill materials that retained more moisture than the surrounding sandy soil layers.

resistivity, while features that impede the flow (e.g., stone foundations) have high resistivity. The level of resistance, measured in ohms (Ω), is recorded on a data logger. These data are later downloaded into specialized software to produce a plotted map of features that have higher or lower resistivity than their surroundings (Figure 6.12).

Although a recent controlled study demonstrated success using electrical resistivity to locate graves containing pig cadavers (Jervis et al., 2009), there are a number of disadvantages to using this method for forensic applications (Killam, 2004). Coverage of larger survey areas is slower than using EM induction methods because ground contact is required. Also, because there is a minimal amount of surface destruction, this can result in damage to evidence at shallow depths. Resistivity methods work best on flat ground, but this type of survey can also be conducted on uneven terrain using soil resistivity electrodes that are not mounted on a frame. There can also be interference from metal and electrical sources such as power lines and above-ground metal objects, although they are less sensitive to this kind of signal noise than EM induction methods. In addition, graves may have such a low resistivity contrast with the surrounding soil that they may not be detected.

6.4   Magnetometers

Magnetometers (MAGs) are passive geophysical tools that measure small variations in the Earth's magnetic field, which are caused by ferrous concentrations (e.g., iron, steel, and nickel), burned soils and clays, and detect subtle anomalies in magnetic susceptibility caused by disturbed soils or concentrations of decayed organic matter (Clark, 1996). For example, burning permanently changes the magnetic properties of the surrounding soil by altering the magnetism of minute iron particles. If this soil is moved, either through natural or mechanical processes, the soil magnetism will vary in relation to the general magnetic background of its new location. However, magnetometry only works when past activities produce a measureable pattern of magnetic contrast.

Most MAGs do not transmit a signal into the ground and therefore do not have a transmitter. Instead, they have a single or paired receiver that detects the magnetic field of buried ferrous objects. MAGs that contain paired receivers, which are usually separated by a distance of 2 to 3 feet (60 to 90 centimeters), are more commonly called gradient magnetometers or gradiometers. There are a variety of commercially available MAGs such as proton precession magnetometers (PPMs), fluxgate magnetometers, and cesium vapor magnetometers. Of these, the PPM is most often used in archaeological contexts.

Data are collected in the field along a grid with readings taken every meter or half-meter along grid transects and then downloaded to a computer for processing in special software. Anomalies can be recognized on a contour magnetic intensity map via contrasts between the target and the magnetic background of the surrounding soil. To avoid contaminating data, individuals conducting the survey and those surrounding the survey area must be free of magnetic materials, such as credit cards and metallic jewelry, clothing fasteners, eyeglasses, and shoe eyelets.

Detecting magnetic anomalies is a function of the differences in contrast due to the magnetic properties, size, shape, orientation, and distance between a ferrous object and point of measurement (Davenport, 2001b). In forensic contexts, a MAG survey is most useful in detecting weapons. Magnetometry will not directly detect a grave, as the process of burial usually involves putting the same soil back into the grave after it is dug out, leaving little to no measurable variation. However, magnetometry may be helpful in locating a grave if ferrous materials are also buried with the remains or if the remains have been cremated. An advantage of a MAG over a metal detector or magnetic locator is that it provides quantitative measurements used to create a map indicating magnetic anomalies. The major disadvantage of a MAG can be interference or noise from cultural features (e.g., fences, pipes, power lines, and metal debris) and geological features in the vicinity. Davenport (2001b) recommends using a gradient magnetometer in forensic contexts because this equipment has a number of advantages over a traditional MAG with a single receiver. For example, the gradiometer's two receivers decrease the noise from surface debris and cultural features, and they provide increased resolution of subsurface features.

6.5 Magnetic Locators

Magnetic locators, also called valve-and-box locators, are passive instruments that operate on principles similar to a gradient magnetometer. Manufacturers design this equipment as a walking staff, usually 35 to 42 inches (89 to 106 centimeters) in length with a small control box at the top end (Figure 6.13). The shaft contains two sensors that respond to changes in magnetic fields surrounding buried ferromagnetic objects, including metallic weapons that are in close proximity to the shaft. The readout and sound operate similarly

Figure 6.13 Author John Schultz demonstrating the use of a magnetic locator, which is swept from side to side when searching for buried metal objects.

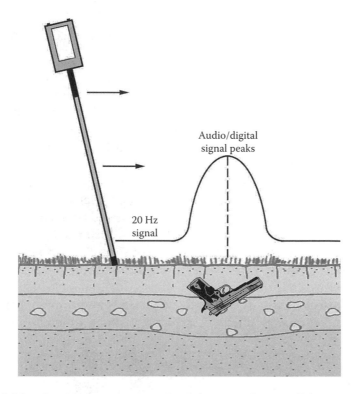

Figure 6.14 When operating a magnetic locator, there will be a pronounced audio signal and an increase in the digital readout when the sensors respond to changes in the magnetic field as it passes over a buried target.

to a metal detector; as you move closer to a metal target, an audible sound gets louder or a digital readout increases (Figure 6.14). During use, the shaft should be swept from side to side in front of the operator.

In comparison to a MAG, a magnetic locator is a less-expensive option and a much easier piece of equipment to operate when searching for ferromagnetic objects. A magnetic locator can locate larger objects at deep depths, such as a large steel container drum up to 8 feet (2.44 meters) deep (Schonstedt Instrument Company, 2001). Smaller objects can only be detected at shallow depths, and handguns may only be detected at depths of less than 1 foot (30 centimeters) (Schonstedt Instrument Company, 2001). However, controlled research with a commercially available magnetic locator has shown that large handguns can be detected at depths greater than 30 centimeters, and long guns (e.g., rifle, shotgun) can be detected at depths of 60 centimeters or greater (Rezos et al., 2011). Before using a magnetic locator for a weapons search, it is important to first determine if the suspected weapon is composed of ferromagnetic components. If the suspected weapon were a handgun primarily composed of a nonferromagnetic metal, or the composition is unknown, then an all-metal detector would be a better option to use for this application.

6.6   Metal Detectors

Metal detectors are the most common geophysical tools because they are relatively inexpensive and easy to use when compared to other equipment. For these reasons, they are very popular with law enforcement (Figure 6.15). Metal detectors operate on the same principle as other EM equipment. The basic metal detector consists of an adjustable stem with a control box near the handle and an antenna that is pointed toward the ground. The antenna head, or search coil, contains transmitting and receiving coils. An EM field is transmitted into the ground from the transmitting coil (Figure 6.16). The EM field encounters a conducting object (e.g., a knife) and creates circulating eddy currents across the object's surface. The eddy currents receive their power from the transmitted primary EM field, which results in a detectable power loss (Garrett, 1998). In addition, these eddy currents generate a secondary EM field that flows outward into the surrounding soil and is detected by the receiver coil.

Metal detectors will detect conductive metals and some minerals, with more expensive models able to discriminate among different metals. One

Figure 6.15 Orange County Sheriff's Office homicide detective Dave Clarke uses a metal detector during a forensic search.

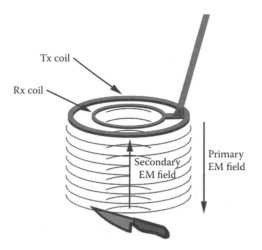

Figure 6.16 On a typical metal detector, an electromagnetic field is transmitted into the ground from the transmitter (Tx) coil. When the field encounters a conducting object, such as the knife shown here, a secondary electromagnetic field is created flowing outward into the surrounding soil and is detected by the receiver (Rx) coil.

popular metal detector is an all-metal detector that electronically balances out or rejects, either manually or automatically, the natural mineral content of the soil or ground surface. The average all-metal detector does not discriminate between ferrous and nonferrous metallic objects; therefore, many indicated targets result in shallow buried trash metals. In contrast, many high-end metal detectors have discriminating capabilities that can accurately indicate the type of target or metal composition, thereby reducing the number of false positives by ignoring signals from small iron and aluminum trash metals. Furthermore, computerized models can also be helpful in determining the precise location and depth of targets (Garrett, 1998).

One option available with most metal detectors manufactured today is the ability to change the antenna head for specific targets. Large heads, 10 to 18 inches (25 to 45 centimeters) in diameter, can penetrate deeper but only locate larger objects. Larger heads do not detect smaller objects because they are treated as noise. Conversely, smaller heads (e.g., 5 inches or 12 centimeters in diameter), are better for detecting smaller objects but only penetrate shallower depths. A general-purpose head is typically 7 to 9 inches (18 to 23 centimeters) in diameter depending on the manufacturer and type of detector. It should be lightweight, respond to a number of different target sizes, and have good scanning width (Garrett, 1998). Other options may be available to increase detection depth, such as depth multiplier attachments that can easily attach to existing heads. Various manufacturers also offer special metal detectors called two-box systems that are designed to locate large objects (e.g., buried steel container drums) at much greater depths than a traditional metal

Figure 6.17 When using the metal detector, the head should be held in front of the operator, parallel and as close to the ground as possible for maximum coverage and depth.

detector. A two-box system consists of separate transmitting and receiving coils that are mounted on either end of a pole with the complete unit measuring approximately 50 inches (125 centimeters). Submersible antenna heads are also available and can be useful when searching in a shallow water environment where a gun or knife may have been discarded.

Before using a metal detector, it is important to first calibrate the machine to local soil conditions per manufacturer directions. The use of headphones is also recommended to enhance audio perception while simultaneously masking potential interference in noisy areas (Garrett, 1998). When using the metal detector, the antenna head should be held in front of the operator, parallel and as close to the ground as possible for maximum coverage and depth (Figure 6.17). The head should be moved in sweeping motions with at least one half the diameter of the head overlapping the adjacent search lanes to ensure 100% coverage of the search area (Figure 6.18). When operating a metal detector, there will be a pronounced audio signal and an increase in the analog or digital readout when the antenna head passes over a buried target. The audio signal will be loudest when the head is directly over the target. To pinpoint the exact location of the target, move the search coil across the area from different directions using an x-pattern.

Law enforcement should have a high-end metal detector as part of their toolkit for searches and may have a number of different-sized antenna heads available. This equipment is best for detecting small objects that are buried at shallow depths. Metal detectors are helpful in locating shallow buried bullets, bullet casings, weapons, and other buried metallic forensic evidence. Controlled research with a commercially available all-metal detector has shown that large handguns can be detected down to 40 centimeters in depth,

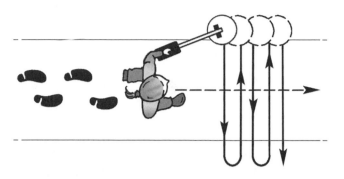

Figure 6.18 The head of a metal detector should be moved in sweeping motions with at least one half the diameter of the head overlapping the adjacent search lanes to ensure 100% coverage of the search area.

and long guns (e.g., rifle, shotgun) can be detected down to depths of 45 to 55 centimeters (Rezos et al., 2010). In addition, metal detectors can be useful when used in combination with more sophisticated geophysical equipment (Davenport, 2001b). They can be used prior to and after conducting magnetic, electromagnetic induction, or GPR geophysical surveys by delineating near-surface objects and trash that can produce interference in other equipment. The greatest disadvantage of this method is that metal detectors will not be able to directly detect a grave unless there are metal objects in the grave at a shallow enough depth. In terms of training, a basic all-metal detector generally requires minimal training before use. However, high-end computerized models with discrimination capabilities will require advanced operator training before use in a weapons search.

6.7 Side-Scan Sonar

Side-scan sonar is a marine geophysical tool that uses sound waves to produce a detailed graphic image of the seafloor surface, riverbed, or lake bottom, similar to an aerial image. The system includes a torpedo-shaped towfish (Figure 6.19), a data collection control unit or computer, a tow cable, and a power supply. Using a differential GPS to establish a survey grid over the

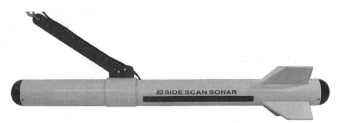

Figure 6.19 Example of side-scan sonar towfish.

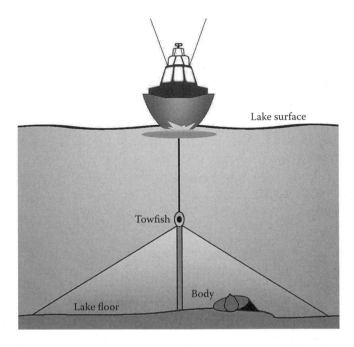

Figure 6.20 The sonar pulse from the side-scan sonar towfish is fan shaped and is projected directly under the towfish and to either side.

search area, the towfish is towed in the water behind a boat at a depth of 10 to 20 feet (3 to 6 meters) above the seafloor or lakebed. The side-scan sonar towfish contains a transducer with a transmitter and receiver that projects high- or low-frequency bursts of acoustic energy on both sides of the towfish in thin, fan-shaped beams (Figure 6.20). The sound pulses, or echoes, reflecting off of the relief or objects projecting above the bottom surface are received by the transducers, amplified, and transmitted up the tow cable to the graphic recorder on the survey vessel. The strength and travel time of reflected pulses are recorded and processed into an image or picture of the bottom surface.

Side-scan sonar has many uses but has become an important tool when conducting underwater searches in archaeological and forensic contexts. For example, side-scan sonar is routinely used to search for old shipwrecks, archaeological sites, downed aircraft, and submersed vehicles. This method has also been used to successfully locate drowned victims lying on the underwater ground surface (Figure 6.21). The major advantages of sonar include the following: it can be used in both fresh- and saltwater, and in deep waters, it is not affected by murky or black water, and it also provides a representative picture of the submersed object. Disadvantages of side-scan sonar include poor detection of objects completely buried beneath the seafloor, and extremely rocky, grassy, or irregular underwater surfaces make it difficult to interpret sonar returns.

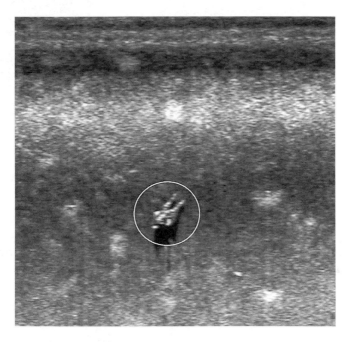

Figure 6.21 Side-scan sonar image of a drowned victim located on the bottom of a lake floor. (Photo courtesy of G. Ralston.)

6.8   Locating a Geophysical Survey Consultant

It is important to note that surveys using geophysical tools must be performed and interpreted by experienced operators. Unfortunately, the high cost of a number of geophysical tools, particularly GPR systems, means that it is not feasible for most law enforcement agencies to own their own equipment, and they must bring in an outside consultant to perform a geophysical survey. In most instances, GPR systems will be the best tool to use for body searches if site conditions are favorable. Law enforcement agencies can search for a geophysical specialist or GPR operator by inquiring at local universities, environmental or archaeological firms, or by performing an Internet search. The most limiting factor when using geophysical tools for forensic applications is the operator's experience. When selecting a consultant for a geophysical survey, it is important to make inquiries about the consultant's experience and how he or she will conduct the geophysical survey. Preference should be given to operators who have experience searching for small subsurface objects buried at shallow depths, such as bodies and archaeological features. Conducting a GPR survey for objects routinely encountered in forensic and archaeological contexts requires additional training, not only in interpreting the results but also in setting up grid transects and conducting the survey. A consultant who only has experience searching for large geologic features may not have training in archaeological search methods or be familiar with the parameters used in forensic searches.

A body buried within the survey area may not be detected if the proper survey methods are not used. The investigator should be aware that forensic geophysical surveys require use of a grid with appropriate transect spacing. Transects should be spaced close enough so that the forensic target in question will be detected and not missed between transects. When searching for adult remains, the preferred maximum transect interval spacing is 50 centimeters (20 inches), and for small children the spacing should be 25 centimeters (10 inches). This method will provide 100% coverage if performed in a single cardinal direction (e.g., east-to-west or north-to-south) and, if time permits, performed in both cardinal directions (e.g., east-to-west and north-to-south), which will provide 200% coverage. The best chance of success for finding a body or clearing an area will only be achieved by choosing a qualified and experienced consultant who will perform a controlled geophysical survey using proper methodology.

Case Study 6: Concrete Cover-Up

In December 2003 author Schultz was requested by the Orange County Sheriff's office (OCSO) to perform a GPR search at a residential home. The case involved a son who was accused of killing his father 15 years earlier and more recently killing his mother. Homicide detectives had received a number of tips that led them to believe that one body, the father's, had been buried under the concrete slab in the garage. One informant, a neighbor, had noticed that the cement floor in the garage had been repaired and was told by the son that a leaking water pipe had been repaired. However, this was suspicious because water pipes did not run under the concrete slab in this area of the house. In addition, the son had contracted with a stone specialist to surface the entire garage floor surface with Chattahoochee stone, which is a common patio surface for in-ground pools and not garage floors. Furthermore, the stone specialist reported that half of the garage floor, the right side, was lined with 4- by 8-foot (1.2 × 2.4 meter) sheets of diamond-plated steel. The son did not want the steel plates removed prior to surfacing the floor, but rather wanted to have them concealed by the Chattahoochee stone surface.

Homicide detectives also believed that the mother, who had been missing for approximately three months, was buried in the backyard of the residence. When detectives and crime scene personnel conducted a preliminary search, it was noted that two recently poured concrete slabs were present in the backyard. It was decided to first perform a GPR survey of the smaller of the two slabs in the backyard. Results of the survey indicated that a grave was not present under the slab, and therefore this

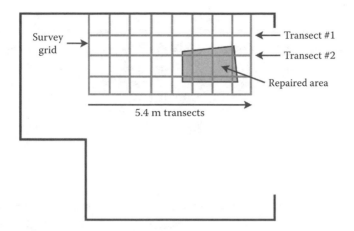

Figure 6.22 Garage plan showing transect grid over the area of interest that included the floor repair concealed by diamond-plated steel sheets and Chattahoochee stone. Ground-penetrating radar (GPR) signal profiles for Transects 1 and 2 are shown in Figure 6.23.

area was eliminated from further searching. While preparing to survey the second slab in the backyard, law enforcement received a tip that the second body was located at a second residential home, which was confirmed later that evening.

Prior to performing the GPR survey in the garage, a cadaver dog had alerted on the floor in an area where the concrete slab had been repaired. The Chattahoochee stone along with the diamond-plated steel sheets that lined one side of the garage were removed, revealing the patched cement floor. Multiple GPR transects were laid out and data were collected in this area (Figure 6.22). The results from the area directly under the repair showed a large enough disturbance to indicate a buried body (Figure 6.23). After the positive results from the GPR survey, OCSO personnel were comfortable with the decision to break the cement floor and excavate the area of interest. Careful excavation of the area revealed a skeleton that was later positively identified as the father. The son eventually pled no contest to killing both of his parents.

Case Study 7: Trash Not Treasure

Author Schultz was requested by OCSO to assist with a search for two weapons, a long-gun and a handgun, thought to be in a residential backyard. No information was provided as to the specific make or model or to the metallic composition of the weapons. Due to the unknown composition of the weapons, Schultz used an all-metal detector for the search. A controlled survey of the backyard was performed using 1-meter wide

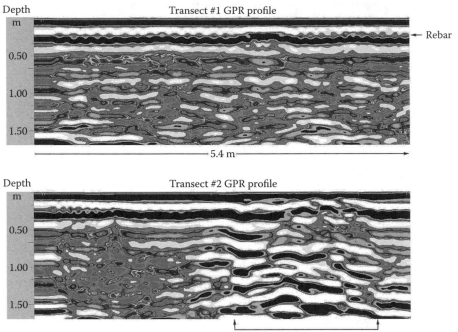

Figure 6.23 Ground-penetrating radar (GPR) reflection profiles of garage floor, with Transect 1 showing the rebar embedded in the concrete slab and no indications of a buried body, while Transect 2 shows the point source reflection of the buried body directly under the area where the floor had been repaired. Note the lack of rebar in the repaired area over the body.

(3½ feet) survey lanes set up with flagging tape. This spacing allowed for overlapping of adjacent search lanes when sweeping the metal detector antenna head during the search. In addition, crime scene personnel assisted Schultz by placing nonmetallic flags at the locations of all detector hits (Figure 6.24). Once a lane was completed, additional personnel intrusively checked all flagged locations. Because an all-metal detector was used, numerous shallow buried trash metals were detected, but no firearms or other weapons were located, and this area was cleared from further searches.

Figure 6.24 Author John Schultz conducting a survey for weapons using an all-metal detector. Note the use of nonmetallic flags for marking detector hits during survey.

Key Words and Questions

conductivity
electrical resistivity
EM induction meter
ferrous/nonferrous
geophysical survey
GPR system
MAG
magnetic locator
metal detector
monostatic antenna
planar surface
point source
receiver
reflection
reflection profile
resistivity
ringing
side-scan sonar
sonar

towfish
transmitter

1. You have been asked to perform a GPR survey to locate a clandestine grave of a homicide victim. What information must you ask the homicide detective to determine if you can perform a survey in this area?
2. If you needed to secure the services of a GPR consultant, where would you find a consultant, and what types of information must you determine prior to securing the consultant's services?
3. You have been asked to search for a buried firearm in a remote wooded area. The search area is approximately 1 acre (63 square meters) in size. Law enforcement officers learned through an informant tip that the firearm is a small revolver and that it is buried at a depth of approximately 1 foot (30 centimeters). However, the informant was unsure of the metallic properties of the weapon. Answer the following based on this information:
    • What geophysical tool should you use for the search and why?
    • What are the recommendations you would provide to law enforcement personnel to ensure that a controlled geophysical survey is undertaken?
4. You have been asked to search for a submerged body in a lake using side-scan sonar. How would you recognize a submerged body on a lake floor? How does the data imagery for this method differ when compared to the other geophysical survey methods discussed in this chapter?
5. Compare and contrast the use of EM induction and electrical resistivity methods in a forensic context.
    • What are the advantages and disadvantages of these methods?
    • What is the most appropriate application for each method?
6. You have been informed that a body has been buried in a residential backyard and that the homeowner built a concrete patio over the grave. The lead homicide detective would like to confirm that a body is under the patio prior to actually breaking up a section of the concrete slab. You suggest to the detective that a GPR system is the best tool for this application. However, the detective asks if you will be able to discern a picture of the skeleton. What will you explain to the detective concerning GPR detection and how a trained operator can ultimately discern what is buried in the ground?

Suggested Readings

Cheetham, P. 2005. Forensic geophysical survey. In: Hunter, J., Cox, M., eds. *Forensic Archaeology: Advances in Theory and Practice*, pp. 62–95. New York: Routledge.

Davenport, C.G. 2001a. Remote sensing applications in forensic investigations. *Historical Archaeology* 35:87–100.

France, D.L., Griffin, T.J., Swanburg, J.G., Lindemann, J.W., Davenport, G.C., Tramell, V., Travis, C.T., Kondratieff, R., Nelson, A., Castellano, K., Hopkins D., Adair T. 1997. NecroSearch revisited: further multidisciplinary approaches to the detection of clandestine graves. In: Haglund, W.D., Sorg, M.H., eds. *Forensic Taphonomy: The Postmortem Fate of Human Remains*, pp. 497–510. Boca Raton, FL: CRC Press.

Rezos, M.M., Schultz, J.J., Murdock, R.A., Smith, S.A. 2010. Controlled research utilizing a basic all-metal detector in the search for buried firearms and miscellaneous weapons. *Forensic Science International* 195:121–127.

Schultz, J.J. 2007. Using ground-penetrating radar to locate clandestine graves of homicide victims: forming forensic archaeology partnerships with law enforcement. *Homicide Studies* 11:15–29.

Schultz, J.J., Collins, M.E., Falsetti, A.B. 2006. Sequential monitoring of burials containing large pig cadavers using ground-penetrating radar. *Journal of Forensic Sciences* 51:607–616.

References

Bevan, B.W. 1991. The search for graves. *Geophysics* 56:1310–1319.

Calkin, S.F., Allen, R.P., Harriman, M.P. 1995. Buried in the basement: geophysic's role in forensic investigation. *Proceedings of the Symposium on the Application of Geophysics to Engineering and Environmental Problems (SAGEEP)*, pp. 397–403.

Conyers, L.B., Goodman, D. 1997. *Ground-Penetrating Radar: An Introduction for Archaeologists*. Walnut Creek, CA: AltaMira Press.

Davenport, C.G. 2001a. Remote sensing applications in forensic investigations. *Historical Archaeology* 35:87–100.

Davenport, C.G. 2001b. *Where Is It? Searching for Buried Bodies and Hidden Evidence*. Church Hill, MD: Sportwork.

Dionne, C.A., Schultz, J.J., Murdock, R.A., Smith, S.A. 2011. Detecting buried metallic weapons in a controlled setting using a conductivity meter. *Forensic Science International* 208:18–24.

France, D.L., Griffin, T.J., Swanburg, J.G., Lindemann, J.W., Davenport, G.C., Tramell, V., Travis, C.T., Kondratieff, R., Nelson, A., Castellano, K., Hopkins D. 1992. A multidisciplinary approach to the detection of clandestine graves. *Journal of Forensic Sciences* 37:1145–1458.

France, D.L., Griffin, T.J., Swanburg, J.G., Lindemann, J.W., Davenport, G.C., Tramell, V., Travis, C.T., Kondratieff, R., Nelson, A., Castellano, K., Hopkins, D., Adair, T. 1997. NecroSearch revisited: further multidisciplinary approaches to the detection of clandestine graves. In: Haglund, W.D., Sorg, M.H., eds. *Forensic Taphonomy: The Postmortem Fate of Human Remains*, pp. 497–510. Boca Raton, FL: CRC Press.

Garrett, C.L. 1998. *Modern Metal Detectors*. Dallas, TX: Ram.

Geonics Limited. 2006. *EM38 Ground Conductivity Meter Operating Manual*. Mississauga, Ontario, Canada: Geonics Limited.

Jervis, J.R., Pringle, J.K., Tuckwell, G.W. 2009. Time-lapse resistivity over simulated clandestine graves. *Forensic Science International* 192:7–13.

Killam, E.W. 2004. *The Detection of Human Remains*, 2nd ed. Springfield, IL: Charles C. Thomas.

King, J.A., Bevan, B.W., Hurry, R.J. 1993. The reliability of geophysical surveys at historic-period cemeteries: an example from the Plains Cemetery, Mechanicsville, Maryland. *Historical Archaeology* 27:4–16.

Mellet, J.S. 1992. Location of human remains with ground-penetrating radar. *Geological Survey of Finland* 16:359–365.

Nobes, D.C. 2000. The search for "Yvonne": a case example of the delineation of a grave using near-surface geophysical methods. *Journal of Forensic Sciences* 45:715–721.

Reynolds, J.M. 1997. *An Introduction to Applied and Environmental Geophysics*. New York: John Wiley and Sons.

Rezos, M.M., Schultz, J.J., Murdock, R.A., Smith, S.A. 2010. Controlled research utilizing a basic all-metal detector in the search for buried firearms and miscellaneous weapons. *Forensic Science International* 195:121–127.

Rezos, M.M., Schultz, J.J., Murdock, R.A., Smith, S.A. 2011. Utilizing a magnetic locator to search for buried firearms and miscellaneous weapons at a controlled research site. *Journal of Forensic Sciences* DOI:10.1111/j.1556-4029. 2011. 01802.x.

Schonstedt Instrument Company. 2001. *Instruction Manual: Model GA-52Cx*. Kearneysville, WV: Schonstedt Instrument Company.

Schultz, J.J. 2003. Detecting buried remains using ground-penetrating radar. PhD diss. University of Florida.

Schultz, J.J. 2007. Using ground-penetrating radar to locate clandestine graves of homicide victims: forming forensic archaeology partnerships with law enforcement. *Homicide Studies* 11:15–29.

Schultz, J.J. 2008. Sequential monitoring of burials containing small pig cadavers using ground-penetrating radar. *Journal of Forensic Sciences* 53:279–287.

Schultz, J.J., Collins, M.E., Falsetti, A.B. 2006. Sequential monitoring of burials containing large pig cadavers using ground-penetrating radar. *Journal of Forensic Sciences* 51:607–616.

Shih, D.G., Doolittle, J.A. 1984. Using radar to investigate organic soil thickness in the Florida Everglades. *Soil Science Society of America Journal* 48:651–656.

Sternberg, B.K., McGill, J.W. 1995. Archaeology studies in southern Arizona using ground-penetrating radar. *Journal of Applied Geophysics* 33:209–225.

Vaughn, C.J. 1986. Ground-penetrating radar surveys used in archaeological investigations. *Geophysics* 51:595–604.

Surveying and Mapping Methods

7

During a forensic investigation, one of the most important things to remember is that once something is moved, it can never be put back in its exact position or orientation. For this reason, practical skills in various survey and mapping techniques will allow investigators to maintain a quality record of where every item of evidence was found within a defined area and if necessary, will also assist the investigator in recreating the order of events surrounding the items being recorded.

The end result of all surveying and mapping, in archaeology as well as in forensic contexts, is an accurate scale drawing of the scene. Many investigators incorrectly believe survey and mapping skills to be beyond their ability. However, an overview of the techniques involved and some practice in the field can turn the fledgling into a specialist very quickly. In fact, if an investigator is working without these skills, he or she should not attempt recovery of any remains, whether working with a surface deposit or a burial in a forensic context. The authors would also like to note that there is an enormous amount of technology used today in recording forensic scenes, from laptops and digital cameras, to the Global Positioning System (GPS) and high-resolution laser surveys—all of which have an amazing capacity to fail at the most critical moment in the most remote location. At times, there is no better backup than the traditional scaled drawings and simple compass survey. This chapter is intended to aid forensic investigators in achieving a respectable level of survey and mapping skills with a minimum of technical explanation.

7.1 Units of Measure

In surveying and mapping there are two different kinds of quantities that are measured, distances and angles. Most people are familiar with measures of distance of length, in either feet and meters, or miles and kilometers. Two additional measures of distance are elevation and depth, how far an object is above or below a fixed reference point. Elevation and depth are mainly used when referring to points on a particular piece of land and are presented using contour lines that join points of equal elevation on a map to show valleys, hills, and steepness of slopes. When used in this manner the fixed reference point is usually mean sea level (MSL), or the average height of the ocean's

157

surface. In archaeological survey, elevation and depth are measured from a ground control point called a datum, which is designated by the surveyor. In measures of distance, metric units should always be used in forensic investigations because of the ease of converting measurements of larger areas, as well as smaller features, to the scales available on preprinted graph paper. For this reason, all measurements in this chapter are given in metric units. Please refer to a standard metric conversion chart or calculator for the equivalent measure in U.S. customary units.

When it comes to angles, the measure of reference may not be as well understood. A complete circle contains 360° with the degrees progressing from 0° to 360° in a clockwise fashion. By dividing a circle into quadrants, a spherical coordinate system can be imposed onto the degree marks with north at 0°/360°, east at 90°, south at 180°, and west at 270°. When using this coordinate system, the projected angle from the center of the circle to a distant point of interest is called the azimuth. Most tend to think of angle measurements as only being measured in terms of degrees. However, there are other common systems of angle measurement. For example, the U.S. military favors the use of the angular mil, where a circle is divided into 6,400 equal units. This system is used for artillery range finding and is based on the simple relationship that an angle of 1 mil subtends a distance of approximately 1 meter at a range of 1 kilometer. When selecting field equipment, such as a compass, it is important to check the instrument graduations because many commercially available prismatic compasses are designed for military use and may be marked in radians (i.e., angular mils) rather than degrees.

7.2   Using Maps

Maps are a way of transforming three-dimensional points on the Earth's surface into a flat, two-dimensional plane of reference. It is important to note the specific system used to generate any map that you are using as a reference in archaeology and forensic investigations, as the same grid reference used in a different system will not refer to the same location. For example, the Universal Transverse Mercator (UTM) grid system is a worldwide mapping system that divides the world into 60 equal zones from west to east (Howard, 2007). The GPS uses a coordinate system based on the World Geodetic System (WGS84) (Howard, 2007). If you are using a map created in the UTM system to reference points taken with a GPS using the WGS84 system, the plotted points will not be correct.

In archaeological and forensic contexts, there are several different types of maps that you may encounter when searching for remains (Hester et al., 2008). The most common is a topographic map, which depicts all visible natural and built surface features. This type of map can be found for virtually any area you may need to investigate. Orthographic maps are also commonly used, as they combine aerial photography with topographic information. They can be very useful in a forensic search; however, their coverage is usually restricted to major towns and their immediate environs. Two other types of maps include geological maps that depict rock formations, geological zones, and soil types, and maritime charts that depict underwater formations and the depth of the sea floor.

Each map should contain a directional indicator, usually a north arrow, a scale, and a legend to explain the mapping conventions used to indicate features or objects. Most maps are oriented with the north at the top, south at the bottom, and east and west to the right and left, respectively. Scale refers to the ratio of the size of a feature or object as it is drawn on the map to its actual size. This ratio is provided as a representative fraction, such as 1:100, meaning that one unit of measurement on the map is equal to 100 units of the same measurement on the ground. Maps come in a standard range of scales, although not all scales are available for each area. For example, the most widely used topographic maps in archaeology are from the U.S. Geological Survey (USGS) 7.5 minute series, which is printed in a 1:24,000 scale covering nearly 80 square kilometers (50 square miles). Orthographic maps are also available from the USGS and are typically in a 1:6,000 scale covering approximately 5 square kilometers (3 square miles). In a forensic context, the most widely used topographic maps are based on the U.S. Public Land Survey System (PLSS). These maps refer to a surveyed township unit of land that is approximately 9.7 square kilometers (6 square miles) in size and is further divided into 36 sections, each approximately 1.6 square kilometers (1 square mile) in size.

Many maps are readily available from various government agency websites and are downloadable free of charge. A few agencies that provide this type of service include the USGS, the PLSS, the U.S. Environmental Protection Agency (EPA), and the Land Boundary Information System (LABIS). The maps and photographs available from the EPA are exceptionally helpful when lakes, rivers, canals, and shorelines are the primary focus in a forensic search. The PLSS and LABIS are excellent sources for detailed country area, railroad, side road, or logging area maps.

7.3 Using the Global Positioning System

The GPS was developed by the U.S. military for global navigation and is made up of a linked system of 24 satellites, each taking 12 hours to orbit (Howard, 2007). The system permits electronic receivers to determine exact positions 24 hours a day, any place on Earth, in any weather conditions. A GPS receiver obtains signals from four or more satellites simultaneously to calculate the user's exact position based on time differences in signal uplink and download.

Absolute GPS accuracy was subject to the U.S. Department of Defense Selective Availability Policy until February 2000. This policy required GPS data to be randomly degraded so that the signal uplink and download codes made available to the general public were only 95% accurate or within 16 to 100 meters of the actual ground position (Van Sickle, 2004). Because of the great demand for GPS use in the public sector, many of the newer recreational GPS models (i.e., those not used for commercial survey) provide somewhat increased levels of accuracy when compared to those in use prior to 2000. These readily available recreational models are usually lightweight, waterproof, and shock resistant, but most are accurate only within 3 to 15 meters. Currently, real-time submeter GPS units are commercially available, but this equipment is expensive and requires an experienced operator to process the data. These types of units have an average of 50 centimeters real-time accuracy and can have accuracy as high as 10 centimeters with 20 minutes of satellite tracking time and postprocessing with specialized software (Trimble Navigation Limited, 2010).

If you are using a GPS unit in a forensic investigation, you should always include the make and model of receiver in your notes, as the degree of accuracy varies among different brands. A GPS receiver can be a valuable mapping tool for recording site locations, delineating site boundaries, and recording the position of skeletal deposits or grouped evidence within a site. Coordinates obtained using a GPS receiver can also be used to relocate sites that were recorded in the past. One major advantage of using GPS coordinates for site mapping is that the data can be downloaded and used in Global Information System (GIS) software that integrates your coordinates into preexisting maps. The major disadvantage of using the less-expensive recreational GPS units is that they are not accurate enough to provide the level of precision required in scaled mapping of a grave and its contents or individualized pieces of evidence contained in surface deposits.

When you first turn on a GPS receiver, it should uplink to all available satellites, provided that the receiver has a clear and uninterrupted signal path. Also, most satellites orbit the equator, so when using a GPS in the northern hemisphere, you should hold the unit facing south so that your body does not interfere with the satellite signal. It is recommended that you leave the GPS unit on for a few minutes prior to collecting any data, as sometimes initial readings can be misleading because of delays in satellite signal reception, which may result from atmospheric conditions, accessibility, or signal reflection. You should always set the GPS grid reference system to match the reference system on any published maps used for plotting coordinates, as GPS error rates are variable from unit to unit, and it is a good practice to confirm coordinates using an official published map or a total station while working in the field.

7.4 Using Aerial Imagery

Aerial images of a region of landscape are taken from the air, either at low or high altitudes. High-altitude aerial imagery typically shows details of the types of terrain as well as any built structures or urban development in the area. This type of imagery is an excellent resource to use when developing a strategy for searching a larger area. However, because of the average level of resolution, it is difficult, if not impossible, to detect smaller disturbances, such as graves or surface deposits, using high-altitude images. High-resolution orthographic images are commercially available for download through TerraServer (http://www.terraserver.com). Another option is Google Maps (http://maps.google.com) using the "satellite" mode. This is a quick resource for aerial images of nearly every part of the world, most of which include the names of street and roadways as well as GPS and geo-tags that identify many built structures and landscape features. Keep in mind that coordinates listed in Google Maps are based on the WGS84 system.

Low-altitude aerial images are commonly used in forensic search and recovery. These usually include a smaller region of the landscape and have a better resolution for detecting smaller disturbances or features. In fact, recent low-altitude images can be easily compared with those from an earlier date to determine how much of the terrain has changed or if there are any newly placed features, such as a swimming pool, patio, or barbeque pit. A few resources for low-resolution aerial images include county planning commissions, local and government civil engineering agencies, and local and government water management services.

7.5 Creating Sketch Maps

The first kind of map constructed during any search or investigation is a simple rough sketch, or "mud map" as it is called in archaeology. This kind of map does not need to be drawn to scale but should include measurements of the surroundings and the location of evidence in relation to features or built structures (Figure 7.1). These maps are made quickly to provide an overview of the most significant information and are primarily used in planning a recovery. For example, the entrance and exit routes to the scene of recovery can be quickly determined and marked using the plan view information provided by a mud map. It is recommended that you never rely on a mud map as your primary form of mapping a scene; instead, it should only be used as

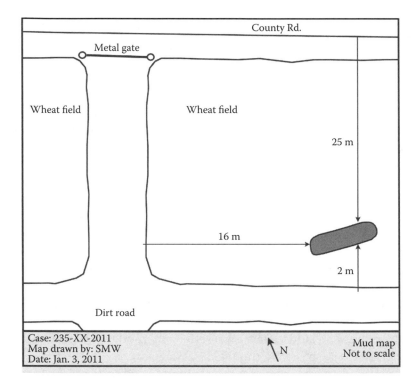

Figure 7.1 Example of a sketch map used in planning scene entrances and exits during the recovery of a surface deposit from a wheat field.

a tool in the staging of the recovery process or as a preliminary form of data collection before creating a more detailed scaled reference map.

7.6   Creating a Site Plan

A site plan is an illustration of all of the features at a site in relation to each other and in relation to a fixed reference point. A clear site plan is an essential part of any forensic investigation and the most effective means of accurately recording spatial information. Site plans are usually constructed using methods of survey, which involve the use of specialized equipment or something as simple as a protractor compass. A good rule to remember is to always map from the whole to the part. In other words, you should establish the site limits and map the site first. Only when this is complete should you create the scaled maps and drawings that contain the details of particular features.

The choice of which method you will use to create a site plan will come down to time and resources. If you were mapping a site that may be destroyed, either from construction work, removal of built structures (e.g., concrete slabs, fence lines), or the process of excavation, then you would want to record everything in minute detail. On the other hand, if you are producing a plan showing a grave or surface deposit in relation to the main physical features of a site that would not be damaged during recovery or any other immediate means, then the greatest amount of time and detail will be in the creation of the scale map and drawing of the evidence being recovered.

7.6.1 Datums, Baselines, and Offsets

To maintain consistency and accuracy in all measurements when mapping a burial or surface deposit, a ground control point should be used. In archaeology, a datum is a fixed point of reference for all elevation, depth, and angle measurements made during survey and excavation. The datum should be permanent, because all measurements within the boundaries of the site are taken from this point, and it may be used in any future work at the site as well. Trees, fence posts, and other seemingly permanent features should not be used as a datum because they can easily be removed. Building corners, utility poles, or datum points that you have added to the scene tend to be the most permanent and reliable points for use. For example, a length of steel rod or pipe is an excellent datum point after being partially driven into the ground and etched with a line at the level of the ground surface. After all work is completed at the site, it can then be driven completely into the ground and easily located later using a metal detector. At that time, it can be reset to its proper height using the etched marking.

All USGS and county survey maps provide the locations of precisely determined elevation points called benchmarks or survey marks (Figure 7.2).

Figure 7.2 Example of a U.S. Geological Survey (USGS) benchmark (left) and a county engineering survey marker (right). Both are permanent disks used to mark a point as an elevation reference.

These marks are established in the field by licensed surveyors and are made of stamped brass disks affixed to rock outcrops, bridges, buildings, sidewalks, or other prominent features. Multiple points can be measured along a distance from a benchmark to obtain an accurate elevation for a datum or to record the exact location of a burial scene in reference to an officially recorded point if needed. This is referred to as "tying in" your datum to official elevations or survey markers. To tie your site datum into a benchmark, use the compass survey method outlined below.

The site datum is often related to an arbitrary line established for the purpose of mapping a larger area. This arbitrary line is called the baseline. The placement of your baseline will depend on the size and shape of the site. If your site is particularly large and spread out, as is the case in some surface deposits, you may need to establish multiple baselines, using a different one to map each heavily localized area of evidence. It is always a good practice to tie in all baselines to the site datum so that each separate map can be combined, showing their relationship to each other in an overall site map if necessary. Any measurement taken from this baseline is referred to as an offset.

7.6.2   Transit Survey Systems

When using transit survey systems for mapping, the instrument operator records the distance, azimuth, and change in elevation between a known reference point and a desired survey point. Reduced to the basics, a transit is a precision telescope that can flip over (i.e., transit the scope) to measure front and back angles. Inside the telescope are vertical and horizontal target crosshairs. This assembly rotates horizontally in reference to a circular lower plate scaled from 0° to 360° and vertically from 0° to 90°. The transit assembly is mounted onto a tripod and is always leveled before obtaining vertical and horizontal measurements.

A transit is used in combination with a stadia rod, which is marked with known measures, so elevations can be measured along with distance and azimuth. These measures are based on two fine stadia cross-hairs that are mounted horizontally inside the telescope. When the operator looks through the telescope, the wires are optically superimposed on the stadia rod marks (Figure 7.3). The operator observes the number of stadia rod marks visible between the cross-hairs and can equate that to the distance between the transit and the stadia rod, as well as determine any elevation changes between the transit point and the base of the stadia rod (Figure 7.4). The azimuth reading marks the horizontal angle from the transit to the stadia rod.

Today, electronic distance measurement (EDM) devices have replaced most mechanical transits. The first EDMs were separate units mounted on

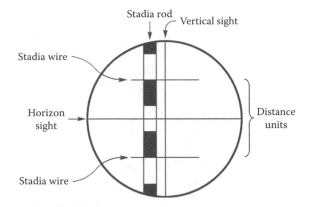

Figure 7.3 Example of cross-hairs seen through the transit telescope superimposed onto the stadia rod held at a distant point.

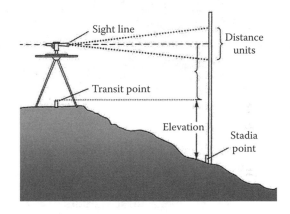

Figure 7.4 Basic schematic of measuring distance, angle, and elevation using a transit and stadia rod.

top of transits, but these were soon replaced with integrated devices, which led to the more common name of "total station," as all necessary measurements could be carried out from a single point (Howard, 2007). Total stations combine electronic measurement of angle with distance and have digital data-loggers and on-board computers (Figure 7.5). Total station transits emit a laser signal directed toward a stadia prism that reflects the signal back to the transit. The unit then calculates the horizontal angle of reflection, vertical angle changes, and any other programmed functions from the transit's position in relation to the stadia prism. The on-board computer typically allows the operator to type in a text identifier for each point as it is measured. The points held in the data-logger are later downloaded into a computer software application for analysis and plotting. Total station transits have become increasingly popular in forensic investigations, as they are

Figure 7.5 Research assistant Jeff Brzezinski using a total station transit. (Photo courtesy of S.B. Barber.)

a very efficient means of mapping forensic scenes, allow for greater detail and accuracy in measurement, and the data can be analyzed in various ways depending on the software applications being used. Figures 7.6 and 7.7 are examples of site plans produced by a total station during a forensic investigation. If a total station is used in the field, it is highly recommended that the information be recorded in field notes as backup just in case any problems occur when downloading data. The total station is, however, considered to be the primary data source if any conflicts occur between the written and electronic records.

High-resolution laser scanning has been in use for some time in archaeology to record the surfaces of such things as gravestones or rock art (Howard, 2007). In the last few years, this technology has extended to indoor crime scene investigations. The scanner is set up on a tripod in the same way as a total station and can be set to automatically record the three-dimensional position of a series of points to define the surface of objects. The resulting point cloud is dense enough to create surfaces between the points. When viewed on a computer screen, details of the target surfaces are clearly visible. At the time of this publication, archaeological and forensic applications of this technology for outdoor survey and mapping purposes are only beginning, but no doubt this situation will rapidly change.

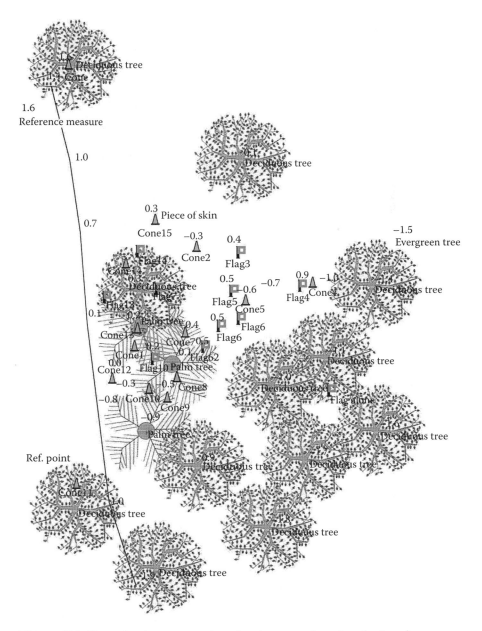

Figure 7.6 Plan of a site map produced using a total station during the recovery of scattered remains from a surface deposit. This plan shows the large trees and the placement of evidence markers within the crime scene. (Site map courtesy of Orange County Sheriff's Office, Florida.)

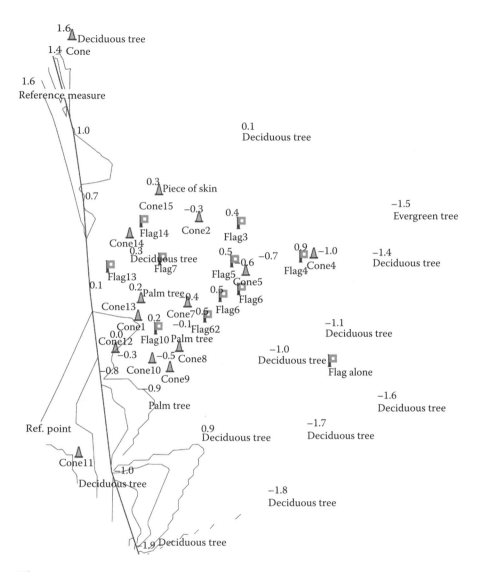

Figure 7.7 Plan of a site map produced using a total station during the recovery of scattered remains from a surface deposit (same plan shown in Figure 7.6). This plan shows elevation contour lines and the placement of evidence markers within the crime scene. (Site map courtesy of Orange County Sheriff's Office, Florida.)

7.6.3 Compass Survey Maps

If particular survey equipment is not available, compass surveying will also allow you to obtain the direction of an object from an established or known point. For example, a field compass used in conjunction with a 50-meter field tape can provide angle and distance measurements that can be used at a later date to relocate a datum from a known point. This method is especially helpful when working in an area where the terrain has heavy ground cover or in cases where the use of flagging tape may draw unwanted attention to the area of investigation. When using a compass, you should always remember that the pointer will pull toward ferrous objects. Compasses cannot be used accurately if you are standing next to a car, beside power lines, or near fencing wire. In some instances, personal belongings, metallic medical implants, or holding the compass in close proximity to a chaining pin can also affect the accuracy of compass readings.

A compass uses a magnetized pointer that aligns itself with the north and south poles of the Earth's natural magnetic field, making it fairly easy to accurately determine the basic directions of north, south, east, and west. The simplest type, a protractor compass (Figure 7.8a), consists of a rotating magnetic pointer, with one end marked for north, and a rotating compass dial, both supported by a handheld base-plate with a sightline and directional markings. This type of compass is typically used for orienteering on a map during outdoor activities such as hiking but can also be used for simple mapping if a more accurate compass is not available. The preferred type of

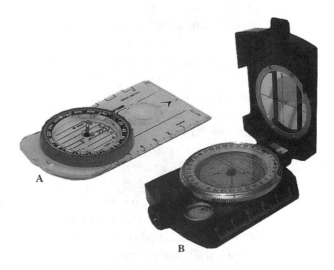

Figure 7.8 Example of a protractor, or baseplate, compass (a) and a prismatic compass (b).

field compass for forensic mapping is a prismatic compass, or pocket transit compass (Figure 7.8b). Most prismatic compasses usually have some sort of forward sighting mark, often incorporated into a hinged lid. The rear sight usually swings up into position or is marked on a baseplate and lines up with the forward sight. The user lines up both sights with the target object, and the prism or mirror then reflects the point where an index line passes through the compass dial, providing the azimuth to the object. The user may also line up the sights on a specific sightline so a distant object can be placed in relation to the point of origin, such as the placement of a chaining pin in a baseline used for mapping. Some of the more expensive prismatic compasses are also designed for survey purposes and can be mounted onto a leveling staff for elevation and distance measurement. When measuring azimuths, most prismatic compasses are accurate to about half a degree.

To align a compass to north, you simply turn the compass dial so that 0°/360°, or "N," on the dial matches the direction of the north end of the pointer. When using a compass to create a simple survey map, use the following steps to determine azimuth and distance measurements:

1. Determine your starting point (point A), such as your datum, a benchmark, or other permanent point, and record its position in your notes.
2. Run a meter tape from A toward the distant point (point B) that you want to record, mark this point with a chaining pin, and write the distance measurement in your notes.
3. Leaving the meter tape in place, return to A and align the sightline of your compass with B. Your sightline should follow the line of the meter tape.
4. Keeping the compass sightline fixed on B, rotate the compass dial so that 0°/360° is aligned with the north end of the compass pointer.
5. The foresight, or the azimuth from A to B, can now be read at the degree mark where the index line crosses the compass dial. Record the foresight azimuth in your notes.
6. Using the same methods, determine the backsight, or the azimuth from B to A, and check your accuracy by calculating the difference of the two readings, which should always equal 180°, although an error of ±2° is often unavoidable. For example, if your foresight from A to B is 60° and the backsight from B to A is 239°, the difference would be 179°. If the difference is within the acceptable error range, continue following the same procedure in foresighting and backsighting until all relevant objects or features in your sight plan are recorded.

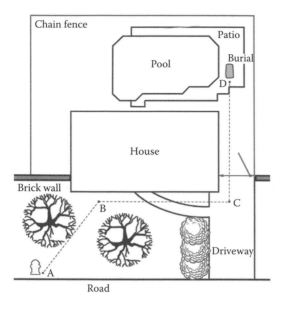

Figure 7.9 A site plan showing the use of the compass survey method to tie a site datum (point D) into a survey benchmark (point A). Starting at point A, foresights and backsights were used to determine the azimuth of each line of sight. Meter tapes were used to determine distance between points, and wooden stakes with depth lines, a stick tape, and mason's line with line levels were used to calculate any changes in elevation.

If you are using this method to tie in your datum to a benchmark or other elevation marker, it is recommended that you use a transit. However, if a transit is not available, this can still be accomplished using wooden stakes, a steel tape or stick tape, mason's line, and a line level. Mark two wooden stakes with an equal depth line and drive these into the ground for the first two points being measured. Starting at the benchmark, you can then use mason's line and a line level to determine changes in elevation based on whether the tops of your wooden stakes are higher or lower than the previous point. When recording the elevation changes, remember to add in the length of the wooden stake from the top to the marked depth line to get the true measure of elevation change. For example, if the top of your first stake is 10 centimeters higher than the benchmark, and the length of your stake to the depth line is 25 centimeters, then the overall change in elevation would be 35 centimeters above the benchmark to the first stake. By keeping a running tally of the changes in elevation as you move from point to point, you can calculate the overall difference between your datum and the benchmark. Figure 7.9 shows an example of a site map where the datum from a recovery scene was tied into a benchmark using the compass survey method.

7.7   Creating Scaled Drawings

When first faced with the responsibility of creating scaled drawings of a specific feature, most beginners are at a loss as to how to start. The secret is to mark the scene limits, determine the types of drawings and scale required to best relate the information in an illustrated form, choose a framework for creating the drawings that would best fit the kinds of evidence being recorded, and then record the details of the evidence using the appropriate steps for your chosen method.

Within a forensic context, there are two forms of detailed drawings that are common; the plan drawing, which is the two-dimensional "bird's-eye" view with which most people are familiar, as it is the view used in most maps, and the section drawing, or the view one would have if an imaginary plane was cut through an object. A third form of drawing called an orthographic project or multiview drawing shows two sides of a feature from an angle. Although these are used in archaeology to depict architectural features or show complex relationships among artifacts, they are rarely needed in a forensic context.

It is important to carefully consider the scale of your plan or section drawing prior to recording any information, because this is the one factor that will determine how accurately the measurements should be read during the mapping process. A ratio of 1:10 (i.e., 1 centimeter on the plan equals 10 centimeters on the ground) is the standard for most burial plan drawings, heavily localized areas of evidence within surface deposits, or any other detailed relationship of evidence. If the burial site is quite large (e.g., a multiple burial), it may be more beneficial to use a scale of 1:20. Drawings of widely scattered evidence are typically recorded in a ratio of 1:50 or 1:100 and usually consist of labeled points within the full limits of the site. It is also good practice to use the same standard size graph paper (e.g., 10 squares per centimeter) as, over time, this creates a familiarity with scale when recording data. Table 7.1 provides a simple reference for the relationship between commonly used scales in plan drawings and real distance. Scale will also make a difference in how accurately you will need to be when measuring and how much detail you will be able to plot on your plan drawing. There is no point in taking the time and trouble to measure something to an exceptional accuracy if it is impossible to plot the work onto the plan with a corresponding degree of accuracy. For example, it might be possible to measure the width of a grave to the nearest millimeter, but on a 1:10 or 1:20 scaled plan drawing, one millimeter will not be discernable. Always be sure that your measurements are reflective of what you can actually record.

It is also important to maintain a sense of neatness in maps, drawings, and corresponding field notes. Notes should be understandable and legible, not only to the person recording the information but to other people.

Table 7.1 Relationship between Commonly Used Scales in Plan Drawings and Real Distance

Scale of Plan Drawing	Scaled Measurement	Real Distance
1:10 (1 cm on paper = 10 cm on the ground)	5 cm on plan	50 cm on ground
	10 cm on plan	1 m on ground
	20 cm on plan	2 m on ground
	30 cm on plan	3 m on ground
	50 cm on plan	5 m on ground
	100 cm on plan	10 m on ground
1:20 (1 cm on paper = 20 cm on the ground)	2.5 cm on plan	50 cm on ground
	5 cm on plan	1 m on ground
	10 cm on plan	2 m on ground
	15 cm on plan	3 m on ground
	25 cm on plan	5 m on ground
	50 cm on plan	10 m on ground
1:50 (1 cm on paper = 50 cm on the ground)	1 cm on plan	50 cm on ground
	2 cm on plan	1 m on ground
	4 cm on plan	2 m on ground
	6 cm on plan	3 m on ground
	10 cm on plan	5 m on ground
	20 cm on plan	10 m on ground
1:100 (1 cm on paper = 100 cm on the ground)	0.5 cm on plan	50 cm on ground
	1 cm on plan	1 m on ground
	2 cm on plan	2 m on ground
	3 cm on plan	3 m on ground
	5 cm on plan	5 m on ground
	10 cm on plan	10 m on ground

Messy maps, incomplete drawings, bad field notes, and the process of copying work into neater formats typically generate errors that can easily be avoided with a little care. Always check your work, and whenever possible, do your error check using an alternate method of measurement or calculation. The easiest alternate method is a sight alignment to see if things are in relative position.

7.7.1 Establishing Limits and Using the Datum

The first concern is marking the limits of the scene surrounding the evidence being mapped. A rectangle or square is typically constructed using wooden corner stakes and brightly colored mason's line to mark the limits (Figure 7.10). It is recommended that you start your limits well outside of the area containing any evidence to ensure that everything will be easily included in your drawing. If possible, it is also recommended that you orient

Figure 7.10 Author Sandra Wheeler (left) assists a student in setting up a baseline using a compass and meter tape.

your marked area in either a north–south or east–west direction to simplify measuring angles when mapping.

When constructing rectangular or square limits, trilateration is used to ensure that 90° angles are formed in each corner. Many people confuse trilateration with the process of triangulation. Triangulation involves the measure of the angles of a triangle, while trilateration involves the measure of the sides of a triangle. Trilateration is based on the calculation of the hypotenuse length of a triangle when the length of the base and one side are known. Common lengths of baselines and the associated hypotenuse lengths can be found in Table 7.2. To construct limits around evidence, use the following steps:

1. Position the first corner stake in the ground and establish a north–south or east–west line with a meter tape extending out from this point.
2. At a whole meter point along this line, position the stake that will form the second corner of your limit. Whole meter measures are

Table 7.2 Common Baseline Lengths and Associated Hypotenuse Measures for Constructing Scene Limits or Grids for Mapping

Side Length	1	2	3	4	5	6	7	8	9	10
1	1.41	2.24	3.16	4.12	5.10	6.08	7.07	8.06	9.06	10.05
2		2.83	3.61	4.47	5.39	6.32	7.28	8.25	9.22	10.20
3			4.24	5.00	5.83	6.71	7.62	8.54	9.49	10.44
4				5.66	6.40	7.21	8.06	8.94	9.85	10.77
5					7.07	7.81	8.60	9.43	10.30	11.18
6						8.49	9.22	10.00	10.82	11.66
7							9.90	10.63	11.40	12.21
8								11.31	12.04	12.81
9									12.73	13.45
10										14.14

recommended to make your calculations easier in setting the final corner of your limit. This first side of your limit is called the baseline.

3. Secure a meter tape (tape A) to the first corner stake and using your compass extend it out at a 90° angle from the newly established baseline. Find the nearest whole meter mark outside of the area containing evidence.

4. Using the length of your baseline and the distance to the whole meter mark obtained from tape A, find the hypotenuse length for your measures in Table 7.2. For example, if your baseline is 5 meters long and your distance mark on tape A is 4 meters, then your hypotenuse length found in Table 7.2 is 6.4 meters.

5. Secure an additional meter tape (tape B) to the second corner stake and run it out at an angle toward the distance mark on tape A.

6. Holding tape A in one hand and tape B in the other, bring them together as level as possible. Keeping tape A at a 90° angle to the baseline, align the mark on tape B, indicating the hypotenuse length, with the distance mark on tape A. The point where these two measures intersect is the point of position for the third corner of your limit.

7. Remove tapes A and B and move to the second corner stake. Using the second corner stake, repeat the same process in steps 3 through 5 to determine the position of the fourth corner of your limit.

Figures 7.11 and 7.12 provide examples of trilateration when constructing limits prior to mapping a burial scene.

After scene limits have been set, a datum can be established if one was not already set during site mapping. If a previously set datum is too distant from the feature being mapped, a secondary or temporary datum can be established and later tied into the original site datum. The datum used for

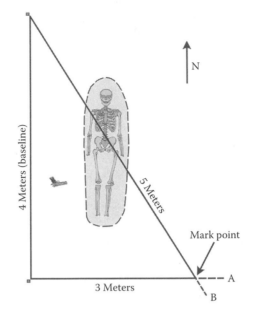

Figure 7.11 An example of trilateration in constructing limits when mapping a burial scene.

Figure 7.12 Author Sandra Wheeler (right) assisting students in setting up the meter tapes for measuring the hypotenuse and setting the final corner in the scene limits.

scale drawings should be in a location clear of all obstructions in relation to the evidence and be positioned above any elevation changes in the ground surface. In many cases, the first corner stake set in the baseline is used as a datum. To measure relative elevations and depths of evidence from the datum, use the following steps:

1. Tie a length of mason's line, long enough to reach the farthest point of your limit, to the datum. This is called the datum line. If you are using a wooden stake, place a nail in the end of the stake to hold the datum line. If you are using a metal rod or pipe, use electrical tape to secure the position of the datum line.
2. Mark the ground surface onto the datum and record the height of the datum line above the ground surface.
3. Attach a line level to the datum line and extend it out over the surface contour or object to be measured.
4. Keeping the datum line level, place the zero end of a stick tape or steel tape on the point to be measured and adjust so that the tape is at a 90° angle to the datum line. If the depth of the object or contour is greater than 1 meter, it is recommended that you carefully hold a plumb bob along with the tape to maintain a 90° angle when measuring.
5. Read the measure where the datum line crosses the tape and record the elevation or depth of the contour or object above or below the datum.
6. Repeat this process for any contour or object that is of interest throughout the mapping and recovery stages.

Figure 7.13 provides an example of a depth measurement taken from a datum. Always remember that all depth measurements taken in this manner should have the height of the datum subtracted when reporting actual depths from the ground surface.

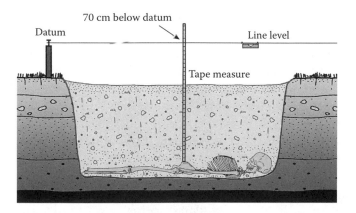

Figure 7.13 Example of measuring the depth of an object using a datum line.

7.7.2   Frameworks for Drawing to Scale

There are two primary frameworks in the methods of drawing to scale. These frameworks are directed toward putting a scaled plan or section drawing on paper as accurately as possible to represent what occurred and what was found at the scene. The first framework, control-point mapping, is concerned with finding the position of an object or feature in relation to a known point. When using this framework, investigators locate evidence and make the best possible record of it. Control-point mapping typically involves survey equipment or simple mapping tools when evidence is spaced out across a larger area, such as surface scatters or in areas surrounding a grave. There are two approaches to control-point mapping: one involves the use of azimuths and a centralized datum as the control point, while the other uses the baseline of your limit as the control point.

The second framework, grid-system mapping, is concerned with laying out grid squares over the scene to control the work area and record evidence in great detail. Grid-system mapping is usually best applied over a grave or heavily localized areas of evidence in a surface deposit as the level of detail is much greater than the level of detail recorded using control-point mapping. However, the same basic principles for scale drawing are used in both frameworks.

7.7.2.1   Azimuth Control-Point Method

The azimuth control-point method, also known as polar coordinate mapping (Hochrein, 2002), is a simple and accurate approach to recording scattered surface remains or other scattered types of evidence when a total station is not available. This method uses a meter tape, mason's line with a line level, and an azimuth board to determine the distance, elevation, and azimuth of each piece of evidence from a fixed center point. A typical azimuth board (Figure 7.14) has a rotating 360° dial attached to a base and includes small stakes or suction cups to keep the board in place during use. Although this method is primarily used with the azimuth board placed at the center of the area being mapped (e.g., Hochrein, 2002), we also recommend placing the center point of azimuth board at the center point of a baseline if there is no clearly defined space free of evidence in the area being mapped. In this instance, you would only be using 180° of the azimuth board, but the steps taken to record the evidence would be much the same.

When mapping using this method, it is best to have one person determine angles and record data at the azimuth board and another to call out distances and elevations. It is also recommended that you start with evidence farthest from the azimuth board and then move in a clockwise manner to avoid damaging or displacing any evidence during the mapping process. To create an azimuth control-point plan drawing of scattered surface remains, use the following steps:

Figure 7.14 An azimuth board used in azimuth control-point mapping. There are holes at each corner of the board for stakes or suction cups, which hold the board in place during use, and a hole at the center point of the azimuth dial, which holds a chaining pin that is used as a datum.

1. Establish the limits of the area to be mapped using the method described above. Using the proper scale, draw the limits of the scene on your graph paper.
2. Locate the center point of the scene and ensure that it is free of evidence prior to placing the azimuth board on the ground. If there is evidence that would be displaced or damaged by the board, place the center point of the azimuth board at the center of the established baseline. If the center is clear of evidence that would be displaced or damaged, position the center of the azimuth board over the center point of the scene. Determine north using your compass and set the 0° mark on the azimuth board to match the direction shown on your compass.
3. Place the pointed end of a chaining pin through the metal D-ring at the start of the meter tape and carefully position the chaining pin through the center of the azimuth board. The chaining pin will serve as a centralized datum. Tie a length of mason's line, long enough to reach the most distant point of your scene limit, to the top of the chaining pin and attach a line level.
4. Starting with evidence that is farthest from the azimuth board, extend the meter tape and datum line out to the object being mapped.

Determine the distance of the object from the centralized datum using the meter tape. While the meter tape is in place, determine the azimuth of the object by reading the degree mark where the meter tape crosses the azimuth dial. Record the distance and azimuth on your graph paper using a protractor and a ruler.

5. After distance and azimuth are recorded, extend the datum line and determine the elevation or depth of the object being mapped. Remember to also record the object's description and any corresponding legend identifier assigned to that object in your field notes.

6. Moving in a clockwise direction, continue in the same manner described above until all evidence has been recorded.

Figure 7.15 shows an example of azimuth control-point mapping used to record a scattered surface deposit. Remember that any elevations taken

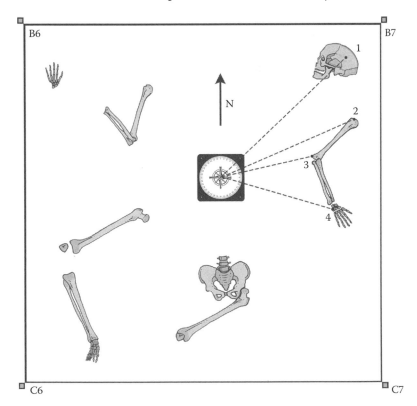

Figure 7.15 Example of azimuth control-point mapping used to record a scattered surface deposit. The surface scatter was contained within a 2-meter grid square of the search area (corner stakes are labeled with grid references). Coordinates were recorded starting with the cranium, which is the skeletal element farthest from the azimuth board, and then moving in a clockwise direction until all elements were mapped.

during the mapping process should be adjusted to reflect the height of the datum above the ground surface.

7.7.2.2 Baseline Control-Point Method

When skeletal elements are found on the ground surface and spaced out with a large degree of dispersal, the baseline control-point method is the most efficient approach to recording this kind of evidence. In some cases, scenes can be quite extensive, and setting a defined limit would serve no real purpose in the mapping process. Instead, large sections of ground surface can be mapped quickly by establishing a single baseline and measuring the distance from the baseline to the evidence. This method works very efficiently with three people: one person working along the baseline, one person working within the scattered evidence, and one person recording the data. On his or her own, an individual could effectively use this method, but it would be a bit more time consuming and cumbersome. To create a baseline control-point plan drawing of scattered surface remains, use the following steps:

1. Determine the limits of the scene. Using the method described above, establish a baseline that extends the full length of the scene. Depending on the level of dispersal of the remains, a baseline can be extended through the centerline of the surface scatter rather than at the side of the scene. Using the proper scale, draw the baseline on your graph paper.
2. Set a datum line at one end of the baseline. If the length of the baseline is quite extensive, you may set a secondary datum at the center point of the baseline, but it should be tied into the original datum prior to its use to ensure accuracy in elevation data.
3. Secure a meter tape to the ground surface along the baseline. Large 1-inch lumber staples can be easily pushed into the ground over the tape, securing it in place without damaging it. If the ground surface is too hard to insert staples, place rocks on top of the tape to keep it from moving.
4. Starting at the zero mark of the baseline meter tape, follow the baseline until you are on a direct sightline with an object that needs to be mapped. Run an additional meter tape from the point where the sightline intersects with the baseline out to the first object being mapped to determine its distance from the baseline.
5. Maintain a 90° angle between the baseline and distance meter tape by using a compass or large, right-angle protractor and record the baseline measure and the distance measure on your graph paper.
6. Using the datum line, record the elevation or depth of the object. Remember to also record the object's description and any corresponding legend identifier assigned to that object in your field notes.

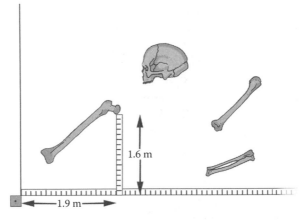

Figure 7.16 Example of measuring the position of an object using the baseline control-point method of mapping.

7. Proceed across the baseline continuing in the same manner described above until all evidence has been recorded. It is good practice to always record measurements in the same order (e.g., baseline point, distance, elevation or depth, description) to avoid any confusion and resulting errors.

Figure 7.16 shows the fundamental aspects of using the baseline control-point method when mapping scattered evidence.

7.7.2.3   Grid-System Method

The grid-system method of recording a burial or other heavily localized areas of evidence is much more time consuming in relation to the previous methods. However, this method allows for a much more refined recording of detail for each object and its relationship to all other objects within a specific area. In most instances, a 3 × 4 meter limit should be large enough to accommodate a grave thought to contain a single individual. The established limits of this size area may also be used as a closed-security area in which to work within a larger site limit. This method also allows for better control over the work area as specific regions within the grid can be mapped with an even higher resolution of detail (e.g., 1:5 scale drawing) if necessary.

Prior to setting up the grid system, ensure that all photographs and notes have been completed for the scene. Extreme care should be taken not to damage or displace any evidence. This method works best with two people: one to measure within the grid system and another to record the data. To set up a grid system and create a plan drawing using this method, follow these steps:

1. Determine the limits of the scene. Using the methods described above, establish a limit around the scene.
2. Along the north–south and east–west sides of the limit, position a wood stake or chaining pin at 1-meter intervals. Tie brightly colored mason's line onto a 1-meter interval stake and string it across the limit to the equivalent stake on the opposite side of the limit. The mason's line should be tied far enough off the ground surface so it does not interfere with any surface features or evidence within the limit.
3. Continue tying mason's line to each pair of stakes in both directions, forming a pattern of 1-meter grid squares within the limit.
4. Label the grid squares along the baseline with capitalized letters. Choose one side that is at a 90° angle to the baseline and label the grid squares along that side with numbers. This is called the *reference number line*. The corner post of the limit where these two lines intersect should then be used to set the datum line for the grid.
5. Using the proper scale, draw the limit on your graph paper. Label the datum, baseline, and reference number line, and label the grid squares along those lines with letters and numbers, respectively.
6. When evidence is encountered within a grid square, its exact position can be determined by measuring from the corner of the square that is closest to the datum along the square's two grid lines that run parallel to the baseline and the reference number line. Using a pair of stick tapes, hold one along the gridline parallel to the baseline with the zero point at the corner closest to the datum. Then place the other so that it intersects at a 90° angle with the first stick tape and the point on the object being mapped. The first measure is the baseline measure, and the second measure is the reference number measure within the grid square.
7. Locate the corresponding grid square on your graph paper. Using the proper scale, plot the point just measured within that grid square using your baseline and reference number measures.
8. Repeat this for each point on the object that needs to be mapped. For example, if you are mapping the position of a femur within a grid square at 1:10 scale, you would want to measure enough points on the femur (e.g., the proximal and distal ends and the midpoint of the diaphysis) to accurately represent its position at that scale.
9. Once the object has been mapped, its depth or elevation should be recorded using the datum line. Remember to also record the object's description and any corresponding legend identifier assigned to that object in your field notes.
10. Proceed throughout the grid continuing in the same manner described above until all evidence has been recorded. It is good

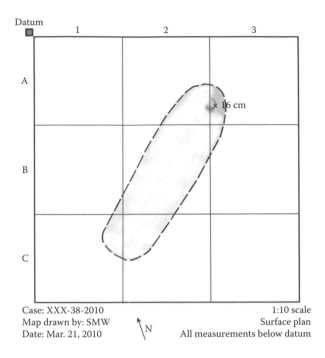

Figure 7.17 An example of a surface plan drawing of a partially eroded and disturbed burial produced using grid-system mapping.

practice to always record measurements in the same order (e.g., baseline measure, reference number measure, elevation or depth, description) to avoid any confusion and resulting errors.

An example of a grid positioned over a partially eroded and disturbed burial is shown in Figure 7.17. When working with burials, we recommend using a series of overlays in plan drawings (Figure 7.18) so that all of the data are recorded in a clear and legible manner. To produce an overlay for your plan drawing, follow these steps:

1. Once the initial surface evidence is drawn, place a sheet of tracing paper over your graph paper. This is referred to as an overlay. Hold it in place with some drafting tape or removable sticky tape.
2. Mark a set of cross-hairs on each end of your graph paper, well outside the previously recorded surface data. Trace these cross-hairs onto your overlay so that it can be realigned with the original drawing at a later date. Label this overlay as "Overlay 1."
3. The graph paper and designated labels for the grid squares should show through the overlay and you can now map the next layer of data on top of your previously recorded data without cluttering the map but still retaining the necessary level of detail.

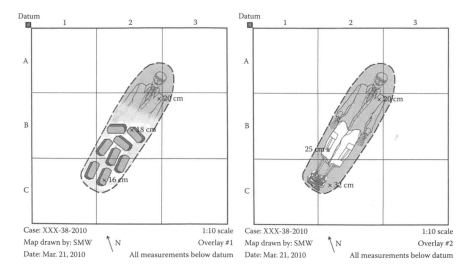

Figure 7.18 After the surface evidence of this burial was recorded on graph paper (Figure 7.17), surface soil was removed and the grid was used with a plan drawing overlay (left) to show the debris covering the body, which was then followed by another overlay (right) showing complete exposure of the skeletal remains and associated evidence.

4. Remove and add overlays in the same manner described above as necessary throughout mapping and excavation process until all evidence has been recorded. Remember to trace the cross-hairs from the original graph paper onto each overlay and label each overlay in consecutive order.

As mentioned earlier, heavily localized areas of evidence can be recorded in higher resolution of detail by using a frame grid placed over the evidence. Frame grids are typically 1-meter square metal frames that have been subdivided into subsquares with wires attached to the frame at either 10 or 5 centimeter intervals. When a frame grid is used, the subsquares are labeled first with the grid square identifier followed by letters and numbers corresponding to the same system as the larger grid system; however, the letters used for the subsquares are in lowercase instead of being capitalized. For example, if a frame grid is placed over grid square B6 to map a heavily localized area of burnt bone, a recorded fragment may be labeled as "B6/d3/–21 cm." This means that the item was found in grid square B6, located in subsquare d3 at a depth of 21 centimeters.

7.7.3 Section Drawings from Mapped Data

Section, or cross-sectional, drawings are used to depict elevation and depth relations among surface contours, objects, and soil layers. These drawings

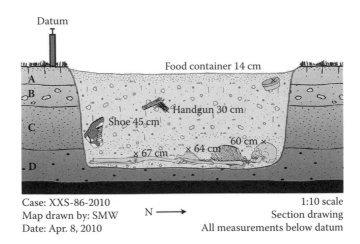

Figure 7.19 An example of a section drawing using depth measurements taken during excavation. This portrays the relative position of the skeletal remains, associated evidence within the grave, and the soil layers encountered during excavation.

can be easily created from the elevation and depth measurements taken during the creation of plan drawings. To create a scaled section drawing from elevation and depth measurements, use the following steps:

1. On graph paper, mark the position of the datum. If you were creating a section drawing that represents depth, it would be placed at the top of the graph paper. If you were recording elevations, it will be placed at the bottom of the graph paper.
2. From the datum point draw a baseline or gridline that represents width of the imaginary section plane used in your drawing. Mark the depth or elevation of surface contours found along this plane, and connect the data points to create a surface horizon line.
3. Below the horizon line, mark the depths of all mapped objects and soil layers. For elevation maps these would be above the horizon line. Be sure to label each point and layer with the corresponding legend identifier to avoid any confusion or resulting errors.

An example of a section drawing using depth measurements taken during excavation is shown in Figure 7.19.

7.7.4   Mapping on a Slope

All of the above techniques assume that your scene has a flat or gently sloping surface. However, forensic investigators are likely to come up against ravines, rock falls, forested hollows, and human-constructed embankments that will call for a certain amount of ingenuity when recording evidence. When measuring on steep slopes, the most important thing to remember is to be very cautious when moving across the slope. It is sometimes difficult to keep the measuring tapes level, and you may find yourself paying more attention to the positioning of the meter tape rather than where you are placing your feet.

It is recommended that a traditional transit or total station be used when recording skeletal remains located on a slope; however, if one is not available, the remains can be accurately recorded by setting a series of intermediate baselines and using the control-point framework for mapping across the face of the slope. This method requires at least three individuals: one working along the baseline, one working upslope from the baseline, and another to record the data. To map evidence located on a slope using this method, follow these steps:

1. Using the methods described above, establish a baseline at the bottom of the slope that extends the full length of the scene.
2. Secure a meter tape to the ground surface along the baseline. Large 1-inch lumber staples can be easily pushed into the ground over the tape, securing it in place without damaging it. If the ground surface is too hard to insert staples, place rocks on top of the tape to keep it from moving.
3. When recording data on a slope, the initial baseline serves as a "zero point" datum, and the elevations of all objects across the slope are calculated from this baseline. Cut a section of mason's line, approximately 3 to 4 meters in length, for use in measuring elevations, and attach a line level.
4. Starting at the zero mark end of the baseline meter tape, follow the baseline until you are on a direct sightline with an object that needs to be mapped. Place the zero mark end of a stick tape at a 90° angle to the baseline at the point where the sightline intersects with the baseline and the object being mapped.
5. Run the length of mason's line with the attached line level out from the object being mapped to the stick tape positioned on the baseline, keeping it level with the elevation of the object being mapped. Read the elevation of the object at the point where the mason's line crosses the stick tape.
6. Run an additional meter tape from the object being mapped out to the elevation mark on the stick tape that was previously recorded. This creates another 90° angle between the stick tape and the meter tape running from the object being mapped, providing a trilateration of the object's distance from the baseline. For example, if the elevation of the object is 2 meters and the distance of the object is

1.5 meters, then the hypotenuse would be 2.25 meters in length. The length of the hypotenuse can be calculated using the equation $a^2 + b^2 = c^2$ because the lengths of two sides ($a^2 + b^2$) of the triangle are known.

7. Proceed across the baseline continuing in the same manner described above until all evidence within a safe upslope distance has been recorded. Remember to also record an object's description and any corresponding legend identifier assigned to that object in your field notes. It is good practice to always record measurements in the same order (e.g., baseline point, distance, elevation, description) to avoid any confusion and resulting errors.

8. Additional intermediate baselines can be established upslope using the methods described above for setting limits. In other words, you would construct a rectangle or square on the slope and use the side parallel with the original baseline as your new intermediate baseline for measurement. Remember to measure the elevation of your intermediate baseline and add its elevation to all elevation measures taken from that point. For example, if your intermediate baseline is 3 meters above your original baseline, and an object's elevation from your intermediate baseline was 50 centimeters, then the actual elevation of that object would be 3.5 meters.

9. Repeat this process moving up the slope until all evidence has been recorded.

An example of the baseline step method for mapping on a slope is shown in Figure 7.20. Once all of the data have been collected from the slope, a plan and section drawing (see Figure 1.1) can be scaled onto graph paper using the recorded elevations and distances to provide details of the distribution of remains across the slope.

Case Study 8: A Bend in the Truth

Authors Wheeler and Williams were involved in the search for and recovery of a missing individual who had been deposited in a wheat field. The information leading to the location of the individual came from a hiker who stumbled across the remains while cutting across the field. The area immediately surrounding the remains was mucky, hard to walk in, and would not have supported a grid system that could be used with any accuracy. The depression holding the remains was filled with water and decomposition fluids, which was host to a large number of insect larvae as the remains were in an advanced state of decomposition. Because of the working conditions, a detailed control-point framework was chosen for mapping, and a baseline was set up lengthwise across the center axis

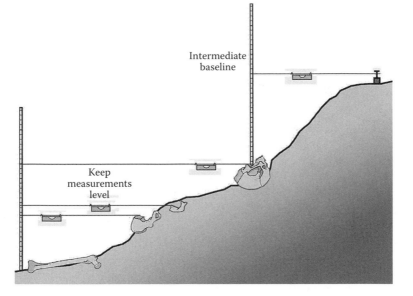

Figure 7.20 Example of using intermediate baselines when mapping remains found on a slope. The stick tape on the left is positioned over the original baseline with skeletal elements in the first step being mapped off of this line. An intermediate baseline is set at the position of the stick tape in the center of the slope and again farther up to safely and accurately map any remaining skeletal elements positioned upslope.

of the remains. A scale of 1:10 was used for the plan drawings. A datum was established and all surface contours, objects, and remains that were encountered during recovery were mapped and recorded with depths and descriptions.

During the initial stages of mapping the remains, it was noted that bent wheat stalks extending out from under the individual's remains appeared to all point in one direction, while the wheat stalks in the area immediately to the south of the body were bent in various directions that centered on one point. The individual was face down with the arms pinned under the front of the body. In addition the back of the shirt that the individual was wearing was pulled up to the shoulders and the individual's boxer shorts were extending out of the beltline of the pants. The individual was wearing a pair of shoes, one of which was partially off of the right foot. All of these details were included in the plan drawing (Figure 7.21). After recovery, all remains and evidence were taken to the Coroner's Office for analysis. There was no identification present on the individual.

Initially during recovery it was thought that the individual's hands may have been bound at one time because of the positioning of the arms and hands; however, during questioning the suspect denied that this was the case and also stated that the individual had been left in the field face

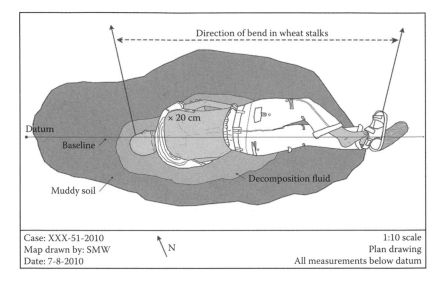

Figure 7.21 Surface plan drawing created using detailed control-point mapping framework from an established baseline that ran through the center axis of the remains. This flexible approach was used because of the working conditions surrounding the remains.

up rather than face down as was the case during recovery. The investigators reviewed the recovery files and noticed that the direction of the wheat stalks and positioning of the clothing as well as the arms did not fit the information provided by the suspect, who later confessed to placing the body in the field. At that point they decided to question the hiker who initially found the remains.

Shortly into the questioning, the hiker admitted to turning the body over by grabbing the edge of the underside of the individual's shirt, which slipped up to the shoulders and displaced the boxer shorts at the beltline of the pants. This action also caused the arms to become pinned under the body and the wheat stalks to be bent in one direction away from the remains. When the body was initially placed in the wheat field, the stalks of wheat were bent in various directions from one center point because the individual was tossed on top of the wheat rather than rolled into the field. The hiker also admitted to stealing the individual's wallet from the back pocket of the pants and waiting approximately two weeks before calling the police to report the location of the remains. In this case, careful mapping and recording of all surrounding evidence explained the differences between information provided in the suspect's confession and the state of the remains at the time of recovery.

Case Study 9: Ashes to Ashes to ... Zipper Teeth?

Authors Wheeler and Williams assisted in the recovery of evidence from a large open fire pit outside the residence where a crime had occurred. The goal of investigating the fire pit was to discern which layers were more recently burned and whether or not the items contained within the topmost layers were related to the crime being investigated. The fire pit was roughly circular, approximately 4 meters in diameter, and approximately 40 centimeters at its highest point from the surrounding ground surface. Four separate concentrations of burned material on the surface layer of the fire pit were noted. There were also a number of items on the surface of the fire pit beyond the limits of the four concentrations. These items were deemed to be in association with the latest burning by virtue of the fact that they rested on top of, rather than being embedded within, the fire pit surface, and by their similarity in nature to the items in the concentrated burn areas. The remains of a couch, mainly the frame and springs, were overlaid on one of the concentrations of burned material, and there was a strong odor of accelerant associated with the concentrated burn areas. After photographing the scene and making notes, a datum was set, a grid was overlaid on the fire pit, and we proceeded to map in the outer limits and all the burnt evidence on the surface of the fire pit. As each item was mapped and photographed, it was catalogued and bagged by the Evidence Officer. After all surface evidence was recorded and removed, the ash was carefully collected and screened and any evidence was bagged and catalogued separately by quadrant according to the grid.

In order to understand the sequences of burn events that took place in the fire pit, a profile was cut from the center of the pit to the outer edge. From this profile, at least seven major burn events could be identified (Figure 7.22). The lower layers contained general debris and household trash. These items were deeply embedded in the fire pit and were not considered to be part of the most recent burn event. The uppermost layer was part of the residue of the last burn event in the fire pit and ranged between 1 and 8 centimeters in thickness. From this layer over 338 items of evidence were mapped, recovered, and identified on a plan drawing (Figure 7.23), including steel toes from a pair of boots, the remains of cells phones, eyeglasses, and a multitude of small metal fragments representing all that remained of various clothing items, such as zipper teeth, snaps, buttons, and shoe eyelets. The items recovered represented the personal items from four individuals involved in the crime that took place. Without using this accurate mapping method, the exact location of the evidence and the defined areas within the most recent burn event would not have been identified or linked to the individuals involved.

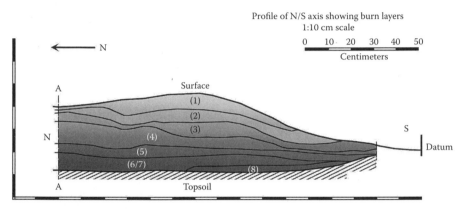

(1) White ashy layer with charcoal inclusions. Most personal items recovered from this layer.
(2) Dark gray layer with charcoal inclusions.
(3) Reddish-brown layer with charcoal inclusions.
(4) Light reddish-brown layer with charcoal inclusions. This layer contains burnt drywall and trash.
(5) Heavy chunks of black charcoal in burn layer. Non-human bone recovered from this layer.
(6/7) Dark brown layer.
(8) Heavy black charcoal layer.
A. Point at which N/S and E/W baselines cross.

Figure 7.22 Section drawing of a profile cut into a fire pit. Note that color change in the ash layers was used to identify the various burn events that took place in the fire pit.

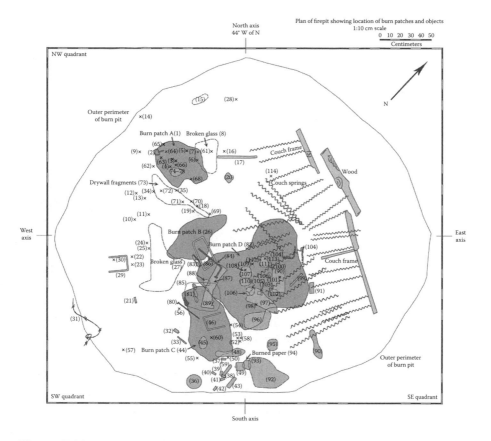

Figure 7.23 Plan drawing of a fire pit. All evidence recovered from the fire pit was recorded with a legend identifier. This legend was cross-referenced with identifiers assigned by the evidence officer at the scene.

Key Words and Questions

aerial imagery
azimuth
baseline
benchmark
control-point mapping
datum
datum line
elevation/depth
foresight/backsight
GPS
grid-system mapping
offset
orthographic map

overlay
plan drawing
prismatic compass
scale
section drawing
site plan
sketch map
topographic map
total station
trilateration

1. Explain the difference between topographic maps, orthographic maps, and aerial imagery.
2. Explain the types of information displayed on a sketch plan, a site plan, and a plan drawing. How does the amount of detail differ among these records?
3. You are assisting during a search, and a primary deposit and two secondary deposits of surface remains were found. One of the secondary deposits is approximately 5 meters away from the primary deposit, while the other secondary deposit is 2 meters away from the primary deposit in the opposite direction. How would you go about selecting a framework for mapping these surface deposits? What additional kinds of information would help you in making this decision?
4. Buried remains have been recovered from the backyard of a residence, as shown in Figure 7.9. Is there a more direct route that can be used to save time when tying in the scene datum to the benchmark located next to the fireplug? Explain the steps you would use in your simplified path of compass survey.
5. You are working in a control-point mapping framework using a baseline to create a plan drawing of a scattered surface deposit. While recording this evidence you come across a heavily localized group of burnt bone fragments and some empty shotgun shell casings, all within a 1-meter square area. What method could you use to map this area with a great amount of detail and then continue with the remaining evidence using the same method with which you started? How would you tie the 1-meter square area into your existing framework of mapping?

Suggested Readings

Ginesse, A., Listi, M.A., Manhein, M.A., Leitner, M. 2006. Use of the Global Positioning System in the field recovery of scattered human remains. *Journal of Forensic Sciences* 52:11–15.

Hawker, J.M. 2001. *A Manual of Archaeological Field Drawing.* Hertford, UK: RESCUE—The British Archaeological Trust.

Hochrein, M.J. 2002. Polar coordinate mapping and forensic archaeology within confined spaces. *Journal of Forensic Identification* 52:733–749.

Kipfer, B.A. 2006. *The Archaeologist's Handbook.* Malden, MA: Wiley-Blackwell.

References

Hester, T.J., Shafer, H., Feder, K. 2008. *Field Methods in Archaeology*, 7th ed. Walnut Creek, CA: Left Coast Press.

Hochrein, M.J. 2002. Polar coordinate mapping and forensic archaeology within confined spaces. *Journal of Forensic Identification* 52:733–749.

Howard, P. 2007. *Archaeological Survey and Mapping.* New York: Routledge.

Trimble Navigation Limited. 2010. *Datasheet: GPS Pathfiner ProXT Receiver.* Westminster, CO: Trimble Navigation.

Van Sickle, J. 2004. *Basic GIS Coordinates.* Boca Raton, FL: CRC Press.

Applying Archaeological Methods in a Forensic Context

8

Historically, the analytical expertise of forensic investigators and archaeologists has been combined on numerous occasions. Both fields of research emerged during the 19th century, and both disciplines were concerned with the proper identification of materials encountered during investigation (Davis, 1992; Hester et al., 2008). There is a theme common to the work of archaeologists and the work of forensic investigators; both attempt to understand the nature, sequence, and underlying reasons for certain events in the past. The final goals may differ, but the philosophy is much the same. Both disciplines use and present evidence in order to prove their cases.

Clyde Snow, a noted forensic anthropologist, stated, "… systematic recovery of the materials from burial and surface sites is best accomplished by suitably modifying methods long employed by archaeologists to solve similar problems" (1982: 118). Archaeology and forensic investigation are both based on highly detailed modes of data collection, documentation, data processing, and analysis. In terms of contemporary evidence gathering, it could be said that archaeologists work on some of the coldest cases in existence. It is understood that "each [type of investigation] gathers data in the hope of reconstructing events in order to solve a problem. Each looks for the agents responsible for the physical evidence. Each should operate through the cooperation of many disciplines working together to provide a complete response to the available data" (Davis, 1992: 152). Therefore, successful investigations in both fields are similarly oriented in reconstructing what happened at the scene based on physical evidence. In archaeology, artifacts, which are portable objects made, used, or modified by humans, are used as evidence to understand the behavior of human populations and their relationships with one another and their environment. In forensic investigation, this same type of evidence is used to reconstruct events or to relate an object or a person from one place to another.

The purpose of this chapter is to introduce the general principles and terminology used in archaeology and to provide the basic steps for the most effective and efficient excavation and recovery of remains in a forensic context. In many instances, forensic investigators rarely supervise the recovery of buried remains and are generally not experienced in processing this type of scene. Many times the common tactic is to recover the remains as quickly as possible, which can lead to the destruction and loss of valuable evidence. Most experienced archaeologists will have excavated numerous human remains during their careers, under different conditions and in different soil environments. Archaeologists have been trained how to locate, excavate, and record a human skeleton in order to maximize the information collected during recovery. This information may help in determining its date, the manner of its deposition, or the relationship of any associated objects or surviving elements—all before it is removed from the ground for analysis. An archaeologist who has worked in a forensic setting has the added benefit of fully understanding crime scene protocols and the evidentiary requirements of additional agencies that may be involved in the scene.

Forensic archaeology is the use of standard archaeological principles and methods in locating and recovering human remains and associated evidence within the context of a forensic investigation. The chief concern of both the forensic archaeologist and the forensic investigator is controlled legal acquisition of evidence that can be used to establish connections among suspect, victim, and crime and its potential use in future legal proceedings. The application of archaeological techniques within a forensic context can greatly assist the investigator in accurately and thoroughly documenting and recovering all potential evidence, aid in reconstructing events surrounding an individual's death, and if applicable, substantiate or disprove informant statements concerning the crime. By using methods familiar to both parties, shared resources and cooperation can lead to more effective and efficient results. Table 8.1 provides a summary of advantages for investigators working with a forensic archaeologist in recovering human remains and other kinds of physical evidence. Appendices A through L contain sample forms typically used by a forensic archaeologist during the recovery of remains.

Table 8.1   Summary of Advantages for Investigators Working with a Forensic Archaeologist

- Using a systematic and controlled approach that is easily adapted to any constraint
- Understanding site formation processes
- Recognizing post-burial site disturbances and identifying their cause
- Effectively reconstructing events surrounding and subsequent to burial process
- Providing increased accuracy in collecting skeletal remains and associated evidence
- Preventing damage to skeletal remains and associated evidence during recovery
- Recording and collecting environmental data that can be used by other specialists (e.g., entomologists, botanists, DNA analysts)
- Processing the scene in a professional manner with the shared goal of thoroughly recording and recovering all potential evidence

Source: Modified from Dirkmaat, D.C., Adovasio J.M. 1997. The role of archaeology in the recovery and interpretation of human remains from an outdoor forensic setting. In: Haglund, W.D., Sorg, M.H., eds. *Forensic Taphonomy: The Postmortem Fate of Human Remains*, pp. 39–64. Boca Raton, FL: CRC Press; and Morse et al., 1983.

8.1   General Principles of Archaeology

The goal of any archaeological excavation is to try to understand what may have happened at a site by carefully excavating the material remains that represent past behavior. Traditional archaeology examines changes in societies over long periods, rather than the much shorter time scales of forensic archaeology. However, in both instances, excavation requires great care and patience as each soil layer is slowly stripped away in succession to reveal material evidence. The most basic principle of any excavation is to proceed horizontally first and vertically second. In other words, by removing a single layer in its entirety before proceeding on to the next, as if moving through a layer cake one layer at a time. In addition, much of the evidence recovered in forensic archaeology is not instantly recognizable in a three-dimensional form. For example, subtle changes in soil color may indicate the outline of a grave or the remnants of decomposition fluids from a body. This evidence can be easily lost if proper care is not taken during the excavation process. An understanding of the basic principles of excavation and key terminology used in archaeology will be helpful when applying the following archaeological techniques to the forensic recovery of human remains.

8.1.1   Provenience and Context

Provenience refers to the exact location of an item in three-dimensional space, reflecting its latitude (north–south location), longitude (east–west location), and its vertical position (depth or elevation), as measured in meters (m) or centimeters (cm) (Hester et al., 2008). An item that has not been moved from its original place of deposition is said to be *in situ* (Hester et al., 2008).

Context, one of the most important terms in archaeology, is an object's exact place in time and space and its association and relationship with other items—that is, where it is, when it arrived, and how it got there (Hester et al. 2008). Context is the most easily lost of all potentially recoverable information. If objects are associated, they may be considered to have had a direct rather than circumstantial role in past events. Removing an object from its archaeological context without proper documentation destroys much of its potential in helping reconstruct the behavior that placed it there.

Provenience and context are equally as important in forensic investigations as they have a legal importance in developing the reconstruction of events at a crime scene. Evidence loses most of its value if the provenience and context in which it is found is lost. This is extremely important considering that associated relationships between objects found at a crime scene are not always immediately apparent. In many cases, remains are removed quickly with brief notations on placement within the crime scene, resulting in the loss of the primary depositional context and incomplete scene reconstruction (Dirkmaat and Adovasio, 1997). Compromising the context of evidence can occur as easily as an untrained individual picking up, examining, or removing skeletal elements in an attempt to identify whether they are human. Once an object is moved, it is almost impossible to return it to its exact position and orientation. In some instances, the context of the scene may not always correspond with the evidence (see Case Study 8 in Chapter 7).

8.1.2 Features

Unlike artifacts, which can be removed for later analysis, features have to be fully documented where they are found. In archaeology, a feature is an artifact that cannot be removed from the site (Hester et al., 2008), for example, an animal burrow, posthole, trash pit, or built structure. Although archaeologists cannot remove a posthole from a site, they can learn much about the structure of the site and human behavior from documenting such artifacts.

In crime scenes that involve buried human remains, a grave can be viewed as a feature. It is part of the crime scene that cannot be removed, but if it is excavated properly, valuable information regarding tools used in grave construction, geophysical characteristics, and other changes can be preserved (Hochrein, 1997a, 1997b, 2002).

8.1.3 Stratigraphy and Soils

For an archaeologist, stratigraphy is the primary basis for understanding buried materials and provides the most direct information on how objects came to be buried. Stratigraphy is the analysis of the sequence of deposits in the earth's surface that have formed through natural or human activities (Hester et al., 2008). With time, the gradual buildup of these deposits forms stratified layers one above the other. The strata, or layers, can be viewed as the pages in a book, and the stratigraphy is the story being told (Dirkmaat and Adovasio, 1997).

Soils are particles of broken rock that have been altered by chemical and environmental processes that include weathering and erosion (Hester et al., 2008). Soils are described using a standard method, developed by the U.S. Department of Agriculture's Natural Resources Conservation Service (NRCS), that distinguishes differences in color, texture, consistency, and composition. In archaeology, the color of soil is evaluated using commercially available color reference systems. The most common system, the Munsell color book (see Figure 2.10), uses a set of color chips that are matched with soils and an alphanumeric designation for the soil color identified. Soil color changes along with the amount of moisture it contains; therefore, an estimate of the level of moisture in the soil at the time that the color is referenced should be noted (Soil Survey Staff, 2010). Texture refers to the relative proportions of

Table 8.2   Simple Field Assessment of Soil Consistency

Consistency	Structure of a Moistened Cube of Soil
Loose	Cannot be formed into a cube (i.e., no adherence)
Weak	Crushes easily
Friable	Requires low pressure to crush it
Firm	Requires great pressure to crush it
Hard	Cannot be crushed
Cemented	Crushes easily but bound together with substance other than clay

Source: Modified from Roskams, S. 2001. *Excavation, Cambridge Manuals in Archaeology.* Cambridge: Cambridge University Press.

clay grains (less than 0.002 millimeters), silt grains (0.002 to 0.05 millimeters), and sand grains (0.5 to 2 millimeters) contained in the soil (Soil Survey Staff, 2010). When recording soil texture during excavation, it is more efficient to use a general measure of the soil texture. Most archaeologists use the following rule after lightly moistening the soil being described: clay coheres, silt adheres, and sand does neither. In other words, clayey soils are sticky and plastic, silty soils are smooth, and sandy soils are gritty. Consistency measures the degree of soil compaction and whether it holds together (Roskams, 2001). Table 8.2 provides a list of measures that are easy to use in the field when describing consistency. The composition of soil is an estimate of size of visible particles within the soil, such as fine, medium, and coarse pebbles.

Soil may also be described as a soil horizon, or a specific layer that possesses characteristics that differ from the layers above and beneath. Most soils conform to a similar general pattern of horizons (Soil Survey Staff, 2010) (Figure 8.1):

- Organic matter (O horizon)—litter layer of loose and partly decayed organic matter
- Surface soil (A horizon)—layer of soil with the most organic matter accumulation and soil life
- Subsurface area of leaching (E horizon)—lightly colored zone of leaching from surface soil
- Subsoil (B horizon)—layer of accumulated mineral and organic compounds from above
- Parent rock (C horizon)—layer of large partially altered or unaltered rocks

During excavation, each soil layer and its composition should be described in your field notes. This information aids in identifying any disturbances to soil layers and reconstructing the events that may have caused them. Official soil descriptions for each county in the United States are listed at the USDA NRCS website (http://soils.usda.gov/survey/printed_surveys). By selecting

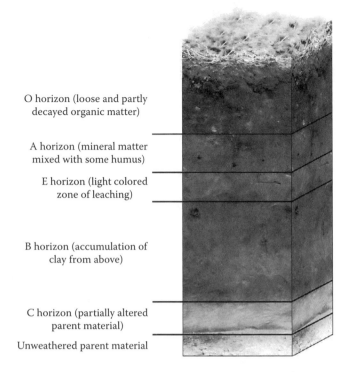

O horizon (loose and partly decayed organic matter)

A horizon (mineral matter mixed with some humus)

E horizon (light colored zone of leaching)

B horizon (accumulation of clay from above)

C horizon (partially altered parent material)

Unweathered parent material

Figure 8.1 Main soil horizons commonly described during archaeological excavation.

your state from the list, you will be forwarded to a list of county soil publications (e.g., maps, local soil taxonomy) that are available for download free of charge.

8.1.4   Principles of Deposition

Depositions of soils that form strata will vary due to climatic and environmental changes, as well as human intervention (e.g., building a road, digging a hole), that can occur over long or short periods of time. However, in archaeology, it is assumed that the order in which the different parts of a site are laid down will reflect the sequence of events that occurred at the site. Figure 8.2 shows an example of stratigraphy encountered during excavation at a forensic scene and the documented reconstruction. The various strata include differing soil layers as well as features, such as an old barn foundation (c), a cement floor (f), and a pit containing human remains (h). From a forensic perspective, digging a grave disturbs the natural stratification of the soil that inevitably makes the gravesite detectable either to the trained eye of the forensic archaeologist or by using specialized equipment, such as ground-penetrating radar (GPR). A grave is typically identified by a burial cut, which

Figure 8.2 Example of a section drawing of the stratigraphy associated with a burial (in order of deposition): (a) bedrock, (b) sterile soil layer, (c) barn foundation, (d) sandy soil layer, (e) barn wall, (f) cement floor, (g) undisturbed debris layer, (h) human remains, (i) chemical layer added to speed decomposition, (j) mixed fill removed during burial and used to cover remains, (k) bricks used to fill hole in cement floor, (l) remaining mixed fill used to conceal hole in cement floor, and (m) topsoil layer and surface vegetation.

is the line of definition between the backfill of the grave and the undisturbed layers through which the grave has been dug. It is impossible to dig a hole and fill it exactly as it was without leaving evidence of disturbance within the soil layers. In most situations, when a perpetrator fills in a grave, the backdirt placed in the hole will consist of a mix of the various soil horizons originally removed from the hole and, in some cases, additional materials from the surrounding surface area. All stratigraphic reconstruction in archaeology is based on four basic principles of deposition: superposition, association, reversal, and intrusion.

8.1.4.1 Superposition

This principle simply assumes that more recent deposits will be laid down on top of older ones (Hester et al., 2008). Because new depositions of soil are usually on top of preexisting layers, the relative date of layers can be determined; for example, an object closer to the surface will typically be more recent than the objects found beneath it. Superposition can easily be applied to forensic recovery, particularly in cases involving multiple individuals and associated evidence. When excavating these types of graves, bodies and objects that are at the top of the grave can be interpreted as being placed last, while those found at the bottom of the grave would have been placed first. The relative dating information acquired through careful excavation of the remains and the soil layers can supply invaluable information to investigators. For example, a bullet casing deposited on the surface of a grave must have been placed there after the burial process was finished, but not before or during the process. Objects found in a layer above, beneath, or with the remains must have been deposited before, after, or at the time of burial. Objects found in any of the layers of a grave may yield physical evidence that should be interpreted relative to the layer in which it was recovered. This information can help reconstruct the events that occurred at the scene; however, the investigator must keep in mind that this principle places items in analytical order based on their sequence of deposition, not on the exact age of the materials in the strata. When excavating, it is also important to keep in mind that new strata, such as a layer of lime or various chemicals, may have been added in an attempt to conceal or aid in decomposition of the remains.

Looking back at Figure 8.2, we can develop a sequence in the burial of a body under the cement floor by using superposition. The cement floor (f) was broken, and the pit was then dug for the body (h). After placing the body in the pit, a chemical substance (i) was dumped on top of the body and the pit was then backfilled using the soil originally removed from the pit, which is now mixed (j). Bricks (k) were placed in the break of the cement floor and then covered with the remaining mixed fill (l). We know from superposition that the body was placed in the pit before the added chemical substance and that the bricks were placed in the burial pit before being covered over with a layer of soil. We can also determine that the surface layer (m) was deposited after the burial took place as it lies on top of the undisturbed debris layer (g) and the burial cut.

8.1.4.2 Association

In archaeology, association presumes that items found together within the same layer are essentially of the same age (Hester et al., 2008). However, this principle must be used with caution, as some items are held for a very long time before they are discarded (e.g., family heirlooms, tools, coins), making these items much older than the other materials with which they are associated. For example, coins are typically in circulation over a fairly lengthy period of time, and most individuals do not throw coins away; still, they seem to work their way into soil layers through various means. If coins are found in association with human remains recovered in a forensic context, the dates on the coins can provide some information concerning the time of deposition, but not the actual date. The individual would have been buried after the latest date on the coins, not necessarily during the year that the latest coin was minted. This same principle applies to other materials that contain dates of copyright, patent, and shelf life.

8.1.4.3 Reversal

In rare cases, objects or materials may have been moved from one location and deposited in another in reverse order. In archaeology, this is called reversal (Hester et al., 2008). The initial process of burial may be used as an example of the principle of reversal in that soil is being removed from its original context and deposited next to the grave in reverse order. Soil erosion is another common form of reversal encountered during the recovery of human remains. If a body is placed in a depression and covered with surface debris, the surrounding soil from higher ground may erode and eventually cover the body as well as the surface debris. This can create a reversal of soil horizons over the remains.

8.1.4.4 Intrusion

Intrusions are disturbances that cut into previous deposits. This principle recognizes that any intrusion must be more recent than the deposit through which it cuts (Hester et al., 2008). During the excavation of remains, it is important to determine whether or not the initial burial cut has been disturbed and identify the cause of any intrusions within the backfill strata. Typically, animal burrows, tree root displacement, and mechanical disturbance during construction, farming, or gardening cause most intrusions. However, in forensic investigations, it is fairly common to encounter intrusions caused by later removal or alteration of the contents of a grave.

8.1.5 Geotaphonomy

Geotaphonomy uses the principles of deposition outlined above to recognize specific geophysical characteristics and changes that affect features and the surrounding environment (Hochrein, 2002). In a forensic context, this type of evidence focuses on the grave and may lead to identifying the initial method of digging as well as recognizing the exact source of any intrusions or disturbances.

8.1.5.1 Bioturbation

Bioturbation is the mixing, displacement, or modification of the position of materials in the soil (Micozzi, 1991). Plants and animals cause the most recognizable forms of bioturbation and can sometimes lead to the determination of season or year when a burial took place. Scavenging animals tend to displace evidence when digging and will often carry skeletal elements back to their burrows or through their tunnels for consumption or gnawing purposes (see Chapter 5). It is sometimes necessary to follow these tunnels or dig into a nearby animal burrow to recover smaller skeletal elements. Root networks from plants can either hold together or displace burial evidence. One commonly overlooked form of botanical evidence is the slice or cut marks in roots that were caused by digging tools during the burial process (Bock and Norris, 1997; Willey and Heilman, 1987).

8.1.5.2 Sedimentation

Water flowing over or through a grave may result in the sedimentation of eroded silts or the formation of fissures. Evaporation of moisture from silty soils may result in cracking patterns that change during wet and dry phases. These patterns can be affected over time by soil and remains settling within the grave, and on occasion the patterns may be used to locate edges of a burial cut (Hochrein, 2002). Careful excavation can also help determine the number of rain events that led to the buildup of silt layers. This information may be matched with local weather records to estimate the postmortem interval (PMI). The formation of fissures from water flows can cause skeletal elements or objects to become embedded in soil layers beneath the grave. When fissures are encountered in a grave, they should be carefully excavated in an attempt to recover any missing skeletal elements.

8.1.5.3 Compaction and Depression

Compaction marks are familiar elements in most forensic scenes and include impressions from such things as a suspect's shoes, tires, and hands and knees, as well as the backs of shovel blades, which are commonly used to pack the fill on top of a grave. In addition, areas of extreme compaction may retain cloth impressions, particularly those from denim, wool, or other types of heavy, coarse-weave fabrics. All compaction marks should be photographed or cast to preserve their details so that they may be later used as evidence in identifying a suspect.

When working with graves, depressions are changes in the surface contours of the soil that usually result from decomposition and settling of the remains. They are typically described as being either primary or secondary (Killam, 2004). Primary depressions form when the freshly dug fill settles in the burial pit, and secondary depressions occur when soil settles as a result of the release of gases and the collapse of the abdominal region during decomposition (see Figure 5.11). Secondary depressions do not always form and can be dependent on the position of the body during burial. Eroded holes made by scavenging animals over the burial are commonly mistaken for a secondary depression.

8.1.5.4 Tool Marks

Tool marks left during the process of burial are routinely overlooked even though they may be well preserved on or beneath the ground surface (Hochrein, 1997b). Understanding how the grave was dug and what tools were used may offer insight into the amount of planning and forethought that went into preparing the grave. Some soils, such as clays and silts, readily retain tool marks; however, sandy soils and gravels are too coarse and dry to retain these kinds of details. Often soil and rock particles adhere to digging tools and may be matched to a specific soil horizon associated with the burial cut.

If there is a possibility that tool mark evidence may be preserved, every effort should be made to avoid contamination or destruction of existing tool marks by excavation tools. In order to prevent this from happening, the forensic archaeologist should clearly define the outline of the burial cut, and excavations should begin inside of this line with small hand tools. When the excavation level is below the areas possibly containing tool marks, small hand tools and brushes can be used to expose the marks for photography and casting. Castings of tool marks are typically made using dental gypsum and a mason's board to form a negative image of the tool mark. These casts often show notches and striae that have formed along the edges of the digging tool, which can be matched with the exact tool or, at the very least, with the class of tool used. In addition, paint chips from the surface of a tool, not evident to the naked eye, may be recovered in the casting process.

8.2   Archaeological Approaches to Recovering Human Remains

As most forensic archaeologists can attest, every crime scene involving human remains is different, and as such, the archaeological techniques used to excavate a site must be adapted to each particular scene. Forensic archaeology makes use of systematic and controlled approaches that can be effectively applied no matter the condition or context of the recovery scene. Flexibility is key when evaluating the environment and working conditions that will be encountered during the recovery process. Although each scene is different, the general methodology of excavation and recovery of remains is similar.

8.2.1   Recovering Surface Remains and Associated Evidence

Human remains that are left on the surface are likely to be disturbed in some manner prior to recovery (Killam, 2004). In these instances, every effort must be made to recover as much evidence as possible, especially in locations where the terrain is difficult and scattering may be extensive. Accurate recording and mapping are also important in these instances so investigators can better understand and reconstruct the events that took place during the postmortem interval. At the start, both the forensic archaeologist and crime scene personnel should keep duplicate records of all scene personnel involved in the recovery (Appendix D), all photographs and all evidentiary materials (Appendices J and K), and chain of custody for any materials recovered by the forensic archaeologist and removed from the scene (Appendix L).

8.2.1.1   Stage 1: Examining and Recording the Recovery Area

Typically, a forensic investigator will determine the perimeter of the scene, and crime scene personnel will carry out all initial documentation of evidence. However, in some cases, the forensic archaeologist will assist in this process. It is recommended that in either instance, the forensic archaeologist should take the following steps to examine and record the scene and recovery area prior to any recovery actions:

1. Record the context of the site and recovery area (Appendix E) and appraise any constraints on recovery (e.g., landscape, weather, time limits, manpower, and equipment availability).
2. Plan any adaptations to archaeological methods for recovery.
3. Determine the extent of the scene associated with the primary surface deposit and designate the perimeter of the recovery area. If possible, determine if there are secondary surface deposits that may be associated with the primary deposit.
4. Establish whether or not restricted routes of access to and from the primary surface deposit, as well as in and out of the recovery area, have been set by the crime scene personnel.
5. Complete detailed descriptions and a general overall sketch of the site and recovery area. It is also recommended that the recovery area and its immediate surroundings be photographed.

8.2.1.2   Stage 2: Establishing Spatial Controls and Recording Secondary Surface Deposits

Provenience and context are equally important in surface and burial recovery. Establishing spatial controls early in the process of surface recovery will help ensure that from the start all data are recorded properly and that the entire scene can be reconstructed with as much accuracy as possible.

1. Construct a baseline and set a datum for mapping surface levels and evidence in the recovery area. In some instances, you may need to construct multiple baselines or reference grids within the site when recording various concentrations of evidence.
2. Record and map any geotaphonomic disturbances and material evidence found on the surface of the recovery area, avoiding the primary surface deposit at this time. Move from the outer perimeter inward in a 1-meter interval spiral pattern to avoid disturbing or damaging any secondary surface deposits in the area.

3. Record and map any secondary surface deposits and any additional evidence that might be disturbed during the next stage when the primary surface deposit is cleared. Use a separate surface deposit recovery form (Appendix F) for each feature.
4. After any secondary deposits or additional evidence within the recovery area have been recorded and mapped, determine the method of mapping that will be used to record the primary surface deposit.
5. Construct a baseline or reference grid for the recovery of the primary surface deposit and set a datum. If time and space permit, it is recommended that a reference grid be used for the recovery and mapping of a primary surface deposit to ensure that all evidence is recorded with the greatest amount of accuracy possible.

During the recording and mapping of evidence within the recovery area, it is recommended that a metal detector be used to locate any bullets, casings, or additional metal-based evidence (e.g., jewelry, coins, medical devices) prior to reaching the screening stage for any removed materials. The screening process can easily abrade metal objects and, especially in the case of bullets and casings, this can damage fine striations that may be used in comparative evidence analysis.

8.2.1.3   Stage 3: Exposing and Recording the Primary Surface Deposit

Extreme care should be used when clearing and exposing the ground surface as small bones, teeth, and hair tend to be swept up in leaf litter or debris. These items should be recovered during proper screening and sorting of the material if this occurs.

1. Remove any loose debris (e.g., leaves, sticks, trash) from the surface of the grid area one square at a time by hand or with a hand trowel; screen or sort through the loose debris, keeping material from each grid square separate.
2. Remove or trim any surface vegetation to expose the remains for recording and mapping; screen or sort through surface vegetation. Take care to record any *in situ* debris or vegetation that may have been purposefully placed over the remains.
3. Record and map all exposed elements and associated evidence.

When searching through any twigs or larger branches, look for signs of "greenstick" breaks and stripping of bark (see Chapter 9 for more information on botanical evidence). These types of marks are a result of breaking and removing branches from living trees and may indicate intentional concealment of the body. Any piles of debris around the remains should also be treated and recorded as possible evidence of concealment.

8.2.1.4 Stage 4: Removing Surface Remains at the Primary Site

It is recommended that the forensic archaeologist and the crime scene personnel review all evidence records and maps prior to removing remains from the primary surface deposit. Any possible errors in recording or labeling can be detected before the primary scene is disturbed.

1. If the skeletal remains overlap each other or if it is suspected that more than one individual may be present, treat the remains as if they were in layers, recording and mapping each layer prior to its removal. If any remains are partially embedded in the ground surface, be sure that each element is carefully loosened from the surrounding soil with small excavation tools before attempting removal. Never pull any evidence out of the soil as this can cause unnecessary damage to the remains and disturb the context of any evidence hidden beneath the ground surface.

2. If the forensic archaeologist is trained in human osteology, the skeletal elements may be inventoried during recovery (Appendices A through C). Otherwise, a summary of the condition of the remains should be completed (Appendix H).

3. During removal, any entomological or botanical samples that are related to the remains should be collected and recorded (Appendix I; refer to Chapter 9 for proper collection methods).

4. Once all of the evidence has been removed from the grid area, a soil sample should be collected from the area thought to be directly below the torso of the remains, and the ground surface should be examined with a metal detector, if available.

8.2.1.5 Stage 5: Examining Soil Layer beneath Surface Deposits

In many instances, smaller elements from a surface deposit may settle into the soil over time and become covered with eroded soils or buried during animal scavenging. In addition, some insects associated with the decomposition of human remains tend to dig into the soil layers beneath the remains during certain stages of their life cycle. For these reasons, it is recommended that the soil layer beneath any surface deposit be thoroughly examined.

1. Using a hand trowel, the ground should be carefully scraped down to a layer of undisturbed soil. All of the removed soil should be

screened. In a primary deposit, soil recovered from each grid square should be kept separate.

2. One final sweep using a metal detector should be done after the soil layer has been scraped to ensure that all metallic evidence has been collected.

3. After the recovery area has been double-checked all materials should be removed from the scene except for the datum. A final photograph should be taken of the recovery area after everything has been removed.

4. Any secondary datum set during recovery should be tied in to the primary site datum.

8.2.2 Removing Buried Remains and Associated Evidence

When excavated properly, graves have many of their own characteristics that can provide vital information to the investigation. Table 8.3 provides a list of questions that a forensic archaeologist usually keeps in mind throughout the recovery process. Recognizing the various types of evidence depends on systematic and careful removal of the burial fill from the original walls and floor of the burial cut. Extreme care should be taken at each step of the process to ensure proper recording and mapping of evidence with nothing being moved or removed without first noting its position and marking it for later identification. Photographs should be used as backup to the written record and not as the principal source of information. The excavation of human remains generally follows a series of stages that are presented here.

8.2.2.1 Stage 1: Examining and Recording the Recovery Area

This stage follows a process similar to the initial steps of surface recovery presented above. Any precautions mentioned in the recovery of surface remains should also be observed when working with buried remains.

Table 8.3 Common Questions Forensic Archaeologists Keep in Mind During Recovery

- How was the grave dug? What tools were used?
- Was the grave dug quickly or was it carefully prepared?
- Was the grave left open for a period of time prior to burial?
- Is there evidence that can be used to estimate postmortem interval?
- Is the burial deliberate or due to natural processes (e.g., soil reversal during erosion)?
- Is there any evidence connecting the grave, individual buried, and gravedigger?
- Is there anything in the soil that is foreign to the original fill (e.g., lime)?
- Is there evidence that could indicate manner of death?

1. Record the context of the site and recovery area (Appendix E) and appraise any constraints on recovery (e.g., landscape, weather, time limits, manpower, and equipment availability).
2. Plan any adaptations to archaeological methods for recovery.
3. Determine the extent of the scene associated with the grave and designate the perimeter of the recovery area. If the grave appears to be disturbed, determine if there are any secondary surface deposits that may be associated with the grave.
4. Establish whether or not restricted routes of access to and from the scene associated with the grave, as well as in and out of the recovery area, have been set by the crime scene personnel.
5. Complete detailed descriptions and a general overall sketch of the site and recovery area. It is also recommended that the recovery area and its immediate surroundings be photographed.

8.2.2.2 Stage 2: Establishing Spatial Controls

This stage is the most important aspect to the excavating and recording processes involved in the recovery of buried remains. Without proper spatial control, associations among recovered evidence and the potential for reconstructing events surrounding the burial process may be lost.

1. Construct a baseline and datum for mapping surface levels and evidence within the site. In some instances, you may need to construct additional baselines or reference grids in areas with a heavy concentration of evidence located away from the primary area of recovery.
2. Record and map any geotaphonomic and material evidence on the surface of the recovery area, avoiding the immediate area surrounding the grave at this time. Move from the outer perimeter of the recovery area inward in a 1-meter interval spiral pattern to avoid disturbing or damaging any surface deposits in the area that may be related to the grave.
3. Using methods in the recovery of surface remains described above, record and remove surface evidence from the recovery area, avoiding the immediate area surrounding the grave. A metal detector should be used over this same recovery area to recover any metallic evidence prior to the start of any screening process.
4. After the surface evidence within the recovery area has been removed, record and map any surface evidence immediately surrounding the grave that might be disturbed during the construction of a reference grid.
5. Construct a reference grid over the grave (Figure 8.3) and establish a secondary datum within the reference grid for use during excavation.

Figure 8.3 Students constructing a grid over a suspected grave at a simulated crime scene.

8.2.2.3 Stage 3: Identifying and Recording the Burial Outline

The second most important aspect in the recovery of buried remains is the identification of the burial cut. In many cases, skeletal elements sustain damage when the ground surface is cleared in an attempt to identify the burial outline. Extreme care should be used when clearing and exposing the ground surface as soil may have eroded to the extent that the remains or associated evidence may be slightly exposed or just below the surface. As a general rule when excavating, whenever you encounter a noticeable change in the soil (e.g., color, texture, consistency, inclusions), stop and assess the situation before you proceed. A feature excavation recovery form (Appendix G) should be used to record all stages of the excavation.

1. Remove loose debris (e.g., leaves, sticks, trash) and surface vegetation from the reference grid area one square at a time by hand or using small hand tools. Screen and sort through all materials removed from the surface of the burial site. Take care to record any debris or vegetation that may have been purposefully placed over the remains as this may indicate intent to conceal the body.
2. Scrape surface soils, no deeper than 1 centimeter, into dustpans and buckets for screening. Keep materials from different grid squares separate during screening so that any evidence recovered during this process can be placed in reference to other items.
3. Continue removing the uppermost soil in 1- to 2-centimeter layers until you can identify outline of the burial by changes in soil color or other characteristics such as cracks, depressions, or tool marks.

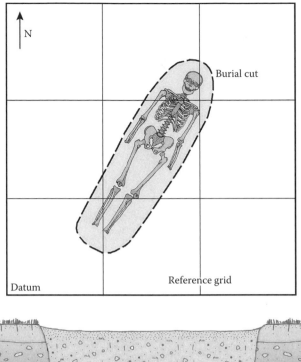

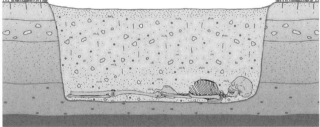

Figure 8.4 Example of a reference grid (top) and profile (bottom) of an exposed burial outline.

4. Once the burial outline has been identified, clear the entire grid area to the same level and map the surface contours, burial outline, and any exposed remains or associated evidence. In certain geographical locations soils may homogenize after a certain amount of time has passed, and the burial outline may not be defined. If this is the case, clear the entire grid area to the same level and map the surface contours and any exposed remains or associated evidence before moving on to the next stage of recovery.

Figure 8.4 shows an example of a reference grid and profile of an exposed burial outline. When screening materials from an excavation, the screening area should be set up on flat ground not too far from the excavation but carefully selected so as not to interfere with the reference grid if, for various reasons, it should need to be enlarged.

8.2.2.4   Stage 4: Excavating and Recording the Burial Feature

At this stage, there are two possible ways to proceed with excavation depending on whether the burial outline can be identified. If the burial outline is evident, it is recommended that investigators excavate the burial feature, meaning that the removal of soil will primarily occur within the defined burial cut (Connor and Scott, 2001) (Figure 8.5). If the burial outline is ignored during the recovery process, there is every probability that materials from surrounding soil layers can contaminate the burial and be mistakenly introduced as evidence.

   If the burial outline is not clearly defined by color differences in the soil or other characteristics, proceed in the following manner:

1. Remove loose debris (e.g., leaves, sticks, trash) and surface vegetation from the reference grid area one square at a time by hand or using small hand tools. Screen and sort through all materials removed from the surface of the burial site. Take care to record any debris or vegetation that may have been purposefully placed over the remains as this may indicate intent to conceal the body.

Figure 8.5 Author Sandra Wheeler (right) demonstrates the proper procedures for excavating a burial feature.

2. Working from a corner and then across the grid, remove soil in 5-centimeter layers one square at a time using a hand trowel. Keep all grid squares at the same depth.
3. Screen all soil from each layer removed from the grid area, keeping materials from each grid square separate during screening. Record the depth of the soil being screened so any associated evidence recovered in this process can be placed in reference to other items.
4. Record and map any artifacts or evidence encountered before moving on to remove the next consecutive layer.
5. If the burial outline is encountered, proceed with the excavation as described below; if remains or any containers or wrappings are encountered, move on to Stage 5 to expose and record the remains.

Excavation of a grave with a defined burial outline should proceed as follows:

1. Initially, only one half of the burial feature should be excavated until remains or any containers or wrappings are encountered. This creates a profile of the position and orientation of the body within the burial feature that can be clearly shown in drawings and photographs (Figure 8.6). Once the profile has been recorded, the other half of the burial may be excavated in the same manner.
2. Excavation should begin in the grid square over the center of the burial feature and move out toward the burial outline, leaving a 3- to 5-centimeter margin of burial fill along the outline. This preserves the burial walls of the burial cut, increasing the possibility of recovering geotaphonomic evidence such as tool marks.
3. The burial fill should be removed in 5-centimeter layers, keeping the excavation within the burial feature at the same depth before moving on to remove the next layer. If the remains are thought to be in an extended position, use extreme care when removing soil from the ends of the grave as one end will contain the skull and the other the feet, both of which can easily be disturbed or damaged if the depth of the grave is unknown.
4. Screen all soil from each layer removed from the burial feature, keeping materials from each grid square separate during screening. Record the depth of the soil being screened so any associated evidence recovered in this process can be placed in reference to other items.
5. After the first 20 to 25 centimeters of soil have been removed from within the burial feature, carefully excavate the remaining fill preserved along the walls of the burial cut. Use small hand tools and brushes to avoid damaging any tool marks that may be present.

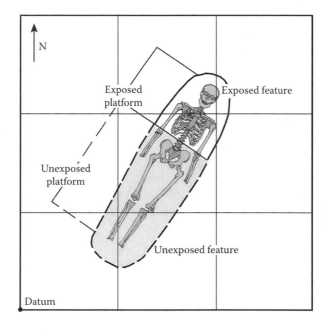

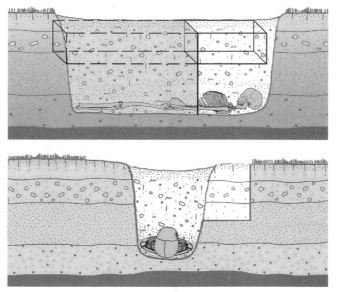

Figure 8.6 A reference grid (top), profile (center), and section (bottom) with half of the burial feature exposed. In this instance, a working platform was created after the wall of the burial cut was examined for tool mark evidence.

Figure 8.7 Orange County homicide detective Dave Clarke (right) uses a datum line to record depth measurements for exposed clothing and skeletal elements at a simulated crime scene.

6. Record and map any artifacts or evidence encountered before moving on to remove the next layer (Figure 8.7). Note any differences in soil layers by placing markers in one excavation wall to assist in recording when creating a scaled section drawing. It is also good practice to photograph these markers.
7. Once remains or any containers or wrappings are encountered, move on to Stage 5 to expose and record the remains.

When excavating, never stand in a burial until the exact burial position is known and the remains have been completely exposed, as it is easy to crush delicate bones or objects that may be associated with the burial. It is usually better to excavate lying on the side of the grave or on planks laid across the exposed burial cut; however, planks should only be used after any tool mark evidence has been recorded. If the depth of the burial increases to the point where it impedes proper excavation (e.g., at depths where the excavator is at risk of falling into the feature), it may be necessary to remove one side of the burial feature in stages to create a working platform as excavation progresses (Figure 8.8). The platform height should always be higher than the surface being excavated, and it should only be lowered after the wall of the burial cut has been recorded at each level.

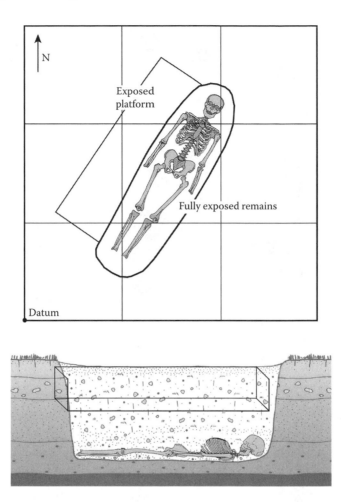

Figure 8.8 A reference grid (top) and a profile (bottom) of a burial feature with the remains fully exposed. A platform area was excavated along the wall of the burial to provide a safe working environment during excavation.

Soils that are heavily compacted or waterlogged (e.g., clays, river sediments, bogs, retention pond materials) may require washing during screening. Water from light-pressure hoses or buckets may be poured over the recovered material to move it through a fine screen. This will help recover fragments or other associated evidence without forcing the soil through a screen. Care must be taken to avoid water overflow, and personnel screening the material must be alert for any evidence that may float on the water surface.

8.2.2.5 Stage 5: Exposing and Recording the Remains
During this stage, all remaining soil surrounding the remains should be excavated. The process of gradually uncovering remains *in situ* is designed to preserve the position of the body and the relationship of any associated

Figure 8.9 Author Sandra Wheeler (front right) and students expose and clean the skeleton for mapping and photography at a simulated crime scene.

evidence, such as wrappings around the remains, containers, or any materials added along with the remains prior to filling the burial.

1. Working carefully with small hand tools, expose all remains within the burial feature (Figure 8.9). Always work from exposed areas toward unexposed areas. Use wood tools or plastic spoons and brushes when working close to bone or preserved soft tissue surfaces to avoid damaging the remains. Excavation notes should contain details of any damage that may occur during recovery to avoid any confusion about tool marks on the remains at a later date.
2. If containers or wrappings are encountered, these should be treated as any other layer within the burial and excavated with care as additional evidence may be collected from the folds or surfaces of the materials.
3. With the exception of smaller items that may impede excavation and that have been recorded and mapped, nothing should be removed at this point.
4. When excavating in areas around the abdominal and pelvic regions, extreme caution should be used, as fetal remains may be present in

Figure 8.10 Author Sandra Wheeler (front left) and students record depths for points on a skeleton using a datum line at a simulated crime scene.

females. These are very fragile and expert handling is recommended (see Chapter 10 for information on collecting juvenile remains).

5. Entomological and soil samples should be taken from the thoracic and abdominal cavity areas prior to fully exposing the area around the pelvis and lumbar vertebrae (see Chapter 9 for proper collection methods). Soil in these areas tends to contain insects and other chemical evidence not easily detected in the field.

6. The following points should be mapped and depths recorded using the datum line: skull, pelvic bones, knees, elbows, shoulders, hands and feet, and any associated objects found with the remains.

7. All remains and associated artifacts should be fully recorded and mapped (Figure 8.10). A summary of the condition of the remains (Appendix H) should be completed before moving on to Stage 6.

Extreme care should be taken when exposing the remains, as many important items may be overlooked if not brought to mind during recovery. Objects such as contact lenses, pacemakers, prosthetic implants, and items associated with surgical procedures are quite common in populations today and most can play a role in the identification of an individual. Any unidentified objects found in association with the individual should be kept as evidence until a medical examiner or forensic pathologist can review the materials.

From this point onward, everyone involved in the recovery should follow health safety protocols for crime scene personnel who come in contact with human remains. Although it is common to wear gloves when working with human remains as a protective measure against viral or bacterial infections, one additional reason to follow this procedure is that certain materials may have been added to the burial in an attempt to speed decomposition or to the body to preserve the remains. For example, many embalming fluids contain high levels of formaldehyde, and in some environments this chemical may oxidize into formic acid that upon contact with skin can cause a reaction equivalent to that of bee stings or fire ant bites (International Agency for Research on Cancer, 2006).

8.2.2.6 Stage 6: Removing the Remains

The following process largely refers to skeletal remains but can be adapted to remains found in various stages of decomposition:

1. To minimize disturbance and damage to an individual in a supine position, the patellae and lower legs should be removed first. The feet should be removed next, keeping the bones from the left and right feet separate. To remove a femur, carefully lift the distal end and gently move it toward the opposite side of the body. This will loosen the proximal portion of the bone from the pelvis. Repeat this for the other side. If the hands are positioned at the sides or placed across the abdomen, they should be removed next, keeping the bones of the left and right hands and wrists separate. The pelvis and sacrum are removed next, followed by the arms and then the ribs. Finally, the vertebrae, hyoid, mandible, and cranium are removed. Take great care in removing the cranium and mandible so that the teeth remain in their sockets. Do not pick the cranium up by the eye orbits or any other opening, as the bones in these areas are very fragile and will easily break. Instead, gently cradle it in both hands and lift with equal pressure on the fingertips and palms of your hands.

2. If the skeletal remains are not in a supine position, the sequence and direction of removal may vary considerably. In cases such as this, skeletal elements that overlap one another should be removed and recorded in layers using the above order when possible.

3. Also be aware that scalp and facial hair may have slipped from position and may be preserved under the cranium or around the lower facial region.

4. When removing the skull, pelvis, and shoulder blades, be aware of possible soft tissue preservation or clothing between these bones and the soil layers beneath the body.

5. Be sure to check for any jewelry, such as necklaces, earrings, rings, or bracelets, which may have slipped into the surrounding soil.

6. Remains held in anatomical position by preserved clothing, such as shirts, pants, shoes, or socks, should be removed as a unit and

investigated under more controlled conditions. Any skeletal elements not contained within clothing should be removed and packaged separately from those contained in preserved clothing.

7. If remains still retain a large percentage of soft tissue, every effort should be made to avoid damage to the existing tissues.

8. A recording sheet of all skeletal elements removed should be inventoried at this time.

9. If the forensic archaeologist is trained in human osteology, the skeletal elements should be inventoried (Appendices A through C) at this time to account for any possible missing elements prior to moving on to Stage 7.

8.2.2.7 Stage 7: Recording and Excavating the Burial Feature Floor

The burial feature floor is often mistakenly thought to be the point at which the evidence stops, but at times it can contain some of the most important evidence within the burial context. Many items or materials may have penetrated the floor in a visually unrecognizable manner (e.g., bullets fired through a victim, permeating toxic chemicals added to enhance decomposition), and at times further entomological evidence may be recovered from these soil layers. The following process will aid in the detection of any remaining evidence within the burial feature:

1. Record soil types and depths of each soil layer and record the depth of any evidence markers placed in the wall of the burial feature to assist in creating a scale section drawing.

2. Collect a soil sample from the floor of the feature that includes soil from at least 5 centimeters beneath the floor surface. A metal detector should also be used over the floor at this time.

3. Using a small hand tool or trowel, scrape all surfaces of the feature and screen for evidence that may have been embedded in the walls or under the body.

4. Scrape the floor of the feature until sterile undisturbed soil is detected across the entire area. Follow any fissures caused by erosion, cracks, or animal burrows to recover displaced remains or associated evidence.

5. Record and map any additional evidence recovered in relation to the burial feature.

6. Once everything has been recorded and collected, determine whether the burial feature should be backfilled at this time. When backfilling, the feature should be filled with the removed soil and leveled with the surface.

7. After the recovery area has been double-checked all materials should be removed from the scene except for the datum. A final photograph should be taken of the recovery area after everything has been removed.
8. Any secondary datum set during recovery should be tied in to the primary site datum.

8.3   How to Use an Archaeological Trowel

Archaeologists use a trowel to define the extent of a deposit and to remove it to expose the underlying layers. The texture and consistency of the soil will determine the most appropriate technique. If soil is loose or sandy, then it is probably easier to scrape the soil away with the edge of the trowel; if it is hard and compacted, then the only option may be to try and break it up carefully with the corner of the trowel. Never use the point of the trowel to remove soil. If you are scraping the soil, the trowel should be held so that the bottom edge of the trowel sits on the soil surface and the top edge is angled slightly away. Always pull the trowel toward you in a smooth motion to avoid digging holes in the ground. For either technique, remember to always keep your dustpan and bucket handy so that you can continually remove the excavated soil as you dig.

Case Study 10: One Person at a Time, Please

Authors Wheeler and Williams assisted in the recovery of human remains discovered in a supposedly empty cemetery plot. Using heavy equipment, gravediggers discovered that the plot reserved for a recently deceased individual was already occupied. The operator of the backhoe noticed some bones in the soil that had been removed from the plot and immediately stopped digging. The cemetery manager notified local law enforcement of the situation. Upon our arrival at the scene, law enforcement personnel had set up a tent with a portable heater over the disturbed grave, as it was winter with a layer of snow on the ground. Our first task was to investigate the pile of soil that had been removed from the plot as well as the backhoe bucket. A few loose teeth, three cervical vertebrae, and a pair of glasses were found. This task was somewhat challenging as groundwater from the snow melt was flowing through the soil and had turned it into a pile of mud.

After clearing the backdirt and bucket of any remains, a ladder was placed down into the grave so that the rest of the remains could be recovered (Figure 8.11). This also proved challenging as a small, ice-cold spring of water was running through the floor of the grave, waterlogging the

Figure 8.11 Author Lana Williams excavating remains discovered in a cemetery plot that should have been empty. Note the water pump hose to the left of the grave and the condition of the soil. A square section of plywood was used to keep investigators from sinking down into the mud while excavating.

soil, the remains, and the excavators. Once the mud surrounding the body had been cleared away, we could see that the skull had been dislodged by the backhoe, but the body had remained largely undisturbed. The individual appeared to be dressed in a suit, tie, and shoes. Coffin handles and large fragments of pressboard were also recovered.

The remains were placed in a body bag and lifted out of the grave. The associated evidence and the previously discovered skeletal elements were packaged separately and all the remains were taken to the Coroner's Office for analysis. The area around and beneath where the body was positioned was investigated further, but no other evidence was recovered. Subsequent investigation of the remains indicated that this individual had been autopsied prior to burial. This treatment and evidence of a coffin suggested that this case was not of forensic significance, but rather was the result of a clerical error on the part of the cemetery, perhaps accidentally burying someone in the wrong plot.

Case Study 11: The Intrusive Inmate

Fourteen-year-old Lisa Brighton* was last seen on May 25, 1987, walking near a convenience store with Wayne Smith. At this time, Smith was already under investigation for the rape of another woman. Formal charges were brought against Smith for this rape and he was sentenced to three years in jail. While Smith was serving his sentence, investigators were building a case against him for the suspected murder of Lisa.

In 1991, Smith was released from prison. Because investigators suspected him in the disappearance and murder of Lisa, they assigned officers to tail Smith in the hope that he would return to Lisa's burial site. One afternoon, Smith escaped the scrutiny of his observers, and during this time he did return to Lisa's grave, dug up her skeleton, and removed certain skeletal elements. Smith had conducted research while in prison as to what skeletal elements were typically used for identifying an individual. If Lisa's skeleton was ever to be discovered, Smith wanted to ensure that investigators could not identify her. Of course, this was before the acceptance of DNA as a viable method for identification. Although they never discovered the location of Lisa's remains, investigators were able to amass enough information to arrest and charge Smith with Lisa's murder six years after her disappearance. Prosecutors convinced a jury of Smith's guilt, without the discovery of Lisa's body, and he was sentenced to death.

In September 2001, 14 years after Lisa's disappearance, a rare and highly unusual plea deal was arranged in which Smith agreed to confess to Lisa's murder and reveal the location of her remains. For his cooperation Smith's death sentence would be converted to a life sentence without parole. At this time, Smith revealed the details of Lisa's murder and also told investigators about the time period in 1991 when he revisited Lisa's grave and removed certain skeletal elements. Under heavy security, Smith identified a wooded lot and the general area in which Lisa was buried (Figure 8.12). Although Smith could not pinpoint the exact location of the burial, as the vegetation had changed dramatically over 14 years, he revealed pertinent details that assisted investigators in their search plan. Smith indicated that he had buried Lisa in a shallow natural depression, with her head beside the root of a large tree. At the time of Lisa's burial, the area around the wooded lot was under heavy construction,

---

* Names have been changed to protect the identity of the victim and her family.

Figure 8.12 The wooded lot identified by Smith as the spot where he buried Lisa Brighton.

and Smith said that he took large strips of metal from the construction site and placed them over her body. He then used a metal bucket to scoop dirt and cover the grave. When Smith returned to the burial site in 1991, he said that he lifted several of the metal pieces and removed Lisa's skull and her right leg in an effort to mask her identity. Smith's rationale for removing these skeletal elements was that Lisa's teeth could be used to make a dental identification, and he removed her leg because when Lisa was younger she had been in a serious car accident that required her right leg to be reconstructed, therefore leaving behind signs of trauma and an orthopedic screw plate that might be used to identify her.

Investigators, including authors Dupras, Wheeler, and Williams, proceeded to search the area using multiple search techniques. First, the area was searched using a strip or line search method. During this time, investigators looked for any signs of burial depression, and also for the descriptors that Smith had mentioned. After the visual search was conducted, a metal detector was used to scan the area, because Smith had described that he used strips of metal to cover Lisa's body. Survey flags were used to mark any metal detector alerts. The last search technique used was a cadaver dog. The combination of all these search techniques indicated a particular area within the wooded lot. At this point, the area was marked with flagging tape and the surface was cleared of debris (Figure 8.13). All the debris removed from the surface was then screened so that no possible evidence would be overlooked (Figure 8.14).

Figure 8.13 After completing the search, the initial work area was delineated by survey tape. Investigators then cleared the surface of any debris. Survey flags mark the areas where the metal detector alerted to a target.

Figure 8.14 Author Lana Williams (left) and a crime scene investigator screen all the debris from the surface.

After clearing the surface, a grid was set up over the area (Figure 8.15) and excavation proceeded. It was not long before several strips of metal (Figure 8.16) were revealed. At each stage, the scene was documented with photos and evidence was mapped on plan (Figure 8.17) and section drawings. After the metal strips were documented and removed, excavations continued, and it was not long before the skeletal remains were revealed. One particularly important piece of evidence, a tooth, was

Figure 8.15 After clearing the area, a grid was established over the area. Letters were placed along the baseline, and numbers were placed along the reference number line to identify each grid square.

Figure 8.16 Excavation with trowels revealed several pieces of metal.

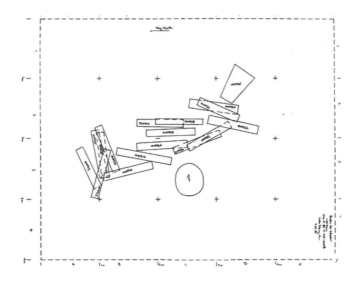

Figure 8.17 Field plan drawing showing the placement of the metal strips in relation to the large tree.

discovered in the thoracic region (Figure 8.18). This tooth may have been missed had improper excavation techniques been employed. Although Smith had done his best to remove all dental evidence, the tooth must have fallen out of the skull as he removed it, and because it was a similar color to the surrounding burial soil, he did not see it. Although not enough to make a dental identification, this tooth was later used for DNA analysis and was the one piece of evidence that enabled a positive identification of Lisa's remains.

Excavations proceeded until the entire skeleton was exposed (Figure 8.19). Once the skeleton was completely uncovered, some of the details of Smith's description were confirmed. For example, the position of the skeleton was such that the skull would have been beside or slightly under a large tree root. In addition, both the skull and the right leg were missing. Detailed plan and section drawings of the skeleton were produced before the skeleton was removed (Figures 8.20 and 8.21). After removal, the skeleton was brought to the local Medical Examiner's Office for further analysis. Lisa's remains were positively identified and then returned to her family. Smith's original death sentence was reduced to a life sentence.

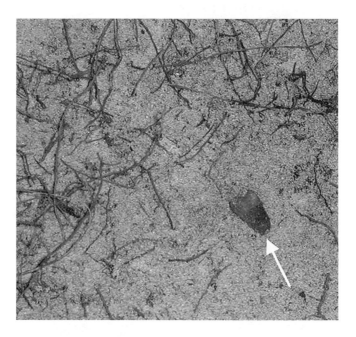

Figure 8.18 The single tooth (arrow) recovered from Lisa Brighton's grave.

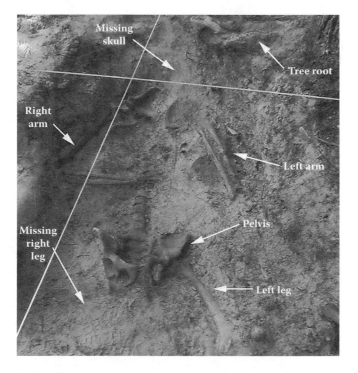

Figure 8.19 The exposed remains of Lisa Brighton. Note the missing skull and right leg.

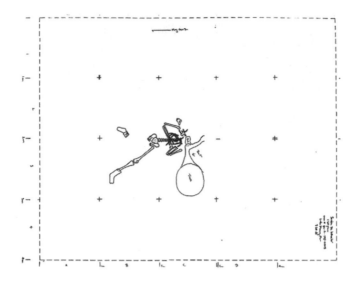

Figure 8.20 Field plan drawing showing the position of Lisa Brighton's remains in relation to the tree.

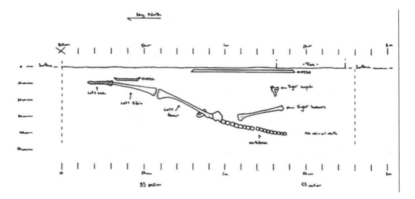

Figure 8.21 Field cross-sectional drawing showing the position of Lisa Brighton's remains in the surface depression used for burial.

Key Words and Questions

association
bioturbation
burial cut
burial outline
compaction
context
depression
feature

geotaphonomy
in situ
intrusion
provenience
reversal
sedimentation
soil
soil horizon
stratigraphy
superposition
tool marks

1. Explain how you would identify clayey, silty, and sandy soils. How would you determine their consistency? Why is this important to record in your excavation notes?
2. During the recovery of a surface deposit located in a ravine, an investigator sat down nearby on a large boulder to have lunch. While seated, he reached down and pulled at a root that was sticking out of the ground and a bone that appeared to be a human ulna popped out of the silty surface soil. What events should occur (after lunch, of course) surrounding the recording and recovery of this newly discovered evidence?
3. Based on information obtained from a suspect, a reference grid was established over an area thought to contain a grave. The soil within the reference grid and across the recovery area is weak, very moist, and has a high percentage of clay content. While clearing away surface debris, you discover a bullet. In the suspect's statement, there was mention of at least seven bullets being fired at the scene. What events should occur to record and recover this evidence and any additional evidence of this type? What precautions should be put in place to avoid damaging this type of evidence?
4. During the recording of a skeleton that was exposed during excavation, you discover that there is a second skeleton located directly beneath the first individual. How would you proceed with the excavation of the first individual? What events should occur concerning the second individual?
5. You are assisting with the removal of a skeletonized individual in a grave over 80 centimeters (2.5 feet) deep. What steps can you take to safely recover the remains and continue with the excavation after their recovery? What evidence should be recorded before these steps are taken?

Suggested Readings

Hochrein, M.J. 2002. Autopsy of the grave: recognizing, collecting, and preserving forensic geotaphonomic evidence. In: Haglund, W.D., Sorg, M.H., eds. *Advances in Forensic Taphonomy: Method, Theory, and Archaeological Perspectives*, pp. 45–70. Boca Raton, FL: CRC Press.

Ruffell, A., Donnelly, C., Carver, N., Murphy, E., Murray, E., McCambridge, J. 2009. Suspect burial excavation procedure: a cautionary tale. *Forensic Science International* 183:e11–e16.

Spennemann, D.H.R., Franke, B. 1995. Archaeological techniques for exhumations: a unique data source for crime scene investigations. *Forensic Science International* 74:5–15.

Stewart, M. 2002. *Archaeology: Basic Field Methods*. Dubuque, IA: Kendall Hunt.

References

Bock, J.H., Norris, D.O. 1997. Forensic botany: an underutilized resource. *Journal of Forensic Sciences* 42:364–367.

Connor, M., Scott, D.D. 2001. Paradigms and perpetrators. *Historical Archaeology* 35(1):1–6.

Davis, J. 1992. Forensic archaeology. *Archaeology Review from Cambridge* 11:151–156.

Dirkmaat, D.C., Adovasio, J.M. 1997. The role of archaeology in the recovery and interpretation of human remains from an outdoor forensic setting. In: Haglund, W.D., Sorg, M.H., eds. *Forensic Taphonomy: The Postmortem Fate of Human Remains*, pp. 39–64. Boca Raton, FL: CRC Press.

Hester, T.J., Shafer, H., Feder, K. 2008. *Field Methods in Archaeology*, 7th ed. Walnut Creek, CA: Left Coast Press.

Hochrein, M.J. 1997a. Buried crime scene evidence: the application of geotaphonomy in forensic archaeology. In: Stimson, P., and Mertz, C., eds. *Forensic Dentistry*, pp. 83–99. Boca Raton, FL: CRC Press.

Hochrein, M.J. 1997b. The dirty dozen: the recognition and collection of tool-marks in the forensic geotaphonomic record. *Journal of Forensic Identification* 47:171–198.

Hochrein, M.J. 2002. Autopsy of the grave: recognizing, collecting, and preserving forensic geotaphonomic evidence. In: Haglund, W.D., Sorg, M.H., eds. *Advances in Forensic Taphonomy: Method, Theory, and Archaeological Perspectives*, pp. 45–70. Boca Raton, FL: CRC Press.

International Agency for Research on Cancer. 2006. Formaldehyde, 2-Butoxyethanol and 1-tert-Butoxypropan-2-ol. In: IARC Monographs on the Evaluation of Carcinogenic Risks to Humans 88, pp. 39–325. Lyon, France: International Agency for Research on Cancer.

Killam, E.W. 2004. *The Detection of Human Remains*, 2nd ed. Springfield, IL: Charles C. Thomas.

Micozzi, M.S. 1991. *Postmortem Changes in Human and Animal Remains, a Systematic Approach*. Springfield, IL: Charles C. Thomas.

Morse, D., Duncan, J., Stoutamire, J. 1983. *Handbook of Forensic Archaeology and Anthropology.* Tallahassee, FL: Rose.

Roskams, S. 2001. *Excavation, Cambridge Manuals in Archaeology.* Cambridge: Cambridge University Press.

Snow, C.C. 1982. Forensic anthropology. *Annual Reviews in Anthropology* 11:97–131.

Soil Survey Staff. 2010. *Keys to Soil Taxonomy,* 11th ed. Washington, DC: USDA–Natural Resources Conservation Service.

Willey, P., Heilman, A. 1987. Estimating time since death using plant roots and stems. *Journal of Forensic Sciences* 32:1264–1270.

Collecting Botanical and Entomological Evidence

9

Within the United States and around the world, forensic botanists and forensic entomologists are being called upon with increasing frequency as vital members of criminal and medicolegal investigation teams. When properly collected, preserved, and analyzed by an experienced and trained team member, plant and insect evidence gathered from and around human remains can provide some of the most valuable information concerning the victim's death. In particular, both can provide important information in determining manner and locality of death and time since death or postmortem interval (PMI).

We recognize that experts in these areas of specialization are not always readily available to assist in recovery during an investigation. Therefore, the primary aim of this chapter is to familiarize the reader with the kinds of botanical and entomological evidence that may be present in a forensic context. In addition, we included appropriate collection procedures with the intent of an expert later examining and interpreting the evidence. It is essential that qualified plant or insect taxonomists or a certified forensic botanist or forensic entomologist should make any species or PMI determinations for forensic casework. If further references are needed for field documentation or collection procedures, the following are written by specialists within each field: *Forensic Botany: Principles and Applications to Criminal Casework* edited by Heather Miller Coyle (2004a), *Forensic Entomology: An Introduction* by Dorothy Gennard (2007), and *Forensic Entomology: The Utility of Arthropods in Legal Investigations* edited by Jason Byrd and James Castner (2010a).

9.1 Forensic Botany

Forensic botany uses plant life to gain information pertinent to legal investigations and to answer questions regarding possible crimes (Bock and Norris, 1997; Coyle, 2004b). The use of botanical evidence in legal investigations is relatively recent. It has been suggested that the first botanical testimony to be heard in a North American court concerned the analysis of the wood from the ladder used in the kidnapping of Charles Lindbergh Jr., and led to the conviction of Bruno Hauptmann for the crime in 1935 (Gardner, 2004).

Today, forensic botany can include many subdisciplines of plant science, such as dendrochronology, limnology, palynology, and molecular biology (Coyle, 2004b). Botanical evidence can be found in a wide variety of crime scenes, and knowledge of plant locality, seasonality, and life cycle can be used to reconstruct key elements of the scene or validate a suspect's alibi (Ladd and Lee, 2004). Forensic botany can also assist in clarifying the circumstances surrounding a homicide and those involved (Lane et al., 1990). The identification of plant remains adhered to clothing or pollen granules in the respiratory tract may be used to trace a victim's last steps, or if the botanical remains are not native to the area where the body was recovered they may indicate the victim's region of origin (Ashage and Caulton, 2009). The determination of PMI is another area in which botanical material can provide significant information. In particular, tree roots can be used to determine the length of time a body has been in a specific environment (Willey and Heilman, 1987), and certain types of seeds can indicate when a body was moved from one location to another (Gunn, 2009).

9.1.1   Sources of Botanical Evidence

Sources of botanical evidence are highly dependent on the type of crime being investigated and the location of the crime scene. Some types of botanical evidence are easier to identify, such as leaves that have been damaged or removed from a plant during the process of burial or broken branches used to conceal a body. Other types of botanical evidence are not as easily distinguished, for instance, plant materials that are foreign to the crime scene or seeds and pollen that are displaced from plants in the vicinity.

9.1.1.1   *Macrobotanicals*

For most cases involving botanical evidence, the plant material can be seen with the naked eye and typically does not require magnification for analysis. This type of botanical evidence is referred to as macrobotanicals.

9.1.1.1.1   Woody Plants   Woody plants share a common trait of annual secondary growth, or growth rings, being recorded in their tissues. These growth rings occur because growth cells, or xylem cells, become progressively smaller as the growth season leads into the dormant season (Willey and Heilman, 1987). Following the dormant season, there is an abrupt change in cell size from small to large, which makes the growth rings visible in wood. This means that even though a woody plant may no longer be increasing in length or height, its trunks, branches, and roots are still capable of increase in girth. The number of growth rings provides the plant's age, and the variation in the width of each ring reflects the environmental conditions during its growth. The study of tree ring patterns is called dendrochronology. Dendrochronology does not involve counting tree rings but rather comparing ring patterns among trees or wood products. As mentioned earlier, during the case involving the kidnapping of Charles Lindbergh Jr., the annual ring pattern in the wood used to construct the ladder was matched to that of a shortened floorboard found in Bruno Hauptmann's attic (Gardner, 2004).

Roots from woody plants also exhibit growth rings that can be used to estimate PMI (Willey and Heilman, 1987). For example, when a grave is dug, the roots from surrounding plants can be disturbed or damaged but still continue growing. In most cases, this will leave a permanent scar, and any growth rings that form after the scar may indicate the number of growing seasons that have passed since the damage occurred (Quatrehomme et al., 1997). In addition, roots found in direct contact with the remains or personal items can be cross-sectioned at the point of contact to determine the number of growth rings present, establishing a minimum PMI estimate. When using this method, the roots must have penetrated the clothing, bones, or other evidence in order for the estimate to be valid (Willey and Heilman, 1987). For example, if a root grew through the nasal opening of a skull (see Figure 5.10) and the cross-section of the root revealed five growth rings, the PMI estimate would be at least five years. The actual PMI could be much longer because there is no way to know how long the body was buried before the root grew into the skeletal remains. Annual longitudinal growth has also been used to estimate PMI by measuring the length of the root from its point of contact with the remains, to its originating end in the plant root system (Quatrehomme et al., 1997). However, this method requires expert analysis by a forensic botanist who specializes in the specific plant type and geographic region associated with the remains.

9.1.1.1.2 Flowers, Fruits, and Seeds Many plants only flower once a year and form their fruits and seeds over a restricted period of time, providing good temporal evidence if they are found in association with human remains. Flowers tend to fall near the parent plant, and dried or rotten flower fragments can easily become adhered to clothing, shoes, or tools. Plant fruits and seeds are relatively large, may be produced in quantity, and for the most part tend to fall close to their parent plant. Many fruits and seeds have casings with hooked spines called burs that cause them to cling to an individual or animal passing by the parent plant. When recovering human remains, special attention should be paid to the cuffs of clothing and the seams or welds in shoes. Any adhered plant material may contain evidence that was transferred from a different location. For example, if remains were found with a shirt that has many small goosegrass (*Galium aparine*) burs attached to the cuffs and back, it would indicate that the individual was recently in an area where goosegrass was seeding. However, if the remains were found in an area where goosegrass was not present, it would indicate that the body had been moved to a different location.

Some fruits and seeds may disappear via animal consumption or germination, but the fruit or seed casings may still be evident. For example, Conker, or horse-chestnut, trees (*Aesculus hippocastanum*) produce seeds that have a soft, spiky outer casing that easily peels away from the seed during consumption or falls away when the seed germinates. If a body is found near a Conker tree and has empty mature casings on top of it, the body would have been present beneath the tree before autumn, when the seeds usually drop from the tree. Taking into account the condition of the remains (i.e., decomposing soft tissue or skeletonized remains), it may be possible that more than one year of seed casings may have accumulated; however, if some of the seeds have germinated over the remains, it may be possible to estimate the number of years past based on the growth of the seedling plants.

In some instances, a plant's reproductive strategy may depend on the fruit of the plant being consumed by animals and the seeds being disbursed in the animals' fecal material. Most fruits digest easily, while the cellulose in leaves or seed casings is much more resistant to gastric breakdown (e.g., kaffir lime leaves, watermelon seeds), allowing these structures to pass through the gut without much change in morphology. During the recovery of human remains, fecal matter should be carefully collected as it may contain undigested evidence of foods eaten shortly before death, some of which may be indicative of specific types of cuisine or seasonally available foods.

9.1.1.1.3 Fungi Fungi are one of the largest and most heterogeneous plants, with a wide range of habitats and forms. They lack chlorophyll and can grow in dry or wet conditions. The majority of fungi, such as mushrooms, toadstools, molds, rusts, and smuts, are multicellular organisms consisting of long filaments called hyphae. Yeasts, another form of fungi, are unicellular and consist of long, thin buds called pseudohyphae. It is widely accepted that there are over 1.5 million species of fungi in the world (Stephenson, 2010).

Most fungi are saprophytic (i.e., they feed on dead organic matter) and are associated with all stages of human decomposition from immediately after death to the skeletonized or mummified remains (Said al Na'imi, 2008). It has been suggested that some fungi species can be used as indicators of clandestine graves and in the estimation of PMI (Hitosugi et al., 2006). While fungal growth on decomposing human remains in outdoor settings has provided positive results in PMI estimation, there is great debate concerning which species of fungi should be considered when found in association with decomposing human remains, as geographic location and environmental conditions must be taken into account (Hitosugi et al., 2006; Menezes et al., 2008; Said al Na'imi, 2008).

Fungal spores, which are produced in large numbers like pollen, have morphological traits that allow species identification by a forensic botanist. Some fungi have very restricted habitats and ecological requirements, which dictates production of spores during certain seasons of the year. The presence of these types of spores may be useful in associating a person with a specific location or crime scene. However, it is important to remember that certain types of blowflies (e.g., *Calliphora*), which often contribute important entomological evidence to PMI estimates, can also distribute fungal spores and, in some instances, may be fungal breeders (Gunn, 2009).

9.1.1.2 Microbotanicals

In many cases, human remains may not have any readily apparent associated botanical evidence. However, as forensic methods of investigation and analyses improve, the collection of microbotanicals is becoming more prevalent. Microbotanicals are plant remains that cannot be seen with the naked eye and require some form of magnification for analysis. Most microbotanicals are collected during autopsy or in the laboratory rather than at the scene, but it is important for investigators to understand the various sources and the kinds of information they can provide.

9.1.1.2.1 Pollens Forensic palynology, a subdiscipline of forensic botany, uses pollen and spores as evidence in legal investigations (Ashage and Caulton, 2009; Milne et al., 2004). Although the full potential of forensic palynology remains underutilized and ignored in some instances, it can provide associative evidence to establish or disprove links among people, places, and objects (Horrocks et al., 1998; Milne et al., 2004). It can also help determine where drugs, food, and merchandise originated and where gardening tools have been used (Agashe and Caulton, 2009; Milne et al., 2004).

Pollen grains are very small particles that vary in shape, structure, color, and ornamentation pattern. The volume of pollen released from a plant is related to its mode of pollination. Autogamous and cleistogamous, or self-pollinating, plants produce very few pollen grains and are rarely encountered in forensic cases because of the reduced sample size (Milne et al., 2004). Anemophilous, or wind-pollinating, plants can produce tens of thousands of pollen grains per flower, some of which have air sacs that aid in dispersal (Milne et al., 2004). In this instance, so many grains of pollen are formed that any object within the general area will be affected by "pollen rain." In addition, this type of pollen is commonly breathed in and can be recovered from the respiratory system during autopsy (Agashe and Caulton, 2009). Cannabis plants (*Cannabis sativa*) are an example of anemophilous plants. If grown in enclosed spaces, these plants will disburse pollen across every surface area and on the clothing of anyone who enters the space (Agashe and Caulton, 2009; Milne et al., 2004). The presence of these plants can also be detected long after they have been removed, as the pollen granules can be found in air filters, cracks and crevices, and door hinges (Milne et al., 2004).

Zoogamous (animal-pollinating) plants release much more pollen than autogamous plants, but not nearly as much as anemophilous plants (Milne et al., 2004). Zoogamous pollen is particularly useful in a forensic context, because direct contact between the plant, object, person of interest, or pollinator is necessary for the pollen to transfer. If a relatively large volume of zoogamous pollen is collected in a forensic sample, it is most likely not from environmental contamination and can be used as a method of pinpointing a particular location (Milne et al., 2004). For example, although dandelions (*Taraxacum* spp.) and foxglove (*Digitalis pururea*) are plants morphologically suited to insect pollination, the pollen from these plants is typically only found close to the parent plants (Agashe and Caulton, 2009; Wiltshire, 2006). If both of these pollens are detected on a person's clothing, the individual either had direct contact with the plants or the soil in their vicinity. For this reason, it is often possible to be very specific about where a person or thing has been from the pollen types that occur together in a sample. Because many types of pollen are produced seasonally and can be readily identified, they have great forensic potential. However, forensic palynology has its limitations. It can be very difficult to identify some kinds of pollen at a species level. In addition, some species of plants take years to mature and produce pollen; therefore, a pollen profile may not fully represent the plant species present in a suspected area of activity.

9.1.1.2.2 Algae and Diatoms Algae are a large and diverse group of simple organisms ranging from unicellular to multicellular forms. Although algae are commonly found in most terrestrial and aquatic ecosystems, the major group of unicellular forms known as diatoms tends to be used as evidence in forensic cases. Diatoms are characterized by uniquely patterned cell walls made of silica, which are called frustules. There are approximately 100,000 species of living diatoms (Graham et al., 2008), each with a specialized frustule design that facilitates their identification by a forensic botanist. They occur in virtually every environment that contains water, including oceans, seas, lakes, streams, and soils in moist terrestrial habitats. Most live in open water, but some live as surface films at a water–sediment interface, such as tidal pools or lakebeds. The relative abundance and species composition at various locations is dependent on temperature, salinity, pH, and available nutrients.

The presence of individual species or combinations of diatoms or algal growth in a forensic sample, whether taken from water sources, soils, or associated clothing, can provide investigators with valuable information about a specific type of habitat or locality at a particular time of year, information concerning manner of death and PMI, and possibly connect a suspect to a victim or to a crime scene. Relative densities of diatoms in an individual's lungs, stomach, major organs, and bone marrow have been used as an indication that the victim may have drowned (Hürlimann et al., 2000). By comparing the diatoms found in the victim's tissues during autopsy with those sampled from a suspected water source or body of water where the remains were recovered, it may be possible to provide corroborating evidence on the locality of the drowning (Ludes et al., 1999). For example, freshwater diatoms found in remains recovered from a marine environment would indicate that the victim most likely died at a different location. However, diatoms may also enter into tissues due to degradation during prolonged submersion of remains in water (Krstic et al., 2002). Furthermore, diatoms are also found in many manufactured products, such as insect repellents, foodstuff, and construction materials. Therefore, diatoms may be aspirated or ingested from additional kinds of material contact and would consequently be found in tissues of persons who died from some manner other than drowning (Yen and Jayaprakash, 2007). Yet, even in these instances, information about proximity to certain types of contaminants or specific foodstuffs encountered or ingested during life could be helpful to an investigation. Diatom composition of mud and lake soils found on clothing, footwear, or a motor vehicle has been used to associate or disassociate a suspect with a crime scene (Siver et al., 1994). It has been suggested that rates of algal growth are a potential means of estimating the amount of time remains or associated objects have been submerged (Haefner et al., 2004). In addition, the presence and density of blue-green algae, more correctly known as cyanobacteria, has received some attention in estimating the length of time that bones have been exposed to the natural environment (Haglund et al., 1988).

9.1.2   Collecting and Preserving Botanical Evidence

Even though it is recommended that a forensic botanist be directly involved in the collection and preservation of botanical evidence, this is not always possible. If this is the case, all botanical evidence collected at the scene should be transported to an expert for identification or analysis as soon as possible. During collection, every effort should be made to avoid possible contamination of samples. All collecting equipment, including soil corers, root clippers, and plankton nets, must be scrupulously cleaned before use. Many of the microbotanicals discussed above will require collection during autopsy. It is recommended that items such as clothing or shoes be handled with extreme care at the point of recovery and bagged immediately to avoid any cross-contamination with pollens or soil diatoms. In addition, the location and condition of any botanical evidence must be thoroughly documented prior to its collection. Written documentation should include a brief description of the material's original condition and any other relevant information, such as the location of any nearby flowering plants or shrubs, broken tree branches, trampled areas, and plants bearing seeds or fruits. Photos should be taken of the surrounding landscape and of any botanical evidence prior to collection.

Fresh leaves or other vegetation should be placed into individual paper bags that are labeled with the date, time of collection, coordinates of the location, and the case number or investigator's name. Larger forms of botanical evidence, such as tree branches or roots, should be individually tagged and photographed prior to removing them from the scene.

Larger forms of fungi, such as mushrooms or toadstools, located around the grave or surface remains should also be collected in paper bags and transported to a forensic botanist for identification as soon as possible, as the specimen will rot very quickly, especially if they are damp. Smaller fungi, such as molds and rusts, should only be collected from remains by the medical examiner or forensic pathologist. These specimens are typically identified microscopically and may need to be cultured; in some instances, they may also be identified using methods of molecular taxonomy.

Many algae and diatoms grow in seasonal blooms, which can be short-lived. Therefore, it may be necessary to take sequential seasonal samples from the suspected water source to attempt matching species composition recovered from the remains to a specific locality. In cases of freshwater sources, samples should be taken both above and below the site at which the remains were found, as there may be differences in the algal flora and water currents may have moved the remains away from the original site of deposition. Blanks, or sample vials of distilled water, should be prepared in the field and processed to test whether samples collected as evidence are free of contamination and carry over.

9.1.3 Locating a Forensic Botanist

Finding a forensic botanist is not as easy as finding a forensic archaeologist, forensic anthropologist, or forensic entomologist, each of whom have their own recognized board for certification. When choosing a forensic botanist, it is important to select an individual with a Ph.D., extensive experience in botanical taxonomy identification, and with experience in forensic casework. At the same time, it is also important to choose a specialist who is familiar with your particular geographic region. Because most forensic botanists hold positions in biology or botany departments at universities, one avenue to finding a forensic botanist is to call your local university and inquire. In addition, archaeology departments may lead to recommendations of specialists in your area who also work with local cultural resource management firms. Many specialists advertise their services, so an Internet search may help in locating someone in your area; however, we recommend further inquiries as to the person's qualifications just as you would for any professional.

9.2 Forensic Entomology

Forensic entomology uses information about insects to answer questions pertinent to the investigation of legal cases, although on occasion the term may be expanded to include other arthropods, such as spiders, centipedes, or scorpions (Byrd and Castner, 2010b; Gennard, 2007). The use of entomological evidence in forensic casework is not a recent development. The first known report of its use is from China during the mid-10th century (Greenberg and Kunich, 2002). In fact, the use of insects as evidence in death investigation gained such importance by the 13th century that it was included in a training manual, *The Washing Away of Wrongs*, written by Sung Tz'u (translated by McKnight, 1981). It was not until the late 19th century that the value of the relationship between human decomposition and the succession of insects colonizing a body after death was fully realized with the publication of *La Faune des Cadavres: Application de l'Entomologie à la Médicine Légale* by Mégnin (1894). Since then, many insect and arthropod species have provided forensic evidence concerning time since death, season of death, geographic location of death, movement or storage of remains, specific sites of trauma on the body, sexual molestation, the use of drugs, and DNA analysis (Catts and Haskell, 1990; Gennard, 2007; Goff, 2000). Two principal approaches are used to obtain this information. The first involves the life cycle of insects, which is influenced by temperature and environment, and the second concerns the generally predictable patterns of colonization during decomposition (Hall and Huntington, 2010).

9.2.1 Insect Life Cycle

The identification and collection of insect life stages, specifically those of flies and beetles, will assist in a calculation of the number of insect generations, thus allowing for a more precise determination of PMI. Insects develop in stages, starting with an egg and ending as an adult. The metamorphosis in physical appearance and the time spent in each stage differ among species and with environmental conditions. For example, in high temperatures, early developmental stages become much shorter in interval, which is why collection of weather data is an integral part of entomological evidence. Laboratory and field studies have generated baseline developmental rates under differing temperature regimes and for various environments (e.g., Hwang and Turner, 2005).

9.2.1.1 Flies (Order Diptera)

Flies undergo a complete metamorphosis in their life cycle (Figure 9.1). The cycle starts when the adult female lays clumps of 150 to 200 eggs in protected areas near moisture and a food source. An adult female may lay several thousand eggs over the course of her life. Fly eggs are typically a shiny white and range in size from 1 to 1.5 millimeters long (Gennard, 2007). The most common locations where eggs are deposited on a body include exposed orifices (e.g., nasal passages, corners of the mouth, and the eyes), open wounds, folds of clothing located near wounds or the face, hair in contact with the ground, and sheltered areas formed by the ground–body interface (Catts and Haskell, 1990). As a result, these areas will decompose faster than other areas because of insect colonization. After the eggs are laid, they will hatch within a few hours giving rise to the first of three larval stages, or instars, which are more commonly referred to as maggots (Figure 9.2). Although the size of larvae is dependent on the amount and quality of food available, the first instar tends to be less than 2 millimeters long, while the second instar is 2 to 9 millimeters long, and the third instar can be up to 22 millimeters in length (Green et al., 2003). During the third instar, the mature larvae finish feeding and migrate away from the remains toward somewhat dark and cooler areas. Mature larvae have been known to migrate up to 6 meters from decomposing remains in an outdoor setting (Gennard, 2007). The larvae then burrow into the soil, folds of clothing, or floor coverings and enter the pupal stage, where a hardened outer casing, known as the puparium, develops from the larval exoskeleton. Over time, the puparium shrinks, hardens, and darkens in color

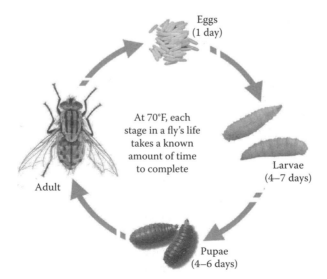

Eggs
(1 day)

At 70°F, each
stage in a fly's life
takes a known
amount of time
to complete

Adult

Larvae
(4–7 days)

Pupae
(4–6 days)

Figure 9.1 Life cycle of a fly in optimum environmental conditions.

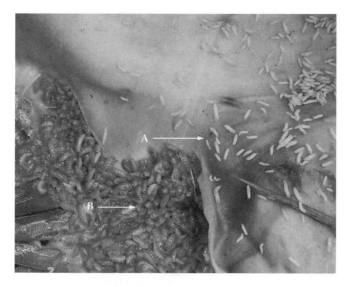

Figure 9.2 Fly larvae (maggot) development on a decomposing pig cadaver. Different instar stages of development are present: (a) younger larvae and (b) older larvae.

from brown, to reddish brown, to almost black. The adult fly emerges up through the soil after several days of development, leaving behind the empty puparial case, and successive life cycles continue as newly hatched females lay eggs on the remains after copulation. In optimal conditions, adult flies emerge from the pupae completing the process of egg to adult in about 7 to 10 days, with adult flies usually living from a few weeks to several months (Gennard, 2007; Gunn, 2009).

9.2.1.2   Beetles (Order Coleoptera)

Beetles also undergo complete metamorphosis, developing through an egg stage, multiple larval stages (environment and species dependent), and a pupal stage before becoming an adult (Figure 9.3). Beetle eggs tend to be oval or spherical in shape and are often hidden in protected areas. The larvae are not readily visible and are often found underground or under the remains in areas soaked with decomposition fluids. Beetle larvae can be distinguished from other insect larvae by their minute legs and hardened, often darkened head with pincer-like mandibles (Figure 9.4). In some cases, as in the rove beetle, the larvae are extremely mobile and forage for their own food source, while in other species, like the carrion beetle, adults must still care for larvae until they are mature (Castner, 2010; Gennard, 2007). Beetle larvae dig into the ground or move to a protected area to pupate, with puparial casings changing from light yellowish in color to a darker brown as they mature. Most species of beetle reproduce only once a year. The length of the life cycle can vary

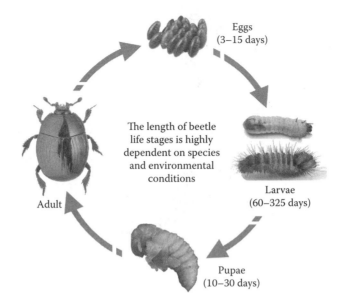

Figure 9.3 Average life cycle of a beetle.

Figure 9.4 Fly larva (left) and beetle larva (right) are different in many ways. In particular, beetle larvae have pairs of legs and readily visible chewing or pinching mouthparts.

greatly, with some species developing from egg to adult in 7 to 10 days (e.g., rove beetles) and others taking up to a year and living for another two to three years after reaching adulthood (e.g., dung beetle) (Castner, 2010; Gennard, 2007). Beetle frass, or adult beetle feces, appears as dry and crumbly brownish strands and may be used by some experts in determination of PMI.

9.2.2 Insects Significant to the Recovery of Human Remains

Numerous entomological species are attracted to human remains with the purpose of feeding on the decaying tissues, preying on other insects and their larvae, and consuming feces from the remains and any larger scavenging animals, or frass from the insect colony. Table 9.1 contains a summary of insects commonly associated with decomposing human remains and their generally predictable pattern of colonization. Insects typically not associated with the decay process may become trapped in clothing or, alternatively, inside wrappings or a container in which the body is placed. Some insects have a restricted geographical distribution, are associated with very specific habitats, or are active at only specific times of year and can provide evidence of association with a particular locality at a particular time. In addition, insects can also have an antemortem association with the individual due to unsanitary living conditions. In order to ensure that all possible evidence is collected and preserved, it is recommended that the reader become familiar with which insects colonize human remains and also know something about their habits and environments. Unless otherwise noted, the following descriptions are based on the work of Byrd and Castner (2010b) and Gennard (2007).

9.2.2.1 Detritivores

Detritivores are organisms that obtain nutrients by consuming decomposing organic matter. Human remains represent an accessible source of food for detritivorous insects. These insects rapidly consume the easily degradable tissues until there is not enough material left to support their high reproductive rates and short life cycles. The following are brief descriptions of some of the more common detritivores associated with human remains. Figure 9.5 shows a number of detritivores commonly associated with human remains.

9.2.2.1.1 Blowfly (Family Calliphoridae) This group of flies contains over 1,000 species and can be found worldwide around trash and wastes during warmer seasons of the year (Byrd and Castner, 2010b). Blowflies are attracted to decomposing tissues and are usually the first insects to arrive at a corpse, colonizing remains that are fresh or at the early stages of decomposition. They are the most important species in providing information relating to accurate estimation of PMI, as they have been recorded arriving at remains within minutes of their exposure (Byrd and Castner, 2010b). Adult

Table 9.1   Summary of Most Common Insects Associated with Human Remains

Flies (Diptera)	
Blowfly	• Lay eggs during early stages of decay
	• Larvae feed during early, active, and late stages of decay
Flesh fly	• Lay larvae during early and late stages of decay
	• Larvae feed during all stages of decay
House and latrine fly	• Lay eggs in wounds or on soiled clothing and feces
	• Larvae feed on feces and liquefied regions of remains
Scuttle fly	• Lay eggs during early and late stages of decay
	• Larvae feed during all stages of decay
	• Can colonize buried bodies
Skipper fly	• Lay eggs at end of active decay and start of drying stage
	• Larvae feed at end of active decay and through dry stage
Soldier fly	• Lay eggs at start of drying stage
	• Larvae feed through dry stage
	• Can colonize buried bodies
Beetles (Coleoptera)	
Carrion beetle	• Lay eggs during early stage of decay
	• Adults and larvae feed on remains and other insects or larvae
Clown beetle	• Lay eggs during early and late stages of decay
	• Adults feed on larvae; larvae feed on remains and other larvae
Rove beetle	• Lay eggs during early and late stages of decay
	• Adults and larvae feed on remains and other insects or larvae
Hide and skin beetle	• Lay eggs at start of drying stage
	• Adults and larvae feed on remains
Wasps	• Lay eggs in larvae and pupae of flies
	• Feed on other insects and remains in early stages of decay
Ants	• Predatory on other insects and larvae
	• Adults feed on remains during early stages of decay
Moths	• Lay eggs at start of drying stage
	• Larvae feed through dry stage

Source: Adapted from Gunn, A. 2009. *Essentials of Forensic Biology.* Hoboken, NJ: Wiley-Blackwell.

Note: Insects may arrive or depart earlier or later depending on individual circumstances of decomposition process.

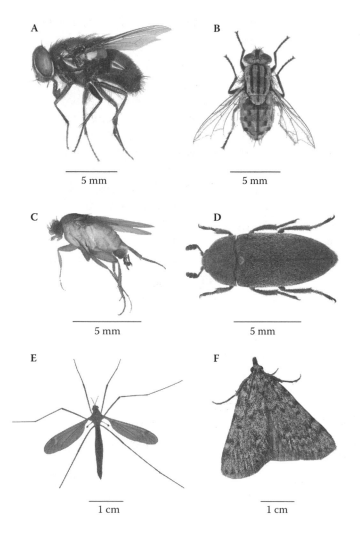

Figure 9.5 Detrivorous insects commonly associated with human remains: (a) blowfly, (b) flesh fly, (c) scuttle fly, (d) larder beetle, (e) crane fly, and (f) clothes moth.

flies range in size from 6 to 14 millimeters in length with the adult size being dependent on species and availability of food during larval stages. Most adult blowflies are a brilliant metallic blue or green in color, commonly called blue bottle or green bottle flies, with bristly bodies and large reddish eyes. Some species also exhibit a metallic bronze or shiny black hue. Adult females tend to lay their eggs in natural body openings and in areas of trauma, causing uneven tissue removal during decomposition. Although the adult flies may feed on dried remains, the females will not lay eggs in conditions with little to no moisture. In some species, the larvae may be predatory and cannibalistic of other larvae. Mature larvae are 8 to 23 millimeters long, ranging in color from white or cream to a darker grayish brown, and may have prominent fleshy protrusions along their body.

9.2.2.1.2   Flesh Fly (Family Sarcophagidae)   Over 2,000 species of flesh flies are found throughout the world, most of which are found in tropical or warmer climates (Castner et al., 1995). These flies are active in wet weather, unlike blowflies, and as a result, are also among the first insects to colonize human remains. They can be found on decomposing tissues during both the early and late stages of decomposition and are also commonly found on remains located indoors. Adult flesh flies are medium sized, ranging in length from 2 to 14 millimeters, have brightly colored eyes, and are grayish in color with dark stripes or a checkerboard pattern. In contrast with other flies, they do not lay eggs (Byrd and Castner, 2010b). Flesh fly eggs develop in the female fly's reproductive tract and are laid as first instar larvae. The larvae range from white to yellowish in color and from 3 to 19 millimeters in length.

9.2.2.1.3   Scuttle Fly (Family Phoridae)   There are over 2,500 species of scuttle flies known worldwide (Disney, 1994). Scuttle flies are small, about 1.5 to 6 millimeters in length, and run rapidly in erratic patterns (i.e., scuttling motion) before taking flight. Adults may be grayish-brown, blue, or yellow in color and are easily recognizable by their humpbacked appearance, giving them an alternate name of "humpback flies" (Byrd and Castner, 2010b). The larvae are somewhat flattened in appearance and have a pair of horns on the anterior end. Some species are predacious or parasitic, but most typically develop in human, animal, or vegetative decomposing matter. Several species are also known as coffin flies, which burrow through soil and colonize buried remains up to 100 centimeters deep (Byrd and Castner, 2010b). Coffin flies have also been known to congregate on the soil surface of graves, making them a possible indicator when locating buried remains (Byrd and Castner, 2010b).

9.2.2.1.4   Skipper Fly (Family Piophilidae)   There are only 69 known species of skipper flies found throughout the world (Byrd and Castner, 2010b). They are usually associated with human remains at the end of active decay when the remains are starting to dry out. The adults are 2.5 to 4.5 millimeters long and shiny black in color but in certain light may appear as metallic blue or green. The larvae may grow up to 10 millimeters in length and are much thinner than typical blowfly larvae. Some species are more commonly referred to as "cheese skippers" due to the mature larvae's ability to bend round and grasp their posterior with mouth hooks, quickly release their grip, and snap or leap up to 15 centimeters into the air and almost twice as far in distance (Gennard, 2007).

9.2.2.1.5   Soldier Fly (Family Stratiomyidae)   More than 250 species of soldier flies are found worldwide, with the adult flies ranging in size from 5 to 20 millimeters (Byrd and Castner, 2010b). They tend to colonize remains after blowfly activity has declined, during the late and dry stages of decomposition. Adult soldier flies are brightly colored with dorsal spines on their body and are sometime referred to as "wasp flies" because of their similarities in appearance and behavior. The larvae vary greatly in size, from 4 to 40 millimeters in length, and have a flattened, segmented appearance with coarse hairs on each body segment. They can be found in both aquatic and terrestrial environments, depending on the species. More mature larvae are gray to brown in color, with a hard, leathery surface, and are commonly found on buried bodies or in the soil under surface deposits (Lord et al., 1994).

9.2.2.1.6 Hide, Skin, Carpet, and Larder Beetles (Family Dermestidae) Over 500 species of dermestid beetles are found throughout the world (Byrd and Castner, 2010b). They are somewhat small, ranging in size from 2 to 12 millimeters in length, with an elongated, oval shape. Some adults may have distinctive colorful patterns across their body. Their life cycles are strongly influenced by environmental conditions, at times experiencing over six instar larval stages. The larvae, commonly called "woolly bears," are approximately 5 to 15 millimeters long and are brown to black in color with dense tufts of hair of varying length over their body (Gennard, 2007). Dermestid beetles are known to quickly skeletonize remains that have started to dry out. The larvae are found on remains during dry and skeletal stages of decomposition, typically away from light and in available cavities or recesses. Adult dermestid beetles are cannibalistic of their own eggs and larvae, as well as other species, and should be kept separate when collecting specimens. The presence of sawdust-like frass indicates that adults have been feeding on tissues for an extended period of time, and it is frequently found on remains from indoor environments (Byrd and Castner, 2010b).

9.2.2.1.7 Winter Crane Fly and Winter Gnat (Family Trichoceroidae) Approximately 110 species of these cold-hardy flies, also commonly called "daddy long leg flies," can be found around the world (Erzinçlioğlu, 1980). Winter crane flies and gnats are typically seen in wet or cold environments. They tend to be active in the cooler months of the year, including winter, with adult males often seen swarming in clouds over open areas in late afternoon sunlight. They are often mistaken for mosquitoes because of their appearance. The adults have long slender bodies, up to 12 millimeters in length, with fine, spider-like legs and long, glassy wings. These species lay their eggs in decaying organic matter and have been known to colonize human remains when other species are no longer active due to low temperatures (Erzinçlioğlu, 1980). Their larvae are very thin and long with well-developed heads.

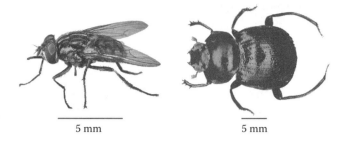

5 mm   5 mm

Figure 9.6 Coprophagous insects commonly found in association with human remains: housefly (left) and dung beetle (right).

9.2.2.1.8 Meal and Clothes Moths (Order Lepidoptera)   Adult meal and clothes moths and their larvae are sometimes associated with remains that are completely dry or skeletonized (Gunn, 2009). They tend to feed on the keratin in hair and nail and any remaining dried tissues still adhered to bone. Depending on the environmental conditions, the larval stage can last up to four years, after which the mature larvae often spin a protective silken tube around themselves to pupate.

9.2.2.2 Coprophiles

Coprophiles are organisms that consume their own feces or that of other animals. Although some insects, such as dung beetles, use feces as their primary food source, most coprophile insects also feed on other sources of decomposing organic matter. Coprophile insects usually colonize a body as a result of fouled clothing at the time of death or when gut contents are exposed through trauma or decay. Figure 9.6 shows two coprophiles commonly associated with human remains.

9.2.2.2.1 House   and   Latrine   Flies   (Family   Muscidae   and Fanniidae)   These families of flies are represented by over 4,000 species found worldwide and are closely associated with human habitats (Byrd and Castner, 2010b). These flies feed on decaying plants and animals, dung, and blood. They are commonly found around garbage, sewage, and unsanitary living conditions and are drawn to human remains if clothing is soiled with urine or feces, or if gut contents are exposed. Adult house and latrine flies are usually small, averaging between 3 and 10 millimeters in length, and dull gray in color with darker lines running down the body. The life cycle of these flies requires relatively high temperatures, and under optimal conditions the entire life cycle may take as little as 6 to 8 days from egg to adult emergence. The larvae are white, cream, or yellow in color and range in size from 5 to 12 millimeters in length. Maggots of these species typically have flattened bodies with protuberances that assist with flotation in semiliquid materials, with mature larvae seeking out drier areas in order to pupate. Often the larvae can be found in fluid-soaked soils below or surrounding the remains. Some species of larvae have been known to prey on eggs and larvae of other insects.

9.2.2.2.2 Dung Fly (Family Scathophagidae) Over 250 species of dung flies are known, almost all of which are found in the Northern Hemisphere (Byrd and Castner, 2010b). Dung flies are attracted by ammonia in urine and feces on soiled clothing and ammonia released during later decomposition of remains. Adult dung flies, approximately 7 to 10 millimeters in length, are reddish or yellowish in color with hairy bodies. The adult females tend to avoid depressions when laying their eggs, preferring raised surfaces. The eggs hatch into predatory larvae that feed on other insect larvae as well as dung. Mature larvae burrow into dung, other decomposing materials, or soil to pupate. The adult flies are also predatory and will feed on other fly species.

9.2.2.2.3 Scavenger Fly (Family Sepsidae) Scavenger flies have a worldwide distribution of over 240 species (Byrd and Castner, 2010b). Adults are small, approximately 3.5 to 5 millimeters in length, and have a shiny black, purple, or red appearance. The adult flies are often mistaken for flying ants and have the habit of waving their wings outward as they walk, which lends to the more common name of "waggle flies." These flies are attracted to dung and decaying organic matter, often occurring in large numbers during active stages of decomposition. Mature larvae are small, approximately 3 to 6 millimeters long.

9.2.2.2.4 Dung Beetle (Family Scarabaeidae) There are more than 7,000 species of dung beetle found throughout the world, most of which are also known as scarab beetle or "tumblebugs" (Cooter and Barclay, 2006). Dung beetles are noted for their habit of rolling dung or decayed organic material into spheres, which are then used as a food source and as brooding chambers for larvae. The adults of species associated with human remains are generally dull black in color and are robust and rounded in shape, approximately 1 to 2.5 centimeters in length. Some iridescent green species have been found with human remains but are not as prevalent (Byrd and Castner, 2010b). Along with robust pincers, a few species of adult males will also develop anterior horns. Adult females lay their eggs in the collected ball of dung. The larvae, which are fat and white with a brown head, tend to curl into a C-shape and are commonly called "grubs." Larvae may pupate within dried dung or other dried organic material.

9.2.2.3 Scavengers and Parasitoids

Over time, detritivores and coprophiles are replaced with insect species that have longer life cycles and lower reproductive rates, which are able to scavenge and exploit the larvae from other insects and any remaining human tissues. Parasitoid insects, in contrast, lay their eggs in the bodies or pupae of

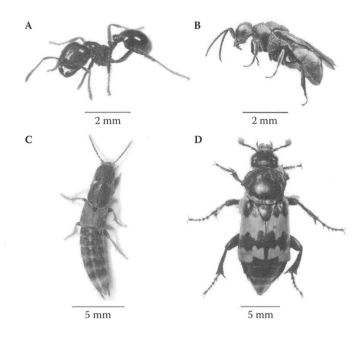

Figure 9.7 Scavenger and parasitoid insects commonly found in association with insect colonization of human remains: (a) fire ant, (b) parasitoid wasp, (c) rove beetle, and (d) carrion beetle.

other insects, with the larvae using the host as a food source. Figure 9.7 shows a few of the predators and parasites associated with the insect colonization of human remains. Due to the very nature of their food source, the following group of insects should be isolated during live collection in the field.

9.2.2.3.1 Rove Beetle (Family Staphylinidae)   With over 47,000 known species, this family of beetles is among the largest in the world (Byrd and Castner, 2010b). Rove beetles, or the "devil's coach horses," are attracted to human remains during active decomposition, using fly larvae as their food source, but their larvae prefer drier conditions. Adult beetles vary in size from 1 to 35 millimeters, with most averaging 2 to 8 millimeters in length, and have a slender, elongated shape. Most species range from yellow to reddish-brown or black in color. They are quick moving and are strong fliers. Some adult rove beetles, when disturbed, curl their abdomen up over their back making them look aggressive (Gennard, 2007). They are also able to emit a very disagreeable odor when alarmed. The larvae are long, slender, and pale in color with darkened heads and have been known to also be predacious on other larvae species.

9.2.2.3.2 Carrion Beetle (Family Silphidae)   Carrion beetles, with over 1,500 species distributed worldwide, can detect a dead organism at a considerable distance and are among the first to colonize human remains (Byrd and

Castner, 2010b). Adult beetles may arrive early in the decomposition process, often within 24 hours after death. They are large, robust beetles, averaging 10 to 35 millimeters in size, with a flat, colorful body, which has yellow, orange, or red markings. A few species, however, are completely black in color. They are commonly called "burying beetles" because adults typically chew out pieces of tissue and bury them, with adult females laying eggs directly above the buried remains. In other instances, the adult female will make a depression in tissues to house the eggs and developing larvae. The adults protect and rear the young through the initial larval stage, with most larvae ranging between 15 and 30 millimeters in length. Larvae exclusively feed on decomposing remains; however, adult carrion beetles will consume larvae as well as decomposing remains, which can heavily influence blowfly larvae numbers and instar distribution (Gennard, 2007).

9.2.2.3.3 Clown Beetle (Family Histeridae)   There are over 3,900 species of clown beetles found worldwide, and they are known to occupy almost any environment (Byrd and Caster, 2010b). Clown beetles are rounded, small, shiny black or metallic green beetles that are usually only 10 millimeters in length. They are commonly found on actively decaying remains and tend to colonize human remains several days after blowflies. Most adult clown beetles and larvae are nocturnal and can be found under remains during daylight hours. Most species will fake death if disturbed or threatened. Both larvae and adults are highly predatory and cannibalistic. The adults primarily feed on other adult beetles and fly larvae, while clown beetle larvae are known to feed on fly maggots and puparia.

9.2.2.3.4 Wasps and Ants (Order Hymenoptera)   Adult social wasps (family Vespidae) will forage for scraps of tissue from human remains as well as prey on eggs and larvae of other insects. The larvae of social wasps are carnivorous and are fed prey brought back to the nest. Parasitoid wasps, such as the *Nasonia vitripennis*, lay their eggs by boring a hole into blowfly puparia (Grassberger and Frank, 2003). After hatching, the wasp larvae feed on the fly pupa, pupate within the host's puparium, and emerge as adults. Parasitoid wasps typically only lay their eggs in blowfly pupae that are 24 to 30 hours old; therefore, the life cycle of the wasps may also become a determinate of PMI (Grassberger and Frank, 2003).

At times, especially in tropical conditions, fire and acrobat ants may be the most plentiful insects found on human remains during all stages of decay. They may slow blowfly colonization by 3 to 4 days through predation of fly eggs and young larvae (Wells and Greenberg, 1994). They may also feed on human tissues and thereby speed the process of decay. Of note is the fact that some species of scuttle fly (family Phoridae) are natural predators of fire ants and may be drawn to decomposing remains due to ant colonization (Gunn, 2009).

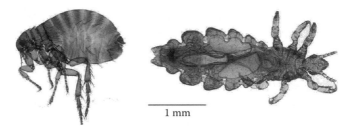

1 mm

Figure 9.8 Ectoparasites such as a human flea (left) or a body louse (right) may be associated with human remains or encountered at various sites in a forensic context.

9.2.2.4 *Ectoparasites*

Ectoparasites, or external parasites, live and feed on the surfaces of their host. The most common ectoparasites encountered in a forensic context are fleas and lice (Figure 9.8). Humans may harbor a few fleas acquired from their pets (e.g., *Ctenocephalides canis* and *C. felis*), while large numbers are usually only present in cases of neglect or unsanitary conditions. Body and head lice (*Pediculus humanus*) are more common, especially in cases of promiscuous sexual contact. Fleas and lice typically vacate a dead host soon after it dies and the body cools. If these insects are found still living in an individual's hair or clothing, it is a good indication that the postmortem interval is very short.

9.2.3 Collecting and Preserving Entomological Evidence

The sampling of entomological evidence should follow standard procedures at all types of death scenes, no matter how diverse the scene environment may appear. Once permission has been obtained from the senior investigator, the remains should be searched in an orderly sequence and all evidence should be collected in conjunction with the crime scene unit or evidence officer. A number of published references provide current detailed procedural instructions for the collection and preservation of entomological evidence (e.g., Amendt et al., 2007; Byrd et al., 2010; Gennard, 2007) and should be consulted if further information is required. The following collection procedures are based upon Byrd et al. (2010).

The process of documentation and collection can be broken down into eight steps (Figure 9.9) that are applicable to most geographic areas and habitats:

- Document the scene and habitat (e.g., plants, water, soil type, landscape, etc.)
- Document the insect colonization of the remains and surrounding area
- Collect environmental data at the scene

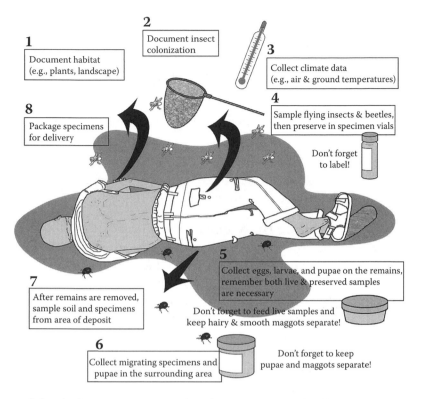

Figure 9.9 The basic steps required in documenting and collecting entomological evidence.

- Sample adult flies and beetles on or near the remains
- Sample eggs, larvae, and pupae on the remains
- Sample specimens migrating into the surrounding area
- Sample specimens and soil samples after removing the remains
- Package specimens for delivery to forensic entomologist for analysis

When dealing with buried remains, there will be some flexibility in the process. An example of a recording form for documenting the scene, environmental data, and sampled specimens can be found in Appendix I. This type of form should be completed as you move through each step in the process. In addition to the documentation form, you should have a grouping of preprinted paper and self-adhesive labels that must be included with each sample. Each label should include the sample number and identifier, date, time, scene location, case number, and the name of the individual collecting the sample (Figure 9.10). Double labeling should be a standard practice, with the interior label placed inside along with the specimen (including jars and vials containing solutions) and a self-adhesive label placed on the exterior of the sample bag or container. Double labeling ensures that the pertinent

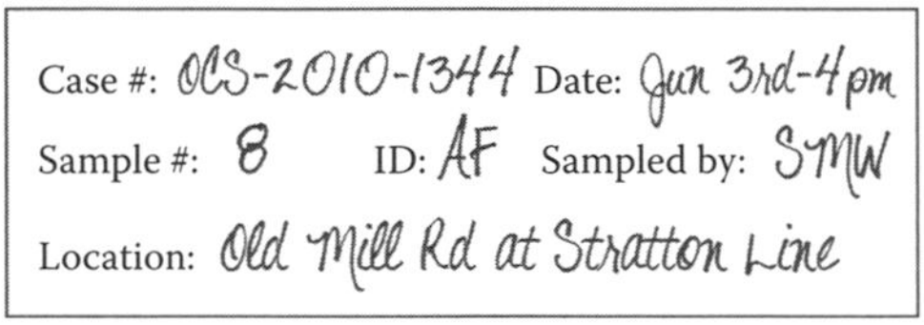

Case #: _OCS-2010-1344_ Date: _Jun 3rd-4pm_

Sample #: _8_   ID: _AF_   Sampled by: _SMW_

Location: _Old Mill Rd at Stratton Line_

Figure 9.10 Example of a preprinted label used to identify each collected entomology sample.

information remains with the sample if the outer label becomes damaged or falls off. All labels should be filled out in pencil, as ink will easily be washed away by the solutions used for killing and preserving samples.

9.2.3.1 Documenting the Scene and Habitat

The first step in the process is a visual observation of the surroundings and documentation of the general habitat where the remains are located. This information is extremely important, as it can help the forensic entomologist in determining which insects should be present in the environment, if there are any anomalous species present, and if certain vegetation may hinder insect presence or development. Habitat documentation includes a general site description, any nearby aquatic sources, the types of vegetation present, the slope and type of groundcover where the remains are located, and whether the remains were wrapped or covered in some way. The current weather conditions at the scene (e.g., sun, shade, rain, snow) should also be recorded. Along with this information, photographs should be taken in a 360° view outward from the remains, starting from the north. In addition, photographs should be taken directly over the remains to show the degree of direct sunlight; however, these should be taken later in the process to keep disturbance of the insect colony at a minimum. Personnel should avoid having their shadow fall across the remains because sudden shifts in light may startle some species and cause them to quickly disperse.

9.2.3.2 Documenting the Insect Colonization

Once the overall scene has been documented, the focus should be on the amount and location of activity within the insect colonization. Documentation should begin at a distance, taking the same precautions discussed above. If available, plastic stepping plates should be used when documenting the insect colonization close to the remains. Written documentation should contain notes on the types of insects present and their relative abundance. Photographs should be taken to accompany the notes, using a photographic scale to assist the forensic entomologist in assessing the size and type of insects present. Byrd et al. (2010) recommend that video not be used as the primary source of visual documentation due to the low-resolution imagery usually obtained from this technology. The fine detail and close-up imagery obtained from still photography is better suited to recording the information needed to assess entomological evidence.

9.2.3.3 Collecting Climate Data

It is essential to have accurate climate data for the scene when estimating PMI from entomological evidence. Temperature and humidity in each particular environment largely determine the time required for various insects to undergo their life-cycle development. In addition to the current climate data collected at the scene, data should be obtained from the scene for three to five days after the body was discovered. Once a PMI is determined, historical climate data for one to two weeks prior to the estimated date of death should also be obtained by contacting the nearest National Weather Service (NWS) station (http://www.weather.gov). The following climate data should be collected at the scene:

- Ambient air temperature and humidity in close proximity to the remains at heights of 1 foot (30 centimeters) and 4 feet (1.3 meters), using a handheld digital temperature and humidity meter
- Ground temperature, by placing a digital probe thermometer directly on top of the surface ground cover
- Body and ground surface interface temperature, by sliding a digital probe thermometer between the underside of the remains and the ground surface
- Body temperature, by placing a digital probe thermometer directly on the body (thoracic and knee areas recommended)
- If observed, larval mass temperatures, by inserting a digital probe thermometer into the center of each mass
- Soil temperatures, taken immediately following the removal of the remains, by inserting a digital probe thermometer into the soil directly under the body to a depth of approximately 2 inches (5 centimeters) and again at a distance 3 to 6 feet (1 to 2 meters) from the remains at a depth of 4 inches (10 centimeters)
- If present, water temperature should be obtained by holding an alcohol thermometer 4 inches (10 centimeters) below the surface

Always shade the thermometer from direct sunlight when taking temperature data. Also, this data should be collected as you move through the process, keeping in mind the precautions for avoiding insect dispersal and disturbance.

9.2.3.4 Sampling Adult Flying and Crawling Insects

The first samples to be collected are the adult flying (flies) and crawling insects (beetles). Typically, sampling of flying insects is done by aerial netting, where an individual sweeps the net rapidly back and forth above the body, or upon vegetation in the area surrounding the remains, and then rotates the net opening 180° after each pass to prevent any collected samples from escaping. Another technique is to approach the insects in a downward swatting motion with the tail of the net up because the natural behavior of the insects is to fly up into the net. Aerial netting should be repeated three or four times above the remains to ensure a representative sample of insects have been captured. Generally, at least two 360° sweeps of the vegetation 5 to 10 feet (1.5 to 3 meters) from the remains is recommended. After the insects are collected, the end of the net should be placed into a wide-mouthed kill jar and the jar is then capped. The kill jar should contain either a few cotton balls or a block of plaster (gypsum cement) at the bottom freshly soaked with ethyl acetate. A few minutes in the kill jar should be adequate for immobilizing the insects. Using light tension forceps, the adult insects should then be transferred into glass vials containing either ETOH or Kahle's solution (Table 9.2) for preservation.

Another method of collecting flying insects is the use of sticky traps. These traps consist of cardboard coated with a heavy glue or adhesive and are either hung across the scene or placed on the ground near the remains. Various forms of adhesive insect traps are available commercially, but they usually are not efficient enough for forensic use. Instead, cardboard-based rodent glue traps are recommended for this level of entomological collection (Byrd et al., 2010). For use in the field, open the trap and fold in half into a V-shape, with the sticky surface on the outside. Place a clothespin at each corner to make legs for the trap. Once all other specimens have been collected and the remains have been cleared from the scene, remove the clothespins and invert the trap with the sticky surface on the inside. Put a crumpled ball of paper towel between the surfaces so the trap does not adhere to itself and place the trap in a large polyethylene specimen bag. The bagged trap can be stored in a freezer until it is transported to a forensic entomologist.

Medium- or fine-point dissecting forceps or gloved fingers can be used to collect adult crawling insects. Many of the crawling insects are quite fast in their movements. It may be necessary to initially have more than one person collecting these adults, as they are likely to disperse into the soil or surrounding groundcover as soon as they detect any disturbance. Any sampled adult beetles can be placed directly in a glass vial with ETOH for preservation. Remember that many adult beetles are predacious and a few are known to consume recently emerged adult flies and other adult beetles. If collected, they should be separated and preserved as soon as possible.

9.2.3.5 Sampling Insects on the Remains

Sampling insects on the remains can be somewhat intrusive and extreme care should be taken when sampling entomological material from the body so no

Table 9.2   Common Entomology Preservation Solutions

ETOH (80% ethyl alcohol)

Commonly known as ethanol; usually purchased in bulk at 95% concentration

Best use:

- Kill and preserve adult specimens
- Preserve eggs
- Preserve larvae after fixing in Kahle's solution or KAAD

KAA (or KAAD)

Best use:

- Kill larval specimens and preserve eggs

Specimens should be transferred to ETOH solution immediately after death

If DNA analysis of samples is a possibility, use of this solution is not recommended

KAA solution can be produced by mixing:

- 90 mL (3.0 fl oz) of 95% ethanol
- 20 mL (0.6 fl oz) of glacial acetic acid
- 10 mL (0.3 fl oz) of kerosene
- Components of solution should be added to ethanol in the above order to avoid any adverse reactions when mixing

Kahle's Solution

Best use:

- Kill and preserve adult specimens
- Preserve larval specimens

Khale's solution can be produced by mixing:

- 30 mL (1.0 fl oz) of 95% ethanol
- 12 mL (0.4 fl oz) of formaldehyde
- 60 mL (2.0 fl oz) of distilled water
- 4 mL (0.1 fl oz) of glacial acetic acid
- Components of solution should be added to ethanol in the above order to avoid any adverse reactions when mixing

Source: Adapted from Byrd, J.H., Lord, W.D., Wallace, J.R., Tomberlin, J.K. 2010. Collection of entomological evidence during legal investigations. In: Byrd, J., Castner, J.L., eds. *Forensic Entomology: The Utility of Arthropods in Legal Investigations*, 2nd ed., pp. 127–176. Boca Raton, FL: CRC Press.

inadvertent postmortem artifacts are left and no other evidence is damaged or disturbed. Insects should be collected from the remains by starting at the head, then through the thoracic region, arms and hands, and moving finally to the legs and feet. Once the upper surface of the remains has been searched and all additional personnel have obtained and recorded information pertinent to body position, the underside of the remains should be examined. Any visible wounds should be described and noted on the evidence collection form. Pockets and folds of clothing should be cursorily examined at the scene if permission is obtained from the senior investigating officer. In some instances, the ME may collect further entomological evidence from the clothing as well as the remains during autopsy.

Sampling of insects directly from the remains usually consists of eggs and larvae. It is important to ensure that a representative sample of eggs and larvae are collected, being careful to select not only the average-sized larvae, but also the largest and smallest larvae present in order to document the range of size variation. Various areas of insect colonization should be sampled and preserved separately, with temperature recordings made at each collection site. After collecting a preserved sample, it is common to then collect an equivalent live sample from the same location if possible.

9.2.3.5.1 Eggs Adult female flies typically lay their eggs in batches, and they can easily be mistaken for mold or sawdust. Eggs can usually be found in dark, moist areas of the body, such as the eyes, nose, ears, hair, joint creases, or the genital and anal regions, and at sites of trauma. They can also be found on clothing that has become soaked with decomposition fluids. Beetles tend to lay their eggs individually, so they may be easily missed in the folds, creases, and cavities of the remains.

The average sample size is 50 to 100 fly eggs or a clump about the size of a pencil eraser. Individual clumps of eggs should be sampled from various sites using a wood tongue depressor or a moistened camelhair brush. The preserved sample of eggs should be collected and placed in a glass vial of ETOH. Carefully place a second equivalent sample of eggs in a glass vial with a moist piece of paper towel to stop the eggs from drying out. Beetle eggs should be collected and preserved in the same manner. Live samples will be reared to adulthood by the forensic entomologist to assist with determining PMI.

9.2.3.5.2 Larvae Larvae have the ability to regulate their environment by forming large aggregates, or larval masses, which help ensure that the larvae develop at an optimum temperature. Larvae are usually collected at the same time as eggs. They also tend to be found in the same regions of the body, but they may also form large maggot masses internally. First instar larvae are the smallest and most fragile and should be collected using light tension forceps or a small moistened camelhair brush. Larvae in the second and third instar stages will mass together and are capable of producing a great amount of heat. Each larval mass encountered should be documented by location, size, and mass temperature prior to sampling. To obtain a mass temperature, gently insert a thermometer directly into the center of a larval mass and wait for the maximum temperature to be measured.

Preserved larvae samples should be collected in batches of 50 to 100 using a plastic spoon or food scoop and then placed in very hot (>80°C/176°F) water for approximately 30 to 60 seconds to achieve the best preservation. Afterward, pour off the water into a waste container and rinse the larvae once before fixing them in a collection jar with Kahle's solution. If hot water is not available at the scene, the larvae should be killed and preserved as soon as possible. Do not place living larvae directly in any of the preserving solutions because the larvae will darken and shrink in a few days due to putrefaction. Larval shrinkage can hide some morphological characteristics and also introduce unwanted error into the estimation of PMI. After fixing the larvae in Kahle's solution, they can be transferred and preserved in a collection jar in either ETOH or clean Kahle's solution.

Live samples of approximately 30 to 50 larvae should be placed in maggot-rearing containers that will keep the specimens alive during transport to a forensic entomologist. Keep in mind that some larvae are predacious, and therefore you should always keep the smooth-bodied larvae from flies separate from the hairy, legged larvae of beetles. Use a 16-ounce plastic container with a sealable, tight-fitting lid and place a layer of vermiculite in the bottom, approximately 1 inch (2.5 centimeters) in depth. Carefully pierce the lid with a metal dissecting probe to form air vents. Next, construct a feeding pouch from aluminum foil by folding a 6 × 7 inch (15 × 18 centimeters) piece of aluminum foil into thirds horizontally, then again into thirds vertically. The end product is a small 2 × 3 inch rectangle (5 × 7 centimeters) that can be unfolded into an open-topped three-dimensional rectangular pouch after crimping together the corners. A small piece of lean pork, about 3 to 5 ounces (90 to 150 grams) is added to the pouch as a food source to keep the larvae alive for approximately 24 hours during transport. Beetle larvae, recognizable by their sets of paired legs, generally feed on fly larvae, which can be collected for use as their food source. The pouch should be tightly crimped to seal the larvae inside and then placed in the prepared container. Polyethylene specimen bags may also be used to hold the feeding pouches and vermiculite, providing that they are properly sealed and that pinholes are created in the plastic for adequate ventilation.

9.2.3.6 *Sampling Insects Migrating from the Remains*

Once insects from the body have been sampled, the area surrounding the body should be investigated. There may be a considerable number of insects still left on the ground surface, hidden under surface debris, or burrowed in the soil. Most migrating larvae and pupae can be found within a radius of 20 feet (6 meters) from the remains and at an average depth of 1 to 2 inches (2.5 to 5 centimeters), but this is highly dependent on the terrain and level of soil compaction. Migrating larvae tend to group in thick clumps of vegetation, around tree trunks, and under rocks or fallen tree limbs. To sample these insects, remove the surface debris with a hand trowel and sift through it to collect any mature larvae or pupae. Topsoil should also be collected and sifted to recover insects that have burrowed into the ground or any remaining insect fragments. The compass direction of migration and distance from the remains should be documented for each sample. Also, it would be a good practice to photograph migrating insects and any groups of pupae *in situ*.

A representative sample of mature larvae should be preserved in the same manner presented above. A second, nearly identical group of mature larvae should be collected as a live sample for rearing. Pupae can be placed in the same type of plastic containers prepared for the larvae. However, you do not need to construct a feeding pouch, as this life stage does not feed. Any remnants of pupal skins, empty puparia, or beetle frass should be stored in polyethylene specimen bags or glass vials with a piece of dry paper towel to absorb any residual moisture.

9.2.3.7 Sampling Insects after Removing the Remains

In cases of heavy insect colonization, many adults (e.g., carrion and rove beetles), larvae, and pupae can still be collected from the soil directly under the body. Any surface litter under the remains should be collected for examination by the forensic entomologist and placed in a cardboard box. Add a layer of vermiculite to the bottom of the box to soak up any residual fluids and seal the box after labeling to prevent any insects from continuing their migration process.

Soil samples from directly under the body can yield various species of insect pupae and can also be used for biochemical analysis of decomposition fluids. Samples should be taken from directly under the head, torso, and extremities, as well as areas directly adjacent to the body and up to 3 feet (1 meter) from the remains. The location of each soil sample collected should be documented. The samples should be about 4 cubic inches in size (10 cubic centimeters) and placed in plastic containers or paper evidence bags. All soil samples should be labeled the same as other entomology samples.

9.2.3.8 Packaging Specimens

Once all of the samples have been collected and properly recorded, they should be placed in a cooling bag or box for transport from the scene. If you are transporting the samples during the hotter months of the year, a small reusable ice pack may be included in the bag or box to keep the temperature fairly stable. Preserved and live specimens from each site on the body should be retained in pairs if possible. Larvae are masters of escape, and each live sample container should have the lid fully sealed with a piece of painter's tape around the edges. Ensure that all samples accepted by the crime scene unit or evidence officer are sealed to preserve chain of custody and ensure that the integrity of the sample is not at risk. All living samples should be transferred to a forensic entomologist for rearing within 24 hours of collection. If it is necessary to ship the samples to an expert, you should consult with the forensic entomologist about proper packaging. In most instances, the samples can be packaged in smaller cardboard boxes and then placed in a larger shipping box. When packaging live samples, be extremely careful not to block the ventilation holes with any extraneous packing materials or other sample boxes.

9.2.4 Locating a Forensic Entomologist

If it is not possible to have a forensic entomologist present during the recovery of remains, it is essential to find one for analysis of material collected from a scene. When choosing a forensic entomologist, it is important to choose one that has a Ph.D. and extensive experience in taxonomic identification of forensic-related insect and arthropod species. At the same time, it is also important to choose a specialist who is familiar with your particular geographic area of the country. The specialist should be active academically and have membership in the American Academy of Forensic Sciences, be a member of the Entomological Society of America (ESA) (http://www.entsoc.org), and be board certified by the American Board of Forensic Entomology (ABFE). Currently there are 15 board-certified forensic entomologists in North America. A list of these individuals and the necessary contact information can be found on the website of the ABFE (http://www.forensicentomologist.org) by selecting the "Members/Bios" tab. You can also access professional biographical information by selecting the individual's name. To locate a forensic entomologist practicing outside of North America or who is familiar with the entomology of various geographic regions of the world, the website of the European Association for Forensic Entomology (EAFE) (http://www.eafe.org) has a list of regular members working throughout Europe and many associate members working throughout the world.

9.2.5 Basic Entomology Collection Kit Checklist

The list of equipment and supplies outlined here will facilitate proper documentation and collection of entomological evidence at the recovery site for later delivery to a forensic entomologist. The equipment listed may be purchased in assembled kits from a multitude of biological supply and scientific equipment companies (see Table 2.1), or a kit can be compiled to suit specific needs. The solutions used in collection and preservation can be purchased separately through the same types of suppliers or prepared prior to field recovery. A component list and their proportions for commonly used kill and preservative solutions can be found in Table 9.2.

- Plastic equipment case
- Plastic stepping and kneeling plates (15 × 15 in, 4 count)
- Disposable gloves

- Insect identification cards
- Hand trowel
- Plastic pet food scoop or large plastic spoon
- Digital temperature and humidity meter (handheld unit)
- 12-in collapsible entomology net with handle extension
- Large rodent paper glue boards (10 count)
- Plastic or wooden spring clothes pins (8 count)
- Small sifting screen (8 × 10 in, #7 mesh)
- Light tension (i.e., "feather touch") forceps
- Medium- or fine-point curved dissecting forceps
- Metal dissecting probe
- Disposable wood tongue depressors (10 count)
- Magnifying lens
- Artist camel hair brush (#2 size)
- 12-in digital probe thermometer
- Disposable eye dropper pipettes
- Glass collecting vials with screw tops (4 dram size, 30 count)
- Wide-mouth glass kill jars with screw tops and plaster block (4 oz and 8 oz, 2 each)
- 6 × 9 in polyethylene specimen bags or 4-oz plastic collection jars (10 each)
- Plastic food containers with lids (16 oz and 32 oz, 15 each)
- Cardboard shipping boxes (shoebox size)
- Painter's tape (0.5 in, 1 roll)
- Aluminum foil
- Packet of vermiculite
- Paper towels
- Cotton balls
- Ethyl acetate (common nail polish remover, 4 oz)
- 80% ethyl alcohol preservative solution (8 oz)
- Kahle's insect preservative solution (6 oz)
- Distilled water (32 oz)
- Large plastic waste bottle (64 oz)
- Small plastic funnel
- Environment and specimen collection forms
- Heavy bond paper labels (interior labeling)
- Self-adhesive labels (exterior labeling)
- Dark graphite (#2) pencils
- Photo scale and white card
- Camera

The following items should be obtained immediately prior to field collection:

- Thermos of boiling water (32 oz)
- Larvae food source (e.g., 9 oz of lean pork or ground beef, room temperature)
- Cooler bag or box with reusable ice packs (for transporting and storing living samples)

Always remember to restock the kit as soon as possible after each use.

Case Study 12: Barking Up the Wrong Tree

Authors Wheeler and Williams assisted in the recovery of a surface deposit that consisted of an unclothed individual found shortly after a winter thaw in a small clearing of a wooded area. A number of various-sized deadfall branches and a layer of leaf litter covered the body. One of the first steps in the recovery was to record the landscape and plant growth surrounding the surface deposit. While recording this information, authors Wheeler and Williams noticed that the concentration of branches over the body was considerably greater than any other location at the site. At this point, there was an agreement among investigators that the branches and leaf litter were most likely used to conceal the body and should be recorded as evidence (Figure 9.11).

After the deadfall branches had been mapped and photographed, they were removed in the reverse order from which they were placed. In addition to the deadfall branches and leaf litter, the entire top half of a sizeable tree sapling had been placed directly over the head and chest of the body. The trunk end of this sapling had an odd appearance when compared to the deadfall branches. Approximately 20 centimeters (8 inches) of wood and bark were stripped away along the length of the trunk, and the remaining wood was frayed at the end, making it obvious that the sapling had been "green" (i.e., living), but the growth rings indicated that the sapling was at the end of a growing season at the time it was used. The lower portion of the sapling was soon found still in the ground not far from the body (Figure 9.12). The top portion of the sapling was matched to this lower portion and both parts of the sapling were collected as evidence.

The remaining branches were then removed, and a substantial amount of animal activity in the gut and upper thigh area was noted. Tufts of animal hair were still attached to the margins of the area damaged by carnivore activity. All of the toes were missing, also the result of carnivore activity. After the remains were recovered, the areas below the remains and surrounding the deposit were searched for additional evidence. Given the botanical evidence and amount of animal activity, it appeared that the body may have been dumped late in the fall season before the

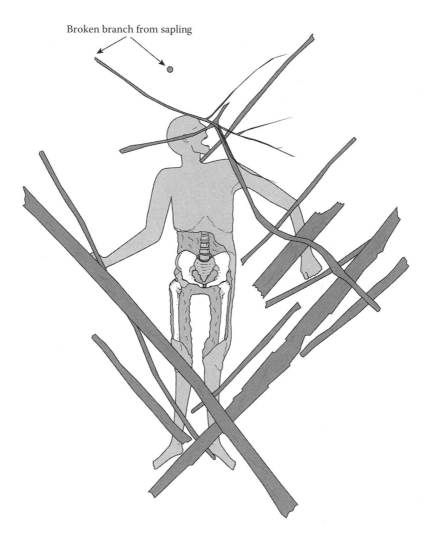

Figure 9.11 The purposeful placement of deadfall branches and broken sapling over remains in a surface deposit. Note the immediate proximity of the sapling trunk to the body.

Figure 9.12 The remaining trunk of a sapling used to conceal remains in a surface deposit. Note the frayed wood and length of stripped wood and bark that resulted from breaking the living wood of the sapling.

first snow, perhaps when the sapling still had its leaves, thus providing greater concealment of the body.

Case Study 13: Sunshine and Sticky Traps

Authors Wheeler and Williams assisted in the recovery of a partially clothed individual deposited on the side of an embankment between an All-Terrain Vehicle (ATV) trail and a canal. The area that the ATV trail ran through was mostly swampy and covered with reeds about 2 meters (6.5 feet) in height. The body was lying halfway down the side of the canal embankment in a slight depression. A wall of reeds separated the body from the canal, suggesting the body had been rolled down the embankment from the ATV trail. The depression had prevented the body from rolling further down into the canal. The body was largely intact but in an advanced state of decomposition with the skin of the limbs and torso partially mummified. The skull, however, was skeletonized. The cranium had separated and rolled a bit farther down slope from the body. There was no evidence of animal scavenging anywhere on the body other than insect activity.

When we initially arrived on the scene, the body had been largely shaded from the sun because of the density and height of the surrounding reeds. Maggots were still visible and there were major breaches in the skin where we could see further evidence of prior insect activity (Figure 9.13), but there were very few flying insects. After initial observations and photography of the site and remains, we decided to cut back the reeds immediately surrounding the body in order to clear a working space and to further record and map the body. Almost immediately after cutting back the reeds and exposing the remains to full sunlight, the insect activity increased dramatically, including the presence of flying insects. Sticky traps were set up in the immediate proximity of the remains and all work ceased for a period of time to minimize disturbance. During this break, the temperature of the remains also increased, which stimulated the remaining maggot masses and caused many larvae to seek out more beneficial environmental conditions (Figure 9.14). After a significant number of flying insects were collected on the sticky

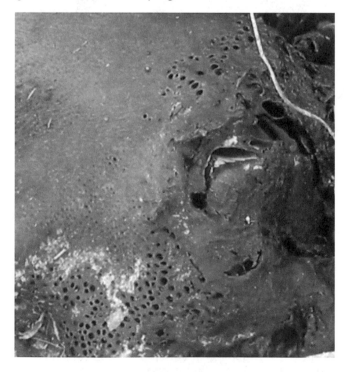

Figure 9.13 Area of skin across the shoulders and back of an individual who had become partially mummified during decomposition. The small holes indicate previous cycles of insect activity, where insects have bored through the skin during larval stages.

Figure 9.14 Area of increased insect activity after the temperature increase from exposure to full sun. Prior to sun exposure, no maggots were visible in this area of the leg; however, soon after exposure the remaining maggot mass became active and was sampled to determine postmortem interval. The smaller holes surrounding the larger opening indicate previous cycles of insect activity.

traps, both live and preserved entomological samples were taken from in and around the remains, including maggots, beetles, and various larvae. When everything was recorded and the entomological sampling of the remains was completed, the cranium was collected and packaged separately, and the body was placed in a body bag so that the original position of the limbs was retained. After the remains were removed, the soil immediately under the body was sampled for pupae. Additional soil samples were collected in areas where additional pupae were detected. The areas around and under the body were searched with a metal detector and excavated with hand trowels to recover any additional items or associated evidence; however, nothing further was found. All of the entomological samples were packaged by the crime scene personnel for transport to a local forensic entomologist for analysis. The results of the entomological analysis later confirmed the PMI estimate based on information obtained from an informant.

Key Words and Questions

ABFE
adults
algae
anemophilous plants
blowfly
carrion beetle
coprophiles
dendrochronology
detritivores
diatoms
ectoparasites
eggs
fixing solution
frass
fungi
instars
larvae
macrobotanicals
maggots
microbotanicals
palynology
parasitoids
preserving solution
pupae/puparium
scavengers
spores
zoogamous plants

1. What are three ways in which the growth of roots might be used to estimate PMI for buried remains?
2. In late autumn, a body in an advanced state of decomposition was found near a lake surrounded by ragweed, oak trees, and goosegrass. Pants and shoes were still associated with the remains, but no other personal possessions were recovered. In this case, what kinds of botanical and entomological evidence should have been considered for collection and why?
3. Why is correct species identification so important in forensic entomology?
4. Describe the differences between fly and beetle larvae. Why is it important to know these differences when collecting live samples?

5. When collecting maggots from human remains, why should you be sure to include the largest maggots present?
6. Why should maggot length be calculated before the specimens are placed in preserving solution?

Suggested Readings

Anderson, G.S., Cervenka, V.J. 2002. Insects associated with the body: their use and analyses. In: Haglund, W.D., Sorg, M.H., eds. *Advances in Forensic Taphonomy: Method, Theory, and Archaeological Perspectives*, pp. 173–200. Boca Raton, FL: CRC Press.

Casamatta, D.A., Verb, R.G. 2000. Algal colonization of submerged carcasses in a mid-order woodland stream. *Journal of Forensic Sciences* 45:1280–1285.

Erzinçlioğlu, Z. 2002. *Maggots, Murder, and Men: Memories and Reflections of a Forensic Entomologist*. New York: Thomas Dunne Books.

Horrocks, M., Walsh, K.A.J. 1999. Fine resolution of pollen patterns in limited space: differentiating a crime scene and alibi scene seven meters apart. *Journal of Forensic Sciences* 44:417–420.

Schroeder, H., Klotzbach, H., Püschel, K. 2003. Insects' colonization of human corpses in warm and cold season. *Legal Medicine* 5:S372–S374.

Willey, P., Heilman, A. 1987. Estimating time since death using plant roots and stems. *Journal of Forensic Sciences* 32:1264–1270.

References

Agashe, S.N., Caulton, E. 2009. *Pollen and Spores: Applications with Special Emphasis on Aerobiology and Allergy*. Enfield, NH: Science Publishers.

Amendt, J., Campobasso, C.P., Gaudry, E., Reiter, C., LeBlanc, H.M., Hall, M.J.R. 2007. Best practice in forensic entomology—standards and guidelines. *International Journal of Legal Medicine* 121:90–104.

Bock, J.H., Norris, D.O. 1997. Forensic botany: an underutilized resource. *Journal of Forensic Sciences* 42:364–367.

Byrd, J., Castner, J.L. 2010a. *Forensic Entomology: The Utility of Arthropods in Legal Investigations*, 2nd ed. Boca Raton, FL: CRC Press.

Byrd, J., Castner, J.L. 2010b. Insects of forensic importance. In: Byrd, J., Castner, J.L., eds. *Forensic Entomology: The Utility of Arthropods in Legal Investigations*, 2nd ed., pp. 39–126. Boca Raton, FL: CRC Press.

Byrd, J.H., Lord, W.D., Wallace, J.R., Tomberlin, J.K. 2010. Collection of entomological evidence during legal investigations. In: Byrd, J., Castner, J.L., eds. *Forensic Entomology: The Utility of Arthropods in Legal Investigations*, 2nd ed., pp. 127–176. Boca Raton, FL: CRC Press.

Castner, J.L. 2010. General entomology and insect biology. In: Byrd, J., Castner, J.L., eds. *Forensic Entomology: The Utility of Arthropods in Legal Investigations*, 2nd ed., pp. 17–38. Boca Raton, FL: CRC Press.

Castner, J.L., Byrd, J.H., Butler, J.F. 1995. *Forensic Insect Field Identification Cards*. Colorado Springs, CO: Forensic Sciences Foundation.

Catts, E.P., Haskell, N.H. 1990. *Entomology and Death: A Procedural Guide*. Clemson, SC: Joyce's Print Shop.

Cooter, J., Barclay, M.V.L. 2006. *A Coleopterist's Handbook*, 4th ed. Kent, UK: Amateur Entomologists' Society.

Coyle, H.M. 2004a. *Forensic Botany: Principles and Applications to Criminal Casework*. Boca Raton, FL: CRC Press.

Coyle, H.M. 2004b. Introduction to forensic botany. In: Coyle, H.M., ed. *Forensic Botany: Principles and Applications to Criminal Casework*, pp. 1–7. Boca Raton, FL: CRC Press.

Disney, R.H.L. 1994. *Scuttle Flies: The Phoridae*. New York: Springer.

Erzinçlioğlu, Y.Z. 1980. On the role of Trichoceridae larvae (Diptera: Trichoceridae) in decomposing carrion in winter. *Naturalist* 105:133–134.

Gardner, L. 2004. *The Case That Never Dies: The Lindberg Kidnapping*. Piscataway, NJ: Rutgers University Press.

Gennard, D. 2007. *Forensic Entomology: An Introduction*. West Sussex, UK: Wiley.

Goff, M.L. 2000. *A Fly for the Prosecution*. Cambridge, MA: Harvard University Press.

Graham, J.E., Wilcox, L.W., Graham, L.E. 2008. *Algae*, 2nd ed. San Francisco: Benjamin Cummings.

Grassberger, M., Frank, C. 2003. Temperature-related development of the parasitoid wasp *Nasonia vitripennis* as a forensic indicator. *Medical and Veterinary Entomology* 17:257–262.

Green, P.W.C., Simmonds, S.J., Blaney, W.M. 2003. Diet nutriment and rearing density affect the growth of the black blowfly larvae, *Phormia regina* (Diptera: Calliphoridae). *European Journal of Entomology* 100:39–42.

Greenberg, B., Kunich, J.C. 2002. *Entomology and the Law*. Cambridge: Cambridge University Press.

Gunn, A. 2009. *Essentials of Forensic Biology*. Hoboken, NJ: Wiley-Blackwell.

Haefner, J.N., Wallace, J.R., Merritt, R.W. 2004. Pig decomposition in lotic aquatic systems: the potential use of algal growth in establishing a postmortem submersion interval (PMSI). *Journal of Forensic Sciences* 49:1–7.

Haglund, W.D., Reay, D.T., Swindler, D.R. 1988. Tooth mark artifacts and survival of bones in animal scavenged human skeletons. *Journal of Forensic Sciences* 33:985–997.

Hall, R.D., Huntington, T.E. 2010. Introduction: Perceptions and status of forensic entomology. In: Byrd, J., Castner, J.L., eds. Forensic Entomology: *The Utility of Arthropods in Legal Investigations*, 2nd ed., pp. 1–16. Boca Raton, FL: CRC Press.

Hitosugi, M., Ishii, K., Yaguchi, T., Chigusa, Y., Kurosu, A., Kido, M., Nagai, T., Tokudome, S. 2006. Fungi can be a useful forensic tool. *Legal Medicine* 8:240–242.

Horrocks, M., Coulson, S.A., Walsh, K.A.J. 1998. Forensic palynology: variation in the pollen content of soil surface samples. *Journal of Forensic Sciences* 43:320–323.

Hürlimann, J., Feer, P., Elber, K., Niederberger, K., Dirnhofer, R., Wyler, D. 2000. Diatom detection in the diagnosis of death by drowning. *International Journal of Legal Medicine* 114:6–14.

Hwang, C., Turner, B.D. 2005. Spatial and temporal variability of necrophagous Diptera from urban and rural areas. *Medical and Veterinary Entomology* 19:379–391.

Krstic, S., Duma, A., Janevska, B., Levkov, Z., Nikolova, K., Noveska, M. 2002. Diatoms in forensic expertise of drowning—a Macedonian experience. *Forensic Science International* 127:198–203.

Ladd, C., Lee, H. 2004. The use of biological and botanical evidence in criminal investigations. In: Coyle, H.M., ed. *Forensic Botany: Principles and Applications to Criminal Casework*, pp. 91–109. Boca Raton, FL: CRC Press.

Lane, M.A., Anderson, L.C., Barkley, T.M., Bock, J.H., Gifford, E.M., Hall, D.W., Norris, D.O., Rost, T.L., Stern, W.L. 1990. Forensic botany: plants, perpetrators, pests, poisons and pot. *Bioscience* 40:34–39.

Lord, W.D., Goff, M.L., Adkins, T.R., Haskell, N.H. 1994. The black soldier fly *Hermetia illucens* (Diptera: Stratiomyidae) as a potential measure of post-mortem interval: observations and case histories. *Journal of Forensic Sciences* 39:215–222.

Ludes, B., Coste, M., North, N., Doray, S., Tracqui, A., Kintz, P. 1999. Diatom analysis in victim's tissues as an indicator of the site of drowning. *International Journal of Legal Medicine* 112:163–166.

Mégnin P. 1894. *La Faune des Cadavres. Encyclopédie Scientifiques des Aide Memoire*. Paris: Villars et Fils, Masson et Gauthier.

Menezes, R.G., Kanchan, T., Lobo, S.W., Jain, A., Bhat, N.B., Rao, N.G. 2008. Cadaveric fungi: not yet an established forensic tool. *Journal of Forensic and Legal Medicine* 15:124–125.

Milne, L.A., Bryant, V.M., Mildenhall, D.C. 2004. Forensic palynology. In: Coyle, H.M., ed. *Forensic Botany: Principles and Applications to Criminal Casework*, pp. 201–237. Boca Raton, FL: CRC Press.

Quatrehomme, G., Lacoste, A., Bailet, P., Grevin, G., Ollier, A. 1997. Contribution of microscopic plant anatomy to postmortem bone dating. *Journal of Forensic Sciences* 42:140–143.

Said al Na'imi, K. 2008. Basics of forensic fungi. In: Coyle, H.M., ed. *Nonhuman DNA Typing: Theory and Casework Applications*, pp. 135–166. Boca Raton, FL: CRC Press.

Siver, P.A., Lord, W.D., McCarthy, D.J. 1994. Forensic limnology: the use of freshwater algal community ecology to link suspects to an aquatic crime scene in southern New England. *Journal of Forensic Sciences* 39:847–853.

Stephenson, S.L. 2010. *The Kingdom Fungi*. Portland, OR: Timber Press.

Tz'u, S. 1981. *The Washing Away of Wrongs* (B. McKnight, trans.) Ann Arbor, MI: University of Michigan Press.

Wells, J.D., Greenberg, B. 1994. Effect of the red imported fire ant (Hymenoptera: Formicidae) and carcass type on the daily occurrence of postfeeding carrion-fly larvae (Diptera: Calliphoridae, Sarcophagidae). *Journal of Medical Entomology* 31:171–174.

Willey, P., Heilman, A. 1987. Estimating time since death using plant roots and stems. *Journal of Forensic Sciences* 32:1264–1270.

Wiltshire, P.E.J. 2006. Consideration of some taphonomic variables of relevance to forensic palynological investigation in the United Kingdom. *Forensic Science International* 163:173–182.

Yen, L.Y., Jayaprakash, P.T. 2007. Prevalence of diatom frustules in non-vegetarian foodstuffs and its implications in interpreting identification of diatom frustules in drowning cases. *Forensic Science International* 170:1–7.

Collecting Skeletal Remains

10

After the discovery and recording of skeletal remains, the next important step in the process is their collection. Skeletal remains should be treated like any other evidence recovered from a scene. It must be collected, packaged, and recorded properly to avoid any potential problems concerning chain of custody. This chapter includes discussions of proper handling, packaging, and storage of all remains including those with soft tissue and cremations.

In this chapter we discuss both human and nonhuman remains. The purpose of including a section on nonhuman skeletal remains is twofold—first, it is included to demonstrate that nonhuman skeletal material can easily be mistaken for human remains, reinforcing the necessity of an experienced osteologist making the final determination; and second, it is included to introduce forensic archaeology students to various examples of nonhuman bones that can easily be confused with human bones.

10.1 Human Skeletal Remains

Proper archaeological recovery methods, such as locating and mapping remains and associated evidence, are followed by proper methods of collecting, packaging, and transporting, as well as storage of skeletal remains if needed. Proper collection methods are vital to not only protect the remains from postmortem damage, but to also maintain chain of custody. While established collection procedures for adult human skeletal remains should be standardized, death investigation personnel may have to modify those methods when recovering and collecting juvenile, fleshed, or burnt remains.

10.1.1 Collecting Human Skeletal Remains

At the time of collection, all remains must be properly recorded with pertinent case information and must be packaged properly to avoid damage and maintain chain of custody. One of the primary goals of the forensic archaeologist during search and recovery is to avoid any postmortem damage to the remains, but at times this may be unavoidable. For example, authors Sandra Wheeler and Lana Williams were asked to assist in the recovery of human remains that were previously discovered by inexperienced personnel who used a spade shovel during their search. Unfortunately, the spade

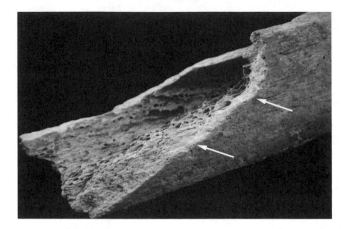

Figure 10.1 Evidence of postmortem damage to bone that occurred during recovery. Note the color change (arrows) where the damaged surface of the cortical bone is much lighter in color than the outer surface, which is stained by the burial environment.

shovel struck one of the long bones and caused severe postmortem damage to the bone (Figure 10.1). If this occurs, either through the actions of inexperienced personnel or the forensic archaeologist, all damage, no matter how slight, should be recorded and the information should be included with the damaged material during packaging. Even though forensic anthropologists may have experience distinguishing postmortem damage from perimortem trauma, the goal should be to avoid any postmortem damage during the search, recovery, packaging, shipping, analysis, and storage phases. In addition, field personnel involved with the recovery may not have experience distinguishing bone from non-bone materials or human bones from nonhuman bones. In these instances, all suspect and associated trash materials must be collected and properly documented so experienced personnel can sort out human bone and related evidence from trash.

10.1.1.1 Packaging Skeletal Remains

During removal from the burial feature, identifying marks should never be placed directly on the bone. Each bone should be identified inside and outside of its package by a tag noting its precise location coordinates either on a control-point or grid-mapping system. Any evidence numbering system that is used by the forensic investigation team should be duplicated in the excavation notes and on the tags for each package to prevent any confusion about identification at a later date.

Packaging guidelines for skeletal human remains free of soft tissue are simple: everything should be placed in labeled paper bags. Place a tag with the pertinent information about the bone inside the paper bag before sealing it. Buried remains are inevitably going to retain some moisture, and packaging in plastic bags or aluminum foil does not allow the moisture to evaporate and will promote the growth of fungus and mold. In addition, the moisture may accelerate the breakdown of skeletal material (Skinner and Lazenby, 1983). The opening of each paper bag should be folded over at least twice and then stapled or sealed with tape at the ends of the fold to prevent bones and evidence from falling out during transport. Small bags can be placed inside large ones, which in turn can be loaded and sealed into clean cardboard boxes or body bags. Padding should be used between packages to prevent breakage and care should be taken in stacking packages on top of one another when placing them in boxes. At a minimum, each bag should be clearly labeled with information regarding the contents, location, case information, and investigator's name. If necessary, crime scene evidence tape and the investigator's signature can be placed over the folded opening of the bag for purposes of chain of custody. Each agency may also have its own mandate for preserving evidence and chain of custody. If this is the case, then the required guidelines should be followed.

The skull should be packaged separately from the other remains to prevent any damage and to retain any soil or other deposits located inside the cranium. This will also prevent the teeth from becoming fractured, broken, dislodged from the tooth socket, or lost during transport. Pelvic bones should also be packaged separately from other elements, taking special precautions with the pubic symphyseal surfaces. When possible, bones from the left and right sides, such as the ribs, hands, and feet, should be bagged separately. If the vertebrae no longer have any connective soft tissue in place, they should be bagged together in cervical, thoracic, and lumbar packages or in packages containing three or four vertebrae to reduce possible damage during transport.

10.1.1.2 Storage of Skeletal Remains

If skeletal remains are to be packaged for shipping or long-term storage, special care must be taken when packing the bones. If bones need to be shipped for analysis, large bones should be wrapped individually in bubble wrap prior to placement in a shipping container. Smaller bones should be wrapped in paper towels or tissue and then placed in ventilated boxes or containers before placement in the shipping container. It is recommended that the shipping container be lined with a clear plastic bag that can be tied closed after packing and that any accompanying forms or shipping paperwork be placed in a separate sealable bag. This is to avoid any possible leakage or staining from the bones during shipment, some of which may still retain fluids or high fat content that could be affected by the transport environment.

Unidentified remains typically need to be packaged for long-term storage, which generally occurs at the medical examiner or coroner offices, or a forensic anthropology laboratory. Bones should be cleaned prior to storage, and depending on laboratory protocols, individual bones may be labeled with the case number. Bones should then be placed neatly in an acid-free cardboard box with the case number on the outside of the box. Additional acid-free packing materials can be used for stabilization during storage. It is important to note that the top of the storage box should allow for ventilation to avoid mold or mildew formation. All skeletal remains in long-term storage should be kept in a fairly stable temperature- and humidity-controlled environment.

10.1.2   Collecting Juvenile Skeletal Remains

The challenges involved in locating and excavating juvenile remains are much greater than those typically encountered when dealing with adult remains. Juvenile bones are not only considerably smaller than adult bones, but there are also numerous bones consisting of multiple unfused elements to allow for bone growth, which results in locating greater numbers of bones. For example, the diaphyses of long bones are not fused to the epiphyses during growth (refer to Figure 3.17). The number of bones present can be misleading, as elements often appear fragmentary and nonhuman in nature. These small skeletal elements are also extremely fragile and do not have the rigidity and hardness often associated with bone. Depending on an individual's developmental age, juvenile bones will be less mineralized than those of an adult, possibly resulting in increased erosion and differential preservation of skeletal elements. The environment and scavenging animals may also easily displace small juvenile remains, especially those of infants. Also, infant and fetal remains could easily be misidentified as items that would typically be seen in a recovery area, such as twigs, pebbles, small animal skeletons, or the remains of a chicken dinner.

As a result of these challenges to the recovery and collection process, it is likely that many juvenile skeletal elements will be missed unless properly identified and collected. It is crucial that great care be taken when processing a recovery site that might involve a juvenile. Identification and collection of juvenile remains by an inexperienced osteologist may prove difficult when confronted with the morphology of the juvenile skeleton and the number of individual unfused skeletal elements. This may also be the case for an osteologist who only has experience with adult skeletal remains. Investigators should work with someone well versed in juvenile osteology, ensuring the proper collection, preservation, documentation, and analysis of this type of evidence.

10.1.3   Collecting Fleshed Remains

There are instances when the degree of human decomposition is such that a different type of approach may be necessary; however, partially decomposed remains should be excavated using the same systematic and controlled approaches as described previously in Chapter 8. Modification of the recovery process usually occurs when the remains are exposed, and minor adjustments may be necessary to preserve as much of the original burial environment as possible when removing the remains for investigation under more controlled conditions.

When the majority of a body is exposed, there is a tendency to want to pull it free from the burial feature. There is a danger that weakened articulations, especially the neck, elbows, wrists, knees, or ankles, may separate, leaving disarticulated portions in the burial feature. This presents the potential for losing important pieces of soft tissue evidence, such as fingernails, fingerprints, and defense wounds or ligature marks. The best method for removal is to completely expose the remains, work around and loosen the areas where the remains are in contact with the floor of the burial feature, then lift the remains as a whole, preferably with a stretcher board support or with many individuals lifting at the same time. Once the body is removed, excavations can continue with investigation of the burial cut and any associated evidence.

Forensic personnel involved in the recovery of bodies and body parts in various stages of decomposition can be exposed to a variety of biological hazards (Galloway and Snodgrass, 1998). All crime scene personnel should take appropriate cautions when working in an environment where they can be exposed to a variety of infectious diseases. Personnel must be up-to-date with their vaccinations and must wear appropriate safety protection (Galloway and Snodgrass, 1998). Safety protection during the recovery of decomposing remains includes disposable protective clothing (e.g., Tyvek chemical resistant suits), examination gloves, masks, eyewear, and face shields if needed.

Remains found in advanced state of decomposition with wet soft tissue still present should be packaged so fluids do not leak during transport. The most efficient method is to wrap the body parts in a sterile cotton sheet or other sterile disposable lint-free material, and then place them into a zippered body bag. Do not seal any plastic bag with tissues inside unless the odor is extreme, and even then, only during the time required for transport. Any associated clothing, wrappings, or containers from the burial should accompany the remains for further investigation and should be packaged accordingly.

10.1.4 Collecting Burnt Remains

The nature of burnt remains differs greatly from other skeletal remains. The temperature of the fire and the length of time that a body is exposed to the fire will determine the appearance of the remains. Bone will change color, crack and warp, and even explode when exposed to high temperatures. Burnt bone is unlikely to have much potential for molecular and chemical analysis, though DNA may still be recovered in some instances (Redsicker and O'Connor, 1996; Smith and Sweet, 2010).

Cremated or burnt remains are found in all sorts of contexts but most are encountered in surface and shallow burials or in containers (Fairgrieve and Molto, 1994; Murad, 1998). Burnt bones are extremely fragile and must be disturbed as little as possible during recovery. A common methodology in fire investigation is to rake through the coals to recover as much as possible as quickly as possible, thus disturbing any relationship that existed between the bones and any other associated evidence. In cases such as this, we recommend that a forensic archaeologist who is familiar with fire recovery techniques and bone identification be used to recover evidence of this type (see Case Study 9).

With a substantial amount of information still able to be gathered from *in situ* burnt human remains, a forensic archaeologist and forensic anthropologist specializing in burnt remains could (Correia and Beattie, 2002; Dirkmaat, 2002; King and King, 1989):

- Identify human versus nonhuman remains
- Establish whether the remains were burned at the scene or burned elsewhere and then redeposited at the scene
- Determine the number of individuals recovered from the fire debris and their locations and orientations during the fire
- Increase the accuracy and precision in the collection of evidence and minimize the damage to bone fragments and associated evidence
- Aid in scene reconstruction with details on fire intensity, duration, and patterns of body and tissue alteration or destruction due to fire exposure

Special care is required when collecting and packaging burnt remains due to the friable nature of the material. Many forensic anthropologists have analyzed burnt remains where crime scene personnel have placed all of the body parts into one body bag during recovery. This collection method results in not only excessive mixing of the remains, but also extreme fragmentation, as the brittle bones are not stabilized for transport. When collecting burnt remains, individual bones must be wrapped separately and placed in a container or box that provides stability. A variety of materials can be used to wrap bones such as paper towels, toilet paper, or aluminum foil. While aluminum foil can provide stability, this material can also trap moisture. If aluminum foil is used to provide stability to fragile bones for transport, the foil must be opened up fairly quickly after arriving back at the lab to allow moisture to evaporate. Additionally, if there is any possibility that chemical testing may be performed on the remains, it is recommended that paper products be used for stabilization as the use of aluminum foil may interfere with test results. Fairgrieve (2008) also suggests using small sterile bottles, or

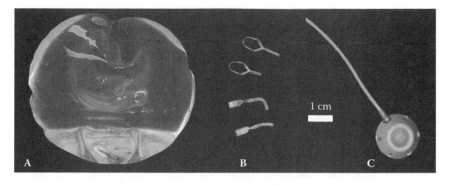

Figure 10.2 Additional materials that may be missed or regarded as refuse during recovery of human remains: (a) saline breast implant, (b) vascular clips, and (c) portacath (injection port).

similar containers, with cotton layering for small fragile items such as dental remains. Large pails with sealable lids should be used for transporting ash or fire debris to the lab for sorting (Fairgrieve, 2008).

10.1.5   Collecting Evidence of Surgical or Dental Modifications

Among the most important items for positive identification include evidence of surgical implants and dental work. Even though larger items, such as joint replacements, plates, and screws to reduce and stabilize broken bones, and dental orthopedics are more easily recognized, there are numerous smaller items that may be unrecognizable to most death investigators as surgical or dental implants if the items are not found attached to bones and teeth. In addition, there may be numerous surgical items added to the body that are never attached to bone, such as breast implants, portacaths (injection ports), and small metallic vascular clips (Figure 10.2), all of which may become disassociated from the skeleton after decomposition. Furthermore, during instances of bone fragmentation, bone erosion, and burnt remains, these forensically important items may be separated from skeletal remains and altered due to taphonomic processes. Most death investigators will be unfamiliar with the range of surgical and dental orthopedics encountered with decomposing bodies and skeletal material. Therefore, we recommend that all unrecognizable "trash" material should be collected at the scene, particularly in cases involving burnt remains, and be examined by knowledgeable personnel.

10.2   Nonhuman Skeletal Remains

Distinguishing between human and nonhuman skeletal remains is a task that should only be undertaken by a forensic anthropologist or other professionally trained individuals experienced in human osteology. In the field, an experienced forensic archaeologist or forensic anthropologist should be able to address one of the most primary concerns: Is the suspect material actually bone? For example, rocks can appear in shapes that mimic some adult skeletal elements (e.g., carpals, tarsals) as well as many elements from juvenile remains (e.g., epiphyses). However, in most cases rock is usually heavier than bone. Many small, irregular, or rounded skeletal elements tend to have greater amounts of cancellous bone in relation to cortical bone, making them significantly lighter than rocks. An experienced forensic anthropologist should have no problem distinguishing bone from other kinds of materials.

More commonly, a forensic anthropologist will be asked to determine whether skeletal remains are human or nonhuman. In many cases, differentiation of human remains from faunal material enables investigators to eliminate cases initially considered forensic in nature; although, in some instances faunal remains may be forensically relevant. William Bass (1995), a noted forensic anthropologist, has stated that as many as 25% to 30% of all cases submitted to forensic anthropologists are determined to be nonhuman, many of which are identified as butchered domestic animals (Figure 10.3). Thus, basic knowledge of the human and nonhuman skeleton can help save time when determining the forensic significance of whole

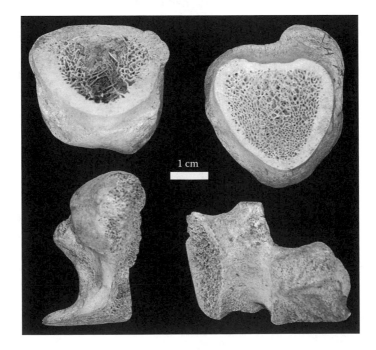

Figure 10.3 Examples of butchered nonhuman remains. Note the sharp edges, which are indicative of saw marks or deliberate dismemberment.

or fragmentary skeletal remains. Nevertheless, a forensic anthropologist should still examine all bones recovered from a scene to confirm whether the remains are human or nonhuman. In particular, when bones are highly weathered, eroded, and fragmented, identification may only be possible by a forensic anthropologist. If you do not have a forensic anthropologist at the scene or readily available, digital photographs of the remains should be emailed to a forensic anthropologist for identification. The remains should be photographed using a scale and *in situ* if possible to avoid damaging or destroying any contextual information. Many forensic anthropologists have reviewed photos via email to assist in identification of human versus nonhuman bones. This can save a tremendous amount of time and resources for everyone involved.

It is important for professionally trained osteologists to be familiar with fauna located in their geographical region when considering the various species that might be confused with human skeletal remains. Osteologists can become familiar with nonhuman skeletal material by putting together a comparative skeletal collection of local known fauna. This collection can then be used to help identify questionable skeletal elements. In addition to comparative collections, or in cases where a comparative collection is not available, there are various books that can be consulted for more in-depth comparative analysis of nonhuman skeletal biology. Two recent guides by forensic anthropologists include *Comparative Skeletal Anatomy: A Photographic Atlas for Medical Examiners, Coroners, Forensic Anthropologists, and Archaeologists* by B.J. Adams, P.J. Crabtree, and G. Santucci (2008) and *Human and Nonhuman Bone Identification: A Color Atlas* by D.L. France (2008). For guides on mammalian osteology, we suggest *Mammalian Osteology* by B.M. Gilbert (2003), *Mammal Bones and Teeth: An Introductory Guide to Methods of Identification* by S. Hillson (1992), and *Mammal Remains from Archaeological Sites: Southeastern and Southwestern United States* by S.J. Olsen (2004a). Also, for information about additional types of faunal remains we suggest *Fish, Amphibian and Reptile Remains from Archaeological Sites: Southeastern and Southwestern United States* by S.J. Olsen (2004b) and *Avian Osteology* by B.M. Gilbert, H.G. Savage, and L.D. Martin (1996).

10.2.1 The Nonhuman Mammal Skeleton

Large mammal bones such as bear, deer, large dogs, and pigs are most often confused with adult human bones, while remains of smaller animals may be confused with juvenile or fetal bones. From an anatomical perspective, because humans are mammals, they possess many of the same skeletal characteristics and can be similar in their skeletal components as nonhuman mammals. For example, bone structure of most nonhuman mammalian long bones includes a diaphysis composed of thick cortical bone and metaphyses and epiphyses composed of cancellous bone, which is similar to that of humans (refer to Figure 3.2). In fact, if a small bone fragment with no morphological indicators were recovered, the only way to identify whether it is human or nonhuman would be through histological examination, protein radioimmunoassay, or DNA analysis (Cattaneo et al., 1999; Ubelaker et al., 2004).

Upon gross examination, there are two main characteristics of bones that can help make the distinction between human and nonhuman bone easy and expeditious: maturity and morphology. Maturity aids in differentiating small nonhuman fauna that, even after reaching adulthood, have bones similar in size to those of juvenile humans. As discussed in Chapter 3, depending on the level of developmental maturity, juvenile human long bones may have separate epiphyses or may not possess any (refer to Figure 3.17). The proximal and distal ends of juvenile human long bones will have a roughened appearance where the epiphyses will eventually fuse to the metaphyses. Conversely, long bones of small adult fauna will have fused epiphyses. As a result, small adult faunal bones can be easily differentiated from those of juvenile humans by examining the level of bone maturity (Figure 10.4).

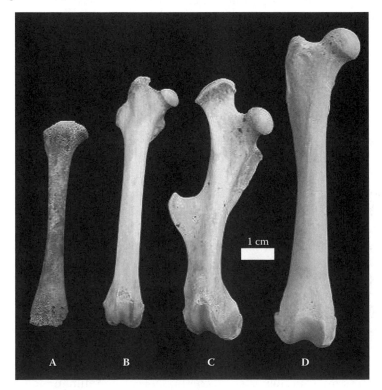

Figure 10.4 Comparison of epiphyseal maturity in the femora of small mammals: (a) human infant, (b) rabbit, (c) armadillo, and (d) raccoon.

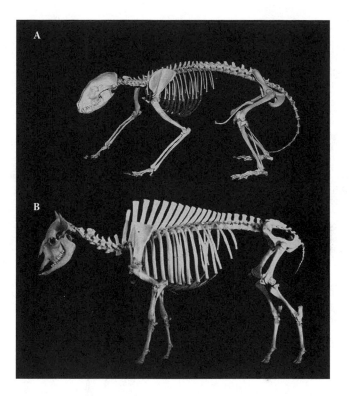
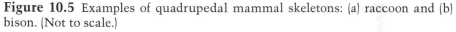

Figure 10.5 Examples of quadrupedal mammal skeletons: (a) raccoon and (b) bison. (Not to scale.)

The second characteristic of bone that aids in the distinction between human and nonhuman mammalian bone is morphology, or the shape of the bone. As mentioned previously, humans and other mammals share many of the same skeletal components, and we also share the same basic architecture (e.g., two femora, two humeri, two scapulae) required by our soft tissue structures. However, because humans are bipedal and walk upright, we have a distinct skeletal morphology that distinguishes us from quadrupeds, which are adapted for four-legged locomotion. Figure 10.5 presents two examples of the generalized mammalian skeleton to illustrate some of the skeletal features related to quadrupedal locomotion in a dog and bison.

When comparing humans with other mammals, the dissimilarity in the shape of long bones (Figures 10.6 and 10.7) and other bones of the body such as the scapula (Figure 10.8) can be very distinct and can quickly lead to a positive identification of human or nonhuman remains. Mammals belonging to the order artiodactyl (i.e., hoofed mammals that have two or four toes on each foot) can be easily distinguished from humans by the presence of a specific skeletal element. In these animals (e.g., deer, sheep, goat, moose, caribou), the third and fourth metacarpals, and third and fourth metatarsals fuse together into one structure early in development. These fused

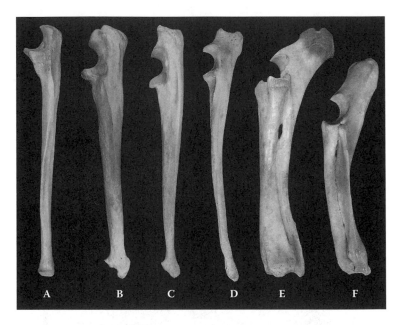

Figure 10.6 Morphological comparison of ulnae (anterior view) in large mammals: (a) adult human; (b) bear; (c) mountain lion; (d) wolf; (e) cow, fused with radius; and (f) domestic pig, fused with radius. (Not to scale.)

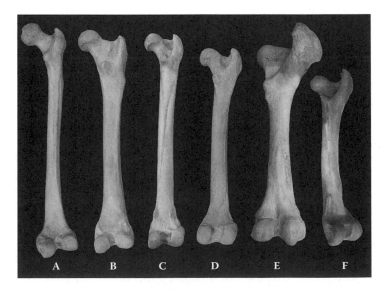

Figure 10.7 Morphological comparison of femora (posterior view) in large mammals: (a) adult human, (b) bear, (c) mountain lion, (d) wolf, (e) cow, and (f) domestic pig. (Not to scale.)

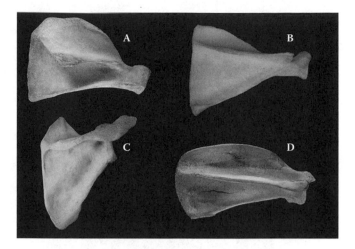

Figure 10.8 Morphological comparison of scapulae in large mammals: (a) pig, (b) sheep, (c) adult human, and (d) dog. (Not to scale.)

structures are called metapodials and are easily recognized by a number of morphological indicators: the shafts are long, thin, and straight, and they still retain a clear groove down the shaft where they have fused; the proximal end is flat while the distal end is unique with double rounded articular surfaces (Figure 10.9). Metapodials are long in certain species and therefore could be mistaken for human long bones.

Morphologically, small nonhuman fauna may have a noticeable curvature in the diaphyses of some long bones. In contrast, long bone diaphyses in a healthy juvenile human should appear straight (Figure 10.10). Also in a number of small nonhuman fauna, the fibula is reduced in size and is fused to the shaft of the tibia (Figure 10.11). Some larger mammal species (e.g., pig, sheep, and deer) have a curved and fused radius and ulna (Figure 10.12). In humans, neither the radius and ulna nor the fibula and tibia fuse together unless there is a pathological condition such as ossification of ligaments that serve to keep both bones articulated. The pelvis is another skeletal structure of small non-human fauna that could possibly be confused with juvenile human remains. If a small pelvis is fused into one unit (i.e., two innominates and a sacrum), it will be faunal, as a comparably sized pelvis in a juvenile human would contain multiple elements that would not be fused (Figure 10.13). In addition, the innominates of the adult human pelvis do not normally fuse to the sacrum unless there is a pathological condition that affects the sacroiliac joints or the pubic symphysis. The human cranium is quite distinct from most other mammals (excluding apes) because humans have a large, rounded braincase and flat, or orthognathic, face when viewed in profile. Because human crania are so distinct from other mammals, and misdiagnosis is unlikely, further differentiation will not be discussed.

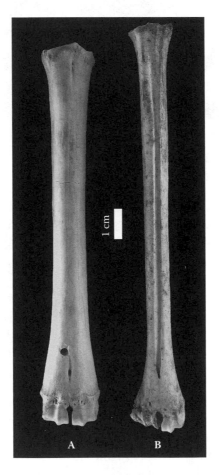

Figure 10.9 Examples of metapodials: (a) sheep metacarpals and (b) deer metatarsals. The large hole located toward the distal end of the sheep metacarpal was drilled to assist in removing fat during the maceration process.

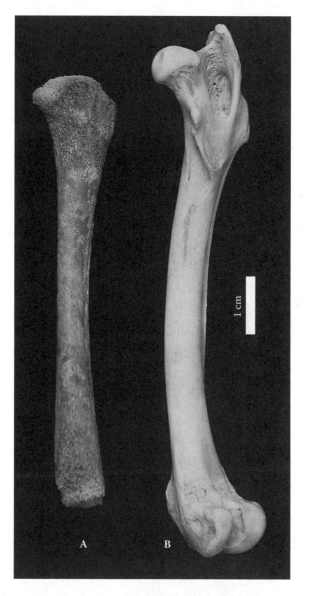

Figure 10.10 Comparison of diaphyseal curvature in small mammal femora (lateral view): (a) human infant and (b) raccoon.

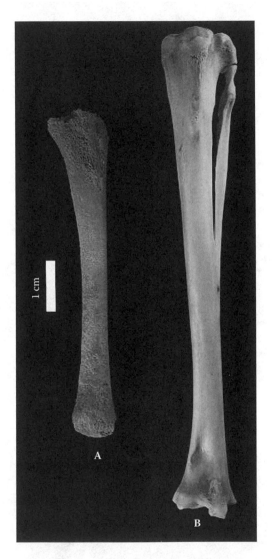

Figure 10.11 Comparison of morphology of tibiae in small mammals: (a) human infant and (b) rabbit with fused fibula (visible at top right).

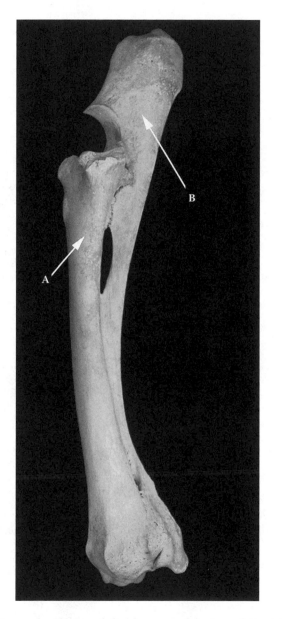

Figure 10.12 Example of curved diaphyses and fusion of the (a) radius and (b) ulna in a sheep.

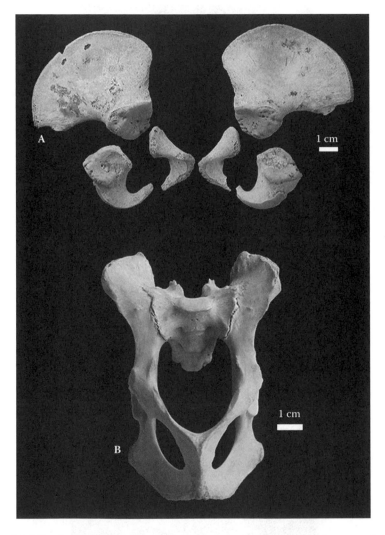

Figure 10.13 Morphological and maturity comparison of (a) a human child pelvis and (b) an adult raccoon. Although roughly the same size, the human pelvis remains unfused in young children, and the sacrum remains as a separate skeletal element.

10.2.2 The Avian Skeleton

There are several differences between a bird skeleton (Figure 10.14) and a human skeleton. Of course, birds have a very distinctive cranium, being the only animal to have a beak. Overall, birds tend to have fewer individual bones than mammals due to the presence of fused bone segments, and almost all bird skeletons are light in weight because they are adapted for flight. Such adaptations include the presence of the furculum (e.g., the wishbone), and the synsacrum, which is the large number of fused vertebrae that form a solid skeletal connection between the axial skeleton, the vertebra, and the pelvic girdle. Another distinct feature is that the bodies of the vertebrae are saddle shaped. On many birds, the sternum has a feature called the carina, a keel-like structure to which the muscles for flight are attached. The forelimb of a

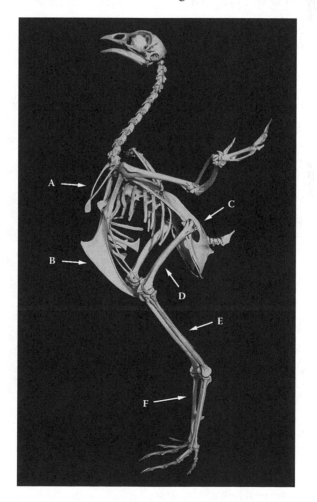

Figure 10.14 Example of an avian skeleton (chicken): (a) furculum, (b) carina, (c) synsacrum, (d) femur, (e) tibiotarsus, and (f) tarsometatarsus.

bird is fused so there is a reduction in the number of bones located in the carpal, metacarpal, and phalangeal regions in comparison with mammals. In addition, the bird skeleton is also unique because the lower limb is composed of three long bone segments: the most proximal being the femur, followed by the tibiotarsus, which is the union of the proximal part of the tarsal bones with the tibia, and the tarsometatarsus, which is the distal long bone segment formed by the fusion of tarsal bones with metatarsal bones.

The long bones of large birds (e.g., stork femora) may be confused with human skeletal elements; however, the unique morphology of bird long bones should preclude them from being misidentified. Bird long bones can be easily differentiated from human long bones because they have an outer surface that is generally smooth except for the ends, which contain irregular articular surfaces and small, roughened muscle attachment sites (Figure 10.15a).

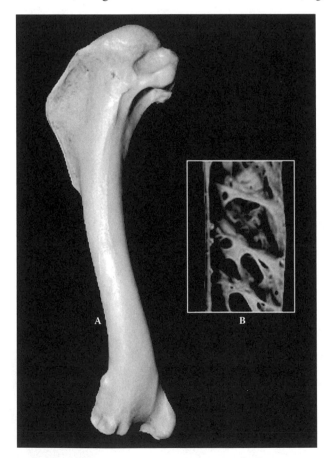

Figure 10.15 A falcon humerus (a) with a very smooth cortical surface, lacking prominent muscle attachments. A cross-section of the humerus (b) shows the thin, lightweight cortical bone and the medullary strut formations that provide structural support. (Not to scale.)

Another differentiating feature is the actual structure of a bird long bone, which is what makes a bird skeleton light. Bird long bones have very thin cortical bone (Figure 10.15b) and are mostly hollow with small struts of bone, called spicules, that cross the medullary cavity and provide structural support like that of an airplane wing. This feature is unique to birds.

10.2.3   The Reptilian Skeleton

Reptiles include animals such as turtles, lizards, snakes, and alligators. Reptiles have many unique skeletal characteristics that make them readily identifiable (Figure 10.16). Reptiles possess ball-and-socket–type joint articulations between their vertebrae, with the cranial side of the vertebra being concave, and the caudal side being convex (Figure 10.17). Unlike the mandible found in adult mammals, the lower jaw of a reptile consists of several skeletal elements. In addition, reptile jaws have conical peg-like teeth that are all the same type, called homodont dentition (Figure 10.18). This dentition is related to their feeding habits, as reptiles do not chew their food; instead they bite, tear, and swallow it.

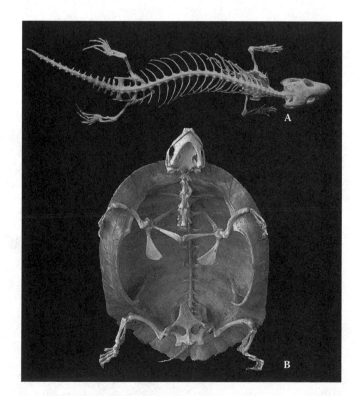

Figure 10.16 Examples of reptilian skeletons: (a) lizard and (b) turtle. (Not to scale.)

Figure 10.17 Alligator vertebrae (a) can be confused with vertebrae from large mammals such as (b) deer and (c) adult humans. Alligator vertebrae can be identified by the concave and convex surfaces (arrows) on the vertebral bodies. (Not to scale.)

Figure 10.18 An example of homodont reptilian dentition from a lizard.

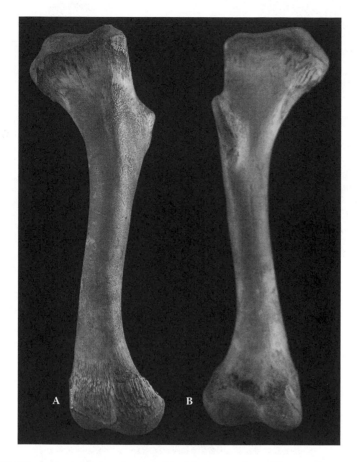

Figure 10.19 Anterior (a) and posterior (b) views of an alligator humerus showing the smooth cortical surface, lack of prominent muscle attachments, and lack of defined epiphyses.

Reptile long bones should be easily differentiated from human long bones. However, eroded and fragmented alligator long bones could cause some confusion in comparison with humans, as alligator bone fragments can be quite large in size. Overall, reptile long bones are moderately heavy with thick cortical bone, a very small medullary cavity, and no epiphyses. In addition, reptile long bones, such as those from an alligator, do not have the roughened and prominent muscle attachment sites commonly seen on human bones (Figure 10.19).

10.2.4 The Amphibian Skeleton

Amphibians include animals such as frogs, toads, and salamanders. Their skeletal elements are very light and few in number (Figure 10.20). There is great diversity among amphibious species in thickness of the cortical bone

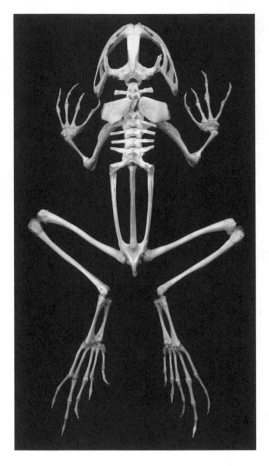

Figure 10.20 Example of an amphibian (frog) skeleton.

and the presence of medullary cavities in the long bones. One consistent feature is that amphibian long bones do not have epiphyses. Some species have cartilaginous ends to their long bones, and once decomposed the bones become hollow tubes. For the most part, there should not be any confusion between amphibian and human skeletal elements as amphibians are usually small and possess unique skeletal morphology.

10.2.5 The Fish Skeleton

There should be no confusion when identifying skeletal elements from fish, because their morphology is very different from any other animal. In comparison with the mammalian skeleton, fish have fewer skeletal elements (Figure 10.21), and as they are adapted to an aquatic environment, all of the bones reflect an adaptation for swimming, such as the absence of cancellous bone and medullary cavities. Like amphibians, fish bones do not have

Figure 10.21 Example of a fish skeleton.

epiphyses. Fish bones are commonly described as being translucent or semi-translucent, and they often emit a fishy odor, which is an uncommon trait in most other animals.

10.3   Common Misidentifications of Human and Nonhuman Bone

There are several nonhuman animals that have bone structures or features that appear similar to human skeletal material. Table 10.1 presents a summary of some of the basic skeletal features that may be used to distinguish

Table 10.1   Comparison of Human and Nonhuman Structural and Morphological Skeletal Indicators

	Structural Comparison		
	Cortical Bone	Medullary Cavity	Epiphyses
Humans	Thick	Small to medium	Distinguished
Mammals	Thick	Small	Distinguished
Birds	Thin	Large	Varies
Reptiles	Moderately thick	Reduced or absent	Varies
Amphibians	Varies	Varies	Absent
Fish	Noncancellous	Absent	Absent
	Morphological Comparison		
	Relative Weight	Muscle Attachments	Translucency
Humans	Heavy	Well developed	Not translucent
Mammals	Heavy	Well developed	Not translucent
Birds	Light	Poorly developed	Not translucent
Reptiles	Moderately heavy	Poorly developed	Not translucent
Amphibians	Light	Almost absent	Not translucent
Fish	Light	Almost absent	Translucent

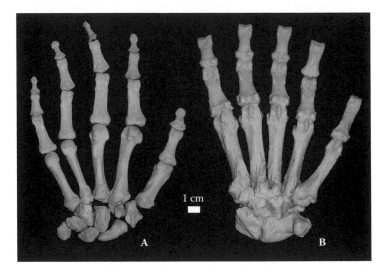

Figure 10.22 Bones from a human hand (a) compared with those of a bear (b).

the different classes of animals. There are some skeletal elements, however, that are commonly misidentified, such as the bones of a bear paw, pig teeth, the knee of a pig, turtle shell bone, and large avian furcula. Disarticulated bear paws are commonly confused with human hands (Figure 10.22). After a hunted bear has been killed, the claws are usually removed as a trophy and the paws are sometimes discarded after they are skinned. There is a striking resemblance between a bear paw and a human hand after decomposition of the soft tissue has started. However, a bear paw can be easily differentiated from a human hand by examining the individual bones, and this can be accomplished without cleaning the soft tissue from the bone. A radiograph will clearly show the differences in morphology between bones in a bear paw and those in a human hand.

Worn pig molar teeth also show a striking resemblance to human molars because pigs, like humans, are omnivorous and their teeth are designed for a generalized diet (Figure 10.23). However, pig molars are larger than human molars and have pointier cusps. The proximal part of the pig tibia, called the tibial plateau, can be easily misidentified as a human tibial plateau by an inexperienced osteologist as they share a similar morphology (Figure 10.24). The tibial plateau of a butchered pig knee or an unfused proximal tibial epiphysis may be easily identified when a portion of the proximal pig fibula is also available for examination. However, if only the very top of the tibial plateau is available without the shaft of the tibia, it can be very difficult to differentiate from a human tibia. Conversely, the tibial plateau of the deer is easily differentiated from the human knee because of the strikingly different morphology (Figure 10.24c).

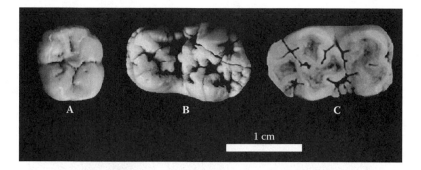

Figure 10.23 Comparison of a (a) human lower molar with that of (b) an unworn pig molar, and (c) a worn pig molar.

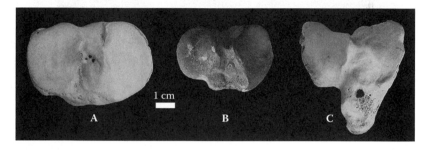

Figure 10.24 Morphological comparison of the tibial plateau in (a) adult human, (b) pig, and (c) deer.

The top portion of a turtle shell is called the carapace, while the bottom portion is called the plastron. Each portion of the shell is made up of fused bone plates covered by an outer layer of keratinized pieces called scutes. When the scutes come off of the shell, the underlying bone may resemble the top of a human skull. This is particularly true if only a portion of the bone layer is visible through the soil and has been bleached from sun exposure (Figure 10.25). Also, fragments of either the carapace or plastron can be easily mistaken for fragments of human cranial bone (Figure 10.26) because the flat shape and thickness is similar in form to human cranial vault fragments. If there are no diagnostic characteristics on the surfaces of the shell fragment, then the cross-sectional morphology of the shell fragment can be used to differentiate it from the unique cross section of human cranial bones.

A furculum from a large avian species can sometimes reach proportions equivalent to the human mandible, especially furcula from swans, geese, storks, and herons. The confusion between a human mandible and a large avian furculum occurs in instances where the lower dentition in a human mandible has been removed or lost and the tooth sockets have been resorbed into the mandible, leaving a smooth curved surface (Figure 10.27). This likeness in whole bone is quite similar; however, in fragmentary remains

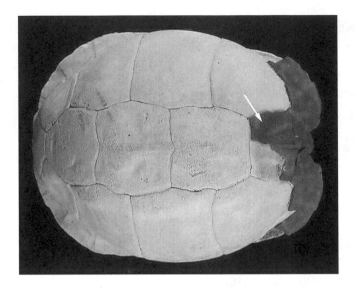

Figure 10.25 Turtle shell with an arrow indicating the remaining portion of the outer keratinized layer, or scute, covering the underlying bone layer.

Figure 10.26 Comparison of materials easily confused in a forensic or archaeological context: (a) turtle shell, (b) shell, (c) human skull, and (d) plastic.

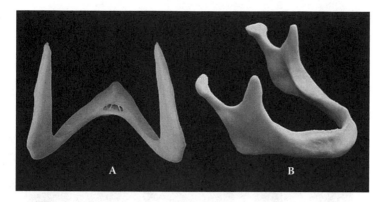

Figure 10.27 Comparison of (a) a goose furculum (posterior view) with (b) an edentulous (toothless) human mandible (lateral view).

it becomes fairly obvious to a trained osteologist whether the fragments are human or avian when the bone structure is exposed. In the furculum the cortical bone is very thin and the cancellous bone reflects adaptations for flight, while in the human mandible there is fairly thick cortical bone and dense cancellous bone.

Case Study 14: The Hog Hesitation

Authors Schultz and Dupras were asked to investigate remains located at a downtown construction site. Heavy equipment was being used to clear multiple large tree stumps when bones were discovered in the disturbed soil (Figure 10.28). The heavy equipment activities ceased and the scene

Figure 10.28 Secured construction site where bones were discovered during the removal of tree stumps.

Figure 10.29 Fragmented skeletal remains identified as pig bones (trowel for scale; pointing to north).

was secured by local law enforcement until we could arrive to distinguish if the remains were human or nonhuman. After examining the scene and the remains, we noted that there were a number of diagnostic bone fragments present including an os coxa, proximal ulna, and second cervical vertebra. The overall morphology of these bones was clearly different than that of a human, such as structural adaptations to quadrupedal locomotion. We determined that all of the fragmented skeletal materials were from a juvenile pig *(Sus scrofa)* (Figure 10.29). At that point we cleared the scene and construction activities resumed.

It is fairly common in forensic settings to distinguish nonhuman remains from potential human remains. Many cases involving questionable human or nonhuman skeletal remains end up with the bones and fragments being removed and transported to the medical examiner's office, where they are then examined outside of their original context. This case was somewhat unique in that we were called to the scene and the bones were left *in situ* so they could be examined in their archaeological context. After we determined on scene that the bones were nonhuman, we suggested that they be collected to avoid any identification issues in the future, which is our standard procedure for nonhuman bone field identification.

Figure 10.30 Flagged remains of a turtle with shell fragments scattered across the ground surface.

Case Study 15: A Nonhuman Human

During a death investigation, crime scene personnel were unsure if they had discovered possible human skull fragments eroding from the ground surface. To be certain, author Schultz was requested to identify the remains. Upon arriving at the scene, it was noted that none of the bone fragments had been moved and crime scene personnel had placed flags in the ground to mark the extent of the discovered remains. The fragments consisted of numerous sunbleached skeletal elements that were small, square, and flat (Figure 10.30). Many of the fragments were adhered to the ground surface by small fibrous roots. The bone fragments were immediately recognized as parts of a turtle carapace and plastron.

Given that land and water turtles are very prevalent in Florida, forensic anthropologists frequently identify this kind of material for law enforcement and medical examiners.

Although a forensic anthropologist is not needed to identify a complete turtle shell, a trained osteologist should always be consulted when identifying turtle shell fragments lacking scutes. In this case, the small fragments were the individual parts of the turtle shell that became disarticulated after the shell dried. Because the fragments were flat, particularly the plastron portion of the shell, they were easily confused with human cranial fragments by someone not familiar with this material. After the bone fragments were identified as nonhuman, the material was collected to avoid any misidentification in the future.

Key Words and Questions

amphibian
avian
ball–socket vertebrae
bone translucency
carapace/plastron
fish
furculum
homodont dentition
mammal
metapodial
reptile
synsacrum

1. You have been asked to assist in collecting and packaging burnt skeletal remains found in a residential house fire that was just extinguished by firefighters and cleared for investigation. What materials will you need for collection and packaging of these remains? What special concerns should be taken into account when collecting and packaging the remains?
2. What are some of the major concerns for the forensic archaeologist when collecting and packaging fleshed remains?
3. What bones of the human skeleton could be mistaken for a metapodial?
4. A construction crew worker found a fragment of a lower jaw during the installation of some new playground equipment. The jaw fragment has three pointy teeth remaining in the tooth sockets. What morphological indications should be considered to determine its forensic significance?
5. A bone, approximately 6 centimeters in length with what appears to be eroded ends, was found during a search for the remains of a missing adult woman in a remote wooded area. The bone was found in association with a concentration of small rocks, some twigs, and a patch of something that looks like fur. What factors should be taken into account in identifying, collecting, and packaging these materials?

Suggested Readings

Adams, B.J., Crabtree, P.J., Santucci, G. 2008. *Comparative Skeletal Anatomy: A Photographic Atlas for Medical Examiners, Coroners, Forensic Anthropologists, and Archaeologists*. Totowa, NJ: Humana Press.

France, D.L. 2008. *Human and Nonhuman Bone Identification: A Color Atlas*. Boca Raton, FL: CRC Press.

Galloway, A., Snodgrass, J.J. 1998. Biological and chemical hazards of forensic skeletal analysis. *Journal of Forensic Sciences* 43:940–948.

Mulhern, D.M. 2009. Differentiating human from nonhuman skeletal remains. In: Blau, S., Ubelaker, D.H., eds. *Handbook of Forensic Anthropology and Archaeology*, pp. 153–163. Walnut Creek, CA: Left Coast Press.

Owsley, D.W., Mires, A.M., Keith, M.S. 1985. Case involving differentiation of deer and human bone fragments. *Journal of Forensic Sciences* 30:572–578.

References

Adams, B.J., Crabtree, P.J., Santucci, G. 2008. *Comparative Skeletal Anatomy: A Photographic Atlas for Medical Examiners, Coroners, Forensic Anthropologists, and Archaeologists*. Totowa, NJ: Humana Press.

Bass, W.M. 1995. *Human Osteology: A Laboratory and Field Manual*. Columbia, MO: Missouri Archaeological Society.

Cattaneo, C., DiMartina, S., Scali, S., Craig., O.E., Grandi, M., Sokol, R.J. 1999. Determining the human origin of burnt bone: a comparative study of histological, immunological and DNA techniques. *Forensic Science International* 102:181–191.

Correia, P.M., Beattie, O. 2002. A critical look at methods for recovering, evaluating, and interpreting cremated human remains. In: Haglund, W.D., Sorg, M.H., eds. *Advances in Forensic Taphonomy: Method, Theory, and Archaeological Perspectives*, pp. 435–450. Boca Raton, FL: CRC Press.

Dirkmaat, D.C. 2002. Recovery and interpretation of the fatal fire victim: the role of forensic anthropology. In: Haglund, W.D., Sorg, M.H., eds. *Advances in Forensic Taphonomy: Method, Theory, and Archaeological Perspectives*, pp. 451–472. Boca Raton, FL: CRC Press.

Fairgrieve, S.I. 2008. *Forensic Cremation: Recovery and Analysis*. Boca Raton, FL: CRC Press.

Fairgrieve, S.I., Molto, J.E. 1994. Burning point: Canadian case studies of intentionally cremated human remains. In: Herring, A., Chan, L., eds. *Strength in Diversity: A Reader in Physical Anthropology*, pp. 385–402. Toronto, Ontario, Canada: Canadian Scholar's Press.

France, D.L. 2008. *Human and Nonhuman Bone Identification: A Color Atlas*. Boca Raton, FL: CRC Press.

Galloway, A., Snodgrass, J.J. 1998. Biological and chemical hazards of forensic skeletal analysis. *Journal of Forensic Sciences* 43:940–948.

Gilbert, B.M. 2003. *Mammalian Osteology*. Columbia, MO: Missouri Archaeological Society.

Gilbert, B.M., Savage, H.G., Martin, L.D. 1996. *Avian Osteology*. Columbia, MO: Missouri Archaeological Society.

Hillson, S. 1992. *Mammal Bones and Teeth: An Introductory Guide to Methods of Identification*. London: University College London Institute of Archaeology.

King, C.G., King, S. 1989. The archaeology of fire investigation. *Fire Engineering* 142(6):70–74.

Murad, T.A. 1998. The growing popularity of cremation versus inhumation: some forensic implications. In: Reichs, K., ed. *Forensic Osteology: Advances in the Identification of Human Remains*, 2nd ed., pp. 86–106. Springfield, IL: Charles C. Thomas.

Olsen, S.J. 2004a. *Mammal Remains from Archaeological Sites: Southeastern and Southwestern United States*. Cambridge, MA: Peabody Museum Press.

Olsen, S.J. 2004b. *Fish, Amphibian and Reptile Remains from Archaeological Sites: Southeastern and Southwestern United States* (No. 2). Cambridge, MA: The Peabody Museum Press.

Redsicker, D.R., O'Connor, J.J. 1996. *Practical Fire and Arson Investigation*, 2nd ed. Boca Raton, FL: CRC Press.

Skinner, M., Lazenby, R.A. 1983. *Found! Human Remains: A Field Manual for the Recovery of the Recent Human Skeleton*. Burnaby, BC: Archaeology Press Simon Fraser University.

Smith, B.C., David Sweet, O.C. 2010. DNA and DNA evidence. In: Senn, D.R., Stimson, P.G., eds. *Forensic Dentistry*, 2nd ed., pp. 103–136. Boca Raton, FL: CRC Press

Ubelaker, D.H., Lowenstein, J.M., Hood, D.G. 2004. Use of solid-phase double-antibody radioimmunoassay to identify species from small skeletal fragments. *Journal of Forensic Sciences* 49:924–929.

Writing the Final Report 11

During the documentation and note-taking process, it is very important to remember that a final report will most likely be required at the end of the investigation. Many law enforcement agencies may request reports even in instances where searches do not produce evidence, as the search process may need to be officially documented during the investigation. There may be cases where a forensic report may not be necessary (e.g., a case deemed to be non-forensic in nature at the end of the investigation), but it is always recommended that every scene should be approached as though some form of final report will be required.

In most cases, the forensic archaeology report will be included as part of a larger report, which is created by the lead investigative author or medical examiner or coroner. When writing a report it is always important to consider to whom the report may be submitted. This will determine the language to be used and the elements that must be included. The language used should be simple and direct, and grammar and spelling errors must be avoided. In some cases it is not possible to avoid using technical language, but care should be taken to make sure that the language used is not at a level that inhibits communication with other law enforcement entities. It should also be remembered that there could be a chance the report you are writing will also be used in a court of law as part of a legal proceeding. As such, a clear, direct approach is best.

11.1 Report Contents

While in the field everything possible should be documented and kept in notes. Appendices A through L are examples of forms that can be used to document information in the field. This information can then be used to construct the final report. Although each case is different, there are some components of the final report that should be consistent. The following can be used as a guide concerning sections that should be included in a report (of course adjusting for the type of case). Images, maps, and illustrations may also be included in each section as appropriate, and extra documentation of this type can be included in appendices at the end of the report or official case file.

11.1.1   Beginning Information

The start of every report should have all possible case numbers. Each law enforcement entity (e.g., Sheriff's Office, Medical Examiner's Office) will have individual case numbers. In addition most forensic archaeologists will have their own case numbering system. All of these numbers should be included in the case report so that there is no mistake in matching all reports together. Information such as location, date(s), and recorder should appear at the beginning of the report. This section should also include information about the person to whom the report will be submitted: their name and contact information.

11.1.2   Case Summary

A simple, straightforward summary of the case should be presented at the beginning of the report. This allows all readers to quickly review the major events and findings of the report without having to search through the entire report. The case summary should include the circumstances in which the investigator became involved in the case (i.e., who contacted them, and on what date, and what was their role in the investigation), the date of the involvement at the scene, methods used for search and excavation, and any findings resulting from those activities.

11.1.3   Participants

All participants at the scene should be listed (see Appendix D). In addition to the participants' names, other information such as affiliation and contact information should be collected. If you are unsure of the individuals at the scene (sometimes this can be hard to track at an active scene when everyone is concentrating on their work), a list is normally kept by one of the attending officers.

11.1.4   Scene Information

Basic information about the scene should be recorded upon arrival (Appendix E). This information should include whether the scene is indoor or outdoor, the topography (e.g., flat area, hills, water features), plant or ground coverage (e.g., wooded, grass, gravel, pavement), architecture, general weather access (e.g., shade, sun), and any miscellaneous factors (e.g., remains in a car, container, etc.). Access to the scene should also be described. If field maps or aerial photos were used to find the scene or to plan search strategies, these should also be listed and may be included in the report as an appendix. Any taphonomical disturbance (human or animal) should be noted and described. Appropriate images for this section might include an aerial photo or orthographic map of the area with the scene highlighted, or overall shots of the location.

11.1.5 Search Summary

Dependent on the case, a search may be required. If so, all search techniques should be documented. This should include any nonintrusive methods (e.g., visual foot searches, cadaver dogs, geophysical methods), and intrusive methods (e.g., probing, shovel or pit testing). Participants in the search should also be listed, particularly if specialists are used (e.g., geophysical equipment experts). Photographs of the search (including grids) would be appropriate in this section.

11.1.6 Surface Deposit

In some cases remains may be discovered as a surface deposit (either during a search, or by individuals who then report their find) (Appendix F). The mode of discovery should be the first thing noted (e.g., accidental discovery, search, witness). In cases where remains are exposed on the surface it should be noted if the deposit is primary or secondary in nature, and if the remains are fully exposed or only partially exposed. If remains are partially exposed, notation of the context (e.g., plant remains, detritus, erosion) must be made. The methods used for recovery of the remains should also be described, including screening techniques. General overview shots of the deposit should be included in this section.

11.1.7 Excavation Summary

If any excavations are performed, copious notes must be recorded. It is important to recognize that any excavation, as with intrusive search methods, will destroy the scene. The notes recorded during excavation, and the final report constructed from these notes, may be the primary means of reconstructing the scene and what happened to an individual. This section should be as detailed as possible (Appendix G). The size and location of the excavated area should be the first thing discussed, including how the area was located (witness, search, etc.). Next a basic description of excavation techniques should be included (e.g., heavy equipment, gridding, hand tools, excavation methods, screen techniques and size, etc.). The description of excavation technique should include whether the feature or grid was excavated, or if a pedestal method was used. Description of the burial feature and matrix is also important. Photographs documenting steps of the excavation may be included in this section.

11.1.8   Remains Recovered

If remains are discovered, it is important to provide a basic description of their context, location, and appearance (Appendix H). Remember that it is not the job of the forensic archaeologist to make any analyses of the remains on the scene, and this should not, under any circumstances, appear in a forensic archaeology report. The mode of deposition (e.g., surface, buried, aquatic, etc.), the condition and completeness of the remains, and the orientation and position of the body should be mentioned. If clothing or other items are associated with the body, this should also be noted.

11.1.9   Associated Evidence

A list of any associated evidence removed from the scene must be documented (Appendix K). This will include any materials gathered during the search for or recovery of remains. The evidence should be listed in order of discovery and should include a description, the individual who logged the evidence, and an evidence number. If the evidence is transferred, there should also be an accompanying chain of custody form, so that evidence mentioned in the report can be traced (Appendix L).

11.1.10   Collected Samples

Samples for future analysis may also be collected during search and recovery. These may include, but are not limited to, botanical samples, soil samples, and entomological samples. Separate collection forms should be filled out for each of these samples. Photographs of samples should also be included in this section.

11.1.11   Photographs/Video

Most law enforcement agencies will take their own photographs, and sometimes video of the scene, search, and excavation procedures. In addition, it is recommended that the forensic archaeologist should also document all procedures with photography (Appendix J). This includes search, excavation, and recovery. A photo log should be kept recording the camera type, card type (if using a digital camera), photo number, and a brief description of the photograph. A CD/DVD of all photos should be included with the report. Select photos are usually included in the report to highlight certain parts of the investigation, as mentioned in certain sections. These can be included in the body of the report or in the appendix. Keep in mind that all photos taken during search and recovery are admissible as evidence; therefore, be sure that the subject matter of all photos is appropriate to the case.

11.1.12 Field Drawings/Maps

Field drawings and maps are also a very important part of the forensic report. In addition to photographs, maps are important to show the location of the remains, and how the remains are associated with any potential evidence. Maps can also document a scene in a way that cannot be achieved with other methods. For example, a cross-sectional map can show how the remains are associated with evidence at different levels, or how remains may be located on a slope, or at different depths. Although we list maps in their section here, they may also be included in the appendices.

11.1.13 References

It may be necessary to include references within the report. For example, if certain published methods are used during the investigation, and are too detailed to include in the report, a reference may be used to supplement the report.

11.1.14 Appendices

Any additional information included in the case file (e.g., aerial photos, topographical maps, case maps, case photos, etc.) that is not in the main body of the report can be included in the appendix section.

11.1.15 Signatures and Dates

There should be a spot for original signatures and date of report completion at the end of the body of the report. This will normally come before the references and appendices, dependent on whether or not these are included in the report.

11.2 Example of a Case Report*

This section includes a sample case report, which is featured as a case study in Chapter 5. This example does not include images or appendices but makes reference to where these should be included.

---

* Some of the names, dates, and places have been changed to protect those involved.

Title: The Good, the Bad, and the Muddy (Featured in Chapter 5)

UCF Case Number: UCF-2001c
ME Case Number: District #9, 01-00003
Orange County Sheriff's Office Number: 2001-000458
Recorded by: Tosha Dupras
Dates: September 7–9, 2001
Report to be submitted to:

Detective Bob Grisham
CID–Homicide
Hardy County Sheriff's Office
555 Willow Street
Orlando, FL 32555
Phone: (407) 555-5551
Fax: (407) 555-5555

Dr. Lauren Green
Chief Medical Examiner
Medical Examiner's Office
555 Sapling Avenue
Orlando, FL 32552
Phone: (407) 555-5552
Fax: (407) 555-5556

CASE SUMMARY

I was initially contacted by Detective Jonathan Sparrow of the Hardy County Sheriff's Office on September 8, 2001, to assist in a search and possible recovery for an individual who had been missing for approximately 15 months. Arrangements were made to meet the following day at the crossroads of Highway 32 and CR #5 in Hardy County. Search for the remains of a missing 22-year-old began at 9:30 AM on September 7, and ensued until September 9 at 2:30 PM when a body was discovered. Search techniques included a visual walking search, cadaver dogs, and heavy equipment. The body was discovered through extensive removal of dirt by the heavy equipment. Once the body was discovered, hand excavations ensued. A pit, 2.5 feet wide, and 4 feet long, was discerned through shovel shining. The body, with the exception of the skull, was still intact due to tissue preservation with adipocere formation. The body was completely removed as a unit and placed in a body bag to be transported to the Medical Examiner's Office. Excavations and body removal were complete at 7:30 PM on September 9. Complete details of the search and excavation are found in the following sections.

PARTICIPANTS

The following participants were involved at the scene (see Appendix A for contact details) and were present throughout the investigation. For logs of exact times and dates, refer to OCSO report #2001-000458.

1. Tosha Dupras, UCF, Assistant Professor, Forensic Anthropologist
2. Lana Williams, graduate student, UCF
3. Sandra Wheeler, graduate student, UCF
4. Jonathan Sparrow, Detective, Orange County Sheriff's Office
5. Bob Grisham, Detective, Orange County Sheriff's Office
6. Richard Lambert, Detective, Orange County Sheriff's Office
7. Jerry Rigs, Sergeant, Orange County Sheriff's Office
8. Dr. Susan Hood, Associate Medical Examiner, District #9 Medical Examiner's Office
9. Kelsey Wells, CSI, Orange County Sheriff's Office

10. Toslitha Hood, CSI, Orange County Sheriff's Office
11. Spencer Styles, CSI, Orange County Sheriff's Office
12. Susan Green, CSI, Orange County Sheriff's Office
13. Reginald Smith, Deputy, Orange County Sheriff's Office
14. Sarah Grewn, Deputy, Orange County Sheriff's Office
15. George Beath, Officer, Canine Unit, Orange County Sheriff's Office
16. Adam Chiboski, Officer, Canine Unit, Orange County Sheriff's Office
17. Jim Roth, Officer, Orange County Corrections
18. Jeffrey Lordes, Inmate, Orange County Corrections
19. Billy Green, Inmate, Orange County Corrections
20. Graham Wordey, Inmate, Orange County Corrections
21. Jesus Pedro Garcia, Inmate, Orange County Corrections
22. Reese Billings, Inmate, Orange County Corrections
23. Goliath Reed, Inmate, Orange County Corrections
24. Todd Breatter, Inmate, Orange County Corrections
25. Tomas Ojek, Inmate, Orange County Corrections
26. Jose Rodriguez, Inmate, Orange County Corrections
27. Zeus Tremble, Inmate, Orange County Corrections
28. Toby Green, Heavy Equipment Operator, Orange County Road System
29. Rocky Onlooker, Incarcerated Inmate (witness), Orange County Corrections

SCENE INFORMATION

The scene (see Appendix B) is located in an abandoned pig farm, located south of Highway 32 on the left side of County Road 5 heading south. A tree line and a fire trench bordered the northern side of the site. The west side was bordered by a dirt road (County Rd #5). East and south sides were covered in low bush cover. The scene is a flat area covered by dense grass and ground cover. The scene was accessed by a dirt road.

SEARCH SUMMARY

SEPTEMBER 7, 2001

Search of the area was initiated at approximately 9:30 AM on September 9, 2001. In attendance was Orange County Homicide detectives Jonathan Sparrow, Richard Lambert and Bob Grisham, and Sergeant Jerry Rigs. Two Sheriff's deputies (Reginald Smith, Sarah Grewn) were present to secure the scene, and two members of the Orange County Canine Unit were present with their dogs.

An initial walkthrough of the area was conducted based on information from one of the suspects who had been on the scene the previous day. The area marked by police as "searchable" measured approximately 75 feet by 50 feet (see figure below). The area was covered in grass, brush, and brambles. Three areas containing features that were anomalous from the surrounding area were identified as possible areas to explore. Brambles and low-lying brush were removed from one area. It was then decided to bring in a large mower to remove all low brush and small trees. Two cadaver dogs searched the scene but did not locate any suspicious areas. A prison detail of approximately 10 inmates was brought in to clear the remainder of the ground cover. One of the areas, previously disturbed by animals, was excavated. A pit containing butchered pig bones was discovered. At approximately 3:30 PM it began to rain very hard and the search was suspended for the day.

SEPTEMBER 8, 2001

I arrived on the scene at approximately 1:15 PM. Lana Williams and Sandra Wheeler were already present with Detectives Bob Grisham and Jonathan Sparrow and other law enforcement personnel. A suspect from the case had been brought back to the scene to describe location of burial. A large earth-moving machine with bucket and hoe was on the scene removing large quantities of dirt. The search had uncovered a large turtle shell but no human remains. The rain began at approximately 3:00 PM and quickly created a large muddy area where excavations were taking place. The search was called off shortly afterwards.

SEPTEMBER 9, 2001

I arrived on the scene at approximately 3:30 PM after receiving a call from Detective Jonathan Sparrow that a human bone had been discovered with the heavy excavation equipment. Upon my arrival I was briefed on the day's search efforts. In my absence that day another canine unit from Tampa's Search and Rescue had searched the area and hit on two possible areas. A large earth-moving machine (Spider) was brought to the scene to explore the area further. A human bone was uncovered by the heavy equipment at approximately 2:30 PM. The search and use of heavy equipment was suspended until a representative from the Medical Examiner's Office arrived. At this point it began to rain, and a temporary shelter was erected over the site. A plastic sheet was placed over the burial area.

EXCAVATION SUMMARY

Dr. Susan Hood from the local Medical Examiner's Office arrived on scene at approximately 4:15 PM. She instructed us to continue with excavations and left a body bag. Location of the burial was documented using GPS.

Shovels with flat blades were used to slowly remove soil from the burial area. As soil was removed a dark discoloration of soil was clearly present and delineated the entire burial pit. The burial pit measured 2.5 feet wide, by 4 feet in length. Once the burial pit was located, the feature was excavated using trowels and small hand tools.

Large quantities of rain made the excavation very difficult. The sides of the excavation area were unstable and continued to collapse. Water ran down the sides of the excavation area and also seeped in from the surrounding walls. Efforts were made to dig trenches around the area to divert water from the burial. Because of these conditions, setting up a grid was impossible

Excavations and removal were completed at approximately 7:30 PM.

REMAINS RECOVERED

Excavations revealed one complete individual lying on the right side in a semi-fetal position. The skull appeared to be skeletonized with some soft tissue and hair present. The infracranial skeleton (with the exception of the left lower arm and hand, and the right foot) was still covered with soft tissue and adipocere. The body was devoid of clothing. The body was exposed and removed as a unit into a body bag. Skeletal elements from left lower arm and hand and right foot were removed and placed in a bag.

ASSOCIATED EVIDENCE

Small shards of glass were removed from the nasal area, and an unidentified piece of material was removed from the occipital region of the skull and recorded as evidence (see Appendix C).

SAMPLES TAKEN

No samples were collected during search or excavation.

PHOTOGRAPHS/VIDEO

Photographs (numbers 2453 to 3532, Appendix D) were taken with a digital Nikon® digital camera and stored on a 1MG SD card. Photographs and video were also taken by crime scene investigation (CSI) personnel on the ground and also from a helicopter.

APPENDICES

Appendix B: Aerial Photos and Maps of Scene and Search Areas
Appendix C: List of Associated Evidence
Appendix D: List of Scene and Evidence Photos

SIGNATURES

Submitted by:

Tosha L. Dupras   **09-18-01**

_____   _____

Dr. Tosha Dupras   Date
Assistant Professor, Department of Anthropology
University of Central Florida
Orlando, FL 32816
Phone: (407) 555-6758
Fax: (407) 555-0006

Appendix A: Adult Skeletal Inventory Form (Field Collection)

Case #:	Agency:	Date/time:
Location:	Collected by:	

Instructions: For single or paired bones (e.g., hyoid, humerus), mark the corresponding box. For grouped bones (e.g., right ribs, left carpals), enter the number present. Any additional notes should be attached to this form.

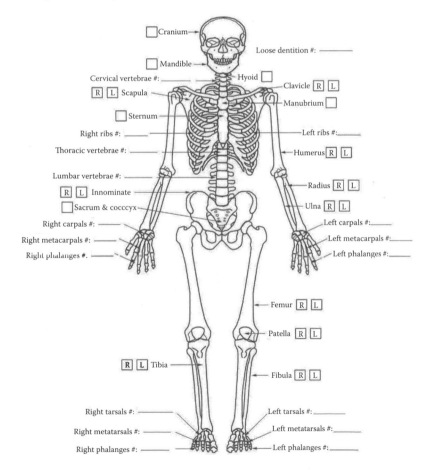

Appendix B: Infant Skeletal Inventory Form (Field Collection)

Case #:	Agency:		Date/time:
Location:		Collected by:	

Instructions: Using the illustration below, fill in the corresponding elements as they are recovered. Any additional notes should be attached to this form.

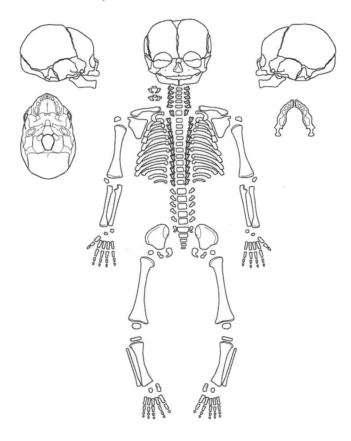

Appendix C: Child Skeletal Inventory Form (Field Collection)

Case #:	Agency:	Date/time:
Location:	Collected by:	

Instructions: Using the illustration below, fill in the corresponding elements as they are recovered. Any additional notes should be attached to this form.

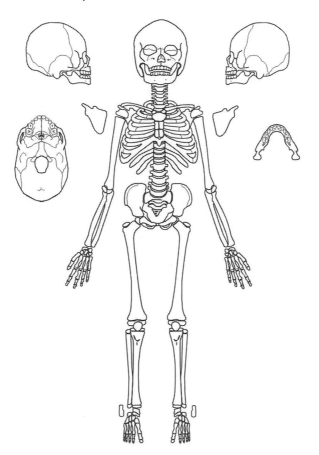

Appendix D: Personnel and Scene Summary Form

Case #:	Agency:
Field #:	Date(s) of recovery:

Scene Personnel

Lead investigator:	Tel: Email:
Lead on recovery team:	Tel: Email:
Additional recovery team personnel (name, title, and contact information): 1. 2. 3. 4.	

Scene Summary

Address or location:
Description of area:

Evidentiary Repositories

Evidence	Name, Title, and Agency	Date
Recovered remains		
Artifactual evidence		
Entomology samples		
Botany samples		
Soil samples		

Appendix E: Recovery Scene Context Form

Case #:	Agency:		Date/time:
Field #:		Recorded by:	

Recovery Scene and Habitat Description

Outdoor:	☐ Forest (wooded area) ☐ Field (pasture/ grassland) ☐ Roadside: ☐ Cemetery: ☐ Aquatic:	☐ Sand ☐ Cleared lot ☐ Leaf litter ☐ Gravel ☐ Pavement	☐ Sun ☐ Shade ☐ Rain ☐ Snow/ice
Indoor:	☐ Barn/stable ☐ Garage/storage area ☐ Single-unit home ☐ Apartment/townhouse Room: Heated: ☐ Yes ☐ No A/C: ☐ Yes ☐ No		☐ Soil ☐ Gravel ☐ Pavement ☐ Carpet ☐ Wood/tile/ terrazzo ☐ Open window ☐ Ceiling fan
Miscellaneous:	☐ Car: ☐ Trash container: ☐ Appliance: ☐ Other:		
Describe access to area:			

Microenvironment Data

Describe groundcover (density and type):
Describe weather conditions (temperature, humidity, precipitation):

Recovery Scene Surroundings

Describe nearby architectural or landscape features:
Field maps or aerial photos used: 1. 2. 3.

Recovery Scene Disturbances

Describe evidence of perimortem/postmortem animal or human disturbance:
Documentation of disturbance:
1.
2.
3.

Appendix F: Surface Deposit Recovery Form

Case #:	Agency:
Field #:	Date(s) of recovery:
Surface Feature #: of	Recorded by:

Surface Feature Description

Feature is:	Feature is partially exposed due to:	

☐ Primary
☐ Secondary
☐ Fully exposed
☐ Partially exposed
	☐ Natural plant growth
	    or detritus
	☐ Purposeful
	    concealment using:
		☐ Aquatic pool or
		    stream
		☐ Burial erosion
		☐ Other:

Size of feature:		
Location of feature:		

Method(s) Used to Locate Feature

☐ Witness identification ☐ Accidental discovery	☐ Visual foot search ☐ Cadaver dog
Remarks:	

Method(s) of Recovery

☐ No excavation required ☐ Removal of plant growth and surface debris	☐ Some excavation required ☐ Extensive excavation required
Size of screen mesh and description of materials screened:	

Associated Evidence

☐ No associated evidence was recovered	☐ Associated evidence was recovered
☐ Evidentiary or ☐ Field collection inventory ID list:	

Feature Photographs/Video

Record log numbers:

Survey Maps/Field Drawings of Feature

1.
2.
3.

Appendix G: Feature Excavation Form

Case #:	Agency:
Field #:	Date(s) of recovery:
Feature #: of	Recorded by:

Excavation Area

Size and location of excavation area:

Method(s) Used to Locate Feature

☐ Witness identification   ☐ Burial erosion
☐ Accidental discovery   ☐ Mechanical exposure
☐ Visual foot search   ☐ Cadaver dog
☐ Other: ☐ Geophysical equipment

Remarks:

Method(s) of Recovery

☐ Hand excavation tools   ☐ Backhoe
☐ Shovel   ☐ Other:

Size of screen mesh and description of materials screened:

Feature Excavation

☐ Direct excavation of feature ☐ Unit area excavation	☐ Pedestal excavation ☐ Other:
Feature size and description:	
Description of burial matrix:	

Associated Evidence

☐ No associated evidence was
   recovered
	☐ Associated evidence was
	   recovered

☐ Evidentiary or ☐ Field collection inventory ID list:	

Feature Photographs/Video

Record log numbers:

Survey Maps/Field Drawings of Feature

1.
2.
3.
4.
5.

Appendix H: Remains Summary Form

Case #:	Agency:	Date(s):
Location:	Recorded by:	

Mode of Deposition

☐ Surface	☐ Partial surface concealment
☐ Buried	☐ Partial burial concealment
☐ Aquatic	☐ Other context

General description:

Condition of Remains

Integrity:	Completeness:
☐ No/minimal decomposition	☐ Completely intact body
☐ Bloating/discoloration	☐ Partially intact or dismembered body
☐ Major soft tissue decomposition/adipose	☐ Complete skeletal articulation
☐ Mostly skeletonized	☐ Partial skeletal articulation
☐ Completely skeletonized	☐ Disarticulated skeleton
☐ Skeletal deterioration	☐ Incomplete remains
☐ Cremains	☐ Unknown

Orientation (Direction/Degrees):	**Clothing Present:**
Head/feet orientation:	
Orientation of body axis:	

Limb Position (Degree of Flexion):	**Hand/Foot Position (Placement):**
R Arm:	R Hand:
L Arm:	L Hand:
R Leg:	R Foot:
L Leg:	L Foot:

Appendix I: Forensic Entomology Data Collection Form

Case #:	Agency:
Field #:	Date(s) of recovery:
Feature #: of	Recorded by:

Scene and Habitat Description

Outdoor:	☐ Forest (wooded area) ☐ Field (pasture/ grassland) ☐ Roadside ☐ Burial ☐ Aquatic:	☐ Grass ☐ Soil ☐ Leaf litter ☐ Gravel ☐ Pavement	☐ Sun ☐ Shade ☐ Rain ☐ Snow/ice

Indoor:	☐ Barn/stable
	☐ Garage/storage area
	☐ Single-unit home
	☐ Apartment/townhouse
	   Room:
	   Heated: ☐ Yes ☐ No
	   A/C: ☐ Yes ☐ No
		☐ Soil
		☐ Gravel
		☐ Pavement
		☐ Carpet
		☐ Wood/tile/terrazzo
		☐ Open window
		☐ Ceiling fan	

Miscellaneous:	☐ Car: ☐ Trash container: ☐ Appliance: ☐ Other:		
Remarks:			

Climate Data

Scene Data:	Sample Temperatures:
Ambient temperature and humidity (30 cm):	Body surface (thoracic):
Ambient temperature and humidity (1.3 m):	Body surface (knees):
Ground surface:	Larval mass 1:
Body/ground interface:	Larval mass 2:
Soil below body (5 cm depth):	Larval mass 3:
Soil away from body (10 cm depth):	Larval mass 4:
Water (10 cm below surface):	

Using the provided sketches, record the following information:
- Clothing (hatched lines ▨)
- Traces of scavenging (SC ⟶)
- Visible wounds (W ⟶)
- Larval masses (LM_1, LM_2, etc. ⟶)
- Sample locations (1, 2, 3, etc. ⟶)

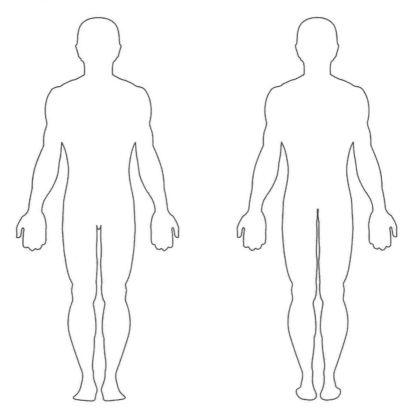

Sample #	Approx. #	Type	PR or LV	Location on Body
		AF ☐ AB ☐ E ☐ L ☐ P ☐ X ☐		
		AF ☐ AB ☐ E ☐ L ☐ P ☐ X ☐		
		AF ☐ AB ☐ E ☐ L ☐ P ☐ X ☐		
		AF ☐ AB ☐ E ☐ L ☐ P ☐ X ☐		
		AF ☐ AB ☐ E ☐ L ☐ P ☐ X ☐		
		AF ☐ AB ☐ E ☐ L ☐ P ☐ X ☐		
		AF ☐ AB ☐ E ☐ L ☐ P ☐ X ☐		
		AF ☐ AB ☐ E ☐ L ☐ P ☐ X ☐		
		AF ☐ AB ☐ E ☐ L ☐ P ☐ X ☐		
		AF ☐ AB ☐ E ☐ L ☐ P ☐ X ☐		
		AF ☐ AB ☐ E ☐ L ☐ P ☐ X ☐		
		AF ☐ AB ☐ E ☐ L ☐ P ☐ X ☐		
		AF ☐ AB ☐ E ☐ L ☐ P ☐ X ☐		
		AF ☐ AB ☐ E ☐ L ☐ P ☐ X ☐		
		AF ☐ AB ☐ E ☐ L ☐ P ☐ X ☐		
		AF ☐ AB ☐ E ☐ L ☐ P ☐ X ☐		
		AF ☐ AB ☐ E ☐ L ☐ P ☐ X ☐		
		AF ☐ AB ☐ E ☐ L ☐ P ☐ X ☐		

Coding key: AF, adult fly; AB, adult beetle; E, eggs; L, larvae; P, pupae; X, frass or insect fragments; PR, preserved sample; LV, live sample.

Appendix J: Photography/Video Record Form

Case #:	Agency:
Field #:	Date(s) of recovery:
Camera:	Data card:

Photographic/Video Evidence

Photo #	Date	Description	Initials

Appendix K: Evidentiary Inventory Form

Case #:	Agency:
Field #:	Date:

Items Collected in Field Recovery

Item #	Description	Initials	Evidence ID #

Appendix L: Evidentiary Chain of Custody Form

Case #:	Agency:
Field #:	Date(s) of Recovery:

Scene Personnel

Lead investigator:	Tel: Email:
Lead on recovery team:	Tel: Email:

Transfer of Custody

☐ Evidentiary or ☐ Field collection inventory ID list:
Description of evidence being transferred:

Transferred from	Transferred to
Name: Title: Agency: Date: Time: Signature:	Name: Title: Agency: Date: Time: Signature:

Glossary

ABFA Diplomat (DABFA): Certified professionals recognized for their special qualifications in forensic anthropology and for meeting the standards set forth by the American Board of Forensic Anthropology

active geophysical method: Transmitting an induced signal into the ground and measuring the returning signal in an effort to detect subsurface anomalies

adipocere: Wax-like insoluble fatty acids resulting from slow hydrolysis of the body's fat during decomposition. Adipocere (grave wax) forms best in an oxygen-free, humid environment, such as in wet ground or a sealed casket

adult: Fully grown or developed organism

aerial imagery: High- or low-resolution images of regions of landscape taken from the air

ala: Wing-like structure

algae: Primitive chlorophyll-containing aquatic organism

alveolus: Angular cavity or pit

amalgam inlay: Dental restoration containing a mixture of mercury with at least one other metal, such as silver, tin, or zinc; also known as a "filling"

American Academy of Forensic Sciences (AAFS): Professional society for people in all areas of forensics and dedicated to the application of science to the legal process

American Board of Forensic Entomology (ABFE): Organization that certifies professionals recognized for their special qualifications in forensic entomology

amphibian: Class of animal that is a four-legged vertebrate, does not have amniotic eggs, and can live both on land and in water

anemophilous plants: Wind-pollinating plants

anomaly (geophysical): An irregularity in the Earth's stratigraphy; detected using geophysical survey tools

antemortem: Before death

anterior: Toward the front

apical: Toward the tip of the tooth root

appendicular skeleton: Bones of the shoulder girdle, pelvic girdle, and limbs

archaeology: Study of past human societies through the recovery and analysis of the material culture, physical remains, and evidence of environmental interactions that they have left behind

articular surface: Where one bone comes in contact with another

articulation: Location where two or more bones make contact, forming a joint (true articulation must have soft tissues connecting the bones; although some may use the term to describe undisturbed skeletal elements, it is more correct to describe the elements as being in *anatomical position*)

artifact: Any portable object made, used, or modified by humans

associated artifacts: Objects that have some direct association with remains (e.g., clothing, personal items)

association: Archaeological principle that presumes that items found together within the same layer are essentially of the same relative age

auditory ossicles: Irregular paired bones of the ears that consist of the incus (anvil), stapes (stirrup), and malleus (hammer); found within the temporal bones of the cranial vault

autogamous plants: Self-pollinating plants

autolysis: Chemical process that results in the destruction of tissues by intracellular enzymes within an organism

avian: Characteristics pertaining to birds

axial skeleton: Bones of the midline; includes skull (cranium and mandible), auditory ossicles, hyoid, ribs, and vertebral column

azimuth: Angular measurement in a spherical coordinate system

azimuth control-point mapping: Method of mapping that uses a 360° spherical coordinate system to record the two-dimensional position of objects on a plan drawing

backfill: To refill a hole or excavation with the material that was taken out of it; also refers to the material itself

backhoe: Heavy excavating equipment consisting of a digging bucket on the end of a two-part arm, which is typically mounted on a tractor or front loader

backsight: A measurement taken back toward a point of known elevation and angle

ball–socket vertebrae: Concave–convex articulation surface found in reptile vertebrae

baseline: Arbitrary line established for the purpose of measuring

benchmark: A precisely determined point of elevation or triangulation point established by a government agency or private survey firm; typically a stamped brass disk affixed to rock outcroppings, bridges, buildings, or other prominent and permanent features

bilateral: On both sides

biological profile: Analysis of skeletal features to estimate the age, sex, ancestry, and stature for an unidentified individual

bioturbation: The mixing of soil or sediments by living organisms

bloating: Recognizable by-product of putrefaction; results in the abdomen swelling with gases that are produced by bacterial flora during decomposition

blowfly: Flies of the family Calliphoridae that deposit their eggs in carrion, decomposing tissues, dung, and open wounds

bone translucency: The characteristic of a bone allowing light to pass through but diffusing it

box screen: A heavy-duty sifting screen that is centrally positioned on a pair of legs so it can be moved back-and-forth to allow for rapid sifting of loose, granular sediments

buccal: Surface of premolars and molars facing the cheek

bulldozer: Continuous tracked tractor equipped with a substantial blade used to push large quantities of soil during heavy construction excavation

burial: The practice of concealing a body in the ground

burial cut: Excavation feature that forms the grave; also known as a grave cut

burial depression: Primary or secondary depression that forms over a burial as a result of settling or decomposition

burial outline: Visible line formed as a result of soil disturbance during burial

cadaver dog: Canine specially trained in detecting the scent of human decomposition and assisting in locating human cadavers, body parts, and body fluids

calcination: Disintegration of bone by heat; calcinated bone is typically grayish-white and crumbly in appearance

cancellous (trabecular) bone: Light, porous interior structure of bone

carapace: Top portion of a turtle shell

carpals: Small, rounded bones of the wrist; each wrist consists of eight bones: scaphoid, lunate, triquetral, pisiform, trapezium, trapezoid, capitate, and hamate

carrion beetle: Beetle from the family Silphidae that feeds on decaying organic matter

caudal: Toward the tail of a quadruped

cemento-enamel junction (CEJ): Point at which enamel ends and cementum begins; found at junction of crown and root of tooth

cementum: Hard tissue covering tooth root; provides attachment surface for periodontal ligament

cemetery: A place where the dead are buried

cephalic: Toward the head of a quadruped

cervical vertebrae: Seven vertebrae that compose the superior portion of the vertebral column; individually abbreviated as C1, C2, and so forth, with C1 (atlas) and C2 (axis) as the most superior

chaining pin: Graduated metal stake with a circular eye at one end and a point at the other

clandestine grave: Grave for which the location has been kept secret or hidden

clavicle: S-shaped tubular paired bones, also known as the collarbones, found in the anterior of the shoulder girdle

clay: Mineral substance made up of small grains; plastic in texture

coccyx: Composed of four or five fused or unfused small bony elements found inferior to the sacrum; also known as the tailbone

Coleptera: The order of insects including the beetles

compaction: Impressions of objects within a material substance; compression of soil layers

condyle: Large, rounded articular projection

context: An object's exact place in time and space and its association and relationship with other items

control-point mapping: Method of mapping that is concerned with finding the position of an object or feature in relation to a known point

coprophile: Organism that consumes its own feces or that of other animals

coroner: Public official who presides over investigations into unnatural deaths

cortical (compact) bone: Dense, thickened outer layer of bone

cranial skeleton: The skull (cranium and mandible) and hyoid

cranium: A skull without a mandible

cremains: Ash, bone fragments, and teeth resulting from remains being cremated

cremation: Process of reducing human remains to bone fragments through burning

crest: Sharp border or ridge

crown: Visible portion of the tooth; covered by enamel

cusp: Elevation on occlusal surface of tooth; primarily found on premolars and molars

datum: Fixed point of reference for all elevation, depth, and angle measurements made during survey and excavation

datum line: Leveling line set from the datum to measure elevation and depth

deciduous teeth: The first set of teeth in a mammal; also known as primary or "baby" teeth

dendrochronology: Scientific method of dating based on tree-ring analysis

dens: Tooth-shaped projection

dental bridge: Fixed or removable partial denture used to replace missing teeth; anchored to adjacent teeth by wires or permanent implants

dentin: Softer core tissue of crown and root of tooth; surrounds pulp chamber

depth: The vertical distance below a known point

detritivore: Organism that obtains nutrients by consuming decomposing organic matter

diaphysis: (*pl. diaphyses*) Shaft of a long bone

diatom: Single-celled algae with cell walls of silica

Diptera: The order of insects including the flies

Disaster Mortuary Operational Response Team (DMORT): Experts in the fields of victim identification and mortuary services

dispersed remains: Remains that have been scattered across a wide area

distal: End of bone farthest from the axial skeleton; toward the posterior of the mouth

disturbed burial: A burial that has had its contents moved by either natural, human, or nonhuman actions; may also have the grave cut marred by the same actions

dorsal: In humans, on the back of the hand or top of the foot; toward the back of a quadruped

ectoparasite: External parasite

eggs: Round or oval bodies laid by a female that provides protection and nutrients for offspring contained inside structure

electrical conductivity: Measure of how strongly a material conducts the flow of electrical current

electrical resistivity: Measure of how strongly a material opposes the flow of electrical current

electromagnetic (EM) induction meter: Geophysical survey tool used to measure differences in the electrical conductivity of the ground

electronic distance measurement (EDM) device: Transit combined with an on-board computer for use in survey; also known as a total station

elevation: The vertical distance above a known point

enamel: Hard, white mineral portion of the tooth; makes up majority of tooth crown

epicondyle: Small projection superior to a condyle

epiphyseal growth plate: Layer of cartilage between metaphysis and epiphysis

epiphysis: (*pl. epiphyses*) End of long bone; separates from metaphysis during development and becomes fused when growth has ceased

etching: Dissolution of a surface by acids; taphonomically associated with the growth and decay of plant material containing humic acid

ethmoid: Small, irregular bone found in the superior portion of the nasal cavity; externally visible on the medial aspect of the eye orbit

evidence: Everything used to demonstrate who is responsible for a criminal act

excavation spoil: Soil dug up from an excavation or a grave cut during burial; also known as backfill

extended position: An individual's legs form a 180° angle in relation to the trunk of the body

facet: Smooth, flattened articular surface

feature: An artifact that cannot be removed from the site without destroying its overall integrity, such as a fire pit, posthole or other man-made structure

femur: (*pl. femora*) Paired long bones that make up the upper portion of the leg; also known as the thigh bone

ferrous: Material containing iron

fibula: (*pl. fibulae*) Paired long bones located on the lateral aspect of the lower leg when in anatomical position

field tape: Metric measuring tape held on a hand reel; typically used in 20-, 50-, or 100-meter lengths

fish: Cold-blooded vertebrate animal living in water and moving with the help of fins and breathing with gills

fixing solution: Used to penetrate the larval cuticle to prevent decomposition in preservation solution

flat-blade shovel: Digging tool with a sharpened blade that is flat and square

flat bones: Bones with broad, flat plates or muscle attachment surfaces such as the parietals or scapulae

flexed position: An individual's legs form an angle of 90° or less in relation to the trunk of the body

foramen: Opening or hole passing through bone

foramen magnum: Large opening found at the base of the cranium

forensic anthropology: The application of the science of physical anthropology and human osteology in a legal setting for the purpose of human identification

forensic archaeology: The use of standard archaeological principles and methods to locate and recover human remains and associated evidence within the context of a forensic investigation

forensic botany: The use of plant morphology, systematics, and growth ecology as evidence in answering questions pertaining to legal issues

forensic context: Interrelated circumstances in which something of medicolegal significance occurs or is found, such as the association and relationship among skeletal remains, personal possessions, location of burial, and environment

forensic entomology: The use of insect and arthropod morphology, systematics, and behavioral ecology as evidence in answering questions pertaining to legal issues

forensic odontology: The examination and evaluation of dental evidence in a legal setting

foresight: A measurement of elevation and angle on a forward point

fossa: Shallow depression

frass: Solid waste products from insect (most often adult beetle or larval) digestion

frontal: Large irregular bone found in the forehead region of the cranium

frontal (coronal) plane: Plane that runs through body from head to feet, dividing body into front and back halves

fungi: Spore-producing organisms

furculum: Sternal element in a bird skeleton; also known as the wishbone

geographic coordinate system: Coordinate system that enables every location on Earth to be specified by a set of numbers, such as latitude, longitude, and elevation

geographic information system (GIS): A set of software application tools that allow users to digitally capture, store, analyze, manage, and present data that are spatially linked

geological map: Map that depicts rock formations, geological zones, and soil types

geophysical prospecting: The study of locating and mapping hidden objects or features that are underground or underwater

geophysical survey: Systematic collection of geophysical data to detect subsurface anomalies, which are recognized as localized areas of contrasting physical properties

geotaphonomy: Use of geophysical principles to recognize specific characteristics and changes that affect features and the surrounding environment

Global Positioning System (GPS): A global navigation satellite system that provides reliable location and time information when there is an unobstructed line of sight to four or more GPS satellites; GPS receivers calculate ground position by determining transit time of the signals sent by satellites

gnawing: Reduction of hard fibrous materials through consistent chewing

gradient magnetometer: Geophysical survey tool that measures small variations in the Earth's magnetic field through paired receivers; also known as a gradiometer

grave: Location where a body has been buried

grave cut: Excavation feature that forms the grave; also known as a burial cut

grid marker: The letter or number identifier placed along the baseline and number reference line in a reference grid; used to identify the position of a single grid square

grid search: A search line that moves across an area and then covers the same area again in a direction perpendicular to the first search

grid-system mapping: Method of mapping that uses grid squares and a datum to record the exact three-dimensional location of an object

groove (sulcus): Furrow on bone surface

ground-penetrating radar (GPR): Geophysical survey method that uses radar pulses to detect anomalies in subsurface layers

grub: Larva of a beetle

hand trowel: Small excavation tool with a flat metal blade; also known as a bricklayer's trowel

historic finds: Materials related to the period of recorded history

homodont dentition: Peg-like teeth all of the same type; found in reptiles

horizontal (transverse) plane: Plane that is perpendicular to median and frontal planes; divides body into upper and lower sections at any level

human remains detection (HRD) dog: Canine specially trained in detecting the scent of human decomposition and assisting in locating human cadavers, body parts, and body fluids; also known as a cadaver dog

humerus: (*pl. humeri*) Paired long bones that make up the upper arm

hyoid: Single U-shaped bone found inferior to the mandible; only bone in the human skeleton that does not articulate with another bone

incisal: Chewing surface of the incisors

indirect evidence: Objects that provide a circumstantial relationship with remains (e.g., weapons, digging tools)

inferior: Lower or below; toward the feet

infracranial skeleton: All skeletal elements except the skull (cranium and mandible) and hyoid

innominate (os coxa): (*pl. os coxae*) Large, flat, irregular paired bones, also known as the hipbones, located laterally in the pelvic girdle; provide an anchor for the legs

in situ: Latin phrase meaning *in the place*; used when remains or associated evidence are still in the position in which they were originally deposited

instar: Stage where the outer layer of larval insect cuticle (exoskeleton) splits from the inner layers (endoskeleton) to allow for growth

intrusion: Archaeological principle that recognizes that any intrusion must be more recent than the deposit through which it cuts

irregular bones: Bones with a peculiar form to support nervous tissue or anchor multiple muscle attachments such as the vertebrae and sacrum

Joint POW/MIA Accounting Command (JPAC): Task force whose mission is to account for U.S. military personnel listed as Prisoners of War (POW) or Missing in Action (MIA)

KAA (or KAAD): A solution for killing larval insect specimens; components of the solution are listed in Chapter 9

Kahle's solution: A solution for preserving dead larvae and for killing and preserving adult insects; components of the solution are listed in Chapter 9

labial: Surface of incisors and canines facing the lips

lacrimal: Small, flat, paired bones located on the medial aspect of the eye orbits; anatomically house the tear glands

larva: (*pl. larvae*) The immature insect stage that emerges from the egg and develops prior to pupation

lateral: Away from the midline

latitude: Geographic coordinate that specifies the north–south position of a point on the Earth's surface; measured in degrees from the equator (0°) to 90° north or –90° south

line (ridge): Long, thin elevation with roughened surface

lingual: Surface of the tooth facing the tongue

long bones: Bones that are longer than they are wide such as a humerus and femur

longitude: Geographic coordinate that specifies the east–west position of a point on the Earth's surface; measured in degrees from the Prime Meridian (0°) to 180° east or –180° west

lumbar vertebrae: Five vertebrae that compose the inferior portion of the vertebral column; individually abbreviated as L1, L2, and so forth, with L1 as the most superior and L5 as most inferior, articulating with the sacrum

macrobotanicals: Plant materials that can be detected with the naked eye and do not require magnification for analysis

maggot: Larva of a fly

magnetic locator: Geophysical survey tool used to measure changes in magnetic fields surrounding buried ferromagnetic objects; also known as valve and box locators

magnetometer: Geophysical survey tool that measures small variations in the Earth's magnetic field

mammal: Class of animal that is warm blooded, has hair, and feeds milk to their young

mandible: Single, irregular bone also known as the lower jaw

maritime chart: Map that depicts underwater formations and depth of the sea floor

mass burial: Burial that consists of disarticulated individuals with the possibility of articulated skeletal elements (e.g., an ossuary)

maxilla: (*pl. maxillae*) Irregular paired bones that make up the upper jaw

medial: Toward the midline

median (sagittal) plane: Plane that runs through body from head to feet, dividing body into left and right halves

medical examiner: Medically qualified government-appointed official who investigates deaths that occur under unusual or suspicious circumstances and performs postmortem examinations

medullary cavity: Central cavity of bone that holds bone marrow

mesial: Toward the anterior or median plane of the mouth

metacarpals: Five short tubular paired bones that form the palm of the hand; individually abbreviated as MC1, MC2, and so forth, with MC1 (base of the thumb) as the most lateral when in standard anatomical position

metal detector: Geophysical survey tool that responds to metal in subsurface layers that may not be readily apparent

metaphysis: (*pl. metaphyses*) Expanded, growth portion of a long bone found between the diaphysis and epiphysis

metapodial: Skeletal element that results from fusion of the third and fourth metacarpals or third and fourth metatarsals in hoofed mammals

metatarsals: Five short, tubular, paired bones that form arch of the foot; individually abbreviated as MT1, MT2, and so forth, with MT1 (base of the big toe) as the most medial when in standard anatomical position

microbotanicals: Plant materials that cannot be detected with the naked eye and require magnification for analysis

monostatic antenna: Antenna where the transmitter and receiver are contained within the same housing

multiple burial: A single grave containing the remains of two or more articulated individuals; may contain a combination of primary and disturbed burials

Munsell color charts: Commercially available color charts used by the USGS as the official color system for soil research; provides a standardized description of soil color

nasal: Small, flat, paired bones that make up the bridge of the nose

nasal concha: (*pl. conchae*) Small, irregular paired bones located laterally in the nasal cavity

natural bristle brush: Brush that is made of animal hair or hog bristles

notch: Indentation at an edge

nutrient foramen: External opening of nutrient canal in bone; facilitates blood and nerve supply

oblique plane: Any plane through the body that is not parallel to the median, frontal, or horizontal planes; divides body diagonally at any level

occipital: Large, irregular, flat bone that makes up the back and base of the cranial vault; foramen magnum feature located on this bone

occlusal: Chewing surface of all teeth

offset: Any measurement taken from a baseline

orientation: Direction in which the head lies in relation to the body's central axis; should be recorded in directional terms using a compass

orthographic map: Map that combines aerial photography with topographic information

osteology: Detailed scientific study of the structure of bones; used in identification of human remains with regard to age, sex, ancestry, stature, and health status

overlay: Tracing sheet placed on top of a plan drawing to superimpose a record of a new layer of stratigraphy or evidence

palatine: Small, irregular, paired bones that make up the posterior of the palate and floor of the nasal cavity

palmar: On the palm of the hand

palynology: Science that studies contemporary or fossil particulate organic matter, such as pollen

parasitoid: An insect whose larvae live as parasites that eventual kill their host

parietal: Large, flat, paired bones found on the superior portion of the cranium

passive geophysical method: Measuring variations within the natural forces of the Earth (e.g., gravitational, magnetic) in an effort to detect subsurface anomalies

patella: (*pl. patellae*) Small, rounded bone, also known as the knee cap, found in the anterior of the knee joint

pedology: The study of soils in their natural environment

pelvic girdle (pelvis): Composed of the left and right innominates

penetrometer: A soil probe with a pressure gauge used to measure soil density

perimortem: At or around the time of death

periodontal ligament: Soft tissue ligament holding tooth in tooth socket

periosteum: Fibrous membrane covering the outer surface of bone

permanent teeth: Second set of dentition in a mammal; also known as adult teeth

pH: Measure of the acidity or basicity of a solution

phalanges: (*sing. phalanx*) Small, tubular bones of the fingers and toes, with a total of 14 phalanges in each hand and foot; identified by position with five proximal, four intermediate (thumb and big toe lack an intermediate phalanx), and five distal or terminal phalanges per hand and foot

photographic scale: Metric measurement tool used to show ratio of an object's depiction to its actual size

Physicians for Human Rights (PHR): Nongovernmental organization that focuses on the health consequences of human rights violations

physical anthropology: Scientific study of the physical and biological aspects of the primate order including humans both past and present

pit: Tiny pocket or depression

plan drawing: Two-dimensional view of an object from directly above drawn to scale

planar surface: Interfaces of stratigraphic horizons detected by a ground-penetrating radar (GPR) system during geophysical survey

plantar: On the sole of the foot

plastron: Bottom portion of a turtle shell

platform excavation: Technique used to create a working space next to a grave

plumb bob: A weight, with a pointed tip, suspended from a string and used as a vertical reference line; also known as a plummet

point source: Small hyperbolic reflections due to smaller features detected using ground-penetrating radar (GPR)

position: Relationship of legs, arms, and head to each other and to the trunk of the body

postcranial: All bones of quadruped skeleton except the skull

posterior: Toward the back

postmortem: After death

postmortem interval (PMI): Amount of time that has passed since death; used as length of time between death and recovery of remains

prehistoric finds: Materials related to the period prior to recorded history

preservation solution: Used to preserve entomological samples

primary burial: A body that remains in the location where it was originally buried and the context of the burial has not been disturbed

primary deposit: Location where remains were originally placed

prismatic compass: Compass that has sighting marks incorporated into the baseplate and lid and uses a mirror or prism to reflect azimuth; typically used for mapping

process: A bony projection

pronation: Rotation of hand so palm faces posteriorly in standard anatomical position

protractor compass: Rotating magnetic pointer and compass dial mounted on a baseplate; typically used for orienteering in outdoor activities

provenience: The exact location of an item in three-dimensional space, reflecting its latitude, longitude, and vertical position

proximal: End of bone closest to axial skeleton

pulp chamber: Inner portion of tooth crown containing blood and nerve supply

pupa: (*pl. pupae*) Insect life stage following the larval stage and prior to the adult stage; final instar transforms into adult structures

puparium: (*pl. puparia*) The final coat of an insect larval instar which becomes hard and dark in color

putrefaction: Decomposition of animal proteins by bacterial flora that spread from the gastrointestinal tract

radius: (*pl. radii*) Paired long bones located on the lateral aspect of the lower arm when in standard anatomical position

ramus: Arm-like bar of bone

receiver: Instrument that detects a signal

reference number line: Line that is at a 90° angle to the baseline and is used to identify reference grid squares

reflection: Nonspecific feature detected using ground-penetrating radar (GPR)

reflection profile: Representation of soil layers and subsurface features produced by a ground-penetrating radar (GPR) system during geophysical survey

remains: Collective term for human and nonhuman tissues recovered from a scene

reptile: Class of animal that is a cold-blooded vertebrate

reversal: Archaeological principle based on the process of materials being moved from one location and deposited in another in reverse order

rib: 12 pairs of curved tubular and flat bones that make up the rib cage; individually identified by side (left or right) and numbered from superior (rib #1) to inferior (rib #12)

rigor mortis: Chemical change in the muscles after death, causing the limbs to become stiff and difficult to move or manipulate

ringing: Prominent horizontal bands of antenna noise seen in a reflection profile produced by a ground-penetrating radar (GPR) system

root: Portion of tooth embedded in jaw; covered by cementum

root canal: Narrow end of pulp chamber at root end of tooth

rounded bones: Bones that are approximately as wide as they are tall such as the tarsals

sacrum: Large, irregular bone composed of five fused bony elements, located at the base of the vertebral column and between the innominates in the pelvic girdle

sand: Mineral substance made up of small grains; gritty in texture

scale: Ratio of the size of an object as it is drawn on a map to its actual size

scapula: (*pl. scapulae*) Large, flat, paired bones, also known as the shoulder blade, located in the posterior portion of the shoulder girdle; provide an anchor for the arms

scavenger: An animal or insect that feeds off of carrion, dead plant material, or refuse

scene: Area within a site where a specific activity took place

scent cone: Concentration of scent dispersing through the environment

scent pool: Concentration of scent either at the point of origin or trapped at a remote location

secondary burial: Consists of skeletal elements that have been removed from their original location of burial by human activity and then reburied in another location

secondary deposit: Location of remains after they have been moved from their primary or original place of deposition

section drawing: Two-dimensional scale drawing that depicts the view one would have if an imaginary plane was cut through an object

sedimentation: Deposition and drying of eroded silty soils

semi-flexed position: Legs form an angle between 90° and 180° in relation to the trunk of the body

shoulder girdle: Set of bones that connect the upper limbs to the axial skeleton on each side; consists of the scapulae and clavicles

shovel shining: Removal of thin layers of soil by keeping the back of a flat-bladed shovel almost parallel with the ground surface; used to delineate the burial outline

side-scan sonar: Marine geophysical survey tool that uses sound waves to produce a graphic image of the sea floor or other water feature

silt: Mineral substance made up of small grains; smooth in texture

sinus: Hollow area within a cranial bone

site: Distinct spatial clustering of human activity

site plan: Illustration of all of the features at a site in relation to each other and in relation to a fixed reference point

skeletonization: Final stage in decomposition; refers to the complete decomposition of soft tissues

sketch map: Illustration of all features at a site in relation to each other and in relation to a fixed reference point

skull: The cranium and mandible

soil: Particles of broken rock that have been altered by chemical and environmental processes

soil color chart: See Munsell color chart

soil-coring probe: Tool used to detect mixing in soil horizons by removing and examining a vertical core of soil

soil horizon: Specific stratigraphic layer that possesses characteristics that differ from the layers above or beneath

sonar: Sound navigation and ranging to navigate, communicate, or detect objects

sphenoid: Large, complex, irregular bone of the cranium forming the posterior and lateral aspects of the eye orbits

spherical coordinate system: System of three-dimensional measurement based on degrees or radians of a circle

spine: Relatively long, slender projection

spore: Asexual reproductive structure of fungi

stadia rod: Graduated wood or aluminum rod used in survey to determine differences in elevation

standard anatomical position: Body standing erect, face forward, feet together, arms slightly raised, palms of hands facing anteriorly

sternum: Small, flat bone composed of three fused or unfused bony elements (manubrium, sternal body, and xyphoid process); located at the midline of the chest and is the anterior anchor site for the ribs

stick tape: Metric foldable ruler; also known as a carpenter's tape

stratigraphy: Analysis of the sequence of deposits in the Earth's surface formed through natural or human activities

strip (line) search: A line of individuals positioned close enough to one another that their field of view overlaps, and they move across the landscape in transects

subchondral bone: Area of bone at the joint covered by cartilage

superior: Upper or above; toward the head

superposition: Archaeological principle that assumes that more recent deposits will be laid down on top of older ones

supination: Rotation of hand so palm faces anteriorly in standard anatomical position

surface deposit: Remains situated either completely on the ground surface or partly exposed, with little or no effort of concealment

surveying: Science of accurately determining the positions of three-dimensional points and the distances and angles between them

suture: Joint between cranial bones

synsacrum: Large number of fused vertebrae that form a solid skeletal connection between the axial skeleton, vertebrae, and pelvic girdle in a bird skeleton

taphonomy: Changes or modifications that occur to bodies, skeletal remains, and any associated evidence, such as clothing or personal possessions, during a postmortem period

tarsals: Small, rounded bones of the ankle; each ankle consists of seven bones: calcaneus, talus, navicular, first cuneiform, second cuneiform, third cuneiform, and the cuboid

T-bar probe: Metal bar probe used to detect variations in the density of subsurface layers

temporal: Large, flat, irregular, paired bones found on the sides of the cranium; contain the auditory ossicles

thoracic vertebrae: 12 vertebrae that comprise the central portion of the vertebral column and articulate with the 12 pairs of ribs; individually abbreviated as T1, T2, and so forth, with T1 as the most superior

tibia: (*pl. tibiae*) Paired long bones located on the medial aspect of the lower leg when in anatomical position

tool marks: Impression left by the contact of a tool on a surface

topographic map: Map that depicts all visible and built surface features

total station: Electronic measurement device that combines a transit with an on-board computer for use in survey

towfish: Geophysical survey component containing a transmitter and receiver for use in side-scan sonar

transit: Surveying instrument used to measure distance, azimuth, and changes in elevation or depth between a known reference point and a desired survey point

transmitter: Electronic device that emits a signal

triangulation: The measure of angles of a triangle

trilateration: The calculation of the hypotenuse of a triangle when the lengths of two sides of the triangle are known

trochanter: Large, blunt elevation for muscle attachment

tubercle: Small, round elevation with roughened surface

tuberosity: Large, round elevation with roughened surface

tubular bones: Bones that are shaped like long bones but are much smaller in size such as the metacarpals

ulna: (*pl. ulnae*) Paired long bones located on the medial aspect of the lower arm when in standard anatomical position

unilateral: On one side

United States Geological Survey (USGS): Scientific civilian federal agency that studies landscape of the United States and produces several series of topographic maps

Universal Transverse Mercator (UTM) Grid: Worldwide mapping system that divides the world into 60 equal zones from west to east

ventral: Toward the chest of a quadruped

vertebra: (*pl. vertebrae*) Any of the 24 bones that make up the human spinal (vertebral) column, which extends from the skull to the sacrum; may be categorized into three types: cervical (C1–C7), thoracic (T1–T12) and lumbar (L1–L5)

vomer: Single, small, flat bone found in the midline of the nasal cavity

weathering: Destruction of bone through natural mechanical and chemical forces in the environment

World Geodetic System (WGS84): Reference coordinate system currently used by the Global Positioning System (GPS)

zoogamous plants: Animal-pollinating plants

zygomatic (malar, zygoma): Irregular, flat, paired bones of the face, also known as the cheekbones

Index

A

AAFS, *see* American Academy of Forensic Sciences
ABFA, *see* American Board of Forensic Anthropology
ABFE, *see* American Board of Forensic Entomology
Adipocere, 69
Adult skeletal inventory form (field collection), 323
Aerial imagery, 161
Algae and diatoms, 242–243
American Academy of Forensic Sciences (AAFS), 10, 12
American Board of Forensic Anthropology (ABFA), 12
American Board of Forensic Entomology (ABFE), 267
Amphibian, 301, 302, 303
Anemophilous plants, 241, 242
Ants, 257
Apical surface, 55, 57
Appendicular skeleton, 40, 42, 44, 46
Archaeological methods, application of in forensic context, 197–235
  advantages for investigators working with forensic archaeologist, 198
  archaeological approaches to recovering human remains, 207–224
    recovering surface remains and associated evidence, 207–211
    removing buried remains and associated evidence, 211–224
  archaeological trowel, how to use, 224
  association, 199, 203, 204, 212
  bioturbation, 205
  burial cut, 202, 204, 205, 206, 213
  burial outline, 213, 214, 215
  case study, 224–226, 226–230
  compaction, 201, 206
  depression, 205, 206

  feature, 200, 202
  general principles of archaeology, 199–207
    features, 200
    geotaphonomy, 205–207
    principles of deposition, 202–205
    provenience and context, 199–200
    stratigraphy and soils, 200–202
  geotaphonomy, 205
  how to use archaeological trowel, 224
  in situ, 199, 209
  intrusion, 203, 205
  key words and questions, 232–233
  provenience, 199, 208
  recovering surface remains and associated evidence, 207–211
    establishing spatial controls and recording secondary surface deposits, 208–209
    examining and recording of recovery area, 208
    examining soil layer beneath surface deposits, 210–211
    exposing and recording of primary surface deposit, 209–210
    removing surface remains at primary site, 210
  removing buried remains and associated evidence, 211–224
    establishing spatial controls, 212
    examining and recording of recovery area, 211–212
    excavating and recording of burial feature, 215–219
    exposing and recording of remains, 219–222
    identifying and recording of burial outline, 213–214
    recording and excavating of burial feature floor, 223–224
    removal of remains, 222–223
  reversal, 203, 204